PRAISE FOR DAVID M. BEERS

"Unbelievable! I could not put this book down. Cal Harris went to trial 4 times for the murder of his wife!!! This book is full of facts and so many lies it's unbelievable. God Bless those who work tirelessly in our justice system and for those who just don't give up."

— JONI

"Great Read!!! I absolutely could not put this book down. I will say it is a top 5 in all the books I have read."

— JUDI

"Well written book, and interesting inside look at an investigation that I followed. Makes you wonder what other cases were handled like this. Good read."

— MATT

"Good read. Kept my attention. Unique perspective from a PI involved in this case. Book focuses more on the behind the scene work of a Private Investigator in a murder case than on the criminal trials. He worked for the defense on a case that went to trial four times."

— MH

REIGN OF INJUSTICE

REIGN OF INJUSTICE

THE CAL HARRIS STORY

DAVID M. BEERS

COPYRIGHT

REIGN OF INJUSTICE: The Cal Harris Story
Written by David M. Beers

Published in United States of America
First edition published 2019
This edition published 2020

Copyright @ 2019 David M. Beers

This is a work of nonfiction, however, some of the names used in this book have been changed to protect those individuals' privacy.

ISBN-13: 978-0-578-73884-0 Paperback
ISBN-13: 978-0-578-73885-7 ebook

Cover design, editing, formatting, and layout by Evening Sky Publishing Services

DEDICATION

For: Michele Harris

May justice prevail and the wrong fail

A NOTE FROM THE AUTHOR

Some of the names used in this book have been changed to protect their privacy.

Although harsh at times, any criticism of the NYSP or any of its members was offered strictly from a professional perspective and should not be construed otherwise.

"Injustice anywhere is a threat to justice everywhere."

— DR. MARTIN LUTHER KING JR.

CONTENTS

PROLOGUE

For the young family of Calvin 'Cal' and Michele 'Shelli' Harris and their four small children, the school year had just started, and like most weekdays, the morning of Tuesday, September 11, 2001, was rather routine. Married for ten years, Cal was 40, and Michele would be turning 36 in a few days. Cal owned and operated two lucrative automobile dealerships. Royal Ford in Owego, NY, and Royal Chevrolet in Cortland, NY. He would routinely work at the Cortland dealership every Tuesday. Before going to Cortland, he dropped off his three oldest children at school in Owego. Then, before heading to Cortland, he checked in at his Owego dealership.

While there, a 'Special Report' flashed across the television, reporting the first plane hitting one of the Twin Towers of the World Trade Center in New York City. Like the rest of the world, Cal was glued to the television, watching the events unfold. Later, while still listening to the radio, he traveled to Cortland, where he worked the rest of the day.

Meanwhile, Michele was home taking care of their youngest child, 18-month-old Tanner. Early that afternoon, Barb Thayer came over to babysit, and Michele left to go to work. Later, Thayer picked up the children after school and watched over them until Cal returned home from work.

Trouble had been brewing in Cal and Michele's marriage for quite some time, and Michele had filed for divorce a few months earlier. For the benefit of the children, they continued to co-exist in the marital home, albeit, sleeping in separate rooms, until the divorce. Michele, claiming that Cal had cut her off financially, had taken a waitressing job at a lower-class bar/restaurant in Waverly, NY called Lefty's.

| Michele Harris

Before leaving Cortland, Cal called Thayer around 5:30 p.m. to tell her he would be home in about an hour. At 6:30 p.m., he arrived home right on schedule. Thayer had already fed the children, so as soon as Cal arrived, she headed home. Cal spent some time playing with the kids. As it was a school night, he readied the kids for bed at about 8 p.m. and tucked them into their upstairs bedrooms. He turned on their 'white noise' machines, which was their routine. Cal worked in his home office, preparing for the next day, then headed to bed around 10:30 p.m.

Meanwhile, around 9:00 p.m., Michele finished her shift at Lefty's as scheduled. After sharing a drink with a co-worker, she left around 9:15 p.m. From there, Michele drove to her boyfriend's apartment in Smithboro, NY, where she remained until about 11:15 p.m. Presumably, after leaving the boyfriend's apartment, she was heading for home.

September 12, 2001, Cal woke up around 6:30 a.m. After showering and dressing for work, he walked downstairs and noticed Michele was not home getting the kids up for breakfast and ready for school. Annoyed, but knowing she had a boyfriend, Cal assumed she was still with him and was just running late. Trying to stay on schedule and knowing he needed help with the kids to get them to school and himself to work, he called Barb Thayer around 7:00 a.m. Cal told her Michele had not come home and asked for her help with the kids. Thayer agreed and said she would be over shortly. While waiting, Cal called Michele's cell phone, which went directly to voicemail. Further annoyed, he hung up, leaving no message.

In the meantime, Thayer left her house and drove the short four-to-five-minute drive to the Harris house, where she saw Michele's van parked near the end of the long driveway. Curious, she parked her car and got out to check to see if Michele was in her van. The van door was unlocked, so she opened it and looked inside. There was no Michele. She then went around and opened the rear hatch to see if she might be 'sleeping-if-off' in the back. But still no Michele. She then got back in her car and drove down the quarter-mile-long driveway to the house.

She parked her car and walked into the house and saw that Cal was dressed and ready for work and asked him if Michele was home. Cal replied, "No, I told you, she didn't come home." She informed him about Michele's van sitting at the end of the driveway. Together, they briefly speculated as to where Michele might be or may have gone. Cal then told Thayer, "Well, we better go get it." They both drove out to Michele's van, and Thayer drove it back, parking it in the garage.

Cal took the three oldest children to school while Thayer stayed with Tanner. Shortly after Cal left, Thayer received a call from Michele's friend Nikki Burdick, who was looking for Michele. Thayer explained what happened. Nikki said that Michele was supposed to be having a meeting later today with her divorce attorney Robert Miller and said, "I better call him." Before calling Miller, though, she called Michele's cell phone, which went right to voicemail. She left this message: "Where the hell are you? You need to call me as soon as freaking possible. I am worried to death about you. You need to call me on my cell phone – goodbye."

At around 8:45 a.m., Burdick called Miller and explained the situation. Miller, in turn, called the New York state police (SP). He spoke with Sr. Investigator Susan Mulvey, advising her that he represents Michele in her divorce action. While speaking with Mulvey, Miller initiated a conference call with Nikki Burdick, who explained the details and concerns to Mulvey. He requested the SP conduct a missing persons investigation. The SP immediately opened a missing person case, and less than an hour later, two BCI[1]investigators walked into Royal Ford to interview Cal.

After a lengthy interview, Cal led the two investigators to his residence. He gave them written consent to search his house, property, Michele's van, and his truck as needed. He returned to work, leaving investigators to do their job. Around 4:15 p.m., he called the house and learned the police were still there. So, he took the kids to dinner, giving them more time to finish. When he returned home with the kids around 7:15 p.m., the police were gone.

> Author's Note: Ordinarily, and more often than not, those who report a missing person, even under suspicious circumstances, are told nothing can be done for 24 hours. However, under the unique and suspicious circumstances here, the SP made an exception and launched their investigation in less than an hour.

As the SP continued and then expanded their investigation, arrangements were made for a variety of search methods. New York State Forest Rangers were brought in to organize a ground search. Civilian volunteers, including friends of the Harris's, familiar with the property, were teamed up with SP investigators and Forest Rangers to search the area. While many searched, on foot, others used ATV's. Divers with SONAR[2] equipment were brought in to search Empire Lake and a small pond off the driveway. K-9 teams, including cadaver dogs, were also used. Flyovers and aerial searches were conducted by helicopter using naked-eye searches as well as FLIR[3] and 3-D scanning technology known as LiDAR[4]. Nothing was found.

Meanwhile, the SP issued a missing person press-release for Michele Harris that included her photograph, physical description, and when and where she was last seen.

On September 14, 2001, the SP applied for, obtained, and executed a search warrant for the Harris residence and surrounding property. After that, members of the Troop 'C' FIU[5] were brought in for a closer look. Crime scene investigators discovered some specks of blood and blood residue just inside the entrance to the residence from the garage. Presumptive field-tests of random samples revealed a positive presence of blood.

BCI field investigators interviewed family, friends, and coworkers of both Cal and Michele. Other investigators re-interviewed Cal and confronted him about the blood they found. Cal, clearly in their crosshairs as the number one suspect, police stepped up their investigation in search of the proof they needed to make an arrest.

At the SP barracks in Owego, a command-post and lead desk were quickly organized, and the investigation officially went into full swing. With two Lieutenants, three Senior Investigators, no less than fifteen

BCI field investigators, and a full contingent of uniformed troopers, a major missing person investigation was launched and underway.

As Michele's husband, Cal knew he was an automatic suspect. Compounding matters was the fact that Michele's family and friends did not like him. In truth, they despised him. He also knew that his character, financial status, and the pending divorce, which included allegations of physical abuse, would all be used to point to him as a suspect. Knowing this, Cal did all he could to cooperate with investigators. He answered all their questions and willingly granted them access to search his house and property.

Cal was concerned as to what may have happened to Michele as the mother of his children. But at that moment, his most immediate concern was his children and what impact her disappearance and the police investigation would have on them. To remain strong and positive for the benefit of his children, Cal was often criticized for his seeming lack of concern for Michele's disappearance. Unsure as to where the investigation might lead, Cal wisely chose to keep his business attorney, Stan Drazen, briefed with updates of any information as it developed and became available to him.

---

1. BCI: Bureau of Criminal Investigation
2. SONAR: Sound Navigation and Ranging
3. FLIR: Forward-Looking Infra-Red
4. LiDAR: Light Detection and Ranging
5. FIU: Forensic Identification Unit

PART I

MICHELE IS MISSING

1

BACKGROUND

Tioga[1] County, NY, with a modest population of 51,000 people, is situated in south-central NY just above the Pennsylvania border between the cities of Binghamton and Elmira, NY. The entire Tioga County is comprised of only nine townships with a few small villages and hamlets. There are no cities. The County Seat is in the small, quaint little Village of Owego,[2] NY, snuggled in along the north side of the Susquehanna[3] River.

Tioga County received some notoriety when, on November 14, 1957, law enforcement raided the estate of a prominent Philadelphia mobster by the name of Joseph Barbara in the small community of Apalachin in the town of Owego. At the raid, 62 men were arrested and later identified as Mafia Chieftains from across the country who had gathered at Barbara's estate for a national 'Crime Boss' summit meeting. In the aftermath, after several years of denial, the FBI was forced to acknowledge the existence of an organized Mafia.

Just west of Owego in the small town of Tioga were two lucrative and well-established automobile dealerships along opposite sides of state route 17C. Royal Chrysler to the North Royal Ford to the South. The Royal Auto Group was a family business started by entrepreneurial business tycoon, R. Dwight Harris, which was later owned and operated by sons, Kevin and Calvin 'Cal' Harris. The third dealership in Oneonta, NY, was owned and operated by older brother Steven Harris.

Calvin 'Cal' Lawrence Harris was born and raised in an affluent upper-middle-class home and attended high school in Vestal, NY. Brothers Steven and Kevin were nine and seven years older than Cal, respectively. As the youngest and smallest of the three, Cal stood five-feet-nine inches tall, weighed 165 pounds, had blue eyes, and sandy-blonde hair. He was a handsome, popular, and talented athlete who excelled in becoming a star lacrosse player. After high school, he attended Hobart and William Smith Colleges, majoring in business and economics. After completing his education, he was groomed into the family car dealer business by his father and later became the owner/operator of Royal Ford.

In 1986, a new girl by the name of Michele 'Shelli' Anne Taylor, was hired by the Royal Auto Group. With beautiful, golden blonde hair and brown eyes, the petite Michele weighed in at a mere 100 pounds and stood only five-foot-two inches tall. Michele was head-turning attractive, personable, flirtatious, well-liked, and loved to party. She grew up in the small, lower-middle-class Hamlet of Tioga Center, NY, with younger brother Greg. After high school, she studied business at Morrisville State College in NY and then took the job with the Royal Auto Group.

When Cal and Michele first met, it was love at first sight. They started dating almost immediately and, within a short time, moved in together. They appeared and were considered by many to be made for each other – the perfect couple.

After living together for four years, they married in August of 1990. Three years later, Cal built Michele, a spacious and beautiful, half-million-dollar, remote, lake-front dream house on Empire Lake, in the rural town of Spencer, NY. Their home, not even visible from the road, was surrounded by more than 250 acres of remote, wooded wilderness. Together, they spent countless hours enjoying and entertaining their friends, families, and children with hunting, fishing,

| Cal and Michele Harris

hayrides, jet-skiing, swimming, ice-skating, camping, and long trail rides on ATVs and snowmobiles.

When Michele Taylor became Michele Harris, she was quickly elevated from her lower-middle-class lifestyle into an upper-middle-class lifestyle. While adapting to her lavish new lifestyle, she began to enjoy many of the finer things in life – limitless designer clothes, fine jewelry, personal hairstylist, new cars, fancy toys, spending money, and of course, a beautiful new home. Her new lifestyle seemed to fit her well.

Not long after settling into their new lake-front home, in April of 1994, they had their first child, a boy named Taylor. By February of 1999, there were three more children, Cayla, Jenna, and Tanner.

| Harris Family - Fall 2000

But problems in their marriage had been brewing for some time. Things became worse when Michele suspected and later learned that Cal was having an affair. Ironically and unbeknownst to Cal, Michele too was having a fling or two of her own. Verbal altercations were increasing in frequency, many of which became heated at times. Their babysitter, Barbara Thayer, witnessed some of the arguments saying they, "got rather nasty, even vulgar at times." She also stated that "it wasn't just Cal." Because Michele could be as verbally abusive to Cal as he was to her, and she had no trouble "holding her own" in an argument.

In November 2000, Michele met and started a secret relationship with a young, new boyfriend from Philadelphia. They started seeing each other regularly and eventually included several secret weekend rendezvous in the Pocono's.

By January 2001, Michele filed for divorce. Cal did not take it well and made several attempts at reconciliation. During much of this time, especially early on, there was little or no communication between them. What conversations they did have usually concerned the children. While cohabitating in the marital home, Cal slept upstairs, while Michele camped out in the downstairs family room.

During April or early May 2001, Michele took a job as a waitress in a lower-class, rather rough-and-tumble bar/restaurant in Waverly, NY, called Lefty's. She told family and friends that she needed the job because Cal had cut her off financially. Unbeknownst to Cal, Michele had opened new credit card accounts, then maxed out her credit limits, with nothing to show for it. Meanwhile, Cal was giving her $400/week spending money and a dealership car to drive. What little income she earned as a waitress ($3.21/hour + tips) wasn't even enough to cover the cost of paying a babysitter while she worked.

Michele's good looks combined with her friendly and fun-loving personality made her a patron favorite at Lefty's. She was well-liked by the clientele and co-workers alike. But Lefty's itself was considered somewhat of a rough establishment, with a reputation to match. Even though Michele was a favorite, she was still deemed by some of her co-workers as being 'out-of-their-league,' while others referred to her as being 'high-maintenance.' Cal expressed his concerns about some of the 'whacky' or 'shady characters' who patronized or worked at Lefty's.

By late August 2001, the divorce was imminent. Even though it was not yet finalized, both Cal and Michele had accepted that the love they once shared for each other was no longer there. There was no hope of reconciliation, and so it was the end of the line. However, the respective love they shared for their children was undeniable. There was an inferred agreement and mutual understanding to move on with their separate lives while maintaining the loving interests of their children that would include joint custody.

---

1. Tioga: Native American (Iroquois – 'teyo:ke') meaning *"at the forks"*
2. Owego: Native American (Iroquois – 'Ahwaga') meaning *"where the valley widens"*
3. Susquehanna: Native American - named after the 'Susquehannock' tribe of the Iroquois Nation.

EARLY INVESTIGATION

K nowing he was the number one suspect, Cal kept his long-time business attorney, Stan Drazen, up-to-date on all events, concerns, and his fear of arrest. Drazen, who shared similar concerns, recommended consulting with a criminal defense attorney. Shortly after, Cal consulted and subsequently retained the services of Joseph P. Cawley Jr. from the law firm of Mlynarski and Cawley. Cawley was a highly qualified, experienced, and well-respected criminal defense attorney in neighboring Broome County, NY. The following day, Joe Cawley called me in as an investigator for the defense and scheduled a joint consult with Cal and his father, Dwight.

We met two days later, and I was brought up to speed on what limited information was available to date. I learned from Drazen that SP Senior Investigator, Susan Mulvey, was named the lead investigator for the case. She had been in his office within the first days of Michele's disappearance with questions. While looking Drazen right in the eye, she said, "I know Cal killed her, and I'm going to prove it."

| Cal Harris

I agreed to open and conduct an independent investigation with a two-pronged objective: (1) Find Michele, and (2) Develop information in support of a defense for Cal Harris should charge(s) be filed. I was retained on the spot, and my own missing person case was adopted. My investigation would start immediately.

In further discussions with Joe and Cal, it became rather apparent that the SP suspected a criminal element in Michele's disappearance. Cal was the number one suspect, yet no charges were filed. He had been cooperative with authorities granting them carte blanch access to his home and property. Preliminary information revealed the SP had used a wide variety of resources to conduct an extensive search of the Harris home and surrounding property, including searches by air, land, and water. All of which had taken place over several days. Their investigation also included the use of forensics[1] crime-scene specialists who had seized various items from the Harris home and property. Preliminary information alleged the discovery and seizure of an unknown quantity of human blood and/or blood residue from the Harris residence.

> Author's Note: Ordinarily, during a criminal defense investigation, a defendant has already been charged with a crime. The attorney is provided 'discovery' material that contains information pertaining to the police investigation and evidence the prosecution intends to use in the People's case against the defendant. Obviously, discovery information is essential in preparation for a defense investigation. Without it, the defense investigator is working blind.

At the time, Cal was not charged with any crime. Therefore, there was no discovery material to examine to know what the police investigation revealed or what evidence was found. From the intensity of the investigation, it was obvious that foul-play was suspected. However, since the case was still classified as a missing person case, the police were under no obligation to disclose any results or findings to the defense. Unless they chose to. Initially, my only source of information would come from Cal, or perhaps snippets from the media. I started by reading in the local newspaper, this press-release provided by the SP:

PRESS RELEASE NEW YORK STATE POLICE
OWEGO, NEW YORK
687-3961
September 12, 2001
The New York State Police are investigating the reported disappearance of
MICHELE A. HARRIS, *age 35, of Tioga Center, New York. Mrs.*
Harris was reported missing this morning. She was last seen on
09/11/01 at approximately 9-30 p.m. leaving work in Waverly, New
York. She was last seen driving a 2000 Ford Windstar van which was
located near her residence. Ms. Harris is described as a white female, 5'2",
thin build, with blonde hair, brown eyes. She was last seen wearing tan
khaki shorts, white sneakers, a navy-blue polo shirt with a red and white
striped collar with a "LEFTY'S" logo, a gold and silver watch, numerous
rings, earrings and bracelets. Anyone with information concerning the
whereabouts of Ms. Harris is asked to contact the New York State Police at
687-3961.

Knowing that I was starting blind, I decided the first step in my investigation was to visit the alleged crime scene. Then spend some one-on-one time with Cal to develop some background information, as well as specific details pertaining to the disappearance of Michele. Cal should be able to provide me with some names and information I would need to start my preliminary investigation.

By now, it was September 21, 2001, and Michele had been missing nearly ten days. I traveled to the Harris residence to conduct an interview with Cal and examine the home and surrounding property. At the time, Hagadorn Hill was a narrow, unpaved dirt road, with a north/south orientation running through the Town of Spencer. The Harris driveway was paved with black asphalt and was a full quarter-mile in length.

Upon entering the driveway, there was a large open field on the north side with a small pond. The south side of the driveway was densely covered with trees and brush. It was only the first day of fall, and the foliage was still full. There was a wooden rail fence along both sides of the driveway for about the first 1000 feet. The driveway then curved in a south-easterly direction and became densely wooded along both sides until reaching a Y intersection. Following the Y to the right led to Dwight's summer cottage. To the left was Cal's house. With the dense woods in between, neither dwelling could be seen from the other.

Similarly, Cal's house could not be seen from Hagadorn Hill Road or vice versa.

| Harris Home

The Harris home was a large, two-story, wood-framed dwelling with natural wood siding. Large double doors led into the main entrance and a large vestibule with a vaulted ceiling. To the right was a long, carpeted stairway leading to the 2nd floor where the children's bedrooms were, as well as the master bedroom. To the left of the vestibule was Cal's home office. Wow! Not a thing out of place and neat as a pin, as if it had never been used. Like something you would see in a *Good Housekeeping* magazine, but then again, the whole house looked like that. I remember thinking my office would never look like that. There was an attached, two-car garage along the south side, with a single man-door leading from the garage into the house.

Upon re-entering the house from the garage, I noticed a small entryway. There was a walk-in pantry to the left, laundry room straight ahead, and the kitchen and main floor area to the right. On the main floor, there was a large formal dining room, beautifully designed and decorated, with all signs that a 'woman's touch' was surely involved. There was a large kitchen in the middle that would make most women envious. I thought, "I better not let my wife see this place." At the other end was a plushly carpeted family room with a beautiful field-stone fireplace. The large picture windows in the dining room, kitchen, and family room, as well as a large elevated deck, overlooked and provided a beautiful panoramic view of Empire Lake about 100 yards east of the house. The lake frontage and surrounding landscape were groomed beautifully, and the trees had been cleared away, allowing for a magnificent view of the lake from the house. A large deck, boat dock, and swimming platform could be seen at the lake's edge.

During the time I was physically viewing the residence and all the surrounding property, Cal gave me a guided tour. Outside, we covered a lot of ground by using one of his larger ATVs, that he called, a 'mule.' During the tour, I told him the SP would likely be speaking with his friends and seeking information about any favorite areas he liked to go to on the property. I also told him that I'd be interested in looking at those areas myself. Over the next few hours, he gave me an extensive tour of his property, including all his favorite spots. There was a lot of area to cover. But this would prove extremely beneficial, not only for my investigation but to better understand what the SP was doing in theirs.

After the physical work was done, at least for now, I had the opportunity to sit down with Cal for a long time. Before discussing the facts and circumstances surrounding Michele's disappearance, I asked about his background and interviewed him on nearly every aspect of his life. Eventually, that brought us back to the matter at hand. As I started to explain the need and purpose of the background information, Cal would interrupt me and say, "Hey, you don't need to explain, I understand, let's do this."

Long before adopting this case, I had heard the name Cal Harris, but I'd never personally met him until he hired me. Somehow though, various aspects of his negative character and reputation had preceded him. Most likely because of him being the owner of Royal Ford. My early years as a young trooper were in the Owego area. At times, I had heard rumblings about his cocky, outspoken, and arrogant character. But I had no personal knowledge or experience of this. With that in the back of my mind, being more of an introvert myself, I wasn't sure if there would be a personality conflict in our relationship or not. We were about to find out.

Before my interview, Cal had already spoken with SP investigators on several occasions. But I was not yet privy to any police documentation related to those interviews. Therefore, I would have to rely on Cal's recollection of what transpired during those interviews. As we sat behind the long kitchen counter on a couple of bar stools, each with a tall glass of ice-tea, I opened my notebook, and we got started. It was apparent from the start that I had his undivided attention. Intently, I listened as Cal laid out his personal, family, and business history in detail, with little prompting from me. He then laid out Michele's family history in the same manner. As we continued, he described how he first met Michele in 1986 when she came to work at Royal Ford. They lived together for four years before getting married in a lake-side ceremony at Empire Lake on August 25, 1990.

Backing up a bit, Cal disclosed that he had been married once before. The marriage had only lasted about six months between 1984-85 before there was a mutual annulment. There were no children. Michele had been engaged briefly but ended up dumping the guy. He was not sure of the reason. He went on to describe having four children with Michele between 1994-99 with the names Taylor, Cayla, Jenna, and Tanner.

He then described how various problems started to develop in the marriage, which led to Michele filing for divorce in January (2001). Additionally, as recent as May or June of this year (2001), she filed an injunction to have him removed from the house, but the judge ruled against her, dismissing the claim for insufficient cause.

Cal admitted that when Michele first filed for divorce, "I did not take it well." There were many heated arguments; as a result, several of which got rather nasty at times. Then, in April or May of this year (2001), Michele started working at Lefty's in Waverly. He believed that she had taken the job, not for the money but rather, "to avoid me and our heated arguments." During his effort to reconcile his marriage, he'd gone to the Taylor's looking for their support. While meeting with them, he expressed his concerns about Michele's 'new' lifestyle and her working at Lefty's with some 'whacky' characters.

Unfortunately, "the Taylor's thought I was trying to place all the blame on Michele for our failed marriage," and his concerns fell on deaf ears. He said, "Michele loved to shop and spend money," but he'd recently discovered several considerable cash advances on credit cards with nothing to show for it. He suspected that she might have been using drugs. His suspicions became so intense he said, "I once searched the entire house for drugs or any related evidence, but never found anything." He also added, "Michele was not very big to begin with, but many, including myself, noticed a significant weight loss (15-20 pounds) in the past few months, plus she was smoking a lot more." Some had even mentioned her sniffling a lot. When asked, the last time he had an intimate relation with Michele was back in October of last year.

He said that for the past several months, even though they were living in the same house, there had been little communication between them. Michele was sleeping on the downstairs sofa. The only contact they had usually concerned the children. He admitted there had been some "heated arguments at times, but more so during the early stage of the divorce proceedings." But over the past several weeks, "things had been running rather smoothly between us with little or no arguing." He believed it was because they were both coming to terms with the imminent reality of the divorce, and were both moving on with their separate lives.

Continuing, he explained how Michele would typically work afternoons and evenings at Lefty's. She'd usually leave between 2:00 or 3:00 p.m. and work until 9:00 p.m. She would generally get home sometime after 10:00 p.m. However, he said, "There were times when she returned in the middle of the night or even the next morning." Adding further that he "could tell when she'd been out all night because she still reeked of booze and was still in her work clothes."

Michele always drove her 2000 Ford Windstar van, which he provided through the dealership. He gave her a new dealership vehicle to drive every few months. But "her vehicles were always a mess," he said, and she never took care of them very well. Adding that, "her housekeeping wasn't much better, and that was one of the things we argued about."

He described a time, a few months earlier, when Michele had been out drinking late one night and drove her van into a ditch down near Halsey Valley Road, a couple of miles away. The van had a broken front wheel and couldn't be driven. Michele had called a neighboring farmer with a tractor to pull her out and bring her home. He said, "The accident was never reported, and I had the van repaired at the dealership."

When asked about her jewelry, he said, "Michele loved jewelry, and sterling was her preference. She regularly wore her diamond engagement ring and other rings, as well as multiple earrings, an ankle bracelet, a toe ring, and other jewelry. He continued with, "She also wore an expensive Rolex watch I had given her as an anniversary gift when we were trying to reconcile our marriage." She also had a tattoo of a sunburst, about the size of a golf ball on her ankle. He was also aware that she had undergone elective breast enhancement surgery a few months earlier.

Cal claimed to have never had any violent encounters with Michele but did acknowledge they had many heated arguments in which they verbally abused each other. "On isolated occasions, it would accelerate to a shove, a slap or the grabbing of an arm, but nothing more," he said. Adding that, "Over the past few months, our relationship was probably the best it had been in several months prior."

Now that I had some background, it was time to shift gears. To get started, I asked Cal to summarize the details of events as he recalled them beginning with the morning of September 11, 2001. With little prompting from me, he explained as follows:

"On Tuesday, September 11, 2001. I took the kids to school in Owego as usual and then stopped at work. I watched the TV coverage of the attack on the Twin Towers for a while and then drove to the Cortland store where I worked the rest of the day. I work there almost every Tuesday. Michele would usually leave for work at Lefty's around 2:00-3:00 p.m., but Barb would have better knowledge of the time. She usually worked until 9:00 p.m. Barb was babysitting the children until I arrived home around 6:30 p.m. I'm pretty sure I called Barb before leaving Cortland and told her I would be home in about an hour, which was the norm. When I arrived home, I parked my truck at the north end of the driveway like I always do. The garage door was open and is usually always left open. Barb had already fed the kids, and I spent some time playing with them. Since it was a school night, I put them all to bed around 8:00 p.m. and turned on their 'white noise' machines also the norm. I worked in my office for a while, but I was tired, and as soon as I knew the kids were all asleep, I went to bed myself around 10:30 p.m.

I woke up around 6:30 a.m. and took a shower. As I was getting dressed, the kids heard me, and they started getting up. When I went downstairs, I noticed Michele was not sleeping on the couch, so I looked in the garage and didn't see her car, and the garage door was still open. This was not the first time this had happened. I was more annoyed than concerned since I thought she was probably still with her boyfriend. I knew she had a boyfriend, but I didn't know who he was, where he lived, or anything about him, and I didn't really care to. I was more concerned about the kids, and since she wasn't there to help, I called our babysitter, Barb Thayer. I told her Michele had not come home and asked if she could come over to help with the kids. She agreed and said she would be right over. I think it was about 7:45 a.m. when she showed up.

As soon as she arrived, she told me Michele's van was parked out at the end of the driveway, but nobody was in it. I drove Barb in my truck out the driveway to pick up Michele's van. I saw the keys were in the ignition. I wish I had felt the hood to see if it was still warm, but I didn't. I had Barb drive it down the driveway and into the garage. I also saw the kid's backpacks in the van. The interior of the van was a real mess, but that was normally how it looked because she never cleaned it out. I left Barb with Tanner, my youngest, and I took the other three to school in Owego as usual. Apparently, shortly after I left, Nikki Burdick called looking for Michele. When I got to the office, I got a call from Shannon (Michele's sister-in-law) looking for Michele. Shortly after, around 10:00 or 11:00 a.m., two investigators showed up at my office, asking questions. I cooperated with them, answered all their questions, and even led them out to my house. I showed them where Michele's van was found at the end of the driveway. They looked around the house and through Michele's van. I left them there to do their thing and returned to work. Later, back at my office, I signed a written consent to search and gave them full access to my house and property. Later, I picked up the kids from school and kept them at work until dinnertime. I then took the kids to dinner, then returned home a little after 7:00 p.m., and the police were gone.

The next morning, I think a family friend, Linda Hyatt, may have come to take care of the two youngest kids while I took the two older ones to school. Linda and her husband were close friends with Michele's mother. After work, I took the kids to Linda's house for dinner. Linda accompanied me back to my house with the kids, and she helped me tell the kids about their mother. Later, Thursday is when the state police came back to me and told me about finding the blood and asking me if I knew anything else. It was also then that they asked me to take a polygraph. I initially told them I wanted to, and I would have, but after speaking with Stan, I was advised not to take the polygraph nor answer any more police questions. On Friday, I took the kids to school, and Barb babysat. The school day was only half-day, so I took the kids to lunch and then to Smart play. I then received a call from Investigator Myers, who wanted to know if they could interview my two older children. I called Stan, who gave the ok, but suggested I be present during the interviews. When I took the kids for their interview, the police said they would prefer to speak to them alone, and I gave them the ok. The interviews only lasted about 10-15 minutes."

I then asked Cal to explain how it came to be that he and the children spent the weekend in Cooperstown, NY, with his brother Steve. He explained as follows

On that Friday, the kids only had a half-day of school. I picked them up and brought them back to work with me. Later, I got a call from the state police advising me they were still working at my house and were likely going to be there through the weekend and asked if I could find a place to stay for few days. I called my brother Kevin and planned to stay at his house temporarily, then go to Cooperstown to stay with my other brother Steve. I knew I was going to need a few things for myself and the kids, so I called the police back, and they said I could come out and pick up what I needed. So, I dropped the kids off at Kevin's house and drove out to my house, where I was met by the investigators. There were quite a few of them there.

After explaining what I needed, including mostly clothing and a few other things, and where they would be located, I was escorted to those areas to collect what I needed. When I went back down to the kitchen, I found some plastic bags, and sat in a chair, packing things up. As I was sitting there packing, I was also kind of looking around, and I noticed the door leading into my garage was open. It looked like 3 or 4 investigators were huddled around some special lighting equipment that was focused on an area of the garage floor. I could see some type of light pattern on the floor. I also saw an area just inside the entrance from the garage that they seemed to be interested in as well. There were some small white measurement strips taped near the bottom of the door and along the wood casing around the door near the bottom. I didn't ask or say anything but assumed these were the same areas where the blood was found that they had questioned me about the day before. I'd only been there about 15 or 20 minutes before I was finished packing. I was then escorted back to my car and drove back to Kevin's house.

Cal went on to say that shortly after discovering the blood, the police questioned him whether he had any knowledge of how the blood got there or who it belonged to. He said he couldn't offer any explanation because he was not aware of any specific incident. He could only speculate that he may have cut himself shaving, or perhaps one of the children had cut themselves.

My first interview with Cal had gone well, and I knew there would need to be many more. I had many more questions, and many more would follow as my investigation progressed. I felt I had established a good working rapport with Cal, and I looked forward to our subsequent interviews. Cal had to get ready to leave for the kids, but before he left, he introduced me to Barbara Thayer, who was still at the house doing some housework. "Ah, the perfect opportunity," I thought, "a face-to-face interview with Thayer. She could be an important witness in this case. With no influence by Cal's presence – let's see what she has to say."

Thayer was in her early 50s. A slight woman with gray hair, soft-spoken, and polite. She lived nearby on Owl Creek Road, about a 4 to 5-minute drive to the Harris residence. As she stood there, folding clothes, I started by asking a few questions but allowed her to do most of the talking. She'd been babysitting and house cleaning for the Harris' for the past four-and-a-half years. On Tuesday morning, September 11, 2011, she was there to babysit and spoke with Michele. Michele told her she had a headache and wasn't sure if she was going to work or not. Michele laid down for a while but then decided she would go to work and left around 4:30 p.m. Michele usually worked Tuesday, Thursday and Saturday and sometimes other days but usually about 3-4 days a week. She had been working for the past few months since springtime and claimed she had to work because Cal cut off her finances.

Thayer remembered that when Michele left for work, she was wearing khaki shorts, a navy-blue Lefty's polo shirt, and white sneakers. She was unsure what jewelry she may have been wearing, but usually, she preferred sterling and often wore necklaces, bracelets, and multiple earrings. She recalled receiving a call from Cal around 5:30 p.m. to say he was leaving work in Cortland and would be home in about an hour. She said, "That was normal because Cal had recently been coming home earlier to spend more time with the children." After he called, she fed the children. Cal arrived home around 6:30 p.m. Once he arrived, he began playing with the kids. He didn't say much of anything to her, but that was also normal. The next morning, around

7:00 a.m., give or take 10 minutes, she got a call from Cal, saying Michele never came home and asked if she could help with the kids. She went right over. She lived nearby, and it only took a few minutes to get there. Around 7:15 a.m., she arrived at the entrance to the driveway and saw Michele's van parked on the driveway near the road. She stopped momentarily and looked in the van but didn't see anybody. She walked around and opened the passenger door to look inside but still didn't see anyone. She then got back in her car and drove to the house and asked Cal if Michele was there. He said, "No, I told you, she didn't come home last night," at which time she told him about seeing Michele's van at the end of the driveway. Cal said, "Well, we better go get it and bring it in."

Cal drove her in his truck out to the van, at which time they discovered the keys were in the ignition. The interior was a mess, but that was normally how it was. She said, "Michele practically lived in her van, and she was not a good housekeeper." As Cal was driving her out to get the van, she suggested Michele may have been drinking and got out and started walking in the wrong direction. Cal replied, "No, she's probably with her boyfriend or friend in NYC." She was worried about his lack of concern but didn't talk any more about it. She drove the van into the garage and parked it where Michele would normally park.

Thayer remembered a week earlier Michele had told her she was planning on going to her friend Lisa's house in NYC, but she wasn't sure when. She also thought it was unusual that the keys were in the van. She said, "Michele's life was in that van. She always locked it up." She then added, "Cal did not seem concerned she was missing but more interested in getting the kids to school."

Cal found Jenna's backpack in the van and commented, "Wow, this thing is a mess." He wanted her to drive the van into the dealership when she came in to pick up Jenna so he could have the van serviced and cleaned top to bottom. Under the circumstances, she thought that was peculiar. Cal left with the three oldest children around 8:15 a.m. Shortly after, Michele's friend Nikki called looking for Michele. After explaining what happened, Nikki said she was going to call Michele's attorney. After that, she took Tanner back to her house and around 10:30 a.m. received a call from Cal saying SP investigators were there.

Thayer said she had a good relationship with Michele, who would often confide in her. She was aware Michele had a boyfriend named Brian, that she'd met last fall. She thought he was younger than

Michele and was from the Philadelphia area, where he might have worked as a surveyor. She'd also noticed and said that "Michele was losing a lot of weight over the past few months and was smoking more heavily. She may have been drinking a little heavier also." But when asked, said there was no indication of drug use.

Thayer knew Michele saw a psychologist on a weekly basis, and she'd been prescribed medications. She also knew Michele had stopped taking her medication because "she didn't like taking it." She then told me there were occasions when she had reason to believe Michele was afraid of Cal. To explain, she said that one time she got a call from Shannon (Michele's sister-in-law) to go to Michele's because Cal was chasing her with a truck. When Barb arrived, Michele was visibly upset but was not injured. Other times Michele called upset over something with Cal, but she couldn't recall anything specific. When describing some of the verbal confrontations she witnessed, she said they were quite nasty at times, but she'd never witnessed anything physical. She then added, "Michele was as verbally abusive to Cal as he was to her."

As I was concluding my interview, she expressed concern about Cal's ATVs in the garage – that they had been re-arranged and placed in different positions than usual. Although I had examined the ATVs before my interview with her, I made a note of her concern to ask Cal. This would conclude my only interview with Thayer. Although she had initially agreed to be re-interviewed further as needed, all future requests for interviews were denied.

Shortly after returning to my office to write up the summaries of my interviews, I received a call from Sr. Investigator John Skinner, one of the lead investigators. Wow! Word sure travels fast. It sure hadn't taken long for the police to learn I had been retained to conduct an independent investigation. I wasn't surprised that Skinner was the one calling me. We knew each other quite well. We had attended the SP Academy together and shared weekend rides back-and-forth during training. Skinner expressed his concerns about an independent investigation going into Lefty's and making accusations against possible suspects. His comment jumped right out at me. Suspects at Lefty's? What suspects? At this stage of my investigation, I didn't even have any names associated with Lefty's. Let alone believe there might have been suspects among them. I assured Skinner I had no intention of doing anything to interfere with their investigation, and my only objective right now was to find Michele.

He went on to tell me that several of Lefty's employees and associates had been interviewed, and Michele's boyfriend Brian had been eliminated as a suspect. He further advised that a registered sex offender, with a felony rape conviction in Arizona, who was employed as a cook at Lefty's, had also been cleared. Even though Skinner didn't provide any names or details, this was good information to have. He also mentioned that it was becoming rather apparent Michele was having sexual relations with others, and those leads were being pursued. Again, good things to know. Skinner also spoke briefly about the search of the Harris property, including searching the surrounding ponds and lake.

The phone call with Skinner only reaffirmed what I already suspected. Even though this was officially a missing person case, it was obviously moving in the direction that a criminal element was involved. I was certainly in no position to rule out criminal involvement, but at the same time, a host of other possibilities would come to mind.

After speaking with Skinner, I had a renewed interest in learning more about Michele and her work at Lefty's, as well as her relationship with co-workers, associates, and patrons. In an effort to learn more, I thought two good sources of information would be Michele's best friend, Nikki Burdick, and Michele's brother and sister-in-law, Greg and Shannon Taylor. My call to Nikki Burdick was rather brief. After identifying myself and the purpose of my call, she said, "I have already told the police all I know. I have nothing more to say to you." Click.

I did speak with Shannon Taylor, who was agreeable initially but wanted to discuss it with Greg. Greg later returned my call and said he was uncomfortable talking with me without an attorney and referred me to Robert Miller, Michele's divorce attorney. I tried to assure Greg that my only objective at this point was to try and find Michele. Again, he referred me to Miller. Of what was he afraid? I then contacted Miller, who quickly berated me before angrily telling me, "I don't want you going anywhere near the Taylor's." Before I could respond, he slammed the phone in my ear. No real surprise there.

Throughout my investigation, I had almost daily phone calls and/or e-mails and face-to-face briefings with Cal and Joe Cawley to keep them up to speed on what I was learning. During an early briefing in early October, Sr. Investigator Skinner called again, requesting a meeting. I met with him at the SP barracks in Owego. We discussed the case in very general terms, both agreeing there was not much to share between us.

Skinner wanted me to know that if I identified a suspect they were not aware of, they would be willing to use their resources and manpower to pursue that lead. Adding that it was possible, some of those they spoke with might share something with a PI that they might not share with the police. I was glad he said that because that had been my experience as well. They were done at Lefty's, and as a result, (without naming names) eliminated some potential suspects. They were also able to identify the last person to see Michele alive (again, no name) and eliminate him as a suspect.

I was a bit puzzled because I understood that the last person known to have seen Michele alive was Brian Earley, the boyfriend. And Skinner already told me that he had been eliminated as a suspect.

As we continued, we briefly discussed the search that was conducted at the Harris property. In addition to the divers, they'd utilized the services of K-9s and NY State Forest Rangers in the ground search. According to Skinner, the Forest Rangers search was very thorough and covered nearly every square inch of the Harris property. He then added, "The Rangers say they're 95% certain that the body of Michele Harris is not on the Harris property."

He further advised that blood was located at the Harris home, and they were waiting for the results of DNA[2] testing, which was currently backlogged due to the attack on the Twin Towers. He felt confident they had enough biological material to establish a DNA profile for Michele. He also added, if the blood they found is determined to be that of Michele Harris, "Cal is going to have a big problem." I then asked, "has any determination been made regarding the volume or age of the blood?" He replied, "I can't comment on that."

Considering that response, I immediately suspected the volume of blood found was *not* significant. Otherwise, I was sure Skinner would have told me. I knew from my own experience that the freshness or age of blood cannot easily be determined unless it's still wet, if at all. So, then the age of the blood was also suspect. Again, had it been fresh, he would have told me. Had it been any different than what I suspected, i.e., fresh blood, or evidence of a massive blood-letting event, Cal would likely have been arrested by that time.

Not having a definitive answer to these questions was troubling. Was there enough blood volume for an expert to say, to any degree of scientific certainty, that it was consistent with serious injury or death? If that's the case, then yes, Cal could have a problem. On the other hand, if the volume is small, or cannot be determined, the likelihood of a minor injury with an innocent explanation presents itself. Had there been evidence of substantial blood loss, questioning its age would become moot. Trying to make this determination will be crucial.

I could clearly understand why the DNA analysis of the blood they found was delayed. But I was suspicious of Skinner's 'no comment' regarding blood volume. We already knew crime scene investigators found blood, but that was over two weeks ago. In my experience having processed numerous blood-letting scenes, I would certainly expect that any volume present would have been reasonably established by now. Therefore, I suspected a volume had been established, but it was not what they expected or hoped to find. In-as-much, they likely needed and were in search of something more.

With only a scant amount of blood, no body, and no murder weapon, the physical evidence was weak at best. The police were going to need something more. But I also knew from experience that blood evidence, no matter how small, if it was Michele's, was ominous. When combined with other known facts relative to motive, means, and opportunity could establish the probable cause needed to bring charges.

The brief meeting with Skinner provided some useful preliminary information, but names and details were lacking and would not be readily forthcoming. Accordingly, there were more questions than answers. Unless, or until charges were filed against Cal, we would be left in limbo, and those questions would remain unanswered. But my effort to find Michele would continue.

Next up – Lefty's. But before I got started, I wanted to learn a bit more about the place. At this stage, I didn't even know who the owner was. So, I turned to the New York State Liquor Authority and the ABC[3] Board. Where I would learn that, according to the ABC Board, Lefty's was officially registered under the name, Jitter's & Lefty's, at 460 Broad St., Waverly, NY. Records also revealed that the owner was one Thomas G. D'Alosio.

Since I did not yet have any names of Lefty's employees that may have known or worked with Michele, it seemed the logical starting point was with the owner, Tom D'Alosio. I met and spoke with D'Alosio, but it was very brief. D'Alosio informed me that his entire staff was fully cooperating with the SP, and a decision had been made during a business meeting that no one would discuss the details of the ongoing investigation with any member of the media or outside investigative agency. It almost sounded rehearsed, like he was expecting me. Most likely because the SP told him I would be showing up sooner or later, and they didn't want to risk that I would learn something they didn't. But why? What did they fear? I thought we had the same objective at this point. This contradicted what Skinner and I had talked about earlier.

This was my second major roadblock in my early investigation. I had little doubt that finding Michele was still a priority for the SP, but this wasn't my first rodeo. It was now evident that even though this was still considered a missing person case, the SP already suspected that Michele was murdered, and Cal was her killer. So, for all-intents-and-purposes, this was now a homicide investigation, and David Beers had become a painful thorn in their side. What did they learn at Lefty's that they didn't want me to know? For now, it would remain a mystery, and I would have to steer my investigation in a different direction.

I reached out to Kevin and Fran Harris, Cal's brother and sister-in-law. Even though Cal had an estranged relationship with his brother, he and Fran were willing to speak with me. I asked a few questions to get started, but for the most part, I let them do the talking.

Kevin admitted that he never had a close relationship with Cal. He said they've always had different interests and ways of doing things. Both Kevin and Fran said they were trying to be open-minded and supportive, but at the same time, they were very concerned about Cal's possible involvement. They'd had a lot of sleepless nights thinking about it. Fran especially was very concerned about Cal's behavior. She mentioned the day she got a call from Dwight Harris, who informed her Michele had been found in a shallow grave near his cottage. When she got off the phone and told Cal, she was taken back by his immediate response when she told him what Dwight said. Cal said, "No way, there's no way they found her there, they already searched there twice" or words to that effect.

Fran and Kevin both admit they thought it strange that ever since Michele disappeared, Cal has not looked them right in the eye and said, "I didn't have anything to do with it." Kevin said that he and a friend, Todd Mansfield, went out to Cal's house that Wednesday night to offer their support and do what they could to help Cal with the kids. Kevin described seeing Cal in the garage, breaking down, saying, "What am I going to do?" Then later, after they got the kids in bed, they were sitting on a bench in the kitchen, and again Cal put his head in his hands, saying, "What am I going do? I don't know what I'm going to do." Kevin said he was not referring to Michele's disappearance but rather, how he was going to handle it with the kids. They decided not to say anything to the kids that night.

Originally, they were going to wait until the weekend to tell the kids. But when the media heard of it, Michele's disappearance was breaking news. The kids still had two more days of school that week, so they thought it best if they said something to the kids sooner before they heard something at school. It was Kevin's understanding that Cal told the kids Thursday night.

Fran recalled a time when Michele brought Cal's guns to their house for safekeeping after she had a problem with him. Michele had confided in her on several occasions that she was afraid of Cal and, at times, feared for her life. She'd tried talking Michele into leaving and going to a shelter with the kids, but she didn't want any part of that. Fran further advised that Cal had problems with his first wife also.

Kevin and Fran were both aware that Cal had a girlfriend, Connie, and how that relationship started long before Michele filed for divorce. They thought it might have been the primary reason that Michele filed. They were also aware that Michele had gone to Dwight for some money with no questions asked, and they'd always wondered what that was all about. They thought perhaps Michele's brother Greg may have been having some financial problems at the time. Both had noticed that after Michele found out about Cal's girlfriend, there was a transition in her appearance and behavior. She started losing weight, smoking more, sniffling, and wearing more seductive type clothing. At about the same time, Cal was becoming involved with a motorcycle group, and he too was acting somewhat differently.

Fran commented that she could never understand how they had four children because they were having problems long before the last two were born. But "the next thing you know, out pops another." She added, "But I will say, Cal and Michele were both very good with their children."

Fran was concerned after learning from Barb Thayer over the past weeks that Cal was clearing the house of all Michele's belongings, including her photographs. Thayer told her, "It's like Michele never existed." She had also told her about Cal asking her to store some of Michele's things in her garage for the winter and suggested having a garage sale in the spring. But Fran also acknowledged that in the last weeks prior to her disappearance, Michele told her "things aren't too bad," and she and Cal were "getting along quite well."

Having hit the roadblock at Lefty's, in my attempt to interview co-workers and associates of Michele, I turned my attention towards Royal Ford, and Cal's co-workers and associates.

It was now October 12, 2001, and Michele had been missing one month. I stopped in to the dealership to speak with Cal and get the names of his co-workers to interview. I also remembered to ask Cal about the ATVs in his garage that Thayer mentioned were out of place. He explained that shortly after Michele went missing, some of his friends went out to his property to help in the search and were teamed up with police officers and used his ATVs. He recalled someone calling him at work from his house, asking him where the keys were to the ATVs. He couldn't remember who called, but he did tell them where the keys were. Later, when his house was turned back over to him, the ATVs were not in the same positions he had left them, so he re-arranged them back to their original positions.

Cal provided me with the names of several of his employees at Royal Ford, most of whom were working there at the time. He briefly introduced me to the employees and then allowed me to use his personal office to conduct private, one-on-one interviews. As each employee came in to be interviewed, I identified myself and the purpose of the interview. I also made it clear that the information they provided would be confidential, and regardless of whether their information was helpful or harmful to Cal, it was important for them to be truthful. They all agreed.

With only a few exceptions, the majority of those interviewed had previously been interviewed by the SP. The police focus had obviously been on Cal, with questioning about their knowledge of any affairs he was having, and/or any witnessing of verbal or physical altercations with Michele.

Additionally, police were inquiring about an alleged affair between Cal and one of his employees there at Royal Ford. None of those interviewed had any knowledge of Cal having an affair. Most had overheard Cal and Michele arguing from time-to-time, but none had witnessed anything physical. Interestingly, when I interviewed the female employee who was the subject of the police inquiry about an affair with Cal, the police never asked anything about it. Others told me that, at times, the police did not like their answers and acted annoyed.

All the employees knew Michele and several described having seen or talked to her shortly before she went missing. She would come into the dealership on a regular basis. At times she would stop in with the children. Other times, she would just stop into gas up her van but would often stick around to chat.

Most described that when they had last seen her, she seemed to be her normal, happy self. A few had noticed her recent weight loss. Several had been challenged, and others accused by police as to why they were protecting or trying to cover for Cal.

They all assured me and had told the police that under the circumstances, they had not, nor would not, do anything to protect or cover for Cal if they knew something.

What a contrast to my experience at Lefty's. Not one person I asked to interview at Royal Ford declined or turned me away. Just the opposite. What was going on here? It certainly seemed to me, at least at this stage, that the SP was, as one witness put it, on a "fishing expedition." They dangled their lines and tried what little bait they had but were not catching anything. I attempted to rationalize my contrasting experience between Lefty's and Royal Ford. If the police were learning nothing of value at Royal Ford, with those who knew Cal the best, what were they learning at Lefty's about Michele, that they don't want to share? I couldn't help wondering. If the police had gleaned important information from Royal Ford employees in their case against Cal, would I have been up against another roadblock? I was briefly encouraged by the Royal Ford interviews, but at the same time, I knew there was a long road ahead.

During one of my status briefings with Joe Cawley and Stan Drazen, Cal and Dwight were there also. We discussed the issue of the polygraph. We knew Cal had been asked to take a polygraph, and Drazen advised against it. Cal was still interested in taking it but expressed his concern about the fairness and reliability of the results since the polygraph examiner was a member of the SP and was directly involved in the investigation. Cal said, "These guys already think I'm guilty, they're just going to tell me I'm lying." I was glad he said it first because that was just what I was going to interject. I've never been a big fan of the polygraph. There are simply too many unknown and changing variables that can affect the reliability of the results.

As we all know, the common generic name for the polygraph is the 'lie-detector.' However, in my experience, I believe a more accurate description would be 'fear-detector.' Additionally, the polygraph is historically unreliable, with many valid reasons why it's use is not accepted in a court of law. Furthermore, the risk of unreliability becomes even greater when the examiner has a biased interest in the results. In my view, any examination by a biased examiner is useless and no better than the flip-of-a-coin. As such, the consensus at our meeting regarding the polygraph was this: If Cal is going to do this, it should *not* be done by the SP. We should seek an independent, highly qualified, and experienced polygraphist. Joe Cawley did some research and contacted such a polygraphist, and arrangements were made for Cal to be examined. Joe then asked me to accompany Cal to his exam.

On the date of his scheduled exam, Cal picked me up early, and we drove to the examiner's studio. He worked out of his home and had a special studio set up in the back for his examinations. He'd been provided with the basic case facts and a list of pertinent questions ahead of time, to prepare for and include in his exam. After the preliminaries, I was escorted into a separate room where I was able to observe the examination on a closed-circuit monitor. Cal was not aware that I was observing.

I watched the entire examination and took a few notes. I thought Cal had done well, but I readily recognized his anxiety and tenseness, which made him visibly uncomfortable. When the exam was completed, the examiner said it would take some time to make his assessment, and he would call Joe later with the results.

As Cal and I walked outside, we hadn't even reached his truck when he shook his head and said, "Oh, wow, I think I really bombed that. I really bombed that." I tried to assure him he had done fine and explained how I had watched the whole thing.

"Really? You watched the whole thing?" he asked.

I said, "Yeah, and under the circumstances, I thought you did fine."

"Well, let's hope so," he said.

Later, Joe was advised that the test results were inconclusive. This came as no surprise to me. After all, I knew Cal was very fearful and under a great deal of stress, knowing he was the prime suspect, and many already believing he was guilty. But with the polygraph behind us, it was time to move forward and continue my investigation.

During one of my many interviews with Cal, he identified his girlfriend as Constance 'Connie' Fellows, of Cortland, NY. I asked him to call and let her know I was interested in interviewing her. She agreed, and I later met and interviewed her in Cortland.

Connie was currently single and living with her 14-year-old daughter. She was working full-time at a lumberyard for the past year-and-a-half and part-time selling cars. She had been married and divorced three times and had known Cal for a little over two years. She was still married to her latest husband at the time and knew Cal was married. Connie had first met Michele when she came to visit Connie at work. After finding out who Connie was, Michele called her on the phone a couple of times before they met in person.

Michele told Connie that she and Cal were trying to work things out, but they couldn't do that with her in the picture. Connie told Michele she wasn't going to interfere with their relationship, but Cal continued to call and see her. She had only seen Cal about six or seven times in the past year. Connie worked at the Cortland dealership for about six weeks back in April and May of 1999. That's where she met Cal. She said, "Cal was always the gentleman" and had always treated her very well. He'd never mistreated her.

In none of their conversations had Michele ever said that Cal was physically abusive or that she was afraid of him in any way. She had never cautioned or warned her of any fears she had of Cal. As we continued, she told me she did have intimate relations with Cal, but it was very infrequent. She described it as more of an 'on-call' type relationship when Cal wanted to have sex. The last time they were intimate before Michele disappeared was near the end of August 2001, after Cal had taken her out to dinner. Then, she didn't see him again for a month.

Connie had only been to Cal's house on two occasions. The first time was in June of 1999. Michele was out of town with the kids at a camp in Ontario. She'd only spent about an hour there, and Cal drove her around the property and showed her the lake on one of his ATVs. The second time was two weeks ago, on September 29, 2001. Cal was alone, and his kids were at his brother's house. He invited her over, but she was reluctant. They talked a few times earlier in the evening, and he kept asking her to come over. She finally decided to go but felt very nervous. She arrived sometime after midnight. As she was parking her car, Cal came out to meet her. She said, "It felt a bit awkward, and I was still feeling a little nervous. But I ended up spending the night and went home the following morning."

She remembered thinking about her car parked in the driveway and asking Cal, "What if she comes home?" And Cal saying, "Well, she's not coming home tonight." She had some regrets going over that night and said she would probably not do it again. While she was there, she hadn't noticed anything unusual. She then talked about her interview with the SP. They had spoken to her on two occasions. The first time they were interested in whether Michele had ever contacted her and when. She told them she had, but it was several months earlier and nothing ever since. They also wanted to know if Cal had said anything about his financial responsibility to Michele in their pending divorce. She knew that Cal had mentioned a preliminary audit or financial statement that was done was to his benefit, but that's all she knew about it.

The SP contacted her again and asked her when the last time was, she was intimate with Cal, and she told them two weeks prior on August 29, 2001. They were not yet aware of her most recent visit to Cal's house on September 29, 2001. In concluding the interview, she recalled having heard a lot of negative comments about her relationship with Cal, but she remains supportive of him.

Cal had also given me the name of Ken 'KC' Carrigan. KC had worked for the Harris family since 1993 and was currently the business manager for the Royal Chrysler dealership, run by Cal's brother Kevin.

Cal believed KC had the 'hots' for Michele and would often see them huddled together, whispering and talking for long periods of time. He wasn't sure but suspected there might have been more to the relationship than just talk.

I found Carrigan at the Royal Chrysler dealership, where he welcomed me into his office for a private interview. He was very cooperative and right away began to explain his knowledge of the situation and his relationship with Michele. He said they would talk often, and they had developed a friendship. They both seemed to enjoy their talks together and found it easy to talk with one another. But he said, "My friendship with Michele never went beyond friendly conversation." Describing it further as more of a brother/sister type relationship saying, "It never went beyond that." Then added, "never any hugging, kissing or sex."

He did say he had a girlfriend at the time who was a bit jealous of Michele, even though nothing was happening. He had no real problems with Cal, except that he was tough to work for at times. He'd been to Cal's house on 4-5 occasions. Usually to fish or ride the jet-skis, and snowmobiles. He'd heard that Michele had a boyfriend, and Cal had a girlfriend named Connie. He'd also heard about Michele's 'boob job' and knew she was having money problems, including trouble making her credit card payments.

KC believed Michele might have borrowed some money from her father recently, possibly to pay her attorney. He'd noticed her losing weight and smoking a lot more but no specific indication of drug use. He knew and told me that Michele would often hang out with Nikki Burdick and her sister-in-law Shannon. Nikki had once worked at Royal Ford but quit and gone to the Simmons-Rockwell dealership in Sayre, PA. It was apparent KC was not fond of Nikki. He said, "Nikki clung to Michele as if she couldn't manage her life without her, and they did everything together." He always felt their relationship was a little strange because he said, "Michele was nothing like Nikki," who he described as "an odd-duck and a real drama-queen." Then added, "Shannon wasn't much different." He also explained having seen Michele out socially on a few occasions, and whenever he did, "Nikki was always right at her side."

He knew all about Michele's 'boob job' and how she seemed to enjoy showing them off, which became a hot topic of conversation for a while. Michele told him about one of the cooks at Lefty's by the name of Micky Kasper, who, after hearing of her boob job, had asked if he could feel them, and she let him. "I remember scolding her for that," he said. Then added, "I told her how stupid it was and just an open invitation for the creep in the future."

KC thought Michele's brother Greg had found her new boyfriend a job but wasn't sure. He'd heard the guy was a surveyor from the Philadelphia area. "Younger than Michele, mid-20s maybe," he said. He'd also heard that they had met at some gin mill when he came up during hunting season to hunt with some cousins in the Nichols, NY area.

He also claimed to have talked to Michelle on the phone hundreds of times. Then reiterated how Michele felt comfortable talking with him and "often came to me just for someone who would listen." She'd told him many things about her and Cal's relationship and said, "It seemed like it was always a mixed bag with them. At times, she said things weren't going well but then later turn around and say things were going much better, and they were trying to get things back together. Other times she would tell me she was afraid of him and needed to get out of there. She even expressed at times that she was in fear for her life." He then added, "I don't feel that Cal would be capable of killing Michele himself."

He also knew Michele was looking for a house of her own in the Owego area. He recalled one time Michele talked about making Cal pay big time, thinking there was a lot of money to be had from the business. Later, however, she kind of turned it around by saying she just wanted it to be over with and was willing to settle for something reasonable.

Continuing, he added, "After Michele found her new boyfriend, her attitude about Cal's relationship with his girlfriend seemed unimportant." She said, "I just don't care." She didn't love him anymore and just wanted it to be over. Her new boyfriend treated her very well, and when he told her he loved her, that's what she needed in her life. As we were winding up, he told me after Michele had her boob job, all her friends joked with her about it. And how she had gone from an A to a C cup. So, in fun, they called her 'C-cup' and he even used to write that in some of his e-mails to her. "Supposedly, Cal found out and took offense to it," he said.

I couldn't get a good read on Carrigan. Upfront, at least, he was a gentleman and very cooperative, and certainly seemed sincere in what he was telling me. But was he being completely honest? I wasn't so sure. I knew Cal was suspicious of his relationship with Michele, and the more I learned about that relationship, the more I began to agree with Cal. To me, it seemed like Carrigan was trying a little too hard to convince me that his relationship with Michele had never gone beyond 'friendly conversation.' I could certainly understand his denial, for fear that if Cal found out, it could make his life difficult.

Michele had now been missing for six weeks. Carrigan had already raised my eyebrow with his information about the cook at Lefty's. What else was there? Skinner told me earlier that others might have had a sexual relationship with Michele. Who were they and how many? Were they eliminated? What were their alibis? So many unanswered questions. But unless or until Cal was charged, those questions remained part of the mystery, at least for now.

At this point, I didn't have much to work with. I was roadblocked in the areas of most interest to me. I would have to continue with the names provided by Cal. Although, I knew it was unlikely they would have any direct knowledge of what happened to Michele. Regardless, their personal history and relationship with Cal and Michele could be important and possibly identify some new leads to follow.

I met Dwight Harris at the early meetings with Joe Cawley and Stan Drazen, but now, I decided it was time to meet and interview him one-on-one. I gave him a call, and he was anxious to meet with me. Later at his house, he laid out the Harris family history much the same way Cal had. He briefly described how he got started in the business world, where he engaged in several different business ventures under the name Harris Enterprises. Eventually, his business expanded into the automobile dealership business, and he started the Royal Auto Group with dealerships in Owego, Cortland, and Oneonta, NY as well as Sayre, PA.

Dwight made a point to tell me that a lot of credit for his success goes to his late wife, Louise. She was the one who held the family together. They both loved Michele and were devastated when they learned Michele wanted a divorce. He said, "We never saw it coming."

They both tried to convince them to try and reconcile, but it failed. Dwight then added, "Cal was especially close to his mother, and her death this past March hit him hard.

He'd spent a week-long vigil at her bedside, making the whole divorce thing that much more difficult."

After each of his three sons completed their education, Dwight groomed them into the family business, where they would eventually take over the ownership and day-to-day operations. He was very supportive of all his sons but was disappointed when they began feuding amongst themselves over various business dealings. Over time, his sons had developed estranged relationships with each other. Dwight tried to remain neutral and did not interfere, hoping they would work things out on their own.

Dwight described one afternoon when Michele came to see him by herself. He thought it might have been in July or August of 2001. She'd asked him if she could borrow some money because she was having trouble with her checking account. He said it was common knowledge among the family that he kept cash in his home safe for emergencies. When he asked Michele how much she needed, she wasn't sure but thought $3,000 would probably be enough. With no questions asked, Dwight opened his safe and counted out $3,000. He hesitated briefly, then counted out an additional $1,000. Then, handed the $4,000 to Michele and said, "Here's $4,000 just in case, I hope it's enough, and everything is OK." She thanked him and assured him that everything was fine. As she was leaving, she said, "I promise to pay you back, but for now, please don't tell Cal." Dwight agreed, and she left.

Cal's two best friends were John Caveny and Todd Mansfield. They had known each other since high school, socialized together, and knew Michele as well. Both had attended his wedding, and Mansfield was Cal's best man.

I spoke with Caveny, who confirmed his relationship with Cal since high school. At the time, he was a financial advisor and had previously handled Cal's account. He'd been out to Cal's several times, even before he built the house. They enjoyed fishing, snowmobiling, ATV rides, and cookouts. He'd also assisted in the search for Michele on the Harris property. Caveny was very concerned about the welfare of the

Harris children. He didn't know what else he could do to help Cal other than an offer to help with the kids, which he did. He expressed valid concerns for the children's welfare and needs, including the uncertainty of whether Cal was aware of or capable of meeting their needs.

Caveny advised that together, he and Cal had a lot of financial success, but when the stock market crashed, they both took a substantial financial beating. Cal was upset with him after that and decided to start making his own financial decisions. I remember commenting, "So, the two of you made lots of money, then lost lots of money?"

"Yep, made millions and lost millions, easy come, easy go," he replied.

Later, in a follow-up interview, Caveny told me that he had confronted Cal with the question, "What happened here?"

Cal's response was, "I think she's in big trouble." Then added, "I'm in big trouble here, I'm fucked, I'm fucked, I'm fucked, if they don't find semen in her I'm totally fucked."

He reiterated his concern for Cal's children, but this time added, "Cal may even be suicidal and could take the kids with him."

I pressed him hard on this, but he could neither explain nor elaborate on why he felt that way.

He just said, "Cal seems to be much more concerned about his business than himself."

> Author's Note: Later, I learned that Caveny didn't fully understand the significance of Cal's answer to his question. What Cal meant was that since he had a vasectomy after his last child was born, unless Michele was found with a presence of semen, he was screwed.

In a future attempt to interview Caveny again, he said, "I don't think I should be talking to you. I've already told Cal that I can no longer be his friend."

I then spoke briefly with Todd Mansfield, who also confirmed his relationship with Cal. He, too, had known Cal since high school and maintained their friendship. Mansfield was also a successful businessman, owning his own physical therapy business in Vestal, NY. He had been Cal's best man at his wedding, and he was also the executor of Cal's will. Like Caveny, he, too, was very concerned about the welfare of the children. He agreed that the children might have special needs that Cal was not aware of or handling well. He offered to help in any way possible, especially when it comes to the welfare of the children. He also said he'd been a part of the volunteer search team that searched for Michele on the Harris property.

It was mid-November 2001, and Michele had been missing a little over two months. Joe called to tell me that he had just learned the SP had obtained and executed a new search warrant on Cal's business at Royal Ford. They seized his laptop computers and financial records. Cal was rather upset when they took his laptop. His biggest concern was for his business records, all of which he kept there. Unfortunately, his records were not backed up on any other device or cloud service. I was not at all surprised. This was SOP. I thought they might have done this before now. It seemed they were zeroing in on the divorce and financial motive. Depending on what they found, could it mean an arrest was near? Not necessarily, but time would tell.

I knew the SP, as part of their ongoing investigation, would obtain all pertinent telephone records from all key players, including both landlines and cell phones. Initially, the top of their list would include the landline phone records from the Harris and Earley residences and Royal Ford. It would also include the cell phone records of Cal, Michele, and Brian Earley. Over time, additional phone records would be included as well.

I knew I would not be privy to these records unless Cal was arrested. Fortunately, Cal still had access to and was able to provide his business and home landline phone records. He was also able to access his and Michele's cell phone records, which were subscribed to and paid for by Royal Ford. They would give me a head start and something to review.

Cal was able to locate and provide many of the financial records he had. More records would be forthcoming from the other financial businesses where he had accounts. Some of those early financial documents I reviewed were already providing helpful information. Like the telephone records, I was interested in going back several months before Michele disappeared. I was looking for any pattern of spending habits, especially once the divorce proceedings had started. I was sure the SP would be looking for the same thing. My attention would focus on identifying both normal and abnormal expenditures by both Cal and Michele. The check-book ledgers and canceled checks Cal provided were a great start. He was very organized and kept excellent records. Again, like the telephone records, any additional financial records obtained by the SP would only be made available through the discovery process, if Cal was charged.

With the cooperation of Stan Drazen, Joe Cawley obtained copies of the divorce proceedings, including Michele's original divorce affidavit and Cal's response affidavit. I knew the SP would be carefully reviewing and scrutinizing these documents, looking to crystallize their theory regarding Cal's motive. Therefore, I would need to do the same. Besides, these documents may shed some light on some of the underlying issues, and perhaps, give me some direction as to what needed to be pursued further.

Michele's affidavit was quite thorough. She briefly described her education and work history and then her history and relationship with Cal and the children. She described various events that were gradually deteriorating their marriage. She discovered Cal was having an affair and how she was devastated upon learning they had spent a weekend together in Daytona, FL. Even though it was around the same time, Michele was having a weekend rendezvous in the Pocono's with Brian Earley.

She then went on to describe how Cal's lifestyle had changed after that, and he'd essentially abandoned her for another woman. It seemed somewhat ironic to me as I wondered whether she even realized how her own lifestyle had changed, and not necessarily in a good way.

Continuing, she claimed Cal had expelled her from his personal life and gradually yet consistently stripped her of her financial security. After describing the details of her financial situation, she went on to describe the alleged details involving incidents of physical abuse. Each incident was alleged to have been preceded by verbal abuse that escalated and resulted in her being injured. The first incident she claimed occurred in December of 2000, where she described Cal chasing her outside, causing her to fall in the driveway and receive bruising. The second incident she described as the 'final straw' had occurred on March 19, 2001 (the day Cal's mother died). It was similar to the first in that there had been an ongoing childish argument. (Notably, this happened two months *after* she had already filed for divorce). Cal had just discovered that his guns were missing, and a month earlier, Michele had removed them and turned them over to another family member. After learning this, Cal grabbed two of her winter jackets, holding them hostage, saying he would return them once she returned his guns. As a result, a childish argument began. They once again ended up out on the driveway, which was now ice-covered. Continuing to argue, Cal jumped into his truck with the jackets. Michele, attempting to retrieve them, reached inside the truck. Cal grabbed her arm and pushed her away. She slipped back and fell on the icy driveway, striking her left hand on the icy pavement, sustaining cuts to her hand.

In my review of Michele's affidavit, I believed many of the elements contained therein were factually accurate. Not surprisingly, she quickly condemned Cal and explained how devastated she was when learning of his affair. Yet, she failed to acknowledge her own six-month affair she was having with Brian Earley at the same time.

As expected, Cal's affidavit was utterly different. He got right to the point. He agreed with much of what Michele laid out in her affidavit and readily accepted blame for Michele wanting the divorce. He also acknowledged the affair with his paramour and how he'd later confessed his infidelity to Michele during a getaway to celebrate their ninth-year anniversary. This was when he bought Michele her Rolex watch, and they had renewed their sexual affection with each other. Believing that Michele had forgiven him, and their marriage was on the mend.

In response to the alleged physical abuse, Cal acknowledged the events Michele described did happen. However, Cal's version of events and descriptive details were different. He admitted that on both occasions, they had argued, and Michele had fallen to the ground. But he denied having any knowledge of her being injured as a result.

I've dealt with my share of domestic-related incidents between husband and wife, boyfriend/girlfriend, etc. This one was no different.

Here, we had a typical, he-said/she-said situation, with conflicting scenarios of what really happened. So, who do we believe? The police were never called, and Michele was never treated for her injuries. Therefore, with no police report or medical records, there was no way to corroborate what truly happened.

When I first read Michele's affidavit, I thought for sure Cal would deny that any of these things ever happened. So, I was surprised when he confirmed they did happen. But more importantly, he went on to explain in much greater detail than Michele, his version of events. I certainly got the impression that Cal's version of events was very plausible. Therefore, whether she was injured or not during either event is unknown. But if she was, it was accidental, and any resulting injury that may have occurred was unintentional.

Interestingly, in Michele's affidavit, she was quick to condemn Cal for his affair. In contrast, Cal's affidavit included nothing about Michele's affair, even though he knew she was having one.

I had little doubt about who the SP would believe in this matter. Michele was missing, and Cal was public enemy number one. They would automatically latch onto anything negative Michele had to say about Cal and use it to build their case against him.

Cal was living day-to-day, fixed under a discriminatory black cloud of suspicion, knowing that the hammer of justice could fall at any moment. Therefore, it was crucial even with what little we had, to be as prepared as possible, should that happen. But it was a challenge trying to stay on top of things while working with such limited information.

---

1. Forensics: the application of scientific methods and principals used and accepted in a Court of Law.
2. DNA: Deoxyribonucleic acid, a self-replicating material present in nearly all living organisms as the main constituent of chromosomes. The carrier of genetic information.
3. ABC: Alcoholic Beverage Control

3

THE SEARCH FOR MICHELE

The initial search for Michele began within hours of her being reported missing on September 12, 2001. Within 24-hours, a temporary command-post was established at the Halsey Valley Fire Department, where the search effort to find Michele was formalized under the command of SP Lt. Robert Galletto. To assist the SP, numerous personnel from other state agencies, surrounding community organizations, and private citizens responded to help in the search. The NYS Forest Rangers, as a division of NYSDEC[1], took the lead in organizing, launching, and directing the massive ground search. The Forest Rangers, under the command of Ranger Terry Figary, responded from Region 7, which encompasses a nine-county area in central NY. Forest Rangers are specially trained in the search for lost or missing persons, or downed aircraft in remote wilderness areas. They also have advanced skills in land navigation through rugged mountainous terrain and valley areas, as well as those downright hard-to-get-at places. Anyone familiar with rural upstate NY knows exactly what I mean.

Some of the other organizations involved included S&R (search & rescue) teams from Tioga, Tompkins, Broome, Cortland and Chenango Counties. They possessed similar skills to those of the Rangers. A vast contingent of SP uniformed troopers and BCI investigators, along with EMT's, firefighters, ENCON officers, and civilian volunteers, teamed up with the experts, to form several search teams.

The immediate area that needed to be searched encompassed an area of more than 250 acres. Except for Empire Lake, a small pond, and a few open fields, most of the search area was densely wooded. With the aid of aerial, property, and topographical maps, organizers divided the search area into eleven search-blocks. These were designated A thru K. All designated search 'blocks' were plotted on maps and assigned to each search team, along with any specific instructions related to their area. Search team leaders were instructed and kept detailed records of the results of their searches. It would take two full days to complete the search. For the most part, individual searchers stuck to very tight linear or grid-line patterns and were usually no more than an arms-length apart at any given time. After completing their assigned search and returning to the command post, team leaders turned in their reports and were de-briefed by the senior organizers.

| Empire Lake

While the massive ground search was underway, additional search efforts were being carried out on other parts of the Harris property. SP divers with SONAR equipment was brought in to search an area pond and Empire Lake. Several bio-sensor K-9 teams, including cadaver dogs, were engaged in the search. Helicopters were utilized for flyovers and aerial searches, using naked-eye searching as well as FLIR and 3-D scanning technology known as LiDAR. After exhausting all the various search methods available by land, sea, and air, there were no signs of Michele or evidence of her demise anywhere.

While several SP investigators were assigned to conduct personal interviews, other investigative functions were being carried out simultaneously by other investigators. Search warrants, for example, were being applied for, issued, and subsequently executed.

So, what exactly were the SP asking to search? There was already one search warrant and a court order applied for and obtained very early in the investigation. On September 14, 2001, to be exact. The first search warrant was rather lengthy and included the authority to search just about anything and everything inside and outside of Cal's house, property, and in his and Michele's vehicles. The SP was leaving no stone unturned. The search warrant was broad enough to grant them the authority to seize just about anything they believed might aid in finding Michele or building a case against Cal. We'll find out later, exactly what they did find.

A court order was also applied for and granted at the same time as the search warrant. The court order authorized the SP to covertly install an electronic tracking device, commonly known as a GPS[2] unit into Cal's Ford F-150 pick-up truck. The GPS unit needed to be installed by hardwiring it directly into the vehicle's electrical system. The order also authorized the installation of an infrared transmitter, known as a VIP[3] or 'fire-fly' device that would allow operatives, using night vision equipment, to track the location and movements of Cal's vehicle at night. The initial SP request for the court order was to allow for enhanced surveillance capability of the suspect – Cal Harris. Police stated in their application that traditional physical surveillance methods in rural areas such as Tioga County were too difficult to conceal from the suspect. Additions made to the application included a paragraph claiming, *"The GPS device would allow investigating officers to offer additional protection to the children of Michele Harris as they are currently in the care of their father, Cal Harris, a suspect in the disappearance of Michele."* Another paragraph claimed, *"use of this device will allow officers to act on all sources of information in a timely fashion."*

These were weak arguments at best. Claiming that this order would provide additional protection for the Harris children was a real stretch. I knew from personal experience that if the SP had even the slightest reason to believe the children of Cal Harris were in any danger, they would have yanked them out in a heartbeat and placed them into protective custody. That being said, I can't disagree with their rationale for wanting to track the whereabouts of Cal. After all, he was the primary suspect. Would their efforts pay off? Would Cal lead them to the incriminating evidence?

During the entire six months of GPS monitoring of Cal's movements in his truck, the SP found nothing of real value. However, during their analysis of the GPS data, they discovered that on September 17, 2001, Cal's truck was in an area they described as an 'unusual location' on the property, some distance from the residence.

Author's Note: Keep in mind that, at this time, the SP was still engaged in their around-the-clock search of Cal's house and property.

While analyzing the earlier GPS data from Cal's truck, the SP extracted what they described as a few 'points of interest' where it had remained stationary. In their attempt to specifically identify these 'points of interest,' SP Investigators Bill Standinger and Steve Andersen flew in a helicopter to get a closer look. The first area of interest was near Lake Timberline in Saint Joseph, PA. Data showed that Cal remained at that location for approximately nine minutes on September 21, 2001. Closer examination revealed that this was an ATV dealership. The second and third locations were both in the general proximity of the Binghamton University Campus along the Vestal Parkway. They were later identified as Denny's Restaurant and Chucky Cheese.

The data also revealed two more points of interest near Cal's residence. Cal visited the fourth 'unusual' location around 9:00 p.m. on September 17, 2001, for two minutes. This area was described as a field, northwest of Cal's residence, and in the general proximity of a nearby pond. Upon closer observation, they described what appeared to be laid-up stone, a hand-dug well, and another area surrounded by brush, which could be the remains of an old house foundation. There was also an area of fresh dirt and some tree stumps on the north side of the pond.

The fifth and final location of interest was located southeast of Cal's residence, just off the driveway leading to Empire Lake. Data had shown that Cal visited this location around 11:00 a.m. on September 23, 2001, for approximately three hours. Upon closer observation, it was described as an open area near the lake, and what appeared to be the remnants of a fire. After completing their aerial mission, Standinger and Andersen returned to the command post, recommending that these areas, specifically the ones on or near Cal's property, be targeted for a more thorough examination.

Four years later, after learning of this aerial search effort, I wanted to see what Cal could remember. After reviewing the lead with Cal, he couldn't recall the exact dates but recognized and confirmed he had been in all those locations. Before Michele disappeared, he took an ATV used by his son Taylor to the ATV dealership for repair, and about a week after she disappeared, he returned to pick it up. He also recalled taking the kids to Chucky Cheese, and later to lunch at Denny's. When I inquired about the location where he had been placed for two minutes on September 17, 2001, at 9:00 p.m., he hung his head and said, "Yeah, that was me." He said, "I know I probably shouldn't have, but it was driving me nuts. They'd already been at my house for a week, and I was just curious about what was taking so long." He'd only been there a couple of minutes trying to get a sneak-peek, but it was too dark. He couldn't really see anything, so he left and returned to Cooperstown. When I inquired about the final location, he couldn't remember a specific date, but there were many times when they would build a fire when they were down by the lake. He also added that it would not be unusual for him to use his truck to haul firewood or the jet-skis down to the lake and park in that location.

Michele had now been missing for two months. The SP devised a new plan. Discouraged from not having found anything of value, the SP's frustration was mounting. All respective search efforts so far, although commendable, had come up empty. It was now time to up the ante, and they tried something new. On November 12, 2001, an application was made for a new, second search of the Harris property. This time, however, they were requesting authority to conduct not only another search of the property but also to conduct surreptitious physical and video surveillance of Cal Harris.

The only new supporting probable cause they had was weak at best. The SP was relying almost exclusively on the GPS analysis that placed Cal in that 'unusual' location at 9:00 p.m. for two minutes on September 17, 2001. But they never explained what was so 'unusual' about it. The application also stated that the physical evidence indicated a *possible* (emphasis mine) struggle in the kitchen/garage area, and the blood spatter contained the DNA of Michele Harris. It also stated that Michele was still missing along with her purse, identification, and jewelry. Even though only two months had passed since the last search, the application claimed that new and enhanced search methods would be used to help locate human remains and physical evidence.

It's important to note that there had already been a steady police presence in Cal's residence and on his surrounding property under search warrant authority for eight straight days since Michele went missing. An extensive search inside and out had already taken place. So, what were they really looking for now? In the final paragraph of the SP application, their real objective was revealed:

> *The investigation will seek to pressure Calvin Harris into making contact with any secreted evidence on his property or elsewhere by asking for his consent and telling his attorney's a massive multi-agency search will be conducted at the property commencing on Wednesday, November 14, 2001. Deponent submits it is more likely that, upon learning of the date, time, and extensive search to be conducted, Calvin Harris will display behaviors consistent with guilt, including the checking of evidence and possible site of Michele Harris' remains.*

The District Attorney, Gerald Keene, also submitted an affidavit in support of the new search order with this additional information:

> *There is probable cause to believe that evidence of the whereabouts of Michele Harris and contact with her assailants and others involved in the criminal activity surrounding her disappearance or abduction/murder will be obtained." And, "The monitoring of his activities after the notice of a second search at his property will provide probative evidence that would not be available by other means..." And, "... it is reasonable to conclude that an assault/homicide commenced at the residence of Calvin Harris and Michele Harris upon her return the evening of September 11, 2001. When notified of the enhanced search capabilities, applicant submits, Calvin Harris may continue to clean, seek to verify, and confirm his clean-up and disposal of the evidence including the remains of Michele Harris.*

Subsequently, the requested search warrant, along with a physical and video-surveillance order was granted by the court. Then, according to plan, through his attorney, Cal was once again asked for consent to search his property. As expected, attorney Drazen, after citing the negative results of their previous weeklong search, denied their request. After that, Drazen was advised that a new 'enhanced' search of Cal's residence and property had been authorized by the court and would commence on November 14, 2001. The snare was set.

This entire initiative involved a great deal of planning, resources, and manpower. It was cleverly and strictly designed not to pressure Cal but rather to provoke him, by pre-announcing their intended search effort. The SP expected that once provoked, his 'consciousness of guilt' would trigger him to lead investigators to the evidence they had been seeking since day one. With the new search warrant and court order, there was a two-fold objective. First and foremost, to monitor Cal's response once the new search was announced. Secondly, to undertake a renewed search for Michele. If their plan was going to work, the renewed search for Michele needed to be convincing.

Learning that the SP had given advanced notice of this new search warrant, I knew exactly what they were up to. It was a tactical maneuver I was quite familiar with from my training. In-as-much, I could have easily crippled their entire initiative by warning Cal of what was about to happen and why. But it didn't require a great deal of thought before deciding I would not do that. Cal had not yet been charged with anything, and I didn't want to be accused of interfering with an ongoing investigation. In the interest of justice, I wanted to see how this would play out. A second, but equally important reason for not saying anything to Cal, was my fear that if he knew what they were up to, he might try something cute, like leading them on a wild goose chase. Thus, tipping them off that he'd been warned and blaming me.

After that, the SP carried out their renewed search of the property surrounding the Harris residence. While simultaneously, covert five or six-man surveillance teams were strategically positioned to observe, monitor visually, and videotape any/all of Cal's activities, day and night. Regular BCI field investigators were teamed up with specially trained members of the SP MRT.[4] All of whom were equipped with camouflage clothing, video cameras, night-vision equipment, and more. They even set up a camouflaged pole-camera, focused on Cal's house. Then, working in shifts around the clock, they began bird-dogging any and all of Cal's activities for the next four days. The renewed search of his property was carried out in nearly identical fashion to the original search two months earlier. It provided an opportunity to re-search those 'areas of interest' identified by the GPS data. The only 'enhanced' search method they used in this new search was the use of a more specialized team of K-9s that we'll learn about shortly.

At this juncture of the SP investigation, this was an excellent investigative strategy. One that I was familiar with and witnessed with some success in the past. Knowing that the SP firmly believed Cal was their man, it made perfect sense, as did the installation of the GPS device on his truck. Unfortunately for them, all of their collective efforts, although stellar, failed. None of their much-anticipated results ever materialized. Considering the herculean-efforts put forth, I could certainly understand their continued frustration. Their planning, resources, and man-hours in this new search, all carried out with the genuine belief in Cal's guilt, would once again be thwarted by a failure to produce the desired results. Frustrated? Disappointed? Discouraged? Indeed.

The days and weeks turned into months, and it was now late September 2002. Michele had been missing for over one year. Prompted by the first anniversary of her disappearance, the SP renewed their efforts to find Michele once again, utilizing several bio-sensor K-9 teams from across the state. Unfortunately, the result was the same – no Michele.

The earlier K-9 searches conducted back on September 12, 2001, as well as a more advanced K-9 search on November 14, 2001, were also both negative. The latter K-9 search had utilized the services of the Ramapo Rescue Dog Association (RRDA) out of Ramsey, New Jersey, under the command of Tim and Penny Sullivan. They used six K-9s with their respective handlers.

The RRDA is a volunteer rescue organization that utilizes air-scenting German Shepherd dogs to help locate missing persons. They've been in business since 1971. The K-9s and their handlers are highly trained to work in wilderness, urban, water, and disaster environments. They're also trained in crime-scene searches, evidence recovery, and the search for cadavers. The RRDA has a lengthy track record and history of success stories. Watching them in action is a great experience. If Michele's remains were anywhere on that property, I'm confident they would have been found.

The SP was not only committed, but they were also persistent in their dutiful pursuit to find Michele Harris. They had already exhausted their earlier water search efforts on the Harris property, including Empire Lake and a small pond near the driveway. It was now time to expand the perimeter of their search. To accomplish this, they obtained both current and century-old property maps of the area. Then they added aerial and topographical maps, identifying any lakes and ponds within the expanded perimeter. Later, respective landowners were identified and contacted by investigators, seeking permission to search the bodies of water on their properties. While speaking with landowners, they also inquired about any open or abandoned wells on their properties. To my knowledge, all landowners contacted were cooperative and granted permission for their properties to be searched. After that, SP divers searched more than thirty lakes/ponds, while other investigators, using remote submersible cameras, searched deep into a dozen or more open or abandoned wells. Another stellar effort, but once again – nothing.

During the ongoing investigation, including all the various searches taking place, Cal was still trying to appear strong in front of his children. He continued his effort to shield them from everything that was happening. With that in mind and for the benefit of himself and his children, he decided to take them on a short vacation. Later, we'll find out what happened when Cal traveled to Disney World with his children.

1. NYSDEC: New York State Dept. of Environmental Conservation
2. GPS: Global Positioning System
3. VIP: Visual Identification Projector
4. MRT: Mobile Response Team

4

THE SEARCH CONTINUES

I t was now late November 2002, and Michele had been missing well over a year.

Several repeated aerial searches had already been completed over the Harris property with negative results. The purpose or what prompted yet another aerial search was unclear. But on November 24, 2002, Sr. Investigator Mulvey went on a helicopter ride, which took her over the Royal Ford dealership, and then out over the Harris property once again. She noted that they had been flying over the Harris property when she observed Cal standing outside.

During part of her observation, she noticed that Cal had a video-camera. She also noted that he appeared agitated and was seen waving his fist in the air. She ended her summation by noting that nothing noteworthy was observed relative to the location of Michele Harris's body. Imagine that. Seriously? Did she really think she was going to find Michele or evidence of her demise from the air more than a year later? Of course not. This was just a joyride. A muscle-flexing exercise and bullying power-play designed strictly to provoke and, as noted, 'agitate' Cal. Writing it up as a 'search' for Michele? Nonsense.

Three days later, Mulvey sent an e-mail to the helicopter pilot. She started by saying, *"Thanks for the great ride on Sunday. I have to document Cal Harris's little 'dance' he did for us. Every little bit helps you know. I still don't think he acted very happy that we were searching for his wife."*

Every little bit helps you know? So, tell me, how was the agitated look on Cal's face, his fist-waving and little dance, considered helpful? Calling this a 'search' for Michele was ludicrous. Mulvey's 'search' scenario was just a sham, disguised to mask her true purpose. Later, it only got worse.

It was now the end of April 2003, and Michele had been missing for nineteen months. As we've already learned, all previous search efforts on and around the Harris property to find Michele, evidence of her disappearance, or proof against Cal were unsuccessful. Other than Mulvey's joyride over Cal's house, the motivation, and commitment by the SP in their effort to find Michele was commendable. Despite all previous failures, they remained undeterred. They were not giving up. In-as-much, they launched yet another massive ground search. Once again, they would be focusing their search along the gas pipeline right-of-way, near the Harris property.

Under the command of SP Lt. Robert Galletto, an extensive foot-search detail was organized. The detail was comprised of two Senior Investigators, three Sergeants, eight investigators, eleven uniform troopers, six more troopers with K-9s, two NY State Forest Rangers, and two ENCON Officers. Assigned members received instructions to report to the command post, dressed appropriately for a foot-search in woods, brush, bogs, and hills. They would be searching both on and adjacent to the gas pipeline area oriented in an east-west direction along nearly a four-mile stretch between Halsey Valley Road and Straits Corners Road, just south of the Harris property. An area the SP knew Cal was familiar with. Once again, after another extensive and exhaustive search, nothing of evidentiary value was found. Other than an old Nokia cell phone that had been lost by a hunter in 2002.

Another year passed. It was now May of 2004, and still no sign of Michele. Sr. Investigator Mulvey organized another ground search. This time, they were searching the area surrounding the Royal Ford dealership, the nearby Lopke Gravel Pit, and St. Patrick's Cemetery. With a contingent led by NYS Forest Rangers, with no less than twenty BCI Investigators and uniformed troopers, the targeted areas were searched. The only thing of interest found was a small bone fragment, which was later determined to be nonhuman.

Another year went by. It was now May of 2005. Time for some more muscle-flexing. Mulvey once again called for an aerial 'search' with the helicopter, in what she would describe as "a continuing effort to locate the remains of Michele Harris." Another joyride. This time, she invited Cal's friend, Todd Mansfield and Tioga County District Attorney (DA) Jerry Keene to accompany her. This was nothing more than a PR stunt. But once again, she flew over the Royal Ford dealership and then out to Cal's place, under the premise of 'searching' for Michele.

While flying over the Harris property, Mansfield pointed out some of the trails he and Cal had ridden on while snowmobiling or riding ATV. Remember, this was 2005. The SP already had that information and searched those areas extensively. From my perspective, this was now part of Mulvey's initial and/or ongoing push to help convince Keene to move forward with the prosecution of Cal Harris. She'd been on the warpath from the get-go. Recall her words to attorney Stan Drazen, "I know Cal killed her, and I'm going to prove it."

From that day forward, the beating of her drum had only become louder. But in her frustration, she was growing tired and running out of patience. Michele had now been missing nearly four years. Despite their best efforts to find Michele, it had not happened. Reluctantly, Mulvey began to accept the reality that maybe she would not be found. As troubling as that was, she remained gung-ho in her pursuit of Cal. For her, the time had come to exercise her authority as lead investigator. Time to convince the DA, even without a body or murder weapon that 'win-lose-or-draw,' the prosecution of Cal Harris needed to move forward.

By April of 2006, Michele had been missing four-and-a-half years. As you'll learn shortly, Cal had previously been indicted for Michele's murder about six months earlier.

In their continued and ongoing efforts to find Michele, the SP organized and assembled a twelve-man team of investigators and troopers to conduct yet another ground search. This time, after getting permission from several local landowners of properties adjacent to the Harris property, SP searchers would once again return to the area around Evelien Hill Road to resume their search. Evelien Hill Road is a dirt road. Its orientation is north and south about one mile behind or east of the Harris residence.

The targeted search area was along a two-mile stretch between Gilke Hill Road, north to the gas pipeline, and then continued north before coming to a dead-end in a remote, densely wooded area. The search of this area and the area along the gas pipeline were justifiable areas of interest that needed to be searched. The SP had learned from several witnesses, that Cal would frequently ride his ATVs and snow-mobiles on remote dirt roads and the open clearing along the gas pipe-line. Considering the surrounding topography, which was mostly densely wooded areas, the cleared dirt roads and gas pipeline area provided ideal riding locations. After another long and exhaustive search on and around Evelien Hill Road, including several adjoining properties, nothing of interest or of evidentiary value was found – another great effort but a fruitless one once again.

All search efforts to find Michele were conducted outdoors, either directly on or near the Harris property and the area around Royal Ford. When considering all those commendable efforts, I couldn't help but think of all the resources and hundreds of man-hours involved, with absolutely nothing to show for it. Even after aggressively searching for more than four years and finding nothing, it was evident the SP remained steadfast in their belief that Cal had killed his wife and disposed of her body. But I had to ask, did they really think Cal was skillful enough to outsmart them? Or clever enough to have found some mysterious or magical place, known only to him, that was so well hidden that it could never be found?

Having struck out repeatedly in all their search efforts had to be discouraging and frustrating. I often wondered whether this had ever prompted anyone on the SP detail to challenge the direction of their investigation or even recommend a new one. The rationale was, "Look, I know you all think Cal did this, but it's been four years, and we haven't found squat. Perhaps, it's time we start looking elsewhere." From my perspective, even if that did happen, Mulvey would have put the kibosh on it instantly, and would likely castigate anyone for even suggesting it. Later, with respect to all their search efforts of the Harris property, I remember Joe Cawley in court saying, "The reason they never found Michele in any of those places is that she was never there. They were looking in the wrong place."

We now know there was no successful search outside, but what did they find inside the Harris home? Let's jump back now to the early part of the investigation as crime-scene investigators entered to conduct an assessment and examination of the inside of Cal's house.

5

MICHELE'S BLOOD

Within the first few hours after Michele went missing, Cal had given the SP unlimited and unrestricted access, in writing, to search inside his home and his surrounding property. He also signed a second consent granting permission to search Michele's van and his truck. After a lengthy interview at his office, Cal led two BCI investigators out to his residence. Before taking them to the house, he stopped at the end of the driveway and pointed to where Michele's van had been discovered earlier. Shortly after that, he gave them complete access to his house, answered a few more of their questions, and then returned to work to allow them to continue their investigation at their discretion.

As previously explained, Michele's van had been driven by Thayer from the end of the driveway to the garage. After looking through the van, investigators arranged to have it towed back to the SP barracks in Owego. There, it underwent a forensic examination by the Troop 'C' FIU, under the direction of Investigator Steven Andersen, assisted by trooper Steven Ryan.

When Andersen and Ryan first arrived at the Owego barracks, they were briefed by Sr. Investigator Mulvey and then started their examination. The examination of the exterior and interior of Michele's van was a lengthy process that was compounded by a large number of items inside her vehicle.

By mid-afternoon on September 13, 2001, they had not yet

completed their examination of the van when Andersen was pulled off and sent to the Harris residence to examine the area where it was found. The examination of Michele's van was put on hold. Upon arrival at the Harris estate, Andersen noted intense ground and aerial searches underway, including the use of K-9s, ATVs, and a helicopter. During his assessment at the end of the driveway, he noted the area was of "no forensic value." He claimed it had been compromised by personnel and vehicles involved in the search.

| Michele's Van Found Here

Author's Note: Although this area had been compromised, I would have to disagree that it was of 'no forensic value.' Even though Andersen found nothing to do at the end of the driveway, he was still at the scene, but for some unknown reason(s), he was never asked to conduct a forensic examination inside the Harris residence. That's still a mystery.

I don't like playing Monday morning quarterback, but to me, this was a lost opportunity. In requesting the services of FIU, someone had realized their priorities got mixed up by starting with Michele's van rather than the area where it was found. By the time Andersen got there, it was too late. Or was it? Conceivably, Michele's van and the area immediately surrounding it was a potential crime scene or extension of a crime scene. As soon as Cal pointed out the area, steps should have been immediately taken to protect the area until it could be examined. All BCI investigators have crime-scene tape in the trunks of their cars.

It's certainly not unusual for a crime scene, or potential crime scene, to be compromised prior to the arrival of the FIU. And I'm not aware of any crime scene that could be considered 'pristine.' It's not unusual to learn that those first responders, such as police, fire, medical, or even relatives or private citizens, have already been at the scene, doing whatever. Despite any known or potential compromise, the scene must still be examined forensically. One of my favorite adoptive quotes, "It's better to have looked and found nothing, than not to have looked at all." So, how can Andersen conclude there was 'no forensic value,' if he never looked for it? He can't.

Andersen left the scene that day, having accomplished very little, only to return the following day, September 14, 2001, under a renewed request. Meanwhile, the clock kept ticking. This time he was requested to examine the interior of the Harris residence. Again, with Cal's written consent. During a cursory assessment, he observed what appeared to be dried red stains on the wall in the garage and just inside the entryway to the kitchen. Presumptive field tests of these stains, using LMG[1] tested positive for the presence of blood (non-species specific).

As a result of Andersen's preliminary findings, Lt. Robert Galletto and Sr. Investigator John Skinner, who were both present, halted the assessment process temporarily to seek a formal search warrant. All personnel exited the residence, and a crime scene log was initiated. No further action was taken pending the issuance of a search warrant. Uniformed personnel was posted as sentries at the door to maintain the integrity of the scene. This was precisely the right thing to do. Unfortunately, it should have been done two days earlier.

Whenever a criminal element (foul play) is suspected, as it was here, time is critical. The more time that passes, the higher the risk that any potential evidence will be compromised, contaminated, lost, or even destroyed completely.

Cal's written consent had no time restrictions to search his house and surrounding property. On the first day, after more than six hours of searching and not finding anything, the SP packed up and left. After that, Cal and his children, along with other family and friends, were prematurely allowed back into the house. Relinquishing control of the house before a forensic examination was conducted was *not* the right thing to do for a couple of reasons.

First, and most importantly, shortly after Michele was reported missing, foul play was suspected, and Cal immediately became the number-one suspect. Therefore, had there been a crime scene at the Harris home, they just gave their number one suspect another window of opportunity to further compromise, clean-up, or destroy any remaining evidence of the crime. Secondly, failure to maintain a continuous police presence at the scene posed a significant risk to the integrity, and probative value of any evidence found thereafter.

The delayed search warrant was applied for by the Troop 'C' MCU[2] and subsequently issued late in the day on September 14th. The warrant would supersede Cal's prior written consent. The authority granted by the search warrant was generously broad and all-inclusive for the entire Harris residence and surrounding property. The next morning, September 15, 2001, under the authority of the search warrant, Andersen and Ryan began a lengthy and much more detailed assessment and processing of the Harris residence and surrounding property. The entire process would take nearly five days to complete. This was in addition to the three days they had already been there. Detailed documentation of the process included notes, diagrams, measurements, photographs, and video. Along the way, they would also identify, examine, collect, preserve, and at times test, various items believed to have evidentiary value.

They began their assessment outside, starting at the end of the driveway. Later, down the driveway, to Empire Lake, where they described a small deck, dock, motorboat, and canoe, all of which were examined with nothing remarkable found. Their focus then shifted to the exterior of the house, looking for any signs of forced entry. They found none.

As they moved their assessment to the interior of the house, their examination continued but would be accentuated much more exten-sively. There, they would examine, describe, and document every room in the house.

Author's Note: Without trying to diminish or minimize the quality or completeness of their work, I'll briefly summarize some of their work, while focusing more on their pertinent findings.

Starting in the basement, then moving to the main floor, the second floor, and then the garage, they examined every room in the house. Along the way, they took notes, photographs and described everything they observed, at times, noting whether anything was remarkable or not.

While examining Cal's office, sports trophies and memorabilia were noted on the shelves along with several photographs of the children. No pictures of Michele were noted. Cupboards containing business, personal investment, and property records were also noted. An unloaded .22 caliber Winchester rifle was located on top of a locked safe. A naked-eye examination of the rifle was conducted for the presence of blood. None was found.

In the kitchen, it was noted, among other items on the island, that a wooden knife block had one slot vacant. Later, the missing knife was found in a drawer.

The second floor consisted of three children's bedrooms and a master bedroom. The master bath also had a master walk-in closet, which contained both his and her clothing. On the shelf, there was an assortment of rifle and shotgun ammunition. As noted, Cal had advised Andersen that the north sink was his, and Michele used the south sink. Next to Michele's sink was an electric toothbrush and a drawer next to it containing combs, hairbrushes, and other toothbrushes utilized by Michele. These were all collected and later submitted to the lab to try and establish a DNA profile for Michele.

Andersen and Ryan then turned their focus back to the kitchen entryway, to pick up where Andersen left off two days earlier. They concentrated their efforts in this area and then moved into the garage. Andersen's assessment provided a detailed description of the garage and its contents, along with supporting photographs. During their assessment, Ryan discovered several tiny specks of red stains in some cracks and crevices on the garage floor close to where Michele would park her van. Random areas were selected, swabbed, and field-tested. Presumptive field-testing revealed a positive presence of blood.

In greater detail, Andersen went on to describe how the concrete garage floor was painted gray. But there were several worn, peeling, or flaking areas, predominately in the higher traffic areas. Along the north wall in front of the man-door leading into the entryway from the garage were two, side-by-side brown throw rugs with stiff rubber borders. Both showed signs of heavy wear and bore visible particles of debris, including some small hairs, likely from the family dog. There was a single step up from the garage floor to the entryway floor, with an aluminum threshold under the door. The door was hinged on the left (west) side and opened inward into the entryway.

Bloodstains were observed on the wall and floor of the garage, as well as in the entryway. Andersen described how some of the suspected blood was under the edges of the loose or chipped paint and within the irregularities of the garage floor. With that, he surmised that an attempted or partial clean-up had occurred. He also surmised that evidence of attempted clean-up was also present in the entryway. And a small amount of spatter was consistent with medium velocity blood spatter, which *could be* (emphasis mine) from an assault. Andersen also added that given the placement of the respective blood spatter in the entryway, the man-door leading to the garage would have been closed at the time the spatter was deposited.

Ryan and Andersen spent the better part of the day on September 15, 2001, looking for and identifying specific areas where the small red stains, believed to be blood, were located. During this early assessment, select areas were swabbed and field-tested positive for blood. During that process, several stains were consumed in their entirety. Unfortunately, no photographs were taken before testing. In-as-much, the elementary crime scene protocol had not been followed.

The following day, absent Andersen, the ongoing assessment was continued by Trooper Ryan, who was now being assisted by Investigator Ken Sosnowski. Even though the first signs of blood were discovered two days earlier, Sosnowski began taking the first photographs of the blood. This was four days after Michele was reported missing. After photographs, additional swabs were taken from randomly selected areas for further testing.

While partially following crime-scene protocol during the collection of forensic evidence, Ryan and Sosnowski obtained random samples directly from the suspect red-stained areas and submitted them to the New York State Police FIC[3] Laboratory in Albany, NY for further testing. As a result, the FIC was able to extract and create a DNA profile which subsequently matched the known DNA profile of Michele Harris. However, they fell short of a more advanced protocol by failing to collect any nearby 'unstained' areas for use as 'control samples.' Sometimes known as a 'blank' or control standard. In other words, a sample that's free from any suspect unknowns.

Forensically, being able to compare a known with an unknown, helps to ensure the reliability of test results. As an added advantage, control samples can be examined further for the presence of other substances. Here, the perfect opportunity presented itself to do just that. The SP was looking for anything that might help corroborate their theory. Specifically, regarding the alleged 'clean-up' in the garage. Conceivably, a forensic examination of one or more control samples could have identified the type of cleaning substance used, if any. Interestingly, a few years later, we learned that a forensics expert consultant had suggested doing this type of examination. But to my knowledge, it was never done, or if it was, it was never disclosed to the defense.

Two forensic scientists from the FIC were called in to assist with the processing of the scene with the use of Fluorescein[4] for possible enhancement of the blood evidence. Briefly, Fluorescein is a chemical reagent that reacts with the iron in the blood and acts as a catalyst, creating a light-producing chemical reaction known as chemiluminescence.[5] Once applied, if there is a reaction, for a limited time, the area will literally 'glow-in-the-dark.' Long enough to visualize and photograph the results. After being photographed, the reactive area can be swabbed for further lab testing.

Fluorescein can be a valuable tool during a crime scene investigation. If properly used and interpreted, it can potentially reveal hidden or cleaned-up areas of blood that can identify shapes or patterns that could help isolate a 'point-of-attack.' Or perhaps, even what sort of weapon was used. It's also capable of revealing latent finger, hand, or footprints. However, there are limitations because Fluorescein is known to react with a variety of other substances, including bleach, copper-based products, cyanide compounds, animal and vegetable proteins, and saliva. As such, it's easy to jump to the conclusion that you've found blood, only to find out later it's something else.

Here, Fluorescein was applied to all areas where alleged or suspected clean-up had taken place in the garage and entryway. As a result, a positive reaction did occur on the ceramic-tile floor in the small entryway. Although initially encouraging, subsequent testing revealed that the reactive substance was not blood. Similarly, there was also a positive reaction of an area treated on the garage floor, which Andersen initially surmised and reported as 'swipe' marks attributed to the blood clean-up theory. However, this area, too, when tested further, revealed no presence of blood.

For all CSI enthusiasts, here's the bottom-line – the application of Fluorescein on all suspect areas where a violent, blood-letting assault was alleged to have occurred, revealed 'no additional presence of blood.' Period. The negative results were indeed not what was expected, hoped for or anticipated. As an experienced CSI, I knew what they were expecting to find and should have found, had there been a major blood-letting event.

Furthermore, had their theory been correct, the application of Fluorescein should have revealed a representative, luminesced image of what the scene looked like *before* any clean-up.

Including, but not limited to, areas of pooling, drops, flow patterns, additional spatter, and distinctive swipe or smear marks, all of which, under subsequent testing, would confirm the presence of blood. The chance of *not* finding any of these things would be extremely remote.

Therefore, with the negative Fluorescein results, they were right back where they started. And all they had left to work with and still be able to call this a 'crime scene' were those tiny specks of blood. Despite the overwhelming lack of supporting forensic evidence, their crime-scene theory remained welded in stone, and abandoning it now was out of the question.

After eight days, the house was released back to Cal. Andersen, and Ryan returned to the Owego barracks to complete their examination of Michele's van. They continued documenting and pouring over the voluminous array of Michele's personal papers and belongings. No blood or suspected blood was located within or upon the vehicle. Andersen also noted that the van was covered with road dust and had not been cleaned.

As a final note upon completing his examination and processing, Andersen wrote, "no wallet, cash, child photographs and/or any personal identification of Michele Harris, such as a driver's license, had been found."

For the first four years, the defense was only privy to a minimal amount of information as it pertained to the alleged 'crime scene' at the Harris residence. We only knew, for example, that some unknown amount of blood was found in the garage and the small entryway. What we didn't know were the answers to the troublesome questions we had regarding the age and volume of blood. Without a body or murder weapon, answering these questions would be critical. Hopefully, a thorough review of the discovery material related to the blood issue will help to answer those questions.

Before reading through all the written reports and narrative descriptions, I wanted to get a visual perspective, so I decided to start with the photographs. I wanted to see for myself everything they had seen.

The blood photos in the garage and entryway were of primary interest. Accordingly, I spent a great deal of time reviewing these photographs. In addition to the photographs, Andersen had prepared a diagram, with precise measurements, that pinpointed the exact locations of the blood. During my review and assessment of everything related to the blood evidence, I identified and documented several issues that would need to be addressed further.

The first thing that jumped out at me was the fact that when Andersen first observed the suspicious red stains on September 13th, they were never photographed or otherwise documented, before being consumed in their entirety during field tests. Then, two days later, Ryan did the same thing. Again, without taking photographs. The argument was that by consuming an entire sample during testing without being photographed first, there's no longer any proof that the suspect areas ever existed or where they came from.

Another significant issue involving the photographs of the blood was that we learned from the photo logs that the first photographs of the blood were not taken until September 16th by Sosnowski. So, at a minimum, the bloodstains were already four days old. Did they look any different three or four days earlier? We'll never know.

The photographs and diagram both documented an area on the garage floor where twelve individual areas of blood were found. Each was alpha-designated, A thru L. Similarly, the six individual areas inside the entryway were numerically designated, 1 thru 6. It was well documented that the size of these bloodstains was extremely small, ranging between sub-millimeter to no more than 1-2 millimeters. Comparatively speaking, for those more familiar with the imperial system, about an eighth-of-an-inch or less.

Importantly, in addition to taking actual size (1 to 1) photographs, due to the small size of the blood specks, progressively enlarged close-ups also needed to be taken to allow for a better visual image. However, without securing the actual surface(s) of where the blood was found, the photographs would be the only reliable means available to preserve the evidence. In-as-much, the accuracy and clarity of the photographs would be crucial.

The most significant issues with the photographs involved various problems, including exposure, contrast, color, and flash. The multiple variations in color and contrast made it difficult, if not impossible, to know what the true color was. With respect to both the age and volume of blood, this was a real problem. Several photos were too dark, suggesting little or no flash. Others appeared just the opposite with colors that were 'washed-out' by too much flash. This obviously affected not only the color of the blood but also the color of the under-lying and surrounding surface(s). As a result, the poor quality of the photographs, with their lack of accuracy and clarity, would later create a great deal of conflict and controversy, even among more qualified experts.

I also discovered that the enlarged or close-up photographs had created another problem. There was nothing in the photo logs to indi-cate what level or degrees of enlargement were used. While some of the enlarged photos included a scale, several others did not. For those that didn't, there was no way to accurately determine their x-ratio, such as 5x, 10x, 100x, or anything between or above. From a defense perspective, we were concerned about how these photographs would be portrayed and interpreted when viewed by a jury.

Except as noted, the overall processing of Michele's van, Cal's truck, the Harris residence, and all the surrounding property was described and examined exceptionally well, using by-the-book protocol and methodology, supported by detailed notes, measurements, diagrams, photographs, and video. Unfortunately, their processing, specifically in relation to the most critical evidence, the blood, was diminished and devalued by the poor quality of the photographs.

With the tiny specks of blood found in the garage and nearby entryway, the SP was alleging that the Harris residence was the 'scene-of-the-crime.' I could certainly understand why they might think that. However, there were some big questions I needed to try and answer. First, was the blood evidence substantial enough to establish that this was, in fact, a crime scene? Second, how long had the blood been there? And finally, could there be a plausible, innocent explanation?

In considering the small amount of blood found, there was nothing to suggest that whoever was injured would have required professional medical treatment. For example, a small cut on a finger, hand, elbow, shin, knee, forehead, lip, or even a nosebleed, could easily explain the presence of such a small amount of blood.

One of the first things I noticed came right from Andersen's report. He was not claiming that the spatter *was* the result of an assault, or even that it was *consistent* with an assault, but rather, it *"could be"* from an assault. Could be? That suggests it could be something else as well. But one of the more self-evident and notable observations of the alleged crime-scene was the absence of a larger volume of blood. Having investigated numerous blood-letting crime-scenes, what I saw here, was not what I would expect at the scene of a suspected homicide – especially one involving a vicious bludgeoning as alleged. The bottom line was there should have been more blood.

I also asked myself if Cal could have cleaned up a large volume of blood so thoroughly that only those few specks would be left behind? From my experience, that did not seem likely. Furthermore, Cal would have had no way of knowing what forensic blood enhancement techniques were capable of in detecting blood that was no longer visible to his naked eye. Many before Cal, who tried, have failed.

As I continued my assessment, I made another interesting discovery. Not in relation to the evidence that *was* found but rather more importantly, what *wasn't* found. In other words, something that should have been present was not. Why? Because the absence of evidence can be evidence itself.

Notably, in Andersen's report, he described everything he saw in detail. When he found the blood in the garage, he carefully documented each respective location with notes, measurements, and photographs and later plotted them onto a scaled diagram. In-as-much, his efforts were by-the-book, and later written into his narrative report. That's all well-and-good, but there was something very important missing.

For a complete and accurate assessment of a suspected crime-scene, in addition to the obvious presence of physical evidence, it must also include that which is *not* present, if anything. In this case, for analytical purposes, due to the tiny specks of blood, that was of particular importance but never done. During my assessment, I identified areas where blood was clearly missing, where more than likely, under their own theory, it should *not* have been. Interestingly, even though these areas were examined and described in Andersen's report, nothing was reported about the absence of blood. And this is important why? A closer examination of these specific areas, including a better understanding of the police theory, should help to answer that question.

Let's break it down. As we've already learned as noted in his report, Andersen described two separate areas where blood was found – in the entryway and on the garage floor. So, let's call the entryway point A and the garage floor point B. Notably, points A and B were separated by a distance of nearly six feet, with those two dark brown rugs in between. Suspiciously, there was no blood on neither the rug nor the nearby pile of family shoes or a baby stroller.

For the purpose of my assessment, I referenced this rug-covered area between A and B as the 'neutral-zone.' It was going to require much closer scrutiny. My first logical question was if Cal did this, how did he get Michele, who was already badly bleeding, across the 'neutral-zone' without leaving any blood? Secondly, if he had carried or dragged her from A to B, knowing that she was already bleeding, how would he know that no blood would fall in the neutral-zone? I think we all know the answer to that question. He wouldn't. Furthermore, if he had meticulously cleaned up blood at both A and B as theorized, logic and common sense would have told him that there would also be blood in the neutral-zone. Even if he couldn't see it on the dark brown rugs, which poses the next logical question, why would he just leave the rugs and not dispose of them along with the body? The short answer is because it never happened.

Following the initial triage of a crime scene, one of the most basic principles in a crime scene investigation is the method of inclusion by exclusion. In other words, before drawing any conclusion about what *did* happen, you must first exclude what *didn't* happen. Failure to do so will leave the door to speculation wide open. As a result, any conclusion drawn could arguably be considered suspect and/or unsubstantiated.

Furthermore, relative to the twelve areas on the garage floor, where specks of blood were documented, the two areas designated as K and L were the greatest distance from the entryway door. Interestingly, their orientation placed them directly *under* the left-front fender of where Michele's van would have been parked. Yet Andersen's report failed to mention that. Additionally, in his final assessment of Michele's van, he noted, *"no blood or suspected blood was located upon, or within the vehicle."* Then also noted her van was *"covered with road dust and had not been cleaned.*" So, the obvious question; how did blood get *under* her van without getting *on* the van? Again, what *didn't* happen here?

Relative to the blood evidence, Andersen had very little to work with. Therefore, the likelihood of a conclusive blood-stain analysis, even by a more experienced expert, would be severely limited and impeded by the fact that many of the necessary analytical elements were missing. For example, there was no evidence of any arterial spurting, or any drip or flow patterns. Additionally, there were no identifiable angles of impact, flight paths, perimeter staining, drag marks, or satellite spatter. And most notably missing were the most common elements associated with a bludgeoning, cast-off and back-spatter patterns.

With the limited blood that was found, Andersen surmised that it was consistent with a medium velocity impact that 'could be' from an assault. Agreed. However, medium velocity 'could be' attributed to any number of innocent explanations as well. Something as simple as cutting your finger and shaking the blood off can create a medium velocity impact. Another example, having a bloody nose and getting blood on your hand while you try and stop the bleeding and then shake it off. Think of your own experiences; we've all had them.

Another area involved the small entryway, where he found those few specks of blood. Notably, this was a rather confined area, only about forty-two-inches square, surrounded on three sides by walls and doors. According to the police theory, this was 'ground-zero' where the attack started. After being struck, Michele would have crumpled to the floor and started bleeding immediately. Being such a small area, one or more parts of her body would likely have made contact with one or more of the surrounding walls and/or doors. But notably, other than those tiny specks of blood, no other trace evidence such as hair, fibers, marks, dents, smears, scratches or gouges, was ever found.

Another area that was not forensically examined was the ATVs. In Andersen's grand jury testimony, he said ATVs had been used in the early search for Michele and admitted that *"any forensic value there may have been, had been compromised."* As the area at the end of the driveway, this was not a plausible excuse for not examining the ATVs. Compromised or not, they should have been examined. To claim there was 'no forensic value' without conducting a proper forensic examination was unacceptable.

Unfortunately, in those 'compromised' areas that were never examined, we'll never know whether anything of value was present or not because it was never done. Compromised or not, a proper forensic examination could conceivably reveal game-changing evidence, capable of steering the investigation in an entirely new direction.

So, the search warrant had been executed, and the results were in. Did the results prove or disprove the police theory? What did it all mean? My job now was to try and put everything into perspective and how it related to the police theory. What was consistent, and what was not?

---

1. LMG: Leuco-Malachite Green; a triphenylmethane dye used to detect blood.
2. MCU: Major Crimes Unit
3. FIC: Forensic Investigation Center
4. Fluorescein: a presumptive blood test used in the detection of latent bloodstains
5. Chemiluminescence: the emission of light during a chemical reaction that does not produce significant quantities of heat.

6

POLICE THEORY

The SP theorized that after leaving Lefty's around 9:15 p.m., Michele drove about eleven miles to her boyfriend's apartment in Smithboro – arriving between 9:30 and 9:45 p.m. Then, after leaving there at about 11:15 p.m., drove the fourteen miles to her residence. Arriving before midnight, she pulled into the garage and parked in the bay nearest the man-door to the entryway. She then got out of her van and walked in the door.

Kitchen Entryway

Cal, waiting just inside, armed with an unknown weapon, immediately struck her with one or two blows, knocking her to the floor, either killing or disabling her instantly. Now bleeding from her wound(s), Cal carried or dragged her out the door, over the threshold, and across the brown rugs to a bare area on the garage floor near her van. Over the next six-plus hours, he engaged in a major clean-up of the spilled blood, in both the entryway and garage. Before disposing of her body, he removed all her jewelry. He then transported her, along with any evidence of clean-up, by some unknown means, to a secret location where he disposed of her body and the evidence.

With the children still asleep (presumably), Cal returned to the house, showered, and dressed for work. Before calling Thayer, he removed Michele's purse, wallet, and remaining jewelry from her van. He then drove the van back out the driveway, parked it near the gate, ran back to the house, and called Thayer.

In my view, the alleged 'scene-of-the-crime' proved their theory was placing a great deal of emphasis on speculation of what little evidence they found. Even during the early stages of my investigation, their theory was ambiguous and somewhat pretentious. It was one that had been formed prematurely and haphazardly. At face value, it was indicative of an early rush-to-judgment, based entirely on conjecture, some guesswork, with wishful thinking, tossed in.

Over the weeks and months that followed, despite its obvious flaws, the SP never changed, modified, or even re-visited their theory. Instead, making matters worse, they locked it in stone, never to turn back, and when necessary along the way, 'crunched' or manufactured evidence to make it fit. This approach is known as 'fake it till you make it.' And it's dangerous. As an investigator, you cannot let yourself fall into that trap. The SP's blinders were firmly fixed in place. They only saw what they wanted to see, but too many things were not adding up. With what I had seen so far, I was far from convinced that the Harris residence was a crime scene, let alone that Cal was responsible.

Believing the police theory was fatally flawed, I decided to break it down further and place it under even closer scrutiny. I wanted to identify its flaws and weaknesses specifically. Paying meticulous attention to the smallest details was important. In that effort, I would virtually have to dissect and closely examine every element.

To start, the SP believed after leaving Earley's apartment, Michele went straight home, yet there was nothing to corroborate this. There was only Earley's word that she left his place when he said she did. Again, no supporting evidence to show that she ever arrived home as claimed.

Presumably, as the last one to see her alive, Earley should have been a suspect with no verifiable alibi. Yet Andersen was never asked to conduct a forensic exam of Earley's person, apartment, vehicle, or property. Failing to do so was not only remiss; it was irresponsible and unprofessional. They also failed to do any of the above with respect to Michael Kasper, another person who had a known relationship with Michele and no verifiable alibi. He should have been a suspect as well. This was not the SP I knew.

The next part of their theory had Michele arriving home and entering the house. With Cal just inside the door waiting for her, she entered and was immediately cold-cocked by Cal with one or more blows from some unknown weapon. Either dead or disabled – blood started flowing.

First, there was no supporting evidence that Michele ever arrived home and parked in the garage. This was guesswork. Second, no evidence to support that any weapon was used. Without a weapon or examination of a body, there was no way to determine what specific weapon may have been used, if any. People do get injured and bleed without the use of any weapons.

Additionally, Andersen reported that the orientation and depositing of the blood on the entry door could only have occurred if the door was in a closed position. Why was that important? As previously noted, the entryway was small. Comparatively, not much larger than a shower stall. Therefore, had the encounter been immediate as theorized, it was highly unlikely Michele would have taken the time or been able to close the door behind her.

Police also theorized that *after* the assault, Michele was transported into the garage where she continued to bleed. Remember points A and B? There was no blood in that between area. How did that happen? Had Michele suddenly or somehow stopped bleeding at A and then started up again at B? Of course not. This was not a crime scene.

Instead, with the absence of blood in the neutral zone, an innocent explanation had clearly presented itself.

Another major part of their theory was that after Cal killed her, he'd engaged in an extensive clean-up. However, even though various cleaning materials were present, none bore any evidence of recent use or blood clean-up. And as previously mentioned, the application of Fluorescein revealed 'no additional presence of blood.'

Furthermore, when Barb Thayer first walked into the garage that morning, followed shortly after by two SP investigators, none of them noted or made mention of smelling the odor of any cleaning product or solution. Had Cal just spent a considerable amount of time cleaning up blood by using bleach, a solvent, or some other type of cleaning solution, he may have gone 'nose-blind' to the smell, but not someone with a fresh nose just arriving at the area. Somewhat like that Febreze commercial, 'You think it smells fine, but your friends smell this.' The nose knows. And we all know that when using bleach during a clean-up project, even when diluted, the smell can linger. So far, I found nothing to support their theory, but let's continue.

Their theory also included that after Cal disposed of her body and evidence, he drove her van out to the end of the driveway, parked it, and walked back to the house. Again, this was just more guesswork, unsupported by any corroborative evidence. Any variety of scenarios may have explained Michele's van being at the end of the driveway. Several of which were speculated on by Cal and Thayer that morning. Just because her van was found at the end of the driveway does not mean Cal put it there.

The SP was convinced the killing of Michele was premeditated and involved several months of careful, masterful planning, which likely started right after Michele filed for divorce. Speculating further, Cal, who had been planning this for a long time, was patiently yet strategically waiting for the 'right moment' to carry out his evil plan. Then, upon learning of the terrorist attacks earlier that day, Cal decided, "OK, tonight's the night, now's the time." They figured Cal had chosen this time because he anticipated, or had some inside way of knowing, the SP would be short-handed and pre-occupied with the terrorist attacks. BCI Captain Mark Lester was later quoted saying, "The events of 9/11 provided a good opportunity to commit this crime."

I wasn't buying into this theory whatsoever. Was it planned and premeditated? No way. Then, dramatizing their theory by inferring that the terrorist attack was in some way the triggering mechanism Cal was waiting for to put his plan in motion? That's nonsense. They were simply using that as an excuse for not being able to find Michele. Indeed. Enough said.

But even if you remove that bizarre element from their theory, what remained was leaking oil as well. Had there been a masterplan several months in the making, other than the overt act of killing and disposing of the body, it would also include other vital components. Not that any of us have ever planned on killing our wives, but other than the act itself, what else might be necessary to the plan? Was anything missing from Cal's masterplan?

To briefly entertain this train of thought, let's say that Cal, once deciding he wanted to kill his wife, needed to come up with a plan. From his perspective and relative to what he knew at the time, right away, Cal knew he would be the main suspect. If anything ever happened to Michele, he, as her wealthy husband, with a divorce pending that included accusations of physical abuse, would be the number one suspect. Therefore, if there was any way to pull this off without getting caught, it would be imperative to remove any element of his suspicion. Or at least, he would have to distance himself as a suspect. That could only happen with the benefit of some careful planning. And what would have been at the top of his list? You guessed it – a rock-solid alibi.

Further along these lines, Cal knew Michele had a regular boyfriend, and she was working with some rather 'shady' characters at Lefty's. With this knowledge, he was equipped with information that could be used to further remove suspicion from himself by making it look like someone else close to Michele was responsible.

His plan could also have included the use of some cognitive behavior that would tend to remove suspicion from himself, i.e., calling Michele and leaving a message, or calling others pretending to be worried and concerned, then asking if they had seen her and seeking their help to try and find her. He might even go a little overboard by showing some exaggerated or pretentious emotion as the concerned and grieving husband. Or perhaps, as some killer husbands have done in the past, turn to the media and plea for her safe return, and take the lead in the search effort to find her.

All that said, Cal's 'masterplan' to kill Michele had been thwarted by the fact that he had no alibi. He'd made no attempt to make it look like someone else killed her, had no explanation for the blood, didn't leave Michele a message when calling her cell phone, and called no one else looking for her. The bottom line here is that there was no masterplan.

To accept the SP's theory, we would have to believe that Cal, failing to include a solid alibi as part of his plan, would instead, expose himself as Michele's killer by placing himself directly in a defenseless window of opportunity of more than six hours. Call it what you will, but to me, that's dumb. A six-hour window of opportunity with no alibi? That would be blatantly foolish, especially when combined with other factors in direct contrast to any masterplan theory. So, which was it? A killer with a masterplan or a bungling idiot? You can't have it both ways.

Underestimating Cal's intelligence would have been remiss. His educational and intellectual acumen, combined with his organizational skills, was what allowed him to become the successful businessman he was. Again, not that any of us are planning on killing our wives, but from a logical perspective, did Cal's theorized master plan make any sense? Lastly, with his four children sleeping upstairs, was this the best way to do it without getting caught? Weren't better, less risky options available? Indeed.

After completing his work at the alleged crime scene, Andersen expressed his concerns and uncertainties with his superiors. Unable to provide definitive answers to the key questions about the blood, Andersen's recommendation to his superiors was to seek the opinion of someone with greater expertise. Accordingly, Troop 'C' BCI Captain, Thomas Kelly Jr, instructed Andersen to prepare a packet, including a complete synopsis of his work at the Harris home, with photographs, measurements, and diagrams. Once completed, Kelly arranged to have the packet sent to the nationally-renowned forensic scientist, Dr. Henry C. Lee, at his Institute of Forensic Science, in West Haven, CT. Along with Andersen's packet, Kelly included this analysis request: *"Through a review of the enclosed photographs and diagrams, it is respectfully requested that the stains present be interpreted:*

1. *Are the observed stains consistent with a clean-up attempt?*
2. *Do the stains indicate an assault?*
3. *Can you determine the type of an assault which could have occurred?*
4. *Are the stains consistent with an assault which could lead to the death of Michele Harris?*
5. *Can a determination be made as to the amount of blood which would have been present?"*

These were great questions. Important questions that needed to be answered because New York's finest were unable to.

But the more significant issue was this: Would Dr. Henry Lee, the nationally-renowned expert in bloodstain analysis, be able to answer these questions? For now, we would just have to wait and see.

I learned later that Andersen hand-delivered his package and personally consulted with Dr. Lee at his Institute in CT. In addition to the package he prepared, Andersen also took a small throw rug he had collected from the entryway floor. Somewhat suspiciously, there was no mention of this rug in any notes, measurements, diagrams, or reports. This was in direct contrast to the thorough documentation of the two brown rugs that were in the garage, the ones he'd described in detail, and later included in his diagram and report.

Prior to taking the rug to Dr. Lee, Andersen conducted his own preliminary examination and identified numerous small, dried red stains believed to be blood. However, this examination was at least *two months after* the rug had been collected from the scene. None of these stains were noticed while it was still at the house. Therefore, there were no photos. In fact, there was no mention of this rug whatsoever until it appeared on the evidence log secured on September 19, 2001. It was also unclear where the rug was for three days, between September 15, 2001, when it was placed in evidence, and September 18, 2001. In addition, it was never reported why the rug was secured as evidence in the first place.

Regardless, Andersen later submitted the rug to the FIC, where random areas of stains were selected and tested positive for human blood. The specks of blood appeared to be in the form of expired or aspirated blood. Expired blood can be associated with multiple varieties of open-bleeding wounds where some force has been applied. Whereas, aspirated blood is associated with blood being propelled from the nose or mouth during coughing or sneezing. Whichever it was, the extracted DNA matched the DNA profile of Michele Harris.

The throw rug was small but had covered the major portion of the ceramic tile floor in the entryway. The rug itself was multicolored, including various shades of blue, pink, and white and fringed at both ends. Interestingly, this rug had an identical twin in size and color that could be seen in photographs on the floor in front of the kitchen sink but was never collected as evidence. Both rugs were reversible and interchangeable. In other words, the same fabric all the way through. There was no distinguishable top or bottom.

I still had to ask why hadn't Andersen or Ryan seen these stains on the rug at the scene? When the defense finally had the opportunity to examine the evidence, I had my answer.

Fortunately, there were a couple of original police photos showing the rug in the entryway *before* it was collected. When comparing the original photos of the rug, to the area on the rug where he found the bloodstains, we learned that the bloodstains had been on the *bottom* side of the rug. It was also noted that the rug had a multitude of other foreign stains on both sides that were not blood. In other words, everyday household dirt and grime, suggesting that the rug had not been laundered recently.

Relative to the non-blood staining on both sides, it appeared as though it might have been picked up, turned over, and replaced on the floor, with the cleaner side up – perhaps more than once. It was also possible that the twin-rugs may have previously been picked up and replaced after cleaning the floor. In so doing, their respective positions may have been swapped inadvertently. But obviously, there was no way to determine whether that ever happened. It did raise the question though of whether the blood could have originally been deposited on the twin rug in front of the kitchen sink – creating another innocent explanation. Anyone ever cut themselves while working near the kitchen sink?

In addition to the small specks of blood found on the bottom of the rug, there was also what appeared to be about a one-inch, square-shaped blood transfer stain. A blood transfer stain is simply when wet blood on one surface comes into contact and transfers to another surface. Here, an unknown square-shaped object left a blood transfer stain on the rug.

The SP quickly surmised that it must have come from the murder weapon. So, what kind of murder weapon might that be? It didn't look like anything I was familiar with. But I was anxious to hear what type of object or 'weapon' they thought it might be. It looked to me as if it could have come from the leg of a chair, the heel of a woman's shoe, or perhaps even a child's toy. Could one of those have been a murder weapon? I suppose, but that certainly didn't seem like a weapon of choice by someone with a plan. To my knowledge, the SP had no better idea or suggestion as to what type of object or alleged 'weapon' may have caused the stain, or when.

At first glance, the blood spatter and staining on the throw rug was a concern. However, under a little closer scrutiny, that concern started to fade. Our blood expert had noticed something during his assessment that I had overlooked earlier. Other than the obvious spatter and transfer stain, he'd noticed no signs of any passive drops or dripping. Of course, why didn't I think of that? He was right. The throw rug was smack-dab in the middle of the kill-zone. If Michele was struck and started bleeding, along with any spatter, there would undoubtedly have been some passive dripping. Again, there was an absence of evidence, where under the police theory, there should not have been.

Furthermore, to accept a criminal element involving the rug, you would have to believe that Cal just happened to forget the blood-spattered rug right at 'ground-zero.' Just like he did with those brown rugs in the 'neutral zone.' Or, after picking it up to clean the tile, he simply flipped it over and put it back, hoping no one would look underneath. Either way, you'd have to be a fool. It makes no sense.

On a related note, remember those brown rugs? Interestingly, there was another development involving the one that was taken and examined by the FIC. During their examination, one small human blood-stain was found. Not on the carpeted surface but instead mysteriously found underneath on the backing. There was no DNA testing performed. Therefore, we were left with two mysterious and unanswered questions: Whose blood was it? And how did it get there? Even if we were to assume it was Michele's, it still doesn't explain how it got there or how long it had been there – raising the likelihood of yet another innocent explanation.

The SP knew that an innocent explanation was plausible but would never acknowledge it. Had the evidence of their assault theory been compelling, their next course of action would not have been necessary. They were trying to find a way to refute any innocent explanations. In that effort, they included in their questioning of witnesses, especially those who had frequent contact with Michele, whether they had any knowledge of Michele having injuries, cuts, or wearing a bandage. Of those questioned, most claimed to have no knowledge of those things. However, when Thayer was asked, she recalled seeing Michele with a bandaid on her knee. But she would quickly try to qualify it by saying it was only a brush-burn from horse-back riding. Who puts band-aids on brush burns? Unless, of course, it's a bleeding brush-burn. Interestingly, when Brian Earley was initially asked if he'd ever seen Michele with any bruising, he said no. Later, however, when testifying before the grand jury, he said yes. He testified that he had seen Michele with minor injuries, including some small cuts, and a couple of times he'd seen her wearing a band-aid.

When Andersen traveled to West Haven CT, he consulted with Dr. Henry Lee, who looked at Andersen's package of photographs, measurements, diagrams, and of course, the small, blood-stained throw rug. After this initial consult, Andersen returned to Troop 'C' Headquarters, leaving Dr. Lee to continue his assessment. Later, we found no formal report of Lee's findings in the discovery material. Therefore, the defense could only assume that any opinions or conclusions he made, had only been offered orally to the SP. Would he be able to answer Captain Kelly's questions conclusively, and if so, how? For the time being, we would have to wait and see.

PART II

CAL'S INDICTMENT | ARREST | TRIAL #1

7

GRAND JURY INDICTMENT/ARREST

I t was now September 21, 2005, and Michele had been missing four years. Attorney Drazen called to inform me that he had just received notice that a grand jury was being seated in Tioga County next week to hear the Harris case.

A grand jury? Wow!!! My mind started racing with so many thoughts and questions. It had been four years. After all this time, had someone found Michele? No, we would certainly have heard about that. So, what do they have now that they didn't have four years ago? If there's an indictment, I guess we were going to find out. At this point, though, it was purely a guessing game. Speculation was flying everywhere. The only thing we knew for sure was the District Attorney, Jerry Keene, was seeking an indictment against Cal and not some other suspect.

As the defense team got together to discuss the latest events, Cal was understandably upset. More so after Joe Cawley explained that the function of the grand jury was to hear and see the evidence presented by the DA. The grand jury had only to decide whether enough probable cause existed to file a formal charge. In this case, even without a body or a murder weapon, the DA was most likely seeking a murder indictment. Cal was advised that he had the right to testify on his own behalf, but Joe's experience led him to advise against it. Cal understood and agreed.

During this meeting, since we had a weeks' notice, I suggested trying to reach out to some of the witnesses we knew would be testifying. Perhaps they might have something new to offer. After that, I spoke with several of those I had interviewed previously. They had nothing new to offer.

Fast-forwarding to September 30, 2005, Joe called to advise that Cal had been indicted on a single count of murder in the Second Degree, a class A-1 Felony. He had been arrested at his business earlier that morning. Armed with an arrest warrant, a host of SP police officers entered Royal Ford to take him into custody. After shackling his hands and feet, he was escorted out of his office and through his business, as both employees and customers looked on. He was then immediately arraigned on the indictment and quickly remanded to the Tioga County jail, pending a bail application hearing. The bail application was being drafted and would be filed before the close of business that day.

The Michele Anne Harris missing person case that started four years earlier had now been officially re-classified as a criminal case of Murder in the Second Degree.

Shortly after Cal's arrest, the SP prepared and published their press release:

New York State Police Owego, New York
Press Release September 30, 2005

FOR IMMEDIATE RELEASE

On September 30, 2005, Tioga County Judge Vincent Squeglia issued a Warrant of Arrest for **CALVIN L. HARRIS** *for the crime of Murder in Second Degree in connection with the disappearance and murder of Michele Harris. Members of the New York State Police arrested Mr. Harris this morning at his business in Owego. The warrant is based on an indictment handed up by a Tioga County Grand Jury. The New York State Police and the Tioga County District Attorney will be available to meet with members of the media at the Owego Town Court room at 2:00 PM. No further information regarding this will be released until that time.*

With Cal's indictment and arrest, the headline news the next day in the *Binghamton Press & Sun-Bulletin* articles read, *"Harris' husband charged with murder,"* with the sub-headline, *"Police tight-lipped about the evidence."* In the article, reporter Scott Rockefeller described Cal's arrest and arraignment before Tioga County Court Judge, Vincent Squeglia. Rockefeller reported that District Attorney Gerald Keene, would not comment on the difficulty of getting a murder conviction without a body, and only said there was enough evidence to secure a grand jury indictment.

Otherwise, he offered little detail about the case against Cal. Rockefeller reported that the SP was equally tight-lipped. He'd also reported that police refused to comment on whether Cal was the only suspect they had looked at over the past four years.

Interestingly, Rockefeller's article was still reporting that Michele was last seen leaving her place of employment at Lefty's around 9:30 p.m. I was not surprised that they refused to comment about other suspects or any recent developments that led to Cal's arrest. However, I was surprised they didn't take the opportunity to say there were other suspects, but they had all been eliminated through the investigation. With respect to any recent developments? That was a legitimate inquiry by Rockefeller. However, I would have posed this more direct question – What do you have now that you didn't have four years ago? I was asking myself the same question. I could have been wrong, but I was not aware of anything new. It wouldn't be long before we would know for sure.

Cal remained in jail for three days as opposing arguments relative to bail were made. Subsequently, the Honorable Tioga County Court Judge, Vincent Squeglia, granted bail in the form of a property bond. Cal signed a $500,000 lien on his lake house property and was released from jail.

With Cal's indictment and arrest, the waiting and uncertainty we experienced over the past four years had come to an end. An indictment was certainly not what we had hoped for, but at the same time, it was not unexpected. I knew the road ahead would be a long uphill battle. I was already anxious to delve into the SP investigation and see for myself what evidence or lack of evidence they had against Cal. A new phase in my investigation was about to begin. It was time to get to work.

8

POST-ARREST

I knew it would take several days or weeks before the defense would start getting discovery materials from the DA. The volume of the discovery materials generated over four years would be massive. Receipt of this material, as well as any new material generated during the ongoing investigation, would likely be spread out over a period of weeks and months right up until the trial. We were anxiously awaiting the first batch of material to get started. We were hoping the early discovery material would reveal the pertinent evidence of their case.

While we waited for the discovery materials, I reached out to a few of the witnesses I had spoken to earlier to inquire about their grand jury experience. I spoke with Todd Mansfield briefly. He said grand jury for him went as expected. All consistent with what we had talked about previously, nothing unexpected and no surprises. He'd only answered the questions asked. He was not asked to offer any opinions and didn't offer any.

Prior to the indictment, I had not interviewed Mike Bulman, another of Cal's friends. I found Bulman at his home in Vestal, NY. Mike grew up and went to school with Cal, along with Mansfield and Caveny. He had both business and social dealings with Cal. Mike first met Michele when Cal started dating her but had met her several times since. He'd been out to Cal's house many times to jet-ski, snowmobile, etc. He worked for Twin-Tier Rehab in Binghamton, NY. He advised that Michele had been a patient there who received Synergy treatment for cellulite.

Mike was aware that Cal's girlfriend Connie was also receiving similar treatments during the same time as Michele, and Cal was paying for hers also. He'd noticed Michele was losing weight and had started smoking heavily. Both Cal and Michele had told him about her 'boob job.' When asked, he said, "Cal never spoke about any concerns about the pending divorce." But he knew they were having problems and had recommended to Michele that she move out. Both him and Caveny had offered her a place to stay, but she declined.

He had never seen any signs of bruising or injury on Michele when she came in for treatments.

He was interviewed by the SP on three or four occasions. Most recently, the past August. He told the police all along that he did not believe Cal did anything to Michele. He learned about her disappearance from Mansfield but didn't think too much about it at the time. He knew from speaking with Cal that there were other times when Michele failed to come home at night. He also recalled going to Cal's office with Mansfield and Caveny, and later the three of them went out to help search for Michele.

Mike was very concerned about the welfare of Cal's children and had spoken with Mansfield and Caveny, who shared similar concerns. When asked, he said he had not testified at the grand jury, "probably because I had told them all along, I didn't believe Cal did anything to Michele," he said.

One of the other names Cal had given me was his friend Mike McKercher. I had attempted to interview McKercher back in 2001, but we never connected. I finally caught up with him at his home in Vestal, NY. He was 3-4 years behind Cal in school but had known him for several years. They became friends when they started playing lacrosse together in a post-collegiate league. He worked for Padgett Pharmaceutical as a sales rep. He'd never met Michele until after Cayla was born. He'd often seen her and the kids at the lacrosse games. He also said that he had been to Cal's business at Royal Ford and out to his residence on several occasions as they have children the same age. He thought he'd first heard about Michele missing from John Caveny, or perhaps on the news. The first time he saw Cal after she was missing was that following Friday. Caveny had invited Cal and his other friends to his house in Vestal to show their support for Cal. He recalled and described Cal looking "as if he'd been hit by a train," and was very concerned about how he was going to handle the children. There wasn't much talk about what happened. He said, "we just got together to be supportive for him and the kids." Then he added, "it seemed like he was just in shock at that point."

In early August of 2001, he and Cal had gone to Lake Placid to play in a lacrosse game, and they each took their oldest sons. They finished playing early and had all afternoon to relax.

They spent some time talking at the poolside drinking beer while the kids were playing. It was during this time that Cal told him about the pending divorce. During the entire conversation, he said, "Cal never once bad-mouthed Michele and even accepted responsibility for her wanting and seeking the divorce." He had told Mike that he understood why she was doing it and couldn't blame her. One of the reasons was the long hours he was spending at work, and another was coming home, expecting the house to be in order and being angry at Michele when it wasn't.

Continuing, he said, "Cal was not concerned about the financial aspect of the divorce," and confided in Mike that it was probably going to cost him $250K or something like that. He wasn't really sure of the amount. Cal told him about Michele getting her own house in Owego, and they'd discussed joint custody of the children. He'd also told him that Michele had a boyfriend and about her boob job. He mentioned Michele was working at Lefty's, and how "he was concerned about her new lifestyle and the 'whacky' characters that hung out there." Cal had also told him that, "if Michele had settled a year earlier, she would have gotten a lot more money." He had just recently lost $1 million in a stock crash; therefore, he wasn't worth as much.

Based on his long candid talk with Cal at Lake Placid and the cookout at Cal's house just days before Michele disappeared, Mike strongly felt that Cal had nothing to do with Michele's disappearance. He was interviewed by the SP, who told him they had found his name in Michele's address book. Even though interviewed, he was never asked to provide a written statement. He said, "I really didn't like it when they tried to influence what I had to say by telling me what other witnesses were saying." I told him about the SP, "well, you're not the first one to tell me that." The last thing he said was, "I would find it difficult to believe that Cal had anything to do with this."

PRE-TRIAL INVESTIGATION

I knew the SP had obtained and executed a search warrant at Royal Ford about two months after Michele went missing. I also knew they seized a couple of Cal's laptop computers, some computer discs, and some financial records. What I didn't know until now, were the details of that search. Not until I reviewed it in the lead narrative.

The narrative described how Cal, during the execution of this search warrant, was in and out of his office, protesting that his laptop computer was being taken away. He was upset because it contained essential work-related material. It also described him being cooperative at times, then going off on tangents where he accused the SP of cutting up his kids' toys and slashing tires when they were at his residence. He complained that someone had defecated in his yard during the search. He then asked, "What next, the Navy Seals?" They also described Cal becoming irate and yelling that they were messing with his kids, and how they were being affected by what they were doing. As he walked freely about his office, he called attorney Drazen, who then spoke with police. Drazen expressed his concern regarding the Corporate Interests of Royal Ford and offered to provide whatever they needed.

I also learned during my review of this lead that two days later, of his own volition, Cal wrote a letter of apology to the SP investigators who had executed the search warrant at his office. It read as follows

Royal Ford
Mercury

Friday, November 23, 2001

Senior Investigator Les Hyman
Investigator's Mike Meyers, Mike Young
NYS Troopers Barracks Owego N.Y.

Gentleman,
    Please accept my sincere apology for what took place in my office this week on Tuesday morning. As you can imagine my life has been turned upside down these last few Months. That coupled with the fact that we still can't find my wife is taking its toll on me.

    My goal, as it has been from the start, is to work together with your staff in Locating Michele as soon as possible. In my opinion the search warrants you have issued These past few months are not necessary. Anything and everything I have will be made Available to you immediately, even if it means coming to me unannounced. All I ask is That we minimize any disruption in the lives of my four young children. Protecting the Children at a time like this would be a top priority for Michele if she were here.

    My family and I truly appreciate all the hard work your people have put into this Investigation. Again my apology's to you all.

Sincerely,

Cal Harris

I was navigating my way through the discovery material for over two months, and still had a long way to go. But I had already acquired a great deal of information that needed follow up. Some with Cal and some with other witnesses. I was meeting with Joe and Cal on a regular basis since the indictment. I was able to get some of my questions answered, but now it was time to talk to some of the other witnesses to see what else I could learn. Hopefully, with the passing of time, those who had no interest in speaking with me earlier would agree to now.

Before I started with the other witnesses, I went back to interview Dwight Harris again. He would call and ask to meet with me on a regular basis. We often met and talked over a cup of coffee at Dunkin Donuts or Starbucks, where he would pick my brain and ask to be brought up to speed on my investigation. On this occasion, I called him and asked to meet. He invited me to his home.

Dwight wanted to start at the beginning. When he first heard about the marital problems between Cal and Michele, he didn't know any details. He thought it was in the fall of 2000 when Cal called him and said, "She's going to do it," adding that, "He was sobbing and called me dad instead of Dwight." He went to Cal's house that night, and Cal was sobbing. Michele was there but was acting cocky with no tears. He also recalled in December 2000, his wife Louise was diagnosed with cancer and given one year to live, but she only lived about 90 days after that.

The last thing he remembered her saying was, "You're not going to get a divorce, are you?" Michele said, "We're going to try and work it out." Michele complained that Cal was unreasonable about her house-keeping, the meals, and how she was spending the money. She also voiced her complaints to her sisters-in-law, Mary Jo and Fran. Louise would always listen to both sides. Dwight said, "Initially, Mary Jo and Fran treated Michele like a tramp, but over time, they gradually accepted her and eventually turned against Cal."

Blood Evidence

Utilizing my own training and experience during my assessment of the dried bloodstains that were found at the Harris residence, I was not convinced that I was looking at a crime scene.

That said, even with the minuscule amount of blood that was found and not knowing how old it was, I knew it could still be problem-atic. Knowing how badly they wanted Cal, I suspected, then later real-ized, the SP was seeking an expert interpretation that would further substantiate their assault/murder theory. And if that happened, it could become the lynchpin of their case against Cal.

Obviously, I was interested in trying to determine the validity of that theory, but at the same time, trying to determine whether there may be an innocent explanation. In what I saw so far, I wasn't sure whether a conclusive interpretation could be made either way. But after speaking with Joe Cawley about the blood evidence, we agreed that it was demonstrably the most powerful evidence in the People's arsenal. And there was no doubt they would be arguing in support of the assault/murder theory. Accordingly, we decided it was time to consult with our own independent expert. During a previous murder case, we had consulted with Dr. Peter R. DeForest, who was a Professor of Criminalistics at John Jay College of Criminal Justice in New York City. Dr. DeForest had impressive credentials and was highly qualified in the field of forensic science. He had a long history serving as a consultant and expert witness for both the prosecution and the defense and was a highly respected professional within the forensic science community. Later, we drove to NYC and consulted with Dr. DeForest.

Cal and I had a lengthy discussion about his friendship with Chris and Lynn Angulas. Upon learning that the SP had interviewed Lynn Angulas shortly after Michele went missing, I was anxious to learn what she would have to say to me.

I located the Angulas's at their home in Owego. They first got to know Cal and Michele about six months before Michele went missing. They often talked about their kids and school, and Michele told Lynn that she was getting divorced, but not a lot of the details. "No real in-depth confiding," she said. Lynn had never seen Michele with any noticeable injuries or bruising, and Michele never told her that Cal had ever been physically abusive to her.

She had helped Michele find the house on Main Street in Owego that she later put a down payment on. She knew Michele had borrowed money for the down payment from a friend, but not who the friend was. She said, "Michele thought the house on Main Street would be convenient for her and Cal because it was close to the children's school and his business."

Lynn had first heard about Michele's disappearance from Cal that same afternoon when he picked up the kids at school. She said, "When I first saw him, he was annoyed that Michele had not come home because it meant he had to leave work early to pick them up."

SP investigators had learned from several witnesses that Michele was actively trying to sell her jewelry during a two or three-week period just before she went missing. This had become common knowledge amongst most of her co-workers as well as some of her regular customers at Lefty's. On September 14, 2001, Art VanRiper, the owner of Broad Street Exchange in Waverly, NY, called the SP to report that Michele Harris had come into his store trying to sell jewelry. Investigator Mike Telfer took the call from VanRiper and interviewed him over the phone. VanRiper explained that Michele Harris had come into his store around August 29, 2001. "She was trying to sell jewelry," he said. He'd looked at her jewelry but didn't buy anything from her. He also added, "this was the second time she had come in." He recalled looking at a steel Rolex watch he believed to be worth $1,500 to $2,000. He'd also looked at a 1.5 karat Solitaire diamond ring worth about $7,000, and a pair of 2-karat diamond earrings worth about $5-6,000. He recalled Michele making the statement that she knew someone in NYC who could sell the items for her. She'd also stated that she had other items to sell and may be interested in selling them. However, she never returned with any other items.

The SP learned early in their investigation that Michele had been frequenting numerous bars in the Nichols and Waverly area as well as others just over the border in PA. Investigator Bill Standinger was assigned a lead that read, "Interview patrons of the bars Michele Harris frequents – Wit's End, Mickey's, and the Lehigh."

This was an important lead worth pursuing or at least should have been. Witness after witness told investigators about all the different bars that Michele went to. Not just Wits End, Mickey's, and the Lehigh. She had also frequented several other bars in the area, including but not limited to: The Rail House, Rock-n-Dock, Night Train Lounge, Marty's, Captain Jacks, Trackside, Candlelight, Rusty Nail, and the Rainbow Lounge. Likely, there were even more. When I read the 'completed' lead, I was shocked. Flabbergasted was more like it. They really dropped the ball on this one. This is how the handwritten, 'completed' lead read:

Guthrie Done 9/18. Photos of Michele Harris displayed to bartenders at Mickey's, Guthrie Inn, Wits End bars. No new information gained – no additional leads generated. Investigator Myers Completed lead. Signed: Investigator Mike Myers

What? That's it? I kept looking through the discovery materials, thinking I must have missed something but found nothing more: no attachments, no notes, no typed-written narrative like all the other leads. Obviously, I was interested in and looking for the names of bartenders and patrons who had been interviewed to learn what they had to say. Again, nothing. And what happened to Investigator Standinger – the one originally assigned to that lead? I'll never be convinced there were no bartenders or patrons that wouldn't have recognized Michele or known something about her night-life activities or associates.

Besides, for insurance and liability purposes, surveillance cameras were routinely installed to monitor and record the activity around bars, both inside and out. That is normal practice. Even well before 2001, I reviewed hundreds of hours of surveillance footage from several bars and a variety of retail and convenience stores. Therefore, I found it rather troubling that out of all the bars in question, not one had a camera? Equally troubling was nary a single lead was ever assigned to even check for cameras at those establishments. Michele's known social activities certainly justified the need to follow up on this.

Checking for cameras is elementary investigative protocol – in other words, a no-brainer. Failure to do so was not only remiss but irresponsible. But even with the remote chance, there were no cameras, or perhaps they existed but were inoperable, those facts should have been noted along with the name of the person who provided that information.

Author's Note: As the story unfolds and more information is developed, a later chapter will address this matter further.

Investigators Scott Pauly and Mike Telfer were assigned to conduct neighborhood interviews around Brian Earley's apartment on Hanna Road in Smithboro. Ryan and Nancy Miller lived in the second-floor apartment at 30-C Hanna Road. They owned the apartment house and were Earley's landlords. Earley lived in the apartment just below them in 30-B.

The Millers described Earley as a model tenant. They had met Michele Harris but didn't know her by name and were unaware of who she was until after she went missing. She had helped Earley find the apartment by inspecting it before he moved in. It seemed the two of them had a good relationship, and they would see Michele at the apartment at least twice a week since Earley moved in on June 15, 2001. On the night of September 11, 2001, neither could recall seeing her. When asked about any suspicious vehicles in the area, Nancy recalled seeing a dark, mid-sized pick-up truck, that she noticed circling the area very slowly at night. The first time she recalled seeing the truck was about two months ago but nothing in the past two weeks. When asked specifically, she was unable to provide a specific color other than a 'dark color.'

I located the Millers, who had since moved to a new address a short distance away from Hanna Road. They still owned and rented the Hanna Road apartment building and confirmed they were the owners at the time Michele Harris went missing. They confirmed for me that Earley was one of their tenants at the time. When showing me their records, they indicated Earley had moved into his apartment on June 15, 2001. Both Millers described Earley as a pleasant young man and a model tenant. They'd never had any problems with him. Occasionally, they would see Michele's light-colored minivan parked outside the apartment, usually during the day.

Neither recalled seeing her van there at night, but they were often settling down for the night early and wouldn't necessarily know if it was there in the late evening. When asked, neither could recall any occasions where arguments or unusual commotions came from Earley's apartment.

Both had often seen Earley leave in the morning, assuming he was going to work. Nancy recalled the morning of September 12, 2001, Earley knocked on her door and appeared very distraught when telling her about Michele's disappearance. They'd both been interviewed by the police. Nancy recalled telling the SP about a dark-colored pick-up truck she had seen "driving slowly around Hanna Road for a few weeks before Michele went missing." Although she could offer no further description of the truck, she did say, "I saw it on several occasions and thought it was unusual because our road is very short and off the main thoroughfare." She also added, "But I never saw it again after Michele went missing."

Author's Note: Initially, because Cal was driving a dark green pick-up truck at the time, the SP surmised this might have been Cal stalking Michele and her boyfriend. But we'll learn much later, who it really was.

───────────

Over a year into their investigation, police learned that Cal hired a new babysitter by the name of Denise Kirby. Investigator Mike Young interviewed Kirby at her home in Owego. She was hired by Cal as a part-time babysitter, to work at the Harris home on Wednesdays and Fridays. She had known the Harris family since Taylor was in pre-school at St. Patrick's, where she worked as a pre-school aide. She further advised that she had a friendly relationship with Michele and was not aware of any problems. Her relationship with Cal was strictly professional, and she'd never had a social or intimate relationship with him. When explicitly asked, she denied that Cal had ever mistreated her and added, "I'm not disposed to be being treated poorly or bullied." Although she was aware of Cal's reputation for having a temper, she had never seen any unusual, or tumultuous behavior from Cal.

Investigator Young returned to re-interview Kirby about eight months later on June 9, 2003. At the time, she was still babysitting the Harris children on Wednesdays and Fridays. She had experienced no unusual or suspicious incidents or circumstances at the Harris home. Kirby reiterated once again that she had no problems whatsoever with Cal. He'd been acting in a rational manner ever since she started working for him. She admitted having gone out to dinner with Cal a few times, but there was no romantic involvement. When asked, she was not aware of whether Cal was seeing anyone socially.

Seven months later, on January 27, 2004, Investigator Mike Myers was assigned to re-interview Kirby once again. He went directly to St. Patrick's school, where Kirby was still employed. She was also still in the employ of Cal Harris as a part-time babysitter for his children. Again, her response was that there were absolutely no problems of any kind at the Harris home. She advised further that personally, she had no problems of any kind with Cal Harris.

Even before I learned what happened next, it had become rather obvious to me what the SP was trying to do. They were conducting these staggered interviews with Kirby, hoping that her relationship with Cal had deteriorated, and she would be willing to disclose something derogatory or incriminating about Cal. In other words, they were trying to turn her into the next Barb Thayer.

Shortly after this final interview, Kirby contacted attorney Stan Drazen, complaining about SP members repeatedly coming to interview her at the school. She described how their open 'question & answer' interview approach created an awkward and embarrassing situation. Not only for her but the children present at the time, including the Harris children. As a result, Drazen drafted and sent a letter to the Jerry Keene, explaining his concerns, and requesting that any further inquiries of Kirby be directed through his office.

Mike Bulman, one of Cal's friends that I had interviewed before the grand jury, had also been interviewed by Sr. Investigator Sue Mulvey. He described his relationship with Cal and his mutual friends, Todd Mansfield, and John Caveny. He described how he had helped in the early search for Michele using their ATVs. When asked if he thought Michele would leave her children, he said, "no." Then added, "But she was running with the wrong crowd, acting like a woman scorned." He'd heard through the grapevine that Michele had a boyfriend, and he'd advised her against it. He also knew that Cal had a girlfriend, but had not offered him the same advice, other than to say, "They were both acting like idiots."

Michele's father, Gary Taylor, had been interviewed by BCI investigators the day she first went missing. Mr. Taylor told investigators that Michele had pulled away from him over the past few months. And she didn't always tell him what was going on. Because he recently lost his wife, his family had been shielding him from all of Michele's problems. What he did hear, he said, came through his friends. The last time he saw Michele was on July 4, 2001. That's when Michele first told him she was seeing someone.

In January of 2005, Gary Taylor was re-interviewed by Sr. Investi-

gator Sue Mulvey and Capt. Mark Lester. After initially laying out the
family history, he explained the background leading up to Michele's
relationship with Cal. He explained how Michele, after high school,
attended and graduated from Morrisville, and found a job at Royal
Ford. He explained it was only a short time before she and Cal started
going out, then started living together and then married. He said,
"Marrying into the Harris family was a whole new experience for
Michele. The Harris family was in a 'different league' than the Taylor
family." He added, "Michele was blown away by the lifestyle she
married into, but at the time, Cal was good to her." He went on to say
that Michele did not often share her problems with him. If she did
have a problem, she would always go to her mother. But she had since
died. So, he said, "I was always the last to know about any problems."

During the forensic examination of Michele's van, shortly after she
went missing, numerous personal papers and documents were recovered. Under closer examination, many of Michele's friends and
associates were identified in the documents. Subsequently, leads were
assigned to contact and interview those identified. After that, dozens of
leads were assigned. One of the leads was developed from information
written on the back of a divorce affidavit. Hand-written on the back
was the name 'Betty,' followed by four numbers, which appeared to be
the last four digits of a telephone number. The lead assignment was to
attempt to identify 'Betty' to determine her association with Michele
Harris.

The name and numbers were quickly determined to be associated
with attorney Betty Keene, of Waverly, NY. When Sr. Investigator
Mulvey contacted Betty Keene, she was asked why her name and
number would be on the back of Michele's divorce affidavit. Betty
advised that she had been retained by attorney Robert Miller, to assist
in reviewing documents associated with the divorce settlement between
Michele and Cal Harris. She admitted having worked on the case for
Miller but claimed she didn't know any details of the agreement.

Having worked in Tioga County as a member of the SP before, I
was able to make a 'keen' observation. Betty Keene was the wife of
Jerry Keene, the Tioga County DA. My very first thought was, this is a
conflict of interest. I was on the phone with Joe Cawley before I was

barely done reading the lead. Too late. Joe had already figured it out and had a call into Keene, who quickly denied any conflict. Of both interest and concern was the fact that the lead in identifying 'Betty' wasn't assigned or completed until the end of January 2002. Why hadn't she called the SP or told her husband of her involvement with the divorce papers sooner? Or had she? Regardless, this lead became our first knowledge of her involvement. It was also interesting to note the lead itself, mentioned nothing about Betty being the wife of the DA.

One of the other contact numbers found in Michele's van was identified as belonging to a Troy Hollenbeck from Newark Valley, NY. Investigators learned that Hollenbeck, who was three years younger than Michele, had met her at a gin mill in Nichols, NY, in early 2001. And afterward, they had a three-month-long relationship. Noticeably missing during his interview, was any information as to whether this three-month relationship had ever become intimate. The SP was certainly aware of Michele's promiscuous sexual behavior. Why wouldn't they ask him that? Hollenbeck also told investigators that he was the one who ended the relationship because he wanted to try and work things out with his wife. He also added that after he broke it off, Michele began seeing someone else.

Hmm? How would he know that? Unless, of course, he returned to the bar where he knew she would be. Knowing the time frame, I think it's more likely he showed up to see Michele and found her there in the arms of Brian Earley, who had just moved into the area.

It was now four years later. I decided to try and find Hollenbeck to see what more I could learn. When he answered the door, I could see a woman in a backroom behind him. When I told him who I was and what I wanted to talk about, he quickly stepped out onto the porch and closed the door. I asked him if that was his wife? He said it was. In speaking with Hollenbeck, he confirmed what he told the police. When asked, he claimed his relationship with Michele never involved sexual intimacy. Other than knowing Michele was going through a divorce and working part-time at Lefty's, he had nothing more to offer. Before leaving, he expressed his concern about being called to testify. He said, "I didn't do anything with her, but my wife doesn't know about this, and I would like to keep it that way." I told him I couldn't make any guarantees but really didn't think his testimony would be required. He said, "I hope so, I'd really appreciate it."

With all I'd learned about Michele, including her active sex-life with various playmates, I found it difficult to believe she would have been involved in a three-month relationship that didn't include sex. With so much at stake, I could certainly understand Hollenbeck's denial. In my view, his relationship with Michele seemed somewhat like that of KC Carrigan. Whether either of them ever had sex with Michele isn't really important. Personally, I believe they did. Not that I'm counting, but I think they should both be included on the growing list of Michele's sexual partners.

10

POLICE INTERVIEWS

Cal Harris Interviews

As mentioned, Cal had been indicted and arrested on September 30, 2005. As expected, we received our first batch of the much-anticipated discovery material, about a month later. We knew from the indictment that Cal was charged with 'intentional' murder, but what were the details? Or what the legal world refers to as the 'Bill of Particulars.' Some of what we learned had briefly been addressed earlier, but now it's time to dig into the details.

It's a given that when a spouse or significant other is found dead or goes missing, the surviving partner is always an automatic suspect. I couldn't agree more, and this case was no exception. But it's also true that the last person to see the victim alive is also a suspect. So, if we're to apply an equal level of suspicion in this case, then at a minimum, we have two primary suspects. Brian Earley fits into both categories as a significant other, and the last one to see Michele alive.

Upon examining the early discovery material, I was anxious to learn what more the SP had developed on Cal, but I was equally interested to learn more about Brian Earley, the boyfriend we heard about. What was his claim to fame, and what was done to eliminate him as a suspect? Before getting to Earley, though, I decided to start by reviewing the SP leads of their interviews with Cal first.

By 9:40 a.m. on September 12, 2001, SP Investigators Mike Myers and Mike Young had already been assigned to the case and were walking into Royal Ford to interview Cal. The following is a summary of each of the four interviews they had with him over the next three days.

During his initial interview, Cal explained that he lived at home with his wife and four kids. But since his wife Michele had filed for divorce, she'd been sleeping on the couch in the living room. She worked at Lefty's and usually finished her shift around 9:00 p.m. but didn't usually return home until 1:00-2:00 a.m. Last night, he believed she went out drinking with her boyfriend after her shift. Other than knowing that Michele had a boyfriend, he didn't know who he was, where he lived, or anything else about him. He thought maybe he lived in the Waverly area. He then told them Michele did not come home at all last night, and he felt it was unusual. He explained about calling the babysitter, Barb Thayer, and her coming over and finding Michele's van at the end of the driveway. He thought Thayer might have arrived at about 7:45 a.m. Then added that he had no clue why Michele's van would have been where it was. He then explained how he drove Thayer out to the end of the driveway, where he saw the van parked at the mouth of the driveway, facing the house. Thayer got out and drove the van back down the driveway and into the garage and parked it where Michele normally did. Together, they looked inside to retrieve the kid's book-bags for school. At the time, he hadn't noticed if Michele's purse or cell phone were in the van. Continuing, he said Michele was always home in the morning to take care of the kids and get them ready for school. But he thought the circumstances were odd with her van parked at the end of the driveway. When asked if he had called anybody to try and locate Michele, he said that he had not.

Cal speculated that Michele might have left her van there, then met and rode with somebody else to go drinking. He added that it was even possible she had been leaving it there on other occasions he wasn't aware of. When asked about boyfriends, he mentioned the name, Ken Carrigan. He and Michele had some type of relationship in the past, but he believed Michele had broken it off with him. Michele had once told him that Carrigan might have been stalking her because she thought she had seen him drive by the house.

Later that day, Cal was interviewed further and told investigators that Michele was planning on visiting one of her college friends in

NYC this coming Thursday or Friday, and her name was Lisa. Her plan was to spend a night with her. But he didn't think she was currently in NYC because she would not leave without telling him. And she would have driven her van to see Lisa. He also explained how he was concerned, and suspected Michele had been using cocaine or some other drugs but didn't know that for a fact.

The SP spent most of that first day at Cal's house and didn't finish for the day until dinner time. Once Cal learned they were gone, he returned home with the children. While at home, the SP called and asked him some follow-up questions over the telephone. Most of the questions pertained to his business, home, and cell phone records. Cal agreed to make all those records available. He also told them there was an unknown caller on his home answering machine and that he would save it and turn it over to them. He also offered and welcomed them to look at his home computer. He thought that there might still be some of the e-mails between Michele and Carrigan. They also asked questions about the gate at the end of the driveway, and he explained how it operated remotely. Although it was operational, they hadn't used it in a long time, and it's normally just left open. To his knowledge, the gate had not been closed in a long time. As they finished up the telephone interview, their last question was when he and Michele last had sex. Cal answered, "Not since October 2000."

On September 14, 2001, Myers and Young re-interviewed Cal at Royal Ford again. They informed him that evidence technicians would be checking his residence thoroughly. He understood and had no problem with that. He was also asked if they could speak to his older children that day, Taylor and Cayla. Cal agreed and made the children available. When asked, he explained that the night before, he told the kids, "Mommy hasn't called in the last few days, and the police are helping look for her." Then added, "the kids took it well."

Continuing, he went on to say, "Michele could not keep a checkbook," and he was currently paying her $400 a week. Michele informed him recently that she opened another checking account. He advised that if Michele was not working, he had no clue what she did or where she went. When asked, he advised that he usually got home between 6:00-7:00 p.m. but had no idea what Michele would be doing because he didn't know her schedule. He added, "We rarely talk, except about the kids." Later, he explained what he knew about the credit cards the two of them had together and two other cards Michele had that he believed were maxed out. He also explained that he had run a credit report on Michele and then turned it over to them. When the topic of the divorce came up, he explained what his understanding of it was. He had made an offer around the end of July 2001 and had not heard anything back. He thought perhaps she would be rejecting it, but he didn't know. He was not aware of any scheduled hearing or other proceeding dealing with the divorce.

Before the interview ended, Cal was asked what he thought might have happened to Michele. He said, "I know she's hanging around with the wrong crowd in Waverly," then suggested they "pump the shit out of them." He also added, "Michele probably knew the person at the end of the driveway, or else she would not have gotten out of her van."

Author's Note: Cal's answer as to what he thought happened to Michele bears greater significance much later.

Near the end of the workday, Myers and Young returned to Royal Ford with new information to share with Cal and to continue their interview. Cal was informed that evidence technicians found the presence of blood at his residence in the garage and in the entryway to the house from the garage. He was told there was evidence showing there had been an attempt to wipe the blood, but some was still present in the cracks on the floor. Several times, Cal responded by saying he had "no idea" while shaking his head. He also said, "Nothing I can think of," when asked if there was some reason why blood would be present in those locations.

He kept rubbing his head in an apparent attempt to try and think of why blood would be there. Then he asked, "Where in the garage?" He was told it was right in the doorway area. He also asked, "Is it recent?" They said they did not have that information. Cal kept saying he had no idea where the blood could have come from and had no recollection of anyone recently being cut or injured in the house. All he could recall was having seen a few small drops of blood in the garage in the past when his son Taylor had cut his finger.

Near the end of the interview, Cal was asked, "Would you be willing to take a polygraph exam?" Without hesitation, he answered, "Yeah." He added that he has been keeping his attorney informed of all that was happening on a regular basis, and he'd advised him that should any legal issues come up, to call him. He then called attorney

Drazen, and they spoke briefly. Cal handed the phone to Myers, who spoke with Drazen. He told Myers he didn't want Cal to be questioned any further, and he did not want him to take a polygraph at that time.

> Author's Note: The last interview with Cal was on September 14th, at which time he was informed and questioned about the blood found on the garage floor. According to the FIU report, the blood in the garage wasn't discovered until the 15th.

In my assessment of the SP interviews with Cal, it seemed as though he had been cooperative and forthcoming in response to all their questions. He maintained an accommodating attitude throughout all the interviews. Never once had he said anything like, "I'm out of here," or "screw you guys, I'm done talking" or, "I want my attorney."

Of special interest to me, was a comparison of the SP interviews of Cal, with those of my own. I found them to be remarkably consistent. But the one thing that jumped out at me was Cal's response to their questions about the blood, where he said, "no idea" and "nothing I can think of." Knowing that the SP was looking for a 'consciousness of guilt,' Cal's inability to offer an explanation or suggesting it may have been from one of his children was *not* what they should have been looking for. Under similar circumstances, I would expect a suspect, knowing the police found some blood he didn't think they would find, to break into a cold sweat, start stuttering and stammering, and, more likely than not, offer some bogus explanation. Cal never did any of that.

In retrospect, Cal could have, guilty or not, offered an explanation that conceivably could not be disputed. Such as, Michele cut her finger, knee or elbow, or had a nosebleed. He could have even said something like, "Oh yeah, I remember now, that was about a week ago, she told me she cut herself, it was no big deal. It bled a little on the floor, and she put on a band-aid, we cleaned it up, that was it, end of the story."

In my experience, if he were guilty, when confronted with the blood evidence, the wheels would start spinning immediately, causing a brief hesitation but then would have offered some explanation. Furthermore, if Cal was Michele's killer, he obviously would have known the blood found was hers. Therefore, it would make no sense for him to suggest the blood might be from one of his children. If Cal was truly demonstrating a 'consciousness of guilt,' he would have offered an innocent explanation that included an injury to Michele.

Nikki Burdick

The SP started their investigation shortly after speaking with attorney Robert Miller and Michele's friend, Nikki Burdick. Investigator Bill McEvoy conducted the first Burdick interview. Other than her age, there was no physical description of Burdick in the lead. Later, I learned that she was five years younger than Michele, and according to Cal, not very attractive. She was shorter than Michele with a stocky build, brown eyes, and medium length, unkempt, dark brown hair. McEvoy had a long interview with Burdick, who explained how she first learned Michele was missing when she tried calling her, and Barb Thayer answered. She told Burdick that she suspected something was wrong right away and called Miller. She then went on to describe all the things she did next in her effort to locate Michele. She immediately called Michele's brother Greg at work to see if Brian was with him. He said he was, and she asked him to have Brian call her. In the meantime, she thought Michele might have spent the night at Brian's, so she went there to look for her. When she arrived, there was no response when she knocked on the door, and it was locked. Then, Greg called her back and said Brian was with him. Brian confirmed that Michele was at his place last night but left just after 11:00 p.m.

Burdick had known Michele since 1997. She described Michele as attractive and would frequently engage in 'innocent' flirting. She also described her smoking and drinking habits but insisted she was not involved with drugs. When asked what she knew about Michele's relationship with KC Carrigan, she believed Carrigan was obsessed with her. She was also aware that Michele was in a relationship with Brian Earley but didn't think Cal was aware of it.

When describing their social habits, Burdick said the two of them would often frequent Wit's End and Marty's taverns in Nichols. They often went out after Michele finished work at Lefty's. Michele enjoyed going to Mickey's Tavern in Waverly or the Lehigh Tavern in Sayre, just across the border, where she liked to sing 'karaoke.' The two of them had been at the Lehigh a few days earlier and stayed until 2:00 a.m. She explained how she tried calling Michele the last night she worked around 9:30 p.m., but Michele didn't answer. She left a message, but Michele never called her back. "That was very unusual," she said.

Nikki knew Michele had secretly purchased a house on Main Street in Owego. But didn't think Cal was aware of this. She also knew Michele received money from her cousin and boyfriend Brian to help make the $10,000 down payment. She advised further that Michele was actively trying to sell her diamond engagement ring and Rolex watch, with plans to go to NYC to see an old college roommate who was going to help her sell them.

During a follow-up interview, Burdick explained how she had once worked for Cal but left her position this past March. She became friends with Michele, who began confiding in her about her marital problems. As a result, she felt she had to choose between Cal and Michele. When asked, she admitted being aware of Michele's weight loss but attributed it to nerves. She went on to say that when Michele was pregnant with their fourth child, she found out Cal was having an affair and knew her marriage was in trouble.

In reviewing some of the attached notes, I learned that Burdick had also told investigators she didn't like any of the girls that worked with Michele at Lefty's – describing them as being weird, divorced, with bad marriages and other strange issues. And because of that, she did not like to associate with them.

Ironically, at least from my view, it seemed as though Burdick was describing herself. She should have fit right in because she had her own set of strange issues. She had a bad marriage, was divorced, and had this weird obsession towards Michele. Compared to Michele, Nikki was an odd duck. Perhaps, she thought that by hanging out with Michele, she was placing herself on a pedestal above the Lefty's girls. In contrast, Michele did not seem to have any difficulty befriending and associating with her co-workers. From my perspective, Burdick was a Michele wannabe, unable to function socially without her. In her obsession, she idolized and practically worshiped Michele. Especially her natural ability to attract young men. Burdick was somewhat jealous, but being starved for male attention, she wanted to be just like her. Therefore, I questioned whether her friendship with Michele was truly genuine or more self-serving.

About a week after I became involved, investigators Jim Conzola and Lori Hochdanner were back speaking with Burdick. They were asking her about other individuals who may have known Michele, and she gave them a couple of names, including a Tom Nabinger, who hung out at the Rock-n-Dock. She and Michele had met him there.

Burdick also told them about Cal's dad hiring a PI who had called her. She told them she'd provided everything she knew about the case to the police and wasn't going to talk to him. That sounded about right. Then added that the hiring of the PI was just a 'front' by the Harris family. She went on to describe going to Lefty's and asking the employees there not to speak to the PI because she didn't want the police case to be 'messed up.' I guess that explained why I got stone-walled at Lefty's. Nikki Burdick, little miss know-it-all. Whether she realized it or not, she was the one 'messing things up.'

In early February 2002, Sr. Investigator John Skinner and Investigator Lori Hochdanner again re-interviewed Burdick. She was asked if she'd ever been romantically involved with Ken Carrigan. With a quirky smile, she admitted they had been sexually involved and 'fooled around' a little bit. When questioned further about Carrigan, she explained how he had a crush on Michele, but she didn't feel the same towards him. She had learned from Michele that Carrigan would call her a lot, and that bothered her at times. But she didn't want to hurt his feelings by telling him not to call so much. She added, "Carrigan was not a person to be trusted," and Michele knew this.

Continuing, Burdick claimed that according to Shannon, Cal did not want her around his children. He had accused her of calling the Child Abuse Hotline. She denied this and claimed Cal never told her exactly what the allegations were but did say they were things only someone close to Michele would know.

The questioning then turned to a man by the name of Kent Cramer. He had worked for Cal at the Ford dealership during the summer of 2000. She admitted being aware of some 'flirtation' going on between them and that Cramer was also part of the group that would go out with her and Michele after work. But she denied knowing anything further.

Author's Note: We knew the Child Abuse Hotline had been called, not once but twice, with complaints about Cal. And CPS[1] had conducted investigations, both of which were unfounded. At the time, we agreed with Cal in assuming it was either Nikki or Shannon. We would only learn much later that we were all wrong – it was Sr. Investigator Mulvey.

Due to Burdick's close relationship with Michele, she was considered a valuable source of information. Investigators often returned to re-interview her for additional information. Each time she was interviewed, more and more information surfaced about Michele. In my review of her earlier interviews, I sensed she was not forthcoming with all she knew. Other than Brian Earley, she denied knowledge of any other relationship Michele was in and was adamant that Michele was not involved in drug use.

After reviewing the lengthy narrative of her last interview with Skinner and Hochdanner as just described, I turned to Hochdanner's notes. There was some valuable information there that did not appear in the narrative. Her notes clearly revealed that Burdick *did* know that Michele was in a relationship with Mike Kasper. Something she'd denied earlier. When questioned about Kasper, she explained that shortly after Michele went missing, she and Shannon went to Lefty's to talk to him. She admitted that Michele told her she was having sex with Kasper. Michele had also said to her that "He didn't like her talking to other men, and he would get mad and be rude to her if she did." When this happened, she said, "Michele would be on egg-shells." Burdick was asked if she knew when Michele and Kasper's last involvement was, and she answered, "Last June."

Apparently, Burdick had a much better recollection of this than Kasper himself, who told police he couldn't remember. When the questioning turned to Michele and drugs, she answered, "She may have smoked some pot with Mike to 'fit in,' but it wasn't a habit." Initially, she denied knowing any of this, and it seemed she was still holding back. At least, Kasper was a person of interest in the case and even on my radar. Knowing that both Nikki and Shannon had immediately gone running to him after Michele went missing was a bit fishy as well. What more did they know? And why weren't they telling the police everything?

I was highly skeptical of the reliability and trustworthiness of any information coming from Nikki Burdick or Shannon Taylor. I was certain they knew more but they were willing to do anything to protect Michele and, at the same time, do anything to destroy Cal. Notably, Burdick had lied to the police earlier when she denied knowledge of a relationship between Michele and Kasper, and likely her relationships with other men as well. Over time, however, she finally admitted that knowledge. Also, she admitted that she and Shannon ran to Kasper right after learning Michele was missing. What was that all about? She also came around a bit, admitting that Michele would smoke some weed just to 'fit in.' What else did she know? For reasons of their own, they were holding back and refusing to share. Interestingly, several years later, Burdick was interviewed by CBS *48-Hours* correspondent Erin Moriarty. When asked what she knew about Michele's relationship with Kasper, she replied, "That, I didn't know about. I think I was as surprised as anybody else to learn about that." Busted! On national television no less.

The Boyfriend – Brian Earley

Next up was Brian Earley. As I thumbed through the lead, I was looking for anything to suggest that the interview with Earley was videotaped. I found nothing. I also looked for a sworn statement. Again, nothing.

The SP caught up to Earley at the home of Gary Taylor, Michele's father, where he was interviewed by Investigator Bill McEvoy. At the time, Earley was 24-years old and 12-years younger than Michele. He was six-feet tall, weighed 170 pounds, had a medium build, with short dark brown hair, blue eyes, and glasses. Earley told McEvoy that he had been dating Michele since the end of November 2000. He described how the relationship evolved quickly, and by December, it included weekend trysts in the Poconos. They took turns paying for the room. "Michele would always pay in cash," he said. He'd moved to the area about three months before. Last night, he said Michele came to his apartment after work, arriving between 9:30 and 9:45 p.m. They sat on the bed and talked about their day's activities and the events in NYC. Michele then left about 11:00 p.m., and he assumed she was going home. He didn't know Cal Harris but was aware he was married to Michele, and the fact they were going through a divorce. He suspected Cal was aware of his relationship with Michele. Explaining further that he believed a man by the name of Ken Carrigan, or KC, who Michele confided in, might have told Cal.

Earley also identified some of Michele's friends, including Nikki Burdick, and some of the girls she worked with at Lefty's. He was also aware of Barb Thayer, Michele's friend Lisa from college, and some of Michele's neighbors. He provided a detailed description of what Michele was wearing, including her jewelry. He was aware that Michele was trying to sell her jewelry and that she had plans later in the week to meet a friend in the NYC area who was going to help her do that.

Later in the interview, McEvoy walked Earley over to his own apartment a short distance away, where the interview continued. There, he told McEvoy he had given Michele a key to his apartment about two months earlier, but she had lost it. So, he gave her a replacement key the night before. He explained how he met Michele and how she became the driving force in his decision to move to NY from Philadelphia. They had even talked a little about marriage. Michele told him that she and Cal argued a lot, and he had once shoved her around, but he'd never struck or injured her.

Earley was then asked if Michele kept any personal items at his apartment. After answering that she did, he showed McEvoy some of Michele's belongings, including a toothbrush, make-up kit, and a few articles of clothing. During the interview, McEvoy was looking around the apartment and observed a 12-gauge shotgun and some ammunition. Earley claimed he used them for hunting. McEvoy picked up the gun and sniffed the barrel. There was no scent of gunpowder to suggest it had been fired recently. Earley then described the different occasions when Michele would spend the night at his place, usually when Cal was out of town with the kids. He said, "Usually, it was just on the weekends, but there was at least one weekday when she stayed over."

Later, in a follow-up interview, Earley was asked if he had given Michele any money for a down payment on the house she was buying. He admitted to giving her $5,000 from his savings. He also knew Michele was working and attempting to sell her jewelry and watch (he believed to be a Rolex) in her effort to raise money for the down payment. Before ending the interview, he was asked about the last time he and Michele had sexual intercourse. He said, "We didn't last night, but we did the night before."

Investigator Jim Conzola joined McEvoy the next day and re-contacted Earley again. Together, they inquired about his hunting property in PA. Earley agreed to take them there, and they followed him to the hunting camp, which was just over the PA border and about a 20-minute drive from Nichols, NY. Once they arrived, he explained how he'd brought Michele to the camp on prior occasions, as recently as last week. He said that he had taken her to see the pond located just behind the camp, perhaps 3-4 weeks earlier. While there,

Conzola and McEvoy made a cursory check of the surrounding area, including a barn and the pond. Nothing remarkable was noted, and surprisingly, no photographs were taken of Earley's properties. Neither the hunting camp nor his apartment back in Smithboro. And of course, no forensic examinations. Why did they even bother going out there?

| Michele and Brian

McEvoy was back again with Earley doing a little followup the next day. While there, he secured some of Michele's belongings. Due to Earley's intimate relationship with Michele, and apparently, the last one to see her alive, McEvoy asked him to take a polygraph. He agreed, and about five days later, McEvoy conducted the examination at the SP barracks in Owego. In his report, McEvoy concluded that Earley had answered the test questions truthfully. Subsequent criminal history checks on Earley were negative.

The police interviews with Earley provided some valuable information, but it was very preliminary, and many unanswered questions remained. As Michele's 'significant other' and the last known person to see her alive, Earley was clearly a suspect. Other than the polygraph, there was nothing that explained what was done to eliminate him as a suspect conclusively.

Barbara Thayer

I knew Barb Thayer was going to be an essential witness in this case. I had interviewed her four years earlier, but I was now anxious to learn what more she had told the SP.

As a key witness, at the same time Cal was first being interviewed, SP investigators Robert DelGiorno and Lori Hochdanner, were interviewing Thayer. Her first interview with the SP was remarkably consistent with my own interview with her previously discussed. Therefore, there is no need to repeat what we already know. Instead, we'll fast forward to what she had to say in subsequent SP interviews.

Thayer's second interview took place at the Owego barracks. After another lengthy interview, an equally lengthy written statement was taken from her. For the most part, her statement detailed the same scenario she described earlier but included a few additional items of interest.

Thayer had become aware that Cal had a girlfriend by the name of Connie, and that Michele had hired a private investigator to try and follow Cal to find out who the girlfriend was. Later, Michele did find out about Connie, and Thayer recalled babysitting for her while she went to confront her.

Thayer stated that Cal was a 'neat freak,' and Michele was not neat. That difference became the crux of many of their arguments. When asked about incidents of physical abuse, she had never seen any. However, there were times when she had witnessed some very heated arguments. Claiming that Cal was verbally abusive to Michele. She then added, "Michele could hold her own in any argument, and she could be as abusive to Cal as he was to her."

Thayer acknowledged, however, that the disputes between Cal and Michele had subsided substantially during the last couple of weeks, compared to earlier in the divorce proceedings. She even described a recent occurrence when Michele said it seemed weird because lately, she'd noticed that she and Cal had not been having their usual conflicts. She'd also been concerned about Cal giving her a hard time about her trip to NYC, but to her surprise, he didn't.

As mentioned, Thayer was an important witness and remained in contact with the SP on a regular basis. I could certainly understand her desire to be helpful, but with the frequency and quality of some of her new information, I was starting to suspect that she might be trying to be a little *too* helpful. Thereafter, I began scrutinizing her information a bit more carefully.

In a later interview by Hochdanner, Thayer disclosed what she had told me a few days earlier. That when Cal was able to return home, one of the things she noticed was how he'd rearranged his ATVs in the garage. Then, she went on to describe how Cal put all of Michele's clothing into garbage bags and placed them in the basement. She had asked Cal if she could store some of Michele's belongings in her barn, and he said it would be alright. He then suggested putting them in a garage sale next summer, and he would split the profits with her. Before the interview ended, Thayer expressed her concerns with Hochdanner, that Cal wanted to clean the boy's rooms out. She feared he was going to remove everything that reminded the children of Michele.

The more I read about the types of things Thayer was telling the SP, the more suspicious I became of her involvement in the case. I began to suspect the SP, knowing she was still working for Cal, had recruited her to be their 'agent eyes and ears' to report anything and everything she could about Cal. My suspicions were also supported when I learned she had been taking her own personal, detailed notes about things Cal said and did. The SP had likely suggested and encouraged her to do so.

Clearly, Thayer loved Michele but despised Cal. As such, she was ready, willing, and able to do anything she could to help the SP build their case against Cal. Sometimes in her notes, after Cal had said or done something she didn't like, where she wrote comments next to it such as "what an ass," or "I can't stand the sight of him." With every passing day, her animosity towards Cal only deepened as she infused herself further into the case. Yet she continued to work for him.

As more time went by, she was trying much too hard to be 'helpful' when she started exaggerating, bolstering, misleading, or simply making things up. But the SP readily embraced anything and everything she had to offer.

In a later interview on October 2, 2001, by Hochdanner, Thayer was explicitly asked if she had called Michele's cell phone on the morning of September 12, 2001, around 7:13 a.m. According to Hochdanner's narrative report, Thayer said she remembered calling her cell phone number that morning but was unsure of the actual time.

During my review, I noticed a significant discrepancy between Hochdanner's typed narrative and her hand-written notes that were attached. Before Thayer was re-interviewed, it was apparent that the SP had received and reviewed Michele's cell phone records. They could see that a 7:13 a.m. call to Michele's cell phone from the Harris residence occurred. Thus, prompting the question to Thayer. In Hochdanner's notes, which were obviously made before the typed version, she wrote, "*phone call @ 7:13 a.m. to Michele's cell phone? No. Barb thought she called it later in the morning.*" Notably, Thayer's original answer of "No" to making the 7:13 a.m. call, as well as the word "later" in the morning, had both been omitted from the typed narrative.

> Author's Note: Prior to being questioned about this 7:13 a.m. phone call, Thayer had already been interviewed more than six times. One of which included a lengthy and detailed written statement. She never once mentioned trying to call Michele. Why all the fuss about this call? Later.

Lefty's

With the large stack of discovery materials, we had received, it was challenging to decide what to review next. So far, I was developing more questions than answers. What I learned from police interviews with Burdick, Earley, and Thayer was very helpful, and a good place to start. But, knowing how I was stonewalled in my interview attempts at Lefty's four years ago, I was anxious to learn why.

The very first Lefty's interview I found was conducted by Investigator Lori Hochdanner, by telephone, on September 12, 2001. She'd interviewed Michael Kasper, who said he was a cook and evening manager. Kasper knew Michele and told Hochdanner she had worked at Lefty's the evening before from 4:00 until 9:00 p.m. Then, around 9:30 p.m., he and Michele and another cook named Mike Hakes walked out to their vehicles together. He watched Michele get into her van like she usually did, and as far as he knew, was headed home. She had not mentioned anything about going out after work, although she would sometimes do that with some of the other girls. None of them were working last night. "Michele seemed normal, nothing out of the ordinary," he said. Over the next several days, Investigators Hochdanner and DelGiorno returned to Lefty's to interview and later re-interview nearly two dozen of Michele's co-workers, both male and female. The majority of those interviewed were other waitresses. While a few only knew who Michele was, most of them had both working and social relationships with her. Collectively, however, what they revealed was very helpful during the early stages of the investigation. As we'll learn in a future chapter, this same information would take on much greater significance, after the discovery of new evidence.

Nearly all of Michele's co-workers knew she was married, had four children, and was currently going through a divorce. Many also knew she had a boyfriend named Brian, who they would see from time-to-time when he came into Lefty's. Several mentioned socializing with Michele after hours and identified several of the bars in the area where they would go with her. They also knew that Nikki Burdick and Michele were close friends, and Burdick was almost always with Michele whenever they went out. Of those who socialized with Michele, they all agreed that the relationship between Michele and Nikki was strange.

They also agreed that Nikki seemed to have this jealous obsession towards Michele. If they weren't together, Nikki would be calling her constantly, demanding to know where she was, what she was doing, and who she was with. At times, when alone with Michele, she admitted that she liked Nikki but didn't like her bugging her all the time. There were times when she said, "I just want to be left alone." One co-worker recalled going out with Michele one night, and she hadn't told Nikki. Later, when Nikki found out, she was furious. She added, "Nikki was jealous, not at all friendly and didn't like Michele making new friends, especially with the other girls at Lefty's." Another co-worker added, "Nikki always acted as if she was too good for the girls at Lefty's."

As police interviews of co-workers continued, much more was revealed about Michele, including both her work and social activities. Information concerning other individuals and happenings at Lefty's was also revealed, especially those involving Michele. Nearly all those interviewed agreed that Michele was well-liked among her co-workers, as well as a favorite among many of the patrons. Especially young men. Michele was frequently seen flirting and interacting with the young male cooks as well as some of the young male customers. Also, she was seen sitting at the bar, enjoying a drink, and engaged in conversation with them after work.

Most of the girls had seen and were able to describe the expensive jewelry Michele wore. While some characterized Michele as 'high-maintenance,' others viewed her as 'out-of-their-league' and questioned why she was working as a waitress. Nearly all knew that for at least a week or two before Michele went missing, she was actively trying to sell some of her jewelry. Most added, "It was common knowledge among most everybody, including many of our regular customers." Even some of the male employees were able to describe Michele's jewelry and knew she was trying to sell it.

When asked about any problems they or Michele may have had with co-workers, Mike Kasper's name popped up right away. He was always hitting on the girls, and if they turned him down, he'd get real nasty with them. At least two girls described Kasper as being arrogant and chauvinistic. He was always pushing Michele to go out with him, but she didn't want to go. Then added, "Kasper was always on the prowl." Some of the other girls either knew or heard rumors that Michele and Kasper were involved in a sexual relationship.

Most of the girls were aware of a former male employee who got fired after exposing himself to Michele. Later, when asked specifically about another cook by the name of Michael Hakes, none of them were aware of any problems or concerns.

In a follow-up interview with Kasper, investigators learned that he worked with Michele the night she disappeared. He was close to her, and they talked often. According to Kasper, Michele had never spoken to him about being physically abused by her husband but knew there were times when Mr. Harris called the restaurant and yelled at her.

Some of the girls who had a closer relationship with Michele than others talked about what they learned from their conversations with her. One had gone through a divorce herself, and Michele had asked her questions and discussed her pending divorce. During one of their discussions, Michele admitted feeling guilty about going out after work and not being home with her children. But then she said the children were all in bed by the time she finished work anyway and she knew they would be okay with their father.

Another knew Michele didn't like going home right after work because she didn't want to get into a fight with Cal. When asked by one of the other girls, Michele said she did feel guilty, but then added, "The kids are home with their dad, so why shouldn't I go out."

Interestingly, when the interviews turned to their knowledge of any problems with customers, nearly everyone mentioned and described two or three young guys who came in regularly, always asking for a table in Michele's section. If one of her tables wasn't available, they'd sit at the bar and wait. They provided physical descriptions of the young men who they believed were in their mid-20s and worked at the local steel plant just west of town.

One of the girls had a more specific recollection of two of the young steelworkers. She thought the older of the two went by the name of Doug. She described him as tall and muscular, with a shaved head and a few moles on his face. She thought the other man, named Stacy, was a little shorter, younger and had short brown hair. Both were regulars at Lefty's. More than once, she had seen them come in together and always ask for a table in Michele's section. On another occasion, she said the one she thought was Doug, made a scene one night at Micky's Bar, about wanting to be with Michele.

The police had not yet interviewed Michael Hakes, the other cook at Lefty's that was identified by Michael Kasper in an earlier interview. I knew from reviewing the lead-log that Michael Hakes would eventually be interviewed. But in the meantime, it was interesting to note what investigators were doing before that happened.

Investigators launched an aggressive campaign in search of any information they could find on Michael Hakes and Michael Kasper. The information and records sought included but were not limited to, federal criminal and civil records, motor vehicle, real property, address histories, and more. They expanded their search to include any files from local police agencies.

NYSPIN[2] and NCIC[3] checks on Michael Kasper revealed no known criminal history. However, an examination of local records at the Waverly, NY Police Department, revealed he had been involved in a domestic dispute with a girl by the name of Margie Quinn, in late June 2001.

The NCIC check on Michael Hakes revealed a great deal more. Hakes had been convicted of a violent sexual assault in Maricopa County, Arizona, in 1990, as a result of numerous felony charges, including forcible rape and sodomy. He was sentenced and served ten years in an Arizona state prison. He was released unsupervised on September 11, 2000, as a registered Level 2 sex offender. The SP immediately contacted the Arizona authorities and subsequently obtained the specific details of his arrest and conviction, which included a detailed case summary.

Briefly, Hakes unlawfully entered the residence of a female stranger, held her captive, and assaulted her physically and sexually. After several minutes of struggling, Hakes forced her into the bedroom where he digitally penetrated her vagina and rectum, then forced his penis into her mouth and then subjected her to sexual intercourse. The victim suffered numerous abrasions and bruises and later suffered a stroke, which permanently limited the use of her left arm and hand.

A follow-up interview with Mike Kasper was conducted by Sr. Investigator John Skinner and Investigator Mike Myers. At the time, Kasper was 24-years old. He was five-feet-seven-inches tall, 150 pounds, with a medium build, medium-length dirty-blonde hair and blue eyes. Kasper told investigators that on the night in question, he, Mike Hakes, and Michele Harris had a drink after work, and then the three of them walked out of the bar together. Hakes left first, and he stayed and talked with Michele for a few minutes in the parking lot. Then they each went their own way. He had not seen Michele since she left around 9:30 p.m.

He told investigators that about two months prior, he was involved with Michele for about a two or three-week period. They did have sexual intercourse on two or three occasions at his apartment. Other than Nikki Burdick, he did not believe anyone else knew of their relationship.

Kasper explained that the relationship only lasted about two or three weeks, and then they just stopped seeing each other. "I was cool with that," he said. They still got along well and continued to talk with each other. When they pushed him to be more specific with the date of this relationship, he claimed he couldn't remember, even to the closest month. He further recalled having seen Michele at the Guthrie Inn.

Investigators caught up with Michael Hakes at his residence in Waverly. During his interview, he admitted knowing that Kasper and Michele did try a relationship, but it didn't work out. He was not aware of any problems Michele was having with any of her co-workers and said he did not have any problems with co-workers. He claimed not to know who Michele went out with after work. He also claimed that generally, he did not go out after work. He knew nothing about Michele having a boyfriend until after she went missing. He also had no recollection of whether Michele left with anyone after work because he usually leaves right after his work is done. On occasion, he'd stay and have a beer.

On the night in question, he finished work around 9:00 p.m. Then recalled seeing Michele get into her vehicle, which he believed was some type of large vehicle. He'd seen Kasper talking to some guy in a pick-up truck but didn't recognize who the guy was. He thought perhaps it was one of Kasper's friends from the Elmira area. On that night, Hakes was driving his father's white Cougar. When he left, he went straight to his girlfriend's house and remained there all night.

Even though I was still in the early stages of my review of the discovery material, I had already learned a great deal. The SP interviews with Lefty's employees were revealing some interesting information. Already, I could see a troubling scene developing, ripened by suspicious characters, circumstances, and activities surrounding Michele. Even with all things considered collectively, it seemed Michele was clueless of her vulnerability, and the risky environment in which she was exposed.

At Lefty's, Michele was clearly in the minority as one of the haves, working in a world of have-nots. The Billy Joel song title, "Uptown Girl," would describe Michele perfectly. That's what she was – an uptown girl in a downtown world. Even with what little I had learned so far, the numerous risk factors contributing to Michele's vulnerability were easy to pinpoint. Any one or combination of these factors could create the potential for her to become a target of a crime. From where I was sitting, criminal activity was likely already brewing at Lefty's. Something bad was on the verge of happening. The stage was set for a crime to occur, including but not limited to sex, drugs, robbery, abduction, or any combination of those. In-as-much, Cal may have been right when the SP asked what he thought happened to his wife, and he answered, "She's hanging around with the wrong crowd in Waverly," and they should, "pump the shit out of them."

As the investigation continued, Lefty's owner, Tom D'Alosio, and his wife Jodi were also interviewed. D'Alosio was friends with Kasper and knew about his sexual relationship with Michele. He'd seen the two of them drinking together at the bar. He was also aware that Michele was trying to sell her jewelry and recalled making a $100 offer on her Rolex. "She just laughed at me," he said.

Both Tom and wife Jodi, who was the floor manager for the waitresses, recalled Michele sitting at the bar having drinks with three young guys they believed were from the local steel plant. Jodi also recalled a separate occasion, seeing Michele after work at the bar, talking with the youngest of the three steelworkers. She couldn't recall any names but said, "They were all regulars."

During one of the interviews at Lefty's, one of the girls identified a man by the name of Tom Nabinger, who allegedly had a brief sexual tryst with Michele. Investigators caught up with Nabinger at the Simmons-Rockwell dealership where he worked. He'd met Michele through Nikki Burdick and later acknowledged having sex with her on a single occasion over Memorial Day weekend.

After learning that one of Michele's co-workers at Lefty's had exposed himself to her at work, investigators identified and interviewed Eddie Tomlin at his residence. After admitting that it did, in fact, happen, he further admitted having done the same thing to another female employee at Lefty's previously.

Subsequent DMV, NCIC, and NYSPIN checks on Tomlin revealed only a conviction for DWI and other traffic violations, but no known criminal history was found.

As mentioned, Michael Hakes was a registered sex offender from Arizona, who was working as a cook at Lefty's at the time Michele went missing. The SP had interviewed Hakes and conducted an extensive background investigation into his past criminal activity. Hakes' girlfriend at the time had given him an alibi, and he'd apparently passed a polygraph examination. As far as the SP was concerned, Hakes had been eliminated as a suspect.

At the time, other than knowing the serious nature of his criminal record, I was not seriously considering Hakes as a viable suspect. But I still wanted to talk with him. Perhaps he could share some additional insight about Michele, her co-workers, or some of the other activities that were going on at Lefty's.

I was able to locate Hakes at his new girlfriend's residence in Broome County, NY. I recognized him when he answered the door from the sex-registry photograph I had with me. At the time, he was 37-years old, about five-foot-seven-inches tall, 200 pounds, with short black hair and brown eyes. After introducing myself and my purpose, Hakes was not sure if he should be talking to me. He said, "The DA told me I didn't have to talk to anyone," or if he did, he should have someone else present. Before agreeing to talk with me, he said he would like to talk to his father about being a witness during the interview, and he would get back to me. I told him that would be fine and encouraged him to do so. Before leaving, I left him my card with all my contact information. He never called back, and my follow-up calls to him went unanswered.

During this same period, I also attempted to interview Michael Kasper. The SP also interviewed Kasper and eliminated him as a suspect as well. I was not convinced of that. I found nothing in the file that showed him having an alibi for the night of Michele's disappearance, or that his apartment, vehicle, and person, had been searched. I located Kasper at his residence in Waverly. When he answered the door, I introduced myself, and he quickly advised it was not a good time since he was getting ready to go to work. I advised him it would only take a few minutes, but he insisted it was not a good time. He said he would check his schedule when he got to work and let me know when it would be more convenient. Before leaving, I told him I could certainly do the interview at his convenience. I left my business card and returned to my car. I suspected he was trying to avoid the interview, so I watched and waited for him to leave for work. He never did. Later, I twice tried calling him back and left messages, but he never called back.

After completing the interviews of the current employees at Lefty's, investigators turned to some of the former employees. Keith Tingley was one of them. While speaking with Investigator Scott Pauly, Tingley advised he had worked with Michele Harris for approximately three months before leaving to take another job. He claimed that he and Michele were friends. Later, he told Pauly about a 'premonition' he had over several days, including a series of visions, where he described seeing only Michele's disembodied head asking for help.

Investigators Mike Myers and Mike Young picked up the interview with Tingley two days later. He told them how Michele would hang around work at times to have a beer with Mike Kasper. He thought they were rather close. He recalled last seeing Michele on Saturday before she went missing. He stopped by Lefty's after it closed and saw Michele sitting at the bar with Kasper.

Tingley admitted having a crush on Michele because she was the first woman he saw after his release from jail for a probation violation and explained they would flirt back and forth. He said there was one time when he fondled her breasts. He claimed she had given him permission after he asked to feel them. He was curious to know what they felt like with implants.

The interview then turned to his 'premonition.' He described seeing Michele's face in a swampy area off Route 34, near Van Etten, NY. He heard her say, "Keith," followed by "help, help." Then he described a location where there was a bridge, along with some other details. Afterward, he led investigators to the area he described, and they searched the area while continuing their interview with him.

For the next two days, they continued their search of the area but found nothing. Knowing that 'visionaries' can at times be the actual perpetrators of a crime, they continued their interview with Tingley.

During the interview, Tingley made a comment regarding DNA evidence on Michele's remains. Specifically, commenting that his DNA would not be found in her mouth or under her fingernails. And that he was sure after her disappearance, she had been raped because she was an attractive woman. He thought that since Michele had long finger-nails, she probably scratched her attacker. When they asked him about his own sexual habits, he said, "I don't care for intercourse due to the prospect of disease and pregnancy, but I do accept blowjobs."

I'm sure their ears perked up a bit when he mentioned Michele being raped, and his DNA would not be found in her mouth or under her fingernails. But after spending a considerable amount of time with

Tingley, they were eventually able to determine there was no credible merit to his 'premonition.'

The Keith Tingley 'premonition' was only one example of the dozens, and I mean dozens of such, that were identified and documented throughout this case. These types of leads are very common, especially in high-profile cases. And this case was no exception. Whether classified as rumors, sightings, psychic readings, visions, premonitions, jail-house snitches, or just gut feelings, each was assigned a lead and properly investigated.

Investigators DelGiorno and Hochdanner, following up on their Lefty's leads, located and interviewed Sarah Nelson. She was the girlfriend of Lefty's cook, Michael Hakes, the registered sex offender from Arizona. In a very brief interview, Nelson told them that Hakes would usually get home from working at Lefty's between 9:15 and 9:30 p.m. She recalled the evening of September 11, 2001, because of the World Trade Center attack, and knew he was home by 9:20 p.m. that night. He remained with her the entire night.

A week later, they returned to re-interview Nelson. She was again asked if she knew the whereabouts of Hakes on the night of September 11, 2001. Nelson again stated that Hakes was with her the entire evening and added that she was aware of his arrest and prison time in Arizona. She further added that she would neither protect him nor lie for him.

During the SP interviews with Lefty's employees, they were all asked about any problems Michele may have had with coworkers or patrons. As previously mentioned, both D'Alosios, as well as several other employees, referred to three young steelworkers who were frequent customers at Lefty's and were often seen interacting with Michele. Accordingly, Investigators Mike Telfer and Scott Pauly were assigned a lead to follow-up on this information. It was now two weeks into the investigation.

Investigators responded to the NUCOR[4] steel plant in nearby Chemung, NY, just west of Waverly. NUCOR was also known as by its subsidiary name, Vulcraft Steel, a division of NUCOR. There, they identified and interviewed two steelworkers by the names of Doug Nagle of Sayre, PA, and Stacy Stewart of Lockwood, NY. Both claimed it had been several weeks since their last contact with Michele at Lefty's. They both met her at Lefty's and seen her out socially with her friend Nikki, at various local bars.

I didn't think much of it at the time, but when I re-visited this lead later, I realized how vague and incomplete it was. There were no other questions of these witnesses. Such as, what interactions, if any, they had with Michele, either at Lefty's or out socially. It was odd that their questioning ended after learning they hadn't seen Michele in several weeks.

The incompleteness of this lead reminded me of one mentioned earlier. Remember the bar lead, where the assignment was to interview patrons of bars frequented by Michele? Other than supposedly dropping off Michele's photograph, not one person was named as having been interviewed. And for some unknown reason(s), the lead was 'completed' by Investigator Myers rather than Investigator Standinger, who was originally assigned. Questionably, if not suspiciously, according to Myers, even though other bars were listed, the only one he specifically noted as being 'done' was the Guthrie Inn. But he never mentioned what it was that he had done. The Lehigh Tavern, one of Nikki and Michele's favorites, wasn't even mentioned.

Not long after leaving NUCOR, Telfer received a call from Jessica Hunsinger, the office secretary. She advised that shortly after they left, Stacy Stewart was acting nervous and asking questions. It's unknown what additional information they may have had, but something prompted the investigators to run a motor vehicle and criminal history check on Stewart before returning to re-interview him. Records revealed that Stewart was on probation for a DWI conviction in the state of Texas, and his probation had been transferred to Tioga County. The DMV check revealed that his license to drive was currently suspended.

Two days later, Telfer returned another call from Hunsinger, who provided even more information. She remembered Stewart calling in sick on a couple of days right around the time Michele was reported missing, but she couldn't recall the exact days. Sometime later, Stewart was re-interviewed, but again, the details were very sketchy at best, much unlike the detailed interviews of other witnesses. Stewart again told investigators he had no contact with Michele for several weeks prior to her disappearance. He claimed he went directly home after work on September 11, 2001, and spoke with his mother in Texas around 7:30 p.m. He further added he went to work the next day September 12th, between 4:00 and 5:00 a.m. That was the extent of his interview.

Author's Note: At the time, this 4:00-5:00 a.m. timeframe bore little significance. Much later, however, as the story unfolds, it becomes very significant.

What other information they may have gleaned from Stewart remains a mystery. There were certainly no details in their lead. What makes this even more interesting was the fact that at some point during this interview or perhaps a subsequent interview, Stewart was asked to take a polygraph. Why? You don't randomly ask someone to take a polygraph. There must have been a good reason. Telfer and Pauly were both trained and experienced Investigators. What had they learned or suspected about Stewart that would prompt them to ask for a polygraph? Something must have raised a 'red flag,' but what was it? For now, it would remain a mystery.

On a related note, there were four others, including Earley, Kasper, Hakes, and Carrigan, who were each asked and later submitted to polygraph examinations. All for a good reason. Three had known intimate relationships with Michele, while the fourth (Hakes) was a convicted sex offender. Polygraphing them as part of the elimination process made perfect sense. Furthermore, their respective relationships or involvement with Michele were clearly outlined in the lead narratives. With Stacy Stewart, that was not the case.

The lead revealed absolutely nothing about Stewart's relationship with Michele. So again, why the polygraph? In reviewing the investigator's attached notes, besides Stewart and Nagle, a few other names appeared along with their respective pedigree and contact information. There was nothing further to indicate whether any of them had ever been interviewed, let alone what they had to say.

Strangely, or perhaps ironically, I had reviewed numerous other leads completed by Pauly and Telfer that always included detailed notes of those interviewed, as well as what they had to say. But other than a few sparse notes in the NUCOR lead, there was nothing about what any of these witnesses told Investigators. Admittedly, I did not fully recognize the vague or incomplete nature of this lead during my initial assessment.

> Author's Note: As the story unfolds, a future chapter will reveal some newly developed information that would lead me back to take a much closer look at the questionable and suspicious nature of both the NUCOR and bar leads. Indeed.

Collectively, the leads from Lefty's had provided a great deal of information. Even though more than four years had passed, I set out to verify what witnesses had told the SP, and perhaps learn something more. Even though I had been blocked from interviewing them earlier, I was now hopeful that after more than four years, they would agree to speak with me.

Michael Hakes' alibi witness was his girlfriend, Sarah Nelson. SP investigators had interviewed her at least twice during the first few days of Michele's disappearance. Since that time, I had learned that Hakes had split with Nelson and moved in with a new girlfriend. My attempt to interview Hakes was unsuccessful. Since Hakes was no longer involved with Nelson, perhaps she would be willing to offer something more.

During my interview with Nelson, she confirmed that Hakes was, in fact, with her on the night Michele went missing. When asked, she said she would not lie for him and had not been coerced or threatened by him to lie. She had not been made aware of his criminal history until the SP told her. That she said, "was sort of the beginning of the end" of their relationship. But the primary reason for their break-up was his drinking problem. On the night in question, she believed Hakes was driving his father's white Cougar but unsure whether he had access to any other vehicles.

I wasn't sure what to expect when trying to interview Brian Earley. By this time, I knew he had returned to PA, married his former girlfriend, and then moved back to live and work in New York. I was able to locate Brian Earley at his new residence in Smithboro, NY. After I introduced myself and explained why I wanted to talk with him, he said it was not a good time, but if I left him my card, he would call me later. He said he needed some time to talk to his wife about it. So, once again, I would leave my card and leave, not holding my breath that I would ever hear back. Surprisingly, two days later, he called me back, and politely said, "I don't want to be interviewed or answer any questions at this time." I told him I understood and thanked him for getting back to me. Before hanging up, I asked, "Perhaps another time?" "Perhaps," he said.

Interesting place this Lefty's. But I sure wouldn't want my wife working there. In the world of haves and have-nots, Michele was clearly one of the haves. But if you're one of the have-nots, you notice. Even though Michele was trying to fit-in, she was clearly 'out of her league.' As a result, she was dangerously vulnerable. Her open, friendly, and flirtatious manner, in combination with her good looks, expensive jewelry, and promiscuous lifestyle, significantly increased the risk and vulnerability of her being targeted by anyone with nefarious and wicked intent.

---

1. CPS: Child Protective Services
2. NYSPIN: New York Statewide Police Information Network
3. NCIC: National Crime Information Center
4. NUCOR: Nuclear Corporation of America: "The Little Steel Company That Could"

11

INVESTIGATION CONTINUED

During the examination of Michele's telephone records, it was determined that before she went to work on September 11, 2001, she had a lengthy conversation with a woman later identified as Brenda Goldman. When interviewed, Goldman acknowledged that she had spoken with Michele that morning. She was aware of the pending divorce and knew Michele had taken a job at a bar or restaurant. Goldman told investigators that things between Cal and Michele had become copacetic, and they were working out the details of the divorce. She explained how she knew Cal and Michele because their sons played lacrosse together. When asked about her phone conversation with Michele, she had first called her at home around 11:30 a.m. They were talking about what happened in New York City.

Michele also told her she was nervous about going to work and that she'd rather stay home. They'd talked about the divorce proceedings. Michele said to her that Cal was taking the divorce much better now. Adding that, "Michele said her, and Cal was getting along better now than they ever had." She added that "recently, Cal had been nice to Michele. He was giving her the divorce, and their fighting had stopped."

During the interview, Goldman explained how she knew Nikki Burdick was a close friend to Michele and had once worked for Cal, but he'd fired her. The reason she said Cal fired her was that she was telling Michele everything he was doing. Additionally, Michele talked about making more money in tips than she did from her regular restaurant pay.

Jumping forward to April 2003, a new lead was assigned to Investigator Jim Conzola to learn more about that 21-minute conversation Michele had with Goldman. Although Goldman reiterated much of the same information from her first interview, she had some interesting new information to offer. She explained it was her understanding, after speaking with Michele, that the reason she had taken a job was that Cal cut off her money. Goldman had recently purchased a new home and recalled talking with Michele about buying her own house in Owego.

As the subject of the interview shifted, she informed Conzola that Michele had a 'wild' side. She described a time when she, Michele, and Nikki Burdick had gone to Syracuse, NY, to celebrate Michele's birthday. Michele had rented a limo. While they were at the Dinosaur Restaurant, a young stranger tried to pick up Michele, who had been drinking heavily and was getting rather drunk. She said, "Michele actually left with the guy who took her on a motorcycle ride." When Michele returned, after being gone for more than an hour, she said they had gone to some other bar to drink more. Later, after leaving the Dinosaur, this same guy and some of his 'biker friends' followed them. After leaving Syracuse, while on their way home, Burdick called some of their 'guy friends,' and they later met up with them. One of the guys, Carrigan, worked at Royal and had given Michele a bracelet. She couldn't recall his name but knew he used to work for Cal and now worked for his brother Kevin Harris.

Goldman spoke about another night when Michele was out with Nikki again when she met another young guy, Earley. It was shortly after this when Michele decided she wanted to divorce Cal. Nearing the end of the interview, she described how Nikki was always overly protective of Michele and thought the relationship between them seemed odd. She described another time when Michele met up with the same guy, Carrigan, who now worked for Kevin, and they had sex in the back of the car while Nikki drove. Later, Michele told her she'd seen this same guy driving past her property.

In my view, it seemed like Goldman was much more forthcoming with information about Michele than Nikki Burdick. Her direct knowledge and observations of Michele's 'wild' side was another example, and further support of Michele's vulnerability at that time from her reckless lifestyle, risk-taking, and behavior. Interestingly, Ken Carrigan had entered the picture once again in Michele's nightlife. Goldman knew that he'd given Michele a bracelet and had sex with him in the back of a moving car. Perhaps their 'cozy' little relationship was a bit more involved than just friendly chit-chats and a few e-mails after-all. I was never convinced that there wasn't something more to their relationship. And I could understand why Cal might think that as well.

Carrigan's continued denials were making sense. He feared Cal finding out as that would not be in his best interest.

Ironically, many were very quick to condemn Cal, including Michele, for his infidelity with Connie. However, when it came to Michele, there was no condemnation. Instead, her infidelity and unfaithfulness were not only protected but spiraled under a cloak of deception and secrecy. And those who welcomed and approved of her behavior not only encouraged and supported it, they helped protect her secrets, even after she went missing.

Another big lead I was anxious to review was the interview with Greg and Shannon Taylor, Michele's brother, and sister-in-law. They had denied my request for an interview four years earlier. For the first time, I was about to learn what they had to say.

Investigator Jim Conzola was assigned and interviewed both Greg and Shannon Taylor. Greg didn't have nearly as much information to share as Shannon. However, he would say that he knew about the pending divorce and that Michele had talked to him about Cal pushing her around. But that conversation had taken place five or six months earlier. He knew that Michele worked at Lefty's and had a boyfriend named Brian Earley. And that she often stopped to see Brian after work. He said Michele was friends with Nikki Burdick and his wife Shannon, and she would confide in them more than himself. When asked, he also told Conzola that Brian Earley was at work with him when they learned that Michele was missing. Brian had said to him that Michele had been to his apartment that night as usual and had left around 11:00 p.m.

Shannon Taylor, as well as being Michele's sister-in-law, described herself as being her good friend. She'd last seen Michele a couple of days earlier. She knew Michele was supposed to be going to a scheduled meeting with her attorney to discuss the divorce settlement. According to Shannon, about three months earlier, Michele told her that Cal had been physical with her before by pushing her to the ground. But she added that Michele hadn't said anything recently about Cal being physical with her. When asked about any recent problems or threats, she wasn't aware of any and claimed there had been very few problems within the past month. Then added, "But if there were, Nikki or I would be the first know."

When she first heard that Michele was missing, she called Cal. He said, "Michele didn't come home" and added that she had been coming home "at all hours of the night reeking of booze." He'd also told her that Michele's purse was missing, but the keys were in her van. Shannon provided the names of Michele's friends and co-workers at Lefty's, and her knowledge of Brian Earley. But nary a word about Mike Kasper.

Shannon knew that Cal suspected Michele had a boyfriend after he said something to her about four weeks earlier. Cal had called and left a message for Michele saying, "Do whatever you have to do with your boyfriend, then get home." According to Shannon, Michele suspected that Ken Carrigan, whom she had confided in about Brian, had told Cal. She went on to describe Carrigan's infatuation with Michele and how Michele believed to have seen him driving out near her house.

A few days later, investigators Bill McEvoy and Bob DelGiorno returned to re-interview Shannon. They learned about a box of papers she had belonging to Michele and was asked to hold on to them. In the box were several letters Michele had received from Brian Earley and some other messages she had started to write to him. There were also miscellaneous scraps of paper with telephone numbers on them. She turned over the box and all its contents to the Investigators.

In one undated, hand-written letter that Brian had written to Michele, he referred to some conflict they were having when he wrote:

Dear Michele,

I'd be really surprised if you're actually reading this. Please be with me. Let's figure this whole mess out soon. I'm extremely happy with you in my life, and I'll do whatever it takes to be in your life. You said if you didn't love me, you wouldn't care. Well, if I didn't care or love you, I wouldn't go through this either. Just talk to me, and we'll work it out.

Love Always,
Brian

Continuing with the interview, Shannon described an incident Michele told her about that occurred at Lefty's. She'd been out on the back deck having a cigarette when a young male employee snuck up behind her. He was about 18-years old and the son of another employee. His pants were down, and he pulled out his penis and asked her to touch him. She reported the incident, and the guy was fired.

A couple more days went by before the SP called Greg and Shannon Taylor into the Owego barracks for further interviews. Shannon told investigators about a payphone at Lefty's that Michele used frequently. She said that Michele and Brian had been buying and using pre-paid calling cards with PINs to call each other. She also explained what she knew about Michele's breast implant surgery. She said one time, Michele came to her upset, telling her that Mickey Kasper, one of the cooks, acted as manager when the boss was not there, and she didn't like that he'd fondled her breasts because he wanted to know what they would feel like with implants.

Shannon added further that there should be more jewelry in Michele's purse beside her engagement ring. She said that Michele kept a dark blue or black velvet jeweler's bag, with two pairs of diamond earrings, an opal bracelet, and a diamond necklace. She'd asked Shannon to keep the bag at her house for safekeeping, until about three weeks ago. She added that "Michele also wore two fine gold chains with a cross and a Virgin Mary medal."

On the first anniversary of Michele's disappearance, brother Greg Taylor had been interviewed by the local media, and his comments had been publicly broadcasted. The following day, after receiving a call from Cal, Greg called attorney Robert Miller to report some threats Cal made. One was that the Taylors would never see the children again. Miller called Sr. Investigator Mulvey, who responded to take a statement from Greg.

According to Greg, Cal had called him after hearing his comments on the news. He claimed that Cal did not appreciate being bashed by Greg telling the media Cal was not cooperating with the police or doing anything to find Michele. He said Cal told him that if he wanted to play that way, he could go on the news and tell everyone how Michele was out four nights a week, doing coke, having sex with a convicted rapist, and was last seen at her boyfriend's house. Greg said that Cal threatened they "would never see his fucking kids again," and hung up. At the end of his statement, Greg added, "I'm sick of seeing things smoothed over for Cal, and I want the truth about his actions to come out."

As Michele's brother, I could understand Greg's frustration and resentment of Cal. After all, his sister was still missing after a year, and he firmly believed Cal was responsible. I'm sure his frustration and resentment had only deepened by what the SP was telling him. At the same time, I can understand Cal's anger when hearing Greg bashing him on the local news, especially when much of what Greg said wasn't accurate.

It was true that Cal had not helped directly in the search for Michele; however, as the prime suspect, he would not have been allowed to anyway. Indirectly, however, he was helping. He was cooperating with the police by answering their questions, consenting to the search of his property, turning over his home computer, as well as his telephone, financial and business records, and allowing his children to be interviewed. He even voluntarily submitted a sample of his DNA. With Cal's knowledge of Michele's suspicious friends, suspected drug use, and reckless behavior, he could have easily smeared her name publicly through the media himself. But he never did that.

Ironically, since Greg raised the issue, there were several others close to Michele, including Greg himself, who never helped in the search. But it was Cal who caught the brunt of criticism for not helping to search. In contrast, there was neither questioning nor criticism of Greg and Shannon Taylor, Nikki Burdick, Brian Earley, Mike Kasper, or even Barb Thayer for not searching. None of them offered to lift a finger in the search for Michele. If that were my sister, I'd be leading the pack.

As I continued, I couldn't help notice that in all the police interviews with Greg, Shannon, and Nikki, they were never asked nor commented about any of the things they did to enable Michele as she pursued her extra-marital affair(s) before the divorce was final. If anything, as her friends and family, they should have been discouraging her.

On a related note, Michele had attended a session with her therapist in mid-January 2001. In his records, he noted, "She continues to talk to Brian on the phone (in Philadelphia) but won't let the relationship develop until the divorce is final." Sounds like an intelligent plan to me. So why would Michele renege on what she told her therapist? It was certainly in her best interest to wait as she said. What changed her mind? Not that I'm trying to point the finger here, but the actions or inactions of Burdick and the Taylors might have been a contributing factor.

During their investigation, the SP learned that Tom and Cindy Turner were neighbors and friends of Cal and Michele Harris. They lived nearby on Halsey Valley Road. Shortly after Michele went missing, BCI Investigator's Bill Standinger and Todd Phillips spoke with Cindy Turner.

The interview with Cindy Turner was very brief and revealed nothing about her relationship with Michele, or the last time she had seen or heard from her. Turner, however, had some information she wanted to provide to the Investigators. She started by telling them there had been domestic violence between Cal and Michele but offered no details as to what it was or how she knew. Turner advised that Michele was always there when the kids got up in the morning and got them ready for school. But didn't offer how she knew this. She mentioned that Michele had life insurance. But again, no details how she knew this. Continuing, she claimed that sometime this past August, Cal had gone missing for a week and thought he might have had a nervous breakdown. I'm sure that investigators would have asked her to elaborate, but she never did. Missing for a week? A nervous breakdown? Where was that coming from, and what was her source? She never said. Later, she advised that she was keeping detailed notes of conversations between herself and Cal. Hmm! I wonder who gave her that idea?

I was surprised they didn't spend more time with Cindy Turner to obtain a more detailed history of her relationship with Michele and the Harris family. This lead merely hinted to having knowledge of things but never revealed any details to prove how she knew. Without supporting details, this information was of no value.

To be honest, I was a bit suspicious of what Turner was telling the SP, especially when she was unable or unwilling to provide any details. But for now, I waited to see if she had anything else to offer.

Cindy Turner re-entered the investigation again about three weeks later on October 9, 2001, when she called and spoke with Investigator Bill Standinger. She said she had some additional information. She started by asking Standinger if they had spoken with Michele's hairdresser Jerry Wilczynski, at the Indulgence Hair Salon. She advised Standinger that she had spoken with Jerry, who told her about an affair Cal had with Pam, the babysitter. According to Jerry, Michele had caught them kissing in the driveway, and he was now having a relationship with her.

Cindy Turner was not re-interviewed again for another year on October 7, 2002. Investigators Myers and Hochdanner interviewed Cindy and her husband Tom at their home. They had new information to offer. Cindy explained how she'd noticed Michele's weight loss, and knew she had a boyfriend, who she thought was from Pittsburgh, but she didn't want her to bring him around. This information was a year old. Why hadn't she told the police this a year ago?

Tom added to the interview, telling how he had helped Cal set up a trampoline back in November of 2001. He said he and Cal talked a little about the case. Tom suggested to Cal that he go on television and tell his side. Cal said, "No, they'd eat me alive, and my attorney said, no." Cal also said, "Why do they suspect me? They only found a bread loaf-size of blood in the garage." Cindy jumped in to say that Cal seemed upset and started asking questions about Barb Thayer. Investigators were advised that Cindy and Barb Thayer talked frequently. Later, Tom added that he and Cal and their boys used to go riding ATVs and snowmobiles around the Evelien Hill Road area. They often camped out in a wooded area near there. "It was one of Cal's favorite places to go," Tom said.

There was some excellent information here. It would explain why the SP focused many of their search efforts on and around the Evelien Hill Road area, albeit without success. Whether Cal had used the description of the blood in the garage as 'bread loaf-size,' would have to be determined.

During my continued review, I thought for sure I'd find some follow-up to Cindy's call with Investigator Standinger last November when she claimed to have learned from Jerry Wilczynski of an ongoing affair between Cal and Pam Brock. Instead, after reviewing the SP interviews with Pam Brock, that we'll learn about shortly, there was no affair. Presumably, that's why the topic never came up.

Cindy told the SP during her very first interview that she was keeping detailed notes about the case. In her notes that she was about to turn over to Myers and Hochdanner, were the details of a conversation she had with Jerry Wilczynski a year earlier on October 5, 2001. She claimed that while speaking with Wilczynski, in addition to the Cal/Pam affair, he'd also told her about a conversation he overheard during a phone call between Cal and Michele when she was there having her hair done. According to her notes, Wilczynski heard Cal say, "Drop the divorce procedures, or I will kill you, and they'll never find you." She also noted how she'd stressed to Jerry that he should call the SP, and he assured her he would.

With Myers and Hochdanner now sitting in her living room, was the perfect opportunity to enquire once again, whether they had spoken with Wilczynski, or to point out what she had written in her notes about the death threat he claimed to overhear. According to the lead, that topic never even came up.

Knowing how crucial the blood evidence was in this case, I knew the SP would be capitalizing on Cal's comment to Tom Turner about the 'bread loaf-size' area of blood in the garage. They would likely be arguing that Cal's comment supports their theory that there had been an initial 'pooling' of blood that Cal later cleaned up. Although more than four years had passed since this conversation between Cal and Tom Turner had taken place, I was anxious to speak with Cal to see what he could remember.

I needed to speak with Cal anyway about several other things, but I wanted to start by taking him back to his conversation with Tom Turner. Cal confirmed much of what Tom told the SP, including helping with the trampoline and the conversation they had, including when Cal said, "Why do they suspect me? They only found a bread loaf-size of blood in the garage." I told Cal that I had a good idea of what he was referring to when he said that to Tom, but I wanted him to explain it to me.

Without any prompting from me, Cal said, "I know exactly where that came from," and he immediately took me back to the day he returned to his house to get some clothes for himself and the kids for their stay in Cooperstown. Again, he described the same scenario he did four years earlier, saying, "To me, it looked like it was about the size of a loaf of bread, and that was the best description I could think of at the time." I asked him if he could remember anything more about the light itself or the shape of the pattern on the garage floor. Cal replied, "All I know is the light itself wasn't very bright, and the shape was oblong like this," as he indicated with his hands a length of 10-12 inches. He then added, "Now that I think about it, it was more like the size and shape of a football, perhaps that would have been a better description."

> Author's Note: What Cal was describing is what's known as a 'Crime Scope' or 'Variable Light Source' instrument, which can be used on a variety of surfaces, using selective and adjustable wavelengths of light to detect foreign particles and/or substances that can't otherwise be seen with the naked eye. Notably, in Andersen's notes, he reported using a crime scope, not only during his forensic exam of Michele's van but at Cal's house as well.

During one of the early interviews with Cal, the SP requested permission to speak with his two oldest children. At the time, his son Taylor was seven, and daughter Cayla was six. Initially, Cal had consulted with attorney Drazen about their request, and Drazen gave his approval but recommended he should be present during their interviews.

Cal was in his office at Royal Ford with his children when Sr. Investigator Mulvey and Investigator Hochdanner arrived to conduct the interview. Due to their young age, Cal expressed his desire to be present during the interview but was told it would be better if they could interview the children alone. Cal consented and left his office.

To start, they were asked what they knew about their mom not being home. Taylor believed that someone picked up their mom and had taken her to NYC to visit her friend, and she had not come back yet.

The interview then shifted as they were asked how their mom and dad got along. "Not too good," Taylor said. Then added, "They argue about mom being on the phone too much and shopping too much." When asked if they had fought recently, Taylor said, "They had a really big fight at one of their friend's wedding." Then added, "The day before the wedding, mom and dad had a really big fight, and they threw stuff around. Then, they both cried, and daddy left." Adding further, "They fight a lot, but they usually go downstairs after we go to bed and argue."

In conclusion, they were asked if they were told to keep any secrets, and they both said no. Then, as a final question, they were asked if there was anything they thought the police should know? They both said no.

Pam Brock

Investigators Mike Myers and Mike Young were assigned to interview Pamela Brock, another Harris babysitter. Brock, who was 21-years old at the time of the interview, had been hired as a teenager and worked as the Harris' babysitter for about two years. She became very close to Michele. They talked frequently. She knew about the divorce and that Michele was anxious for it to go through so she could get out of the house she was living in with Cal. She knew they would argue quite often. Furthermore, Michele confided in her that for the past 5-6 months, she had a boyfriend by the name of Brian. She also knew Cal had a girlfriend.

Myers and Young returned about four months later in January 2002 to interview Brock again. When explicitly asked, Brock denied having any relationship with Cal, elaborating further that he had never tried anything inappropriate with her at any time. She also told investigators that within five minutes after Cal got home, she was on her way out. She had very little contact with him.

Michele had been missing for a little over a year on October 10, 2002, when Investigators Jim Conzola and Lori Hochdanner returned to interview Brock again. At the time, she was still employed by Cal as a full-time babysitter and provided them with her work schedule. According to Brock, Cal had hired a new babysitter by the name of Denise, who worked two days a week.

When Brock was asked if she ever spent the night at the Harris house, she answered, "Yes, but only if Cal was out of town, I would stay over with the kids." She was also asked how her relationship was with Cal, and she said, "It's very good." She was questioned about the rumors of her and Cal having an affair. She said she had heard the stories herself but insisted they were not true and added, "I have a boyfriend." Pushing a little further, they asked if Cal had ever made any advances towards her? She answered firmly, "No, never."

Fast-forwarding to the middle of 2004, Brock had since been fired from her babysitting job, moved to Florida, and found new employment. In an attempt to re-interview her, the SP had contacted her family and friends. But they had not heard back from her for an extended period. Finally, in May 2004, Brock called and spoke with Sr. Investigator Sue Mulvey by phone.

Unlike her previous interviews, Brock did a complete flip-flop. She supposedly told Mulvey she had quit her babysitting job at the Harris' because she was in fear for her safety. She claimed she was afraid because of the way Cal acted towards her. Furthermore, she was convinced there was a leak within the police department and concerned that Cal might be able to locate her if she gave out her phone number.

During this telephone interview, she explained how Cal needed her in the beginning and had treated her well. But in the end, he flipped out and screamed at her. She added further that she had been speaking with Barb Thayer and Shannon Taylor and learned about accusations Cal made against her after Denise Kirby entered the picture. It was shortly after that when she started looking for new employment.

Continuing on, she claimed Cal and Denise were drunk all the time, especially on weekends. At first, she was protective of Cal because she didn't want him to get in trouble and lose the kids. Now she felt he wasn't good for the kids. She explained further that she was still in contact with the children, who told her what was going on between Cal and Denise. Brock advised she was unhappy and did not approve of the way Denise took care of the kids. She also stated that Cal treated Denise like a queen but was no longer nice to Brock, even though Brock had been working there much longer. Was I detecting a bit of jealousy, perhaps?

Notably, Brock's early interviews were all consistent. Cal treated her well and had given her a great deal of responsibility for the children's activities. She had grown comfortable in that position and enjoyed being with the children. But then Denise Kirby entered the picture. Brock began to feel threatened and realized that her lead position was in jeopardy. She did not handle it well. Even though she told the SP that she feared for her safety and quit, that's not what happened. Instead, it was Brock who became angry, and Cal had fired her after learning that she was going behind his back, complaining and feeding lies to the Taylors. Knowing that Brock had frequently been speaking with Barb Thayer and Shannon Taylor may explain some of the animosity she claimed to have.

> Author's Note: Interestingly, long after she'd been fired, Brock came back to town and called Cal, asking to meet with him and the children. Cal agreed, and they all met for over an hour at a local park. There was no fear.

Friends & Family

About ten days after Michele went missing, Investigator Mike Telfer received a call at his residence early one morning. The male caller did not want to identify himself, but Telfer recognized the voice as that of Kevin Harris, Cal's brother. Telfer told him he knew who he was. Kevin neither confirmed nor denied his identity, but went on to express his concerns about Cal.

He told Telfer he was worried about the safety of the children, and said, "If Cal can do this once, he can do it again." He continued by saying since this happened, he had been watching Cal, and something wasn't right. He said Cal was much too confident that Michele would not be found when a rumor of such was going around. He felt Cal might have had some help and to look in the direction of the money. He even admitted to thinking Cal did not do this in rage but planned it out. He ended by telling Telfer he would deny ever making the call. But for his own conscience, he felt obligated to call. He was hoping to be able to call in the future if any new information developed.

Later, Sr. Investigators Skinner and McEvoy contacted Kevin Harris, and arrangements were made for a personal interview. Kevin agreed but requested that attorney Drazen be present. After that, he was interviewed at Drazen's office. Kevin had seen a physical change with Michele in the last few months before she disappeared. She'd lost a lot of weight and was wearing a bunch of earrings and ankle bracelets. It was an "immature look," he said. When asked about the changes in Cal, he said he had become more concerned and stressed.

He said that Cal would keep to himself and was hard to read, adding Cal's change was not nearly as significant as Michele's.

Michele had been missing for five months when Investigators Myers and Young re-interviewed Kevin Harris at his residence. Kevin, along with Todd Mansfield, had gone out to Cal's house. He recalled having a conversation with Cal earlier, when Cal told him the divorce was pretty much set, and he felt the money part of the agreement was handled. Cal told him his biggest concern was the custody issue. He was worried about only having the children on weekends. While he was at Cal's house with Todd, he recalled Cal going upstairs to check on the kids, and when he returned, broke down in tears, sobbing uncontrollably to the point it made him and Todd uncomfortable. Cal said that the girls had asked where their mom was and that caused him to break down again. Kevin recalled earlier that day when he called Cal asking where he thought Michele was, and he said, "I don't know." Kevin then asked, "What do you think happened?" Cal answered, "I don't know, maybe she's with her boyfriend, and maybe she's drinking."

Fran Harris was also re-interviewed. She started the interview by telling investigators she and Kevin were afraid of Cal and that he was 'wacky.' Furthermore, Cal was acting like everything was normal, and that was unsettling to her. The interview turned to her knowledge of Cal's first wife, Leah. According to Fran, Leah had left Cal after a physical altercation with him. She recalled Leah showing up at her house with a reddened neck claiming Cal had just grabbed her. Shortly after that, Leah called her parents, and she was gone.

From there, the interview shifted to the day the police were searching Cal's house. He and the kids came to stay with her and Kevin, and then went on to Cooperstown, NY to stay at Steve and Mary Jo's cottage. While they were all at the cottage, she recalled receiving a call from Dwight, asking if Cal was there, and she said yes. She said Dwight didn't need to talk to Cal but wanted her to tell him that Michele's body had been found in a shallow grave near his cottage. She hung up the phone and told Cal what Dwight just told her. Cal acted like he did not believe it and wasn't worried about it at all. Later, Cal asked her if they found any semen. When she asked why, he said, "I was just wondering if they found semen because I haven't had sex with Michele in six months." She also said that Cal, still in disbelief, called his dad only to learn that it was just a rumor he'd heard from a neighbor.

That same weekend, when it was only the adults present, Mary Jo started asking Cal about a comment he made to Michele about killing her without the use of a gun and nobody ever finding her body. Cal denied making the comment, but Mary Jo kept after him, pointing out that Michele had told several people about what he said. Eventually, Cal admitted saying it but said he was kidding.

Investigators McEvoy and Conzola were assigned to interview Kenneth 'KC' Carrigan. They caught up with him on the first day of their investigation at the Royal Chrysler dealership. He was friends with Michele and had been out socially with her and Nikki Burdick. He knew all about the pending divorce. Carrigan told investigators about a falling out he had with Cal over his ex-girlfriend, Sarah Tymeson, thinking Cal was seeing her. He also knew Michele had a boyfriend because both she and Nikki had told him.

KC was asked where he was on Tuesday afternoon until Wednesday. He claimed to have worked until 7:30 p.m. and then went home and worked on his house, getting it ready for sale. He said he remained at home until going back to work Wednesday morning.

About three weeks later, Carrigan was re-interviewed. In the interim, the SP researched and prepared a biography, which included his criminal history. Records revealed that Carrigan had several previous encounters with law enforcement. Briefly, his record included two misdemeanor charges, one in 1989 and another in 1991, followed by two felony burglary charges in 1992, where he was sentenced to five years probation.

Later, Carrigan was re-interviewed by McEvoy and Hochdanner. He explained that he and Michele became close friends and would talk to each other often on the phone. He'd just gone through a divorce himself, and Michele would ask him divorce questions. Nikki Burdick had told him that Michele had a boyfriend, and he told Cal. When asked why he would do that, he said, "Even though Cal was difficult to work for, I didn't want to see the dealership go down. So, I figured if they got divorced, Michele would get part of the dealership."

Continuing, he said he was aware that Michele had breast implant surgery. Then added that after her implant surgery, she was showing them off to just about everyone at Lefty's. He'd seen them himself one night when he was out with her, Nikki, and some other people from work. He watched her lift her shirt and flash her bare chest for some guy in the bar at the Guthrie Inn. He recalled scolding her, saying, "You're only going to encourage these guys."

When explicitly asked, he firmly denied ever having a sexual relationship with Michele. He did admit, however, "I wanted to, and would have, given the opportunity."

In my review of the Carrigan interviews as well as my own, it was well established that he had a close relationship with Michele. Even though he denied it, their relationship likely included sex. During my review, I found nothing to indicate that Carrigan's alibi had been verified or whether his house, vehicle or his person had ever been searched as part of the elimination process. During his first SP interview, he told investigators that he worked until 7:30 p.m., went home and worked on his house, and returned to work the next morning. That's fine, but what about the hours in between? With twelve hours unaccounted for, I was surprised to learn there was no attempt to determine where he was, who he was with, or what he was doing. He already admitted that on prior occasions, he had been out late with Michele and Nikki in the Waverly and Sayre areas. Oddly, they never even asked if Michele had ever been to his house.

Following-up on Carrigan's interview, investigators located and interviewed his ex-girlfriend, Sarah Tymeson. She acknowledged knowing both Cal and Michele and said, "I was shocked to learn that Michele was missing." She told investigators she had run into Cal at Thirsty's Bar in Binghamton about six weeks ago and had a conversation about Michele and KC. She remembered telling Cal that KC and Michele were planning to start dating after the divorce. She couldn't remember who she heard it from but believed it was someone from the dealership.

She also told investigators that she and KC broke up around July 1, 2001. Elaborating, she stated, "KC is nothing but a liar," which gave investigators the impression there was no love lost between them. She also suspected that the relationship between KC and Michele likely involved more than just friendly conversation.

As an ex-girlfriend with no apparent love lost, I was a bit surprised the SP didn't pursue a more in-depth interview with her to learn more about Carrigan. We learned from Tymeson that Carrigan at least had a suspicious relationship with Michele and had just recently broken up with Tymeson. Furthermore, she referred to KC as "nothing but a liar," and heard of tentative plans for him and Michele to start dating after the divorce. Was this just the scornful ramblings of a disgruntled ex-girlfriend? Perhaps. Or was there something more going on? For now, I would have to place Carrigan on my 'person-of-interest' list.

About eighteen months later, Investigators Conzola and Hochdanner re-interviewed Sarah Tymeson.

Tymeson was first asked if she had ever been employed by any of the Royal dealerships? She said no. Her only connection to Royal was through her dating Carrigan. She'd dated him for about five years before they broke up in July 2001. When asked how she knew Cal, she said she had met him through KC at company dinners and outings. She then added, "Cal had a bad attitude and a wicked temper with his employees, but he'd always been pleasant when speaking with me."

Tymeson continued by offering up the name of Kent Cramer, and a suggestion that he was someone they might want to talk to. She seemed to think he may have had an affair with Michele.

Knowing that Tymeson had dated Carrigan for five years before their breakup, I was disappointed that she was never asked what happened or what caused the breakup. Could Michele have been the reason? Initially, I thought about going back and asking Carrigan, but I changed my mind. The question would go unanswered for now, but I would hold it in reserve. Perhaps we wait and spring it on him on the witness stand.

Several witnesses, including Cal, knew that Michele was planning a trip to NYC to visit her friend from college, Lisa Feuer. Investigator Bill Standinger was assigned to interview Feuer for confirmation. In a telephone interview, Feuer said she had talked with Michele shortly after the attack on the World Trade Center. They made plans for her to come for a visit on Thursday. Cal was aware of the planned trip and was agreeable to it. The purpose of the trip was to help Michele try and sell her engagement ring in the Diamond District of NYC. They were supposed to confirm the details the next day, but Michele never called her back.

According to Standinger's narrative, Feuer said Michele was not a cocaine user and never talked to her about drugs. She was aware of her relationship with Brian, and Michele told her she was in love with him. They were really looking forward to getting together and having a drink. Michele had also told her about the divorce and how nasty it was at times. Nasty enough that she had even filed for an order of protection. When Feuer spoke with Michele, she did not seem at all depressed, and she thought foul play was probably involved in her disappearance.

After reading Standinger's written narrative, I turned to his attached notes. In respect to Michele's drug use, I noticed a discrepancy. His notes indicated that when he asked Feuer about her knowledge of drug use by Michele, her answer was, "Not a regular drug user but partied a little in college." What does that mean? It certainly seemed like a contradiction to what was written in the narrative. This notation, along with other information gleaned from the investigation, would also tend to support the growing suspicion that Michele may have been involved in drug use. It also suggested that Michele had at least experimented with or used drugs recreationally in the past.

Attempting to confirm whether Michele had used or was currently using drugs was not the main issue. It seemed, however, that the SP was doing all they could to prove otherwise. Why? There were two reasons. First, they didn't want to tarnish Michele's image any further. Secondly, they were trying to avoid or eliminate any motive other than Cal's divorce motive. In other words, they were trying to remove any argument that Michele's disappearance was drug-related. Reasonable suspicion alone was enough to argue a drug-related motive.

Circumstantially at least, more than enough information had been collected to believe Michele was involved in drug-related activities. Regardless, whether she was using drugs herself, owed money for drugs, purchased drugs for others, or just hung out with those who did, a drug-related motive could easily present itself. Burdick had already told investigators that Michele might have smoked some marijuana with Kasper just to 'fit in,' and Feuer had said: "Not a regular drug user but partied a little in college."

According to several different witnesses, Michele had been displaying many of the classic signs associated with drug abuse, such as weight loss, heavy smoking, sniffling, cash flow problems, and changes in or lack-of-interest in her appearance. Even Cal's brother Kevin, whose son had an earlier drug abuse problem, recognized similar signs in Michele. Therefore, I was surprised and rather disappointed to learn that the SP was not only steering their investigation away from any drug-related motive, but they were ignoring it altogether.

Even within the first week after Michele went missing, FIU Investigator Steve Andersen recognized the need to address the suspected drug use by Michele. As mentioned previously, during the execution of the search warrant at Cal's residence, Andersen collected several of Michele's toothbrushes, combs, and hairbrushes and submitted them to the FIC lab. From his experience, he knew that human hair is often an excellent source, not only for DNA but drug toxicology as well. On his lab submission form for these items, he requested a two-part examination that included both DNA and drug tox. Subsequently, the FIC was able to extract enough material to establish a DNA profile, which was later determined and reported to be that of Michele Harris. For reasons unknown, his request for drug toxicology was never completed, or if it was, it was never disclosed to the defense.

In October 2001, I had a lengthy interview with Cal's girlfriend, Connie Fellows. With the new discovery materials, I would learn for the first time what she was telling the SP. Connie was a cooperative witness, and the SP had interviewed her on several occasions throughout the first year of their investigation. In late January 2002, Sr. Investigator John Skinner and Investigator Lori Hochdanner sat down with Connie, and she summarized the details of her relationship with Cal.

She had last seen Cal on August 29, 2001, when he came to Cortland, and they went out to dinner. During dinner, Cal became teary-eyed while telling her a story about taking his daughter to the movie *The Princess Diaries*. During the movie, two of the actors were kissing when his daughter turned and said, "Oh, that's like you and mommy." Cal said it made him cry. Connie continued by telling them that Cal was very concerned about losing the kids in the divorce. He told her that he could never handle not seeing them every day. When asked if Cal ever talked about killing Michele or the kids, she said, "No, never." It was her understanding that Cal wanted full custody of the children and was not going to budge. At no point during dinner had he talked about reconciliation with Michele. After dinner, they went back to her house and had sex.

Police then moved to September 11, 2001, and asked her if she was at Cal's house that day? She said, "No, I wasn't there that day." She went on to explain who she was with and other things she did that day. Cal was supposed to call her when he got out of work that day, but she never heard from him.

Connie also told the SP what she had told me about going over to Cal's house on September 29, 2001, sometime after midnight. She'd felt uncomfortable and asked Cal, "What if Michele comes home?" Cal replied, "She's not coming home tonight." She decided to stay and ended up spending the night. They got up the next morning, showered, and went their separate ways by 9:30 a.m. She had not been back since, even though Cal had asked her to. They also talked about their relationship and the concern she had about her three failed marriages and not wanting to get involved in another bad relationship. After that, they decided to be just friends.

Linda Hyatt worked as a payroll clerk for the Owego Apalachin School District. She was a close family friend to both Cal and Michele. She'd been best friends with Michele's mother before she died. After her friend's death, Hyatt remained good friends and a mother-like figure to Michele. Michele had been missing for two days when the SP went to interview her. She'd last seen Michele on Labor Day. Prior to that, she had not seen her much over the summer. Michele had told her about taking the job at Lefty's and what an "eye-opening" experience it was. She and Michele talked about her separation from Cal and the pending divorce. She then explained she had spoken with Cal shortly after he'd been served with the divorce papers and said, "Cal did not want the divorce." He'd talked with her about reading books and doing research about the negative impact divorce could have on the children and his fear for them. "He wanted to stay together for the benefit of the children," she said.

Hyatt heard about the incident where they had been arguing outside, and Michele had fallen to the ground. She added that they would both yell and scream at each other in front of the kids. Later, when she saw Michele on August 1, 2001, she appeared calm and said, "things were going well" and expected the divorce to be final in October.

Hyatt was asked about Cal and Michele's outside relationships. She heard about Cal's relationship with Connie that was supposedly over. She also knew Michele was in a relationship with a man named Brian, who she heard was much younger than Michele. She recalled seeing Michele on Labor Day and learned that she was still seeing Brian but having second thoughts due to their age difference.

To her knowledge, neither Cal nor Michele were involved in drugs. But she had spoken to Cal about Michele's spending and how he'd speculated she might be using drugs. Hyatt continued by telling investigators that when Michele went shopping, which was quite often, she could spend $200 to $300 in a heartbeat. "Michele always had plans to spend money," she said.

Hyatt then described being at the Harris residence the first night after Michele went missing. All the children were there, and she heard Cal tell the children, "We have not heard from mommy in a couple of days." Then he added, "Mommy loves you," and he was sure she was trying to contact them. He also told the children that there were people looking for her. When Taylor asked, "Who?" Cal said, "The police."

About ten days later, Hyatt was re-interviewed. She reiterated what Michele told her on Labor Day about her relationship with Brian and how she was having second thoughts due to their age difference. The interview then turned to her knowledge of Cal and Michele's financial situation. She had learned from Cal that Michele had a real serious problem with money. She'd opened another credit card account that he wasn't aware of and maxed it out. He'd told her that Michele was bouncing 10 to 15 checks a month. He'd finally closed the checking account and opened another without her name on it.

He told Hyatt initially that he would give Michele $750 a week. The money was supposed to be used for paying household bills, babysitters, food, and clothes. Then he told her of the time when the electricity got turned off because she hadn't paid the bill. Later, he learned she wasn't paying the other bills either. He also told Hyatt that after Michele decided to go to work at Lefty's, he reduced her weekly pay to $300 and told her he wasn't going to pay for babysitters or housekeepers, so she could work. Hyatt also knew Michele had borrowed $3,000 from her father to hire a private investigator, but never paid him back. During one of her conversations with Cal, he swore he'd never laid a hand on Michele and never would. He did mention, however, that there was an incident when they were arguing when Michele had grabbed him, and when he pushed her away, she fell.

Michele had been missing for six months when Investigators Young and Hochdanner returned to re-interview Hyatt. She was staying close to the family out of concern for the children. At that time, she said that Cal and the children were talking about Michele more now than when she first disappeared. She had purchased lockets for the girls for Christmas and explained how Cal helped Cayla put a picture of Michele in her locket. When asked if she was aware of any big upcoming events that were planned, she advised that Cal was taking the children to Florida at the end of the month. Later, she added that Cal had asked her and her husband to accompany him to help with the children. They were scheduled to leave February 23, 2002, and would return on March 1, 2002.

The SP spoke to many witnesses who told them Cal had been married before, and there were problems in that marriage as well. Cal's ex-wife had been identified as Leah Grayson. Investigator Mike Telfer was assigned to interview Grayson. He located Grayson in Natick, MA, where she was now living. She had since remarried and went by the name of Leah Frazier. During the telephone interview, Frazier described that she had met Cal at Hobart College, they began dating, and after college, they moved to Vestal, NY. In June of 1985, they married in Syracuse, NY.

According to Frazier, in November of 1985, Cal had told her to go home for a few months while he decided if he wanted to be married anymore. So, she moved back in with her parents. She said after a time, Cal initiated divorce proceedings, adding that she had problems with Cal and his parents during their short marriage. They had stopped seeing each other, and she was living in the Boston area when Cal contacted her mother and said he wanted to get back together. Cal came to Boston to try and work things out. Frazier decided the relationship was unhealthy and told Cal it was over. Six months later, the divorce was final. In the interim, they exchanged mutual letters apologizing and saying good-bye.

Frazier recalled three times when Cal became physical with her. The first was about a month after they were married. Cal had pinned her down on the bed, trying to shut her up. She was crying uncontrollably, as he was holding her neck and his hands were over her mouth. She'd begged him not to hurt her. He did let her up, but the whole family got involved, and her parents came down from Syracuse.

Frazier described a second time when Cal slapped her with his open hand on the side of the head. Right after, he quickly retreated, started crying, and apologized. He gave her some flowers and told her it would never happen again. The third time was in Owego. According to Frazier, they were sitting in a car near the river. Cal had just told her, "you're nothing without me." She didn't want to hear anymore and tried getting out of the car when he grabbed her around the neck. Again, he quickly retreated, started crying, and became very remorseful. It was soon after that when she decided Cal was no longer going to control her. When asked, Cal had never used or threatened to use any kind of weapon on her.

She said that she did not believe Cal was having an affair while they were married. She also said she felt he was under a great deal of pressure from the family and business matters, and ultimately, she thought that was the root of their marriage problems.

Later, I traveled to Massachusetts for a face-to-face interview with Frazier. She refused to speak to me.

Death Threat

Since marrying into the Harris family, Michele had grown accustomed to enjoying many of the finer things in life, including having her hair professionally and expensively done for several years. Her personal hairstylist was a professional in Binghamton, NY by the name of Jerome 'Jerry' Wilczynski. He worked his magic at the elegant Indulgence Hair Salon, on Binghamton's south-side. Michele was one of his regulars and routinely had her hair done there every six-to-eight weeks.

Shortly after Michele went missing, Investigators Bob DelGiorno and Todd Phillips were assigned to interview Wilczynski. He confirmed that he had been Michele's hairstylist for the past four years and told them he never knew Michele to miss an appointment. Shortly after the interview started, Wilczynski expressed his concern about speaking with the police, for fear that Cal would find out, and something might happen to him. In continuing, he advised that because Michele was one of his regulars, he'd become concerned about her weight loss during her last three hair appointments. Even more so, the fact that she did not want to talk about it concerned him. "Michele appeared to be exceptionally skinny," he said.

As he continued, he said Michele would not ordinarily talk about her personal problems, and it had only been during her last two appointments that she started to talk about what was happening at home openly. She shared that she and Cal fought often, but he'd never hit her. She'd told him that Cal was cheating on her with a 24-year-old girl that worked at his dealership, but he didn't know her name. According to Wilczynski, Michele claimed to have hired this girl to babysit. She came out, the kids loved her, and she babysat three times. Later, Michele claimed to have caught her and Cal together in the house. After that, Michele didn't allow her to babysit again. He was asked if he was certain this girl had babysat. Wilczynski was insistent and replied, "Yes, and she originally worked at Royal Motors."

He also told them that during Michele's last hair appointment, he overheard a conversation Michele was having on her cell phone with Cal. He heard Cal say to her, "drop the divorce proceedings and come back to the Harris family fortune." If she didn't, he could "make things very difficult" for her. He also heard him say the kids would never live with her, and that they would live with him. When explicitly asked if he ever heard Cal threaten Michele, he replied, "Yes. He told her she would never get the kids." According to Wilczynski, Michele had also told him the reason she had to take a job was that Cal refused to give her money for school clothes for the kids.

Upon request, Wilczynski provided investigators with a computer printout of his salon records of Michele's hair appointments for the past year. The records revealed Michele's appointment history going back to October of 2000. Moreover, they also showed her last appointment was on May 16, 2001, at noon.

Three days later, on September 28, 2001, Wilczynski called and spoke with DelGiorno, claiming to have additional information. He said he recalled Michele telling him about another affair Cal had. The affair he described during his first interview, between Cal and the young babysitter, was not his first, but according to Michele, "would be his last." He was certain Michele told him this girl had worked at the Owego dealership as a secretary. He now thought her name might be

Christine but wasn't sure. After being fired from the dealership, she went to work for an insurance company.

During this same telephone call, DelGiorno's notes revealed some additional info, although it was not included in his narrative. Wilczynski also told DelGiorno that during Michele's second-to-last appointment, maybe the third, Michele told people that she was already divorced and that the settlement was for half-a-million. Later, however, she took it back and said she wasn't divorced.

After Wilczynski's first interview, I shared the same concerns as the SP. Who was this mystery woman and babysitter that Cal was alleged to have had an affair with? The investigation to date had not revealed anyone by the name of Christine, which was the name Wilczynski thought it might be. The only young babysitter was Pam Brock, who had already been interviewed extensively. And she adamantly denied any inappropriate behavior or relationship with Cal, even when pressed on the issue.

Furthermore, she was still employed by Cal at the time and had never worked at the dealership or an insurance company. Still, Wilczynski insisted that after Cal was caught with this girl, she was no longer employed as their babysitter. Where was this information coming from?

Those closest to Michele including, Barb Thayer and her best friends, Nikki and Shannon, had already been interviewed extensively. None of them knew or had ever said anything about Michele catching Cal in the house with the babysitter, or that he was having another affair. And what was he supposedly caught doing in the house?

It was confusing and concerning. What was really going on here? I learned from the police interview with Cindy Turner, where she claimed to have spoken with Wilczynski on October 5, 2001, just one week after his phone call to DelGiorno. According to Turner, Wilczynski told her that when speaking with Michele, she said, "Cal and Pam have been having an affair for some time now and, it's only a matter of time before they'll have a life together." So, at some point within a one-week period, Wilczynski suddenly remembered the name was Pam and not Christine. Then added the affair had been going on for some time, and it was only a matter of time before they'll have a life together. This was *not* the same story he had just told the SP.

What was even more interesting, is when Turner had this conversation with Wilczynski, she claimed he'd also told her something more.

That Michele had been sitting in a chair at the salon one day when Cal called her. Wilczynski said he could hear the call plain as day, and over-heard Cal saying, "Drop the divorce or I will kill you, and they'll never find you." After learning this from Wilczynski, Turner said she'd stressed to Jerry that he call the SP and tell them what he overheard. Wilczynski had assured her he would make the call right after work. He never did.

Fast-forward four days to October 9, 2001, checking to make sure that Jerry made the call, Turner placed a call to Investigator Standinger and asked if they'd talked with Wilczynski. It's not clear how he answered, but we know they had interviewed Wilczynski just days earlier. Turner continued by telling Standinger what Wilczynski supposedly told her. But she didn't mention the death threat. Only that Cal was having an affair with Pam, and Michele had caught them kissing in the driveway. According to her own notes, that's *not* what Wilczynski told her. So now Turner's story has evolved from Michele catching Cal with Pam in the house to catching him kissing her in the driveway. Where's this coming from?

Now I thought to myself, wait a minute, something was not right here. If Wilczynski had only hearsay knowledge of the Cal/Pam affair, yet direct knowledge of a death threat, why would Turner, when calling Standinger, only share the information about the affair and not the death threat? Come on. What's more important here, another affair, or a death threat? Turner obviously understood the significance of the death threat; otherwise, she would not have stressed to Wilczynski that he report it to the police right away.

For me, things were not adding up. Wilczynski had just been inter-viewed a few days earlier, and when asked specifically, if he'd heard Cal threaten Michele, his response was, "Yes, he told her she would never get the kids." Okay, so there was a 'threat,' but that wasn't a 'death threat.' Why would he omit such an important piece of information? And why hadn't he called the SP? He knew Michele personally and was aware of her current divorce situation. He knew she was missing and had direct knowledge of a death threat. Yet, upon learning of her disappearance, he never called the SP to share that knowledge. Then, even when investigators interviewed him and inquired specifically about his knowledge of any threats, he said nothing.

As I continued looking through the Cindy Turner leads, including her notes, I started noticing some strange similarities to what I'd seen in some earlier leads. Turner was regularly inserting her own derogatory thoughts and opinions of what she deemed suspicious behavior, surrounding everything Cal said or did. This was starting to look familiar. It wasn't long before I discovered why.

It was right there in her notes where she admitted she and Barb Thayer were good friends, and they had been talking daily often several times a day. Well, "that explains a lot," I said to myself. I had no doubt their main topic of conversation was Cal Harris, as they shared and exchanged their inimical thoughts. This also explained why Turner's notes nearly mirrored those of Thayer. The similarities were striking. It was obvious these two had been comparing notes and colluding against Cal. Their collective animus and bias were obvious. Earlier, I had viewed and self-captioned some of Thayer's entries as 'collateral nonsense.' Turner's were much the same. But I think my earlier description may have been a bit too polite. Perhaps a better descriptor would be, 'delusional BS.'

I was still curious as to how Turner knew Wilczynski, and why she would be in dialogue with him and making notes of their communications. I had missed it the first time, but in my second review of her notes, I had my answer. After Turner noted having talked with Jerry (Wilczynski) at Indulgence, she'd also noted in parentheses (Shelli's & my hairdresser). They had the same hairdresser. That explains it. It might explain even more. I was already highly skeptical and very distrusting of anything involving Barb Thayer or Cindy Turner. But now, I had to add Wilczynski as well.

Knowing that Thayer and Turner were speaking daily, then learning that Turner was also sharing information with Wilczynski, my suspicions were growing. I began asking myself if Turner and Thayer could be in cahoots with Wilczynski in a triune effort to 'help the cause?' I was especially troubled by Wilczynski's failure to disclose his direct knowledge of a death threat. As my skepticism grew, I began wondering if Wilczynski's source of information was truly coming from Michele, or was it being fed to him by Turner? I also found it strange that Michele, who was supposedly a close friend with Turner, had never told her of the death threat. In fact, Michele never mentioned a death threat to any of her closest friends, including Barb Thayer, Nikki Burdick, or Shannon Taylor.

If you recall, during an early SP interview with Shannon Taylor, she was asked if she was aware of any threats. Not only had she denied knowing of any threats, but she also made it a point to say, "If there were, Nikki or I would be the first know."

So, other than Wilczynski, Michele never told any of her closest friends about Cal having an affair with Pam Brock. Why? Because there was no affair. So, where was this information coming from? Why would Michele tell her hairdresser, but not her best friends? She wouldn't. By process of elimination, I quickly zeroed in on the only logical source – Barb Thayer. Although Pam Brock never worked at the dealership, Thayer may have assumed she did. Or, by using her own warped imagination, simply created the affair scenario and passed it along to Turner during one of their daily chit-chats.

We already know that Michele had lied to Wilczynski when telling him she had settled the divorce for a half-million, then later recanted. Could this be Michele lying to Wilczynski once again, just to make things a bit more exciting for him? Perhaps. Or was there something more sinister at work here? It was obvious Turner and Thayer both abhorred Cal and were doing anything and everything to 'help the cause' in the case against him. In-as-much, I could not exclude the likelihood that Thayer and Turner, being biased and desperate, colluded and conspired to 'fabricate' the affair between Cal and Pam, as well as the death threat. Turner used her connection with Wilczynski to set things in motion, by feeding him the information and asking him to do the dirty work. Wilczynski agreed but didn't always get the story straight.

Wilczynski was obviously receptive to the Cal/Pam affair scenario and shared that with the SP, even though he couldn't remember her name. The death threat, however, was a different matter. After insistence from Turner that he call the SP with that information, and him assuring her that he would, he never did. Was he feeling a bit guilty, perhaps? Or was he a bit nervous and uncomfortable about lying to the police?

During the SP interview with Turner on October 7, 2002, she turned over all her notes. In these notes, she described her conversation with Wilczynski just two days earlier on October 5, 2002, where she described Wilczynski's direct knowledge of overhearing a death threat. I had little doubt the SP had carefully read every line of Turner's notes, and likely some 'in between the lines' as well. What struck me was the fact that the SP wasn't knocking on Wilczynski's door the next day or sooner. Yet they had just talked to him a few days earlier, and he said nothing about a death threat. I think perhaps they, too, had doubts about the source and reliability of these notes.

There was an entry in Turner's notes where she claimed Wilczynski told her about the Cal/Pam affair. Even though that was *not* what he told the SP. Therefore, I think the SP may have recognized the same problem here as I did. Turner wanted the SP to believe that the information about the affair and the death threat came from Wilczynski. But they were skeptical. Whether they believed she was the actual source of information or not is anyone's guess. Regardless, they still should have followed up with Wilczynski and applied a little pressure for the truth. If you think this part is interesting, then stay with me because it's about to get even better.

We're now going to jump forward to October 1, 2005. As a reminder, Cal had just been indicted the day before for Michele's murder. According to the new lead, Sr. Investigator Mulvey claimed to have received a call from Wilczynski. During the call, he spoke about being interviewed previously but now wanted to share some new information. Three days later, Mulvey interviewed Wilczynski in the parking lot of the Indulgence Hair Salon in Binghamton.

During his interview, Wilczynski explained to Mulvey that the first time he was interviewed, four years earlier by, the other investigators, he felt they (DelGiorno and Phillips) were sympathetic towards Cal Harris. He said it was "almost like they were working for him," so he didn't trust or feel comfortable telling them everything.

> Author's Note: Whoa! Really? He was actually telling Mulvey that the SP was 'sympathetic' towards Cal Harris and may have been working for him? Seriously? Are you kidding me? There was no way in hell. If anything, it was the complete opposite. But he had me on the edge of my seat. I couldn't wait to see what was coming next.

Continuing on, Wilczynski said that during that interview, one of the investigators (DelGiorno) had rolled his eyes and was flippant. He felt maybe DelGiorno didn't like him or discounted what he had to say because he was gay.

He admitted not trusting DelGiorno, yet he called him three days later to provide additional information.

Wilczynski went on to say that Michele never missed an appointment. But she had canceled in August and was crying on the phone when she called. He claimed that during Michele's last hair appointment in July 2001, she told him she was having an affair. However, according to his business records, though, Michele did *not* have a hair appointment in July. The records indicated Michele's last hair appointment was on May 16, 2001. I questioned but could never understand why he was so insistent that Michele's appointment was in July when his own records proved otherwise.

Also, according to Wilczynski, Michele told him Cal had asked if Connie could move in with them, and this infuriated Michele. He said Michele told Cal, "No if you want a life with her, go build her a house." To which Cal replied, "This is my house, and you aren't getting it." Michele told him Cal threw it in her face that she was having an affair, and she snapped back, telling him, "This is your fourth time, not your first." Wilczynski then claimed that Michele had never confided such personal information to him before. Indeed.

This story was getting more bizarre by the minute. So now we were hearing for the very first time, four years later, that Cal had asked Connie to move in. It was nonsense. But more importantly, where the hell was this stuff coming from? It was starting to look more like a last-minute, poorly scripted, low-budget, soap-opera. Did Mulvey really buy into this crap? Please, Jerry – tell us more.

Wilczynski continued his story claiming that while Michele was getting her hair done, she told him she was waiting for a callback from Cal after she'd asked him for some money for the kid's school supplies. She didn't want to wait until the last minute. School supplies? Remember – this was May.

Her phone rang, and Michele tilted the phone, so they both could hear, and she said, "I want you to hear how he talks to me." He then heard Cal say, "You fucking bitch, you either drop all of this or I will kill you. I'm not kidding. You won't see a penny of the Harris money unless you drop this divorce nonsense. Do you hear me?" He said Michele then turned her phone back to her ear and said, "If you're going to talk to me like this, call my lawyer," and she hung up. After the call ended, Michele told him she was afraid of Cal because he hung out with guys that rode motorcycles, and she was uncomfortable around them. Oh, really? He must not have heard about her wild, late-night adventure in Syracuse when she was picked up by a strange biker and taken on a motorcycle joyride, barhopping across town.

I was now beginning to understand why DelGiorno may have

rolled his eyes. I think mine just did as well – perhaps more than once. Normally, I'm not at a loss for words, but how was I to respond to this drivel? My pejorative thoughts lead me right back to the Turner/Thayer connection. This stuff had been smoldering in their scheming little brains for the last four years, trying desperately to 'help the cause' all along. Likely prompted by Cal's recent indictment, Turner and Thayer began by renewing their colluding efforts and resurrecting their earlier plan. They dragged Wilczynski in and convinced him that now was the right time to 'make-the-call.'

But again, why was it that Wilczynski was the only one to hear about the 'death threat, 'Cal/Pam affair,' and most recently, the 'Connie-moving-in' scenario from Michele? Where the hell is this coming from? Even Michele's two best friends, Nikki Burdick, and Shannon Taylor, knew nothing about it. If they had, they would have been first-in-line on the horn to Mulvey. It was looking more and more like a fantasy of someone's warped imagination. Known these days as 'fake news.'

Before the interview was over, Mulvey asked Wilczynski to check his appointment schedule once again and look for the day of Michele's July appointment. His receptionist checked, but there were no additional records, other than the ones he provided earlier, showing her last appointment on May 16, 2001. Obviously, Mulvey had some concern about the discrepancy and was attempting to corroborate what he had told her. As the interview ended, he added that he felt "an obligation" to Michele because he was her hairdresser, and it was a "dilemma" for him to call with this information. Yes, I'd bet it was.

Where was that obligation when he first learned Michele was missing? Why now? Four years later. One day after Cal gets indicted.

Interestingly, Mulvey never asked why he waited until now to call. She also would have or should have known about the alleged death threat from Cindy Turner's notes that were turned over years earlier. I think it's safe to say that Mulvey did read Turner's notes and knew of it. My fear was, knowing how driven she was in her pursuit of Cal, she would anxiously, yet blindly, embrace anything Wilczynski had to say.

I spent a considerable amount of time making the connection between Thayer and Turner. They were two-of-a-kind. Twin troublemakers.

That reminded me of those mischievous characters of Dr. Seuss, Thing 1, and Thing 2. But perhaps more like a couple of 'wolves in sheep's-clothing' who'd been howling behind the scenes for years. Dare I say when Wilczynski entered the picture, he became Thing 3? Together, they were the only common link to the creation and circulation of the fake 'death threat, Cal/Pam affair, and Connie-moving-in' scenarios. In their collective effort to 'help the cause,' and with Mulvey in their corner, they worked to build the most damnable image of the man they abhorred the most − Cal Harris. I could almost picture Turner speaking with Wilczynski saying, "Jerry, we all loved Michele, and we all know that son-of-a-bitch Cal killed her. We need to put him away for good. Will you help us? Please, Jerry, make the call."

Wilczynski was easily exploited into the cause and agreed to help make it happen. Thereafter, they began releasing their bogus information even though they couldn't always keep their stories straight. They may have bamboozled some, but once I pieced it all together, I wasn't buying it − not for a second. Considering their feigned and deceptive information, in combination with their shameful behavior, nothing they offered could even remotely be considered credible. Instead, it reminded me of a quote from W.C. Fields, "If you can't dazzle them with brilliance, baffle them with bullshit." Since there was no hint of brilliance here, they'd obviously opted for the latter.

Author's Note: Interestingly, during a later proceeding, I would learn that Cindy Turner's relationship with Michele was not as close as she claimed. She'd rarely seen Michele once the divorce started. Initially, there may have been some elements of truth in what Thayer and Turner were saying. Over time, however, truth-telling became less important. Holding Cal accountable was all that mattered, and they were not about to let the truth stand in the way.

12

CONFLICT OF INTEREST

C al knew early on my training and experience had come from being an SP investigator. During one of our many meetings, he asked me about some of the investigators currently working on the investigation. He was curious as to whether I knew or had worked with any of them, and what I could tell him about them. At the time, Cal had only recently been indicted, and we had not yet received any of the discovery materials. So, at this point, the only investigators I knew for sure were the three lead investigators, Sr. Investigators Sue Mulvey, Les Hyman, and John Skinner. I also knew that Investigator Steve Andersen was the lead investigator of the FIU and was likely involved in the execution of the search warrant at Cal's house. I knew there would be a host of other investigators and troopers involved, and I would likely know most of them. But I wouldn't know for sure until we had a look at the discovery materials.

I spoke briefly about my work history with the SP and how I knew all three of the lead Investigators. Cal was particularly interested in what I could tell him about Sr. Investigator Mulvey. Her early comment to attorney Stan Drazen, "I know Cal killed her, and I'm going to prove it," was concerning.

I recalled and explained that when she first joined the SP, her name was Susan Andrews. Later, she married another trooper and took the name Mulvey, but had since divorced. I went on to explain how she came from a police family, and several years earlier, her father had once been the Sheriff of Broome County, NY.

Suddenly, Cal leaped to his feet, screaming, "John Andrews! John Andrews is Mulvey's father?"

I knew I had just struck a nerve and quickly responded, "Yes, John Andrews is her father. Why, do you know him?"

Cal's face turned beet red as he started pacing around. He was livid. With fire in his eyes, he said, "Know him? Yes, I know him. That son-of-a-bitch used to work for me, and I had to fire him – it ended badly."

I said, "So, you know he used to be the Sheriff?"

"Yeah, yeah, I knew that. I heard that from my dad, but I didn't know Sue Mulvey was his daughter. This is bullshit. Why is she involved in this?"

"Good question," I said. "We'll have to let Joe know about this."

"You're damn right we do, I'm going to call him right now. This is bullshit."

When Cal called, Joe wasn't available, so he left a message, asking him to call. It took a few minutes, but after he calmed down, he sat, and we continued our conversation. We exchanged information about our respective knowledge of John Andrews and daughter Sue Mulvey.

I started by explaining how John Andrews had once been the Sheriff of Broome County, NY, in the mid-to-late-seventies, before losing his bid for re-election. Then, in 1979, just before the end of his term in office, his daughter Sue Andrews, joined the SP. Later, she met and married another trooper and became Susan Mulvey. I had no details but knew the marriage was short and ended in divorce.

Cal then explained that he was fresh out of college, and still a little wet-behind-the-ears, when he started at the Royal dealership, where his brother Kevin was already working. His father, Dwight, who had groomed him into the family business, was friends with John Andrews, who was now out of a job and looking for work. Dwight had asked Cal to hire him. He was never very confident that John Andrews was the right man for the job and had serious reservations. But at his father's request and recommendation, he hired him on as a salesman. He said, "It wasn't long before problems started happening." Complaints from customers started coming in regularly that Andrews was either lying to them or making promises he couldn't keep. Others reported being rushed, misled, or pushed into buying a more expensive vehicle.

Even though he hired Andrews as a full-time salesman, he soon started complaining that he only wanted to work part-time. Yet he still wanted the perks, like having a demo car to drive. Cal said, "John was always looking for and expecting special treatment, and if he didn't get his way, he'd go whining to Dwight." Later he added, "The biggest problem I had with John was his lack of responsibility and dependability as a salesman." Explaining that after making a sale, all his salesmen were required to personally deliver the vehicle to the customer. "With John, it became a bad habit of his of not showing up for the delivery, and some other salesman would have to step in and handle it." As he thought back, he believed Andrews had worked for him for about a year before he decided to fire him. When that happened, he said, "John did not take it well." Then added, "In retrospect, I probably should never have hired him in the first place, or at least fired him a lot sooner than I did."

I wanted Cal to explain the Mulvey issue to Joe himself, so I didn't stick around during his call. Later, in speaking with Joe, we discussed the matter. We both agreed that Mulvey's personal interest was not just a perceived conflict, but an actual conflict for her to act as lead investigator. Our dilemma was, what do we do about it now? We were already four years into this. The bell had already been rung. Any damage caused by the conflict had already been done. At this point, bringing the conflict to the attention of the SP or DA would likely fall on deaf ears and not change or undo anything. We also agreed that Mulvey would probably deny any conflict, and she would only be backed up by her superiors and the DA. Therefore, we decided it was best to move forward. But at the same time, now aware of the conflict, we would be scrutinizing Mulvey's involvement much more thoroughly. We would also return to the very beginning and look for evidence to determine whether the direction of Mulvey's investigation was prompted by her personal, as opposed to professional interests. With some reluctance and reservation, Cal agreed.

Growing Conflict

As lead investigator, Sr. Investigator Mulvey would typically delegate investigative leads to her subordinate field investigators working on the case, with only a few exceptions. As a result of her obvious conflict of interest, this was one of those leads that should have been assigned to another member. Or perhaps never adopted in the first place. Instead, Mulvey decided to handle it personally. The only information in the lead instructions was to "Document Cal Harris cashing award checks given to salesman."

Mulvey, having assigned herself to the lead, began interviewing John Andrews. That's right, John Andrews – her own father, who was likely the source of the lead. The conflict was apparent, but let's look at what this was all about. During the interview, John Andrews reported to his daughter he had previously worked for Cal Harris selling cars at his dealership. He told her that during an IRS audit of his tax return, he was made aware of unreported income. He claimed the unreported income was the result of award checks issued to him by the manufacturer, for his sales performance. Mulvey then wrote: Investigation revealed that Cal Harris had never given the checks to Andrews but had cashed them and kept the money for himself.

Whoa! Hold on before we go any further. We have a rather significant problem here. What 'investigation' is she referring to? There was no 'investigation.' Had there been, who initiated it and where are the results? At a minimum, it would have included copies of the original complaint, canceled checks, Andrews' tax return, IRS statement, witness depositions, amount of money involved, dealership and manufacturer's records, and of course, the results of the so-called 'investigation.' This information would have been included and attached to the lead in support of any 'investigation.' There was no investigation. And other than Mulvey's misleading say so, there was nothing more.

To the casual observer, this may have gone unnoticed, but for me, it was an insult. Ordinarily, as an introvert, I'm rather passive, and I don't get riled easily, but Mulvey was really pushing-the-envelope here. Obviously, any professional, or ethical integrity she may have had, was long gone. But then again, in her 'it's-all-about-me' world, it's likely there never was any.

Once again, to the casual observer, Mulvey's obvious omissions might go unnoticed. For me, however, her failure to include all the facts was blatantly shameful. Omitting that John Andrews was her father was bad enough. But to falsely say there had been an 'investigation' that supported his claim when there was none, was particularly egregious.

Ironically, there was another lead involving the interviews of several of Cal's current and former salesmen. Nary one of them supported

Andrews' claim that Cal was cashing their bonus checks for himself or had otherwise cheated them. Therefore, the only purpose for the John Andrews lead was Mulvey's self-serving interest to try and further justify her continued retribution against Cal. By her moving forward, knowing there was an apparent conflict of interest, she knowingly and willfully crossed the governing boundaries of professional and ethical conduct. She was in violation of not only the Law Enforcement Code of Ethics but her own oath of office she had sworn to uphold. Unfortunately, this would not be the end of her ignominious behavior.

During my previous discussion with Cal about John Andrews, I thought I had a pretty good idea of what happened. But I was anxious to speak to him again for some clarification. After reviewing the lead with Cal, he couldn't help but laugh and said, "That's so typical, John Andrews." He agreed with me that there never was any investigation, then added, "because it never happened." Cal confirmed that his salesmen did, in fact, get bonus checks from the manufacturer after they sold and later delivered a car. He said, "Bonus checks were only made payable in the name of the respective salesman." The manufacturer sent the checks directly to the dealership. When a bonus check arrived in the mail, the office manager would open it and hand it directly to the person named on the check. Cal added, "There was no reason for me to be involved in that process, and besides, I would have no way of cashing a check with someone else's name on it."

Continuing, he added, "If John Andrews had done his job the way he was supposed to, he would have received his bonus checks like everyone else."

"Anything else?" I asked.

"If he never received any bonus checks, it's his own fault. I had nothing to do with it."

Trip to Disney

More than five months had passed, and the search for Michele was still ongoing. Cal decided to take his children on a short vacation to Disney World in Florida. Getting some relief from the continued stress and anxiety surrounding the ongoing investigation, including the non-stop media bombardment, was as important to Cal as it was his children. Cal had asked family friend, Linda Hyatt, and her husband to accompany him to help with the children. It was late February 2002 when Cal and his children, along with the Hyatt's, boarded a plane in Syracuse and flew to Orlando, FL, for a weeks' vacation at Disney World.

The SP had learned previously from Linda Hyatt of Cal's scheduled trip to Florida with his children. When checking with the airline, it was confirmed that Cal had booked a round-trip flight from Syracuse to Orlando. Leaving on February 23, 2002, and returning a week later in mid-afternoon on March 1, 2002.

It's common knowledge that police are suspicious by nature, especially during a high-profile murder investigation. But that level of suspicion jumps up a notch or two when learning that your number one suspect is about to leave the state. What the SP had learned from Hyatt, gave them more than a week's advance notice of Cal's pending trip. If they believed or suspected Cal's activities in FL might involve more than just a trip to Disney World, they now had enough time to put plans in place and stay a step ahead of him. Accordingly, early contact was made with detectives with the Orlando County Sheriff's Office and a detective liaison at Disney World.

They were giving Cal way too much credit by believing he was clever or ballsy enough to use his young children in this way. They suspected he wanted to make this trip look legitimate, and that would allow him the opportunity to slip away to engage in some secret activity. At the time, with all things considered, it was still a justifiable lead.

During my review, I hadn't found any reports from any of the Florida officials attached to the lead. Other than a few names that appeared in some notes, there was no indication of what they did or what they were asked to do regarding Cal Harris. From my experience, I could only surmise from the few notes that Cal had been surveilled from the Orlando airport to his hotel at Disney World. The notes also indicated that Cal was staying at the Coronado Springs Resort, right on the Disney complex. Another entry showed that he paid for the hotel with his own American Express card. If he was trying to hide something, he wasn't doing a very good job. Other than his stay at the hotel and visiting Disney World with his children, there was nothing to show or suggest that Cal had gone anywhere, met anyone, made other purchases, or did anything of a suspicious nature the entire time he was in FL. Once again, a tangible lead, but unfortunately, not the results they were looking for.

After striking out again in FL, the SP was understandably still disappointed, and likely very frustrated as well. And no one working the case was more frustrated than Sue Mulvey. The bizarre nature of what happened next was just another example of Mulvey's personal, self-serving, and ongoing vendetta against Cal Harris.

On the day of Cal's scheduled, mid-afternoon return trip to Syracuse on March 1, 2002, SP Investigators traveled to the airport to conduct a 'surveillance' of his arrival. In the lead narrative authored by Mulvey, she wrote how Cal was observed exiting the plane with his four children, along with Linda Hyatt and her husband. Upon seeing Investigators, he became visibly upset. He separated himself from the children and the Hyatt's and was observed making a call on his cell phone. Later, as they continued to watch him heading to the baggage claim area, he held out his phone and stated, "Stan wants to speak with you." Mulvey, knowing he was referring to attorney Stan Drazan, said she did not want to speak with him. She described Cal walking away in an animated conversation on his phone. She then wrote, "Cal appeared to be agitated." Sound familiar? They continued to 'surveil' him to the baggage claim area and concluded their 'surveillance' as they watched him loading his luggage and helping his children into a van.

Typically, the objective of a 'surveillance' is to watch and learn, without being seen. If the SP truly believed Cal might demonstrate some 'consciousness of guilt' or otherwise engage in surreptitious activity upon his arrival back in NY, why would they allow themselves to be recognized? They wouldn't. Obviously, this was not actual surveillance. So, what was the real objective here? Was it to 'agitate' Cal as written? If that's the case, then mission accomplished. Otherwise, it served no legitimate investigative purpose whatsoever. Besides, they already knew what he was doing and who he was with long before he arrived, and had just learned that his activities in Florida revealed nothing whatsoever.

From my perspective, this was nothing more than a Friday afternoon joyride. Not unlike Mulvey's helicopter joyrides over Cal's house. Yet under the watchful eyes of two SP investigators with his four children and the Hyatt's all looking on, they thought he might demonstrate a 'consciousness of guilt' by engaging in some secret activity? That's nonsense.

This was not the type of 'investigative' behavior I would expect from the SP. Although I have seen it before, I was disappointed. This so-called 'surveillance' was nothing more than a sham, carried out for the exclusive fulfillment of some personal gratification, as opposed to any legitimate, professional purpose. This was more like a juvenile school-yard bully, strutting and flexing his muscles while taking pleasure in watching the fear come across the eyes of his frightened prey.

Glory Without Honor

From my perspective, Mulvey's personal bias towards Cal had been demonstrated from the very beginning. When she first walked into attorney Stan Drazen's office that day and said, "I know Cal killed her, and I'm going to prove it." Her rush-to-judgment and mind-set would never change. Since then, evidence of her bias not only continued but deeply infused itself throughout her investigation. Believing that Cal had cheated, stole from, and fired her father, she was unable to set aside her animus, hostility, and contemptuous feelings towards him. In-as-much, those vengeful feelings became her motivation and driving force behind the investigation. As a result, the investigation that followed centered more on retribution rather than justice.

Mulvey joined the SP about one year after I did. We had never worked together, but we knew one another and would see each other from time-to-time in passing. Although I'd heard some negative rumblings from others who worked with her, I never had any personal issues with her. As far as I knew, she had none with me.

As mentioned, evidence of Mulvey's bias had been growing steadily throughout my investigation and was becoming increasingly troubling to me. So much so, that I finally reached a point where I temporarily shifted my focus off Cal's case to see what more I could learn about her.

I knew she'd worked with two or more of my trusted colleagues who had since retired from the SP. After reaching out and explaining my concerns, I was reminded of an attempted murder case she'd investigated back in 1996.

Briefly, on October 15, 1996, at 12:30 a.m., a suspected marihuana dealer had been shot and critically injured in his mobile home in the Town of German, Chenango County, NY. SP Investigators Sue Mulvey and Joe Valentine were assigned, but it was Valentine who was first on the scene.

The victim was identified as Larry Smith. After suffering from two gunshot wounds, Smith was initially unresponsive and was quickly loaded into an ambulance and rushed off to the hospital. His 15-year-old stepson Patrick, although visibly shaken, had witnessed the shooting and began anxiously telling his story to Valentine.

As other police personnel arrived to assess the crime-scene, Valentine transported Patrick back to the SP barracks in Norwich for a more thorough interview and to take his statement. Patrick's mother, Carol Witty, was transported to the barracks by another officer but was not allowed to be present during Patrick's interview even though he was a juvenile. During his interview, Patrick was fully cooperative and laid out the specific details of the shooting and later signed a lengthy statement prepared by Valentine. After that, Patrick and his mom were on their way back home with Valentine.

Meanwhile, Investigator Mulvey was notified of the shooting at home and responded to the barracks. By the time she arrived, Valentine had already completed his interview and statement with Patrick Smith and was taking him back home.

Mulvey, upon arriving at the barracks, for no explainable reason, called Valentine and instructed him to return to the barracks with young Patrick. Although somewhat confused, Valentine complied with her instructions and returned to the barracks with Patrick and his mother. Arriving at the barracks, Mulvey separated mother and child by placing mom in a separate room by herself and then took Patrick alone to a local McDonald's for breakfast. There, they spent over an hour talking about 'generalities' before returning to the barracks. Back at the barracks, Patrick was placed into an interrogation room where Mulvey began questioning him about some 'inconsistencies' in his statement. Later, however, she was unable to explain what those 'inconsistencies' were.

Meanwhile, Patrick's mom had once again asked if she could be in the room with her juvenile son and was told, "You don't need to be there." Asking further if she could at least see him, she was told again, "You don't need to be there with him. Because you're going to be questioned too." Patrick himself had asked if his mom could be present and was told, "That's not necessary." After that, Mulvey pushed forward with a lengthy and progressively aggressive interrogation of Patrick, while knowingly violating the SP rules and regulations relative to the interview of a minor.

For the protection of both the juvenile and the investigating agency, the standard interview protocol of juveniles requires that the interview be videotaped. Unfortunately, even though the interview/interrogation rooms at the SP barracks are equipped for videotaping, it was never used during Patrick's interrogation. Or if it was, it was never disclosed.

With only a small single table between two chairs inside a small, windowless, and barren wall interrogation room, Mulvey began her lengthy interrogation of young Patrick. His mother had been illegally prohibited from being with him during police questioning. Even after several grueling hours, Patrick continued to deny any involvement in the shooting of his stepfather. More than once, he told Mulvey, "I'm not stupid enough to shoot my dad." Mulvey had already learned the victim, Patrick's stepdad Larry, had survived the shooting. He was awake and insisted it was not Patrick who shot him. Additionally, both Larry and Patrick were telling the same story. Two black men came barging into the house, and there was a brief confrontation with Larry before one of the men shot him.

During the struggle, Patrick tried to defend his dad. While doing so, he yanked the wristwatch off one of the men. Then he watched as one of the men shot at his dad three times. During the crime scene search, in addition to a nine-pound cache of marihuana, a man's wristwatch was found on the floor close to where the shooting took place. Mulvey simply ignored this and continued with her aggressive interrogation. After more than fourteen-hours of non-stop interrogation, she promised Patrick that if he confessed, he could go home. To further coerce him into a confession, she told him that they (SP) could get him probation and a job coaching a soccer team. But she'd also told him, if he didn't confess, they would have him locked away for a long time. Faced with that ultimatum, having been intimidated and coerced by Mulvey, a very frightened, learning disabled, and sleep-deprived, Patrick Smith caved and confessed to the shooting. But despite Mulvey's promise, he wasn't about to go home.

After signing his false confession, Patrick was arrested, arraigned, and remanded to the local jail. After that, he was issued the standard orange jail jump-suit, shackled and hauled off to a juvenile detention facility near Rochester, NY. A week later, the ink from Patrick's signature on his false, coerced confession was barely dry when Mulvey proudly received her Troop 'C' *Letter of Commendation* for her work on the case. It read as follows:

On October 15, 1996, a call was received regarding a shooting incident in the Town of German, Chenango County involving Larry E. Smith, age 44, at his residence. Subsequent investigation revealed the subject was shot by a fifteen-year-old residing within the household. Further investigation revealed that most of the subjects involved in the case were engaged in a major processing operation of marihuana. Due to the keen investigative skills and insight of the members responding to the scene, the appropriate subjects were arrested.

I wish to commend you for your outstanding efforts. Your response and decisive action which resulted in the arrest for Criminal Possession of Marihuana 2nd and Assault 1st. Your conduct was in keeping, with the highest standards of the New York State Police. I commend you for your efforts.

After reading this letter, authored by the BCI Lieutenant, I was thoroughly disgusted and felt nauseous. Seriously? Keen investigative skills and insight? Outstanding efforts? The highest standards of the New York State Police? Undoubtedly, those are the essential attributes I would expect to see demonstrated during any police investigation. Had Mulvey demonstrated any of those? Not even close. But for a while, the self-aggrandizing 'queen-for-a-day' proudly hung her commendation letter on the wall. Then, she basked in the accolades of her remarkable achievement while receiving fist-pumps, high-fives, and congratulatory kudos from her colleagues and clueless superiors.

The case against Patrick Smith could have ended there with an innocent young man, coerced into a false confession, convicted and incarcerated for a crime he didn't commit. Fortunately, for Patrick Smith, a bizarre chain of events that was about to take place would change all that.

Patrick had been sitting in the juvenile detention facility for several months, still trying to adjust to his unpleasant new environment. He was kicking himself for not sticking to his guns in telling the truth. He now found himself in the company of hard-core, juvenile criminal offenders, including murderers, drug abusers, child molesters, rapists, and more.

Meanwhile, SP Investigators in the SIU[1] were wrapping up a somewhat routine investigation that resulted in the arrest of a male suspect. During his interrogation, he claimed to have information about a shooting and was looking to make a deal. Before agreeing to any deal, he was told they would need to hear what he had to offer. With nothing to lose, he agreed and started to sing. He explained that he knew the identities of three men who had broken into a mobile home to try and rob a drug dealer of his weed. Then, as they were trying to rob the guy, there was a struggle, and one of the men shot the guy and took off. He threw the gun in a lake. But he knew where it was.

Attempting to verify his information, SIU Investigator's discovered the scenario in the Patrick Smith case mirrored the details provided by their suspect. Their next step was to find the gun, which they did. It was in the lake, right where he said it would be. Shortly thereafter, the three men responsible were apprehended. Later, with the help of Patrick Smith's original statement, followed by his own testimony, a Chenango County grand jury returned indictments against all three men on charges of Robbery, Burglary, Weapons Possession, and Assault. The truth about everything that happened had been accurately detailed in Patrick's original statement to Investigator Valentine.

Notably, by mid-February 1997, the SP acknowledged that Patrick Smith had been telling the truth all along. Yet sadly and unjustly, Patrick remained imprisoned for another eight months, which was now the better part of a year, before the charges against him were finally dismissed. He was quietly released from the detention center.

Court of Claims

Later, in mid-April of 1998, litigation was commenced on behalf of Patrick Smith with the filing of a 'Malicious Prosecution' claim with the New York State Court of Claims. As the senior investigator-in-charge, Sue Mulvey was named specifically as the party responsible for Patrick Smith's false and coerced confession, which ultimately led to his malicious prosecution, conviction, and incarceration.

Thereafter, a trial was held. As a result, on February 2, 2000, in the Court of Claims decision by Judge Jerome F. Hanifin, the court found in favor of Patrick Smith and awarded a $150,000 settlement. In the decision, the court addressed Mulvey's defense argument that this was 'just a mistake.' The court said no and wrote,

Indeed (Sue) Mulvey was the senior investigator, so it is unlikely that what transpired was simply the result of inattention or mindlessness. The court also found, *for reason(s) that cannot be gleaned from the record, Claimant was targeted virtually as soon as he returned to the barracks. Mulvey did not just discuss "generalities" at breakfast, she elicited the information.*

But Judge Hanifin didn't stop there as he went on to reference the confession as a sham, and the factual context before the court did not justify the interrogation.

In respect to the malicious prosecution claim, the court finds that the conduct of Mulvey deviated "egregiously from acceptable police activity as to demonstrate an intentional [and] reckless disregard for proper procedure" to the extent that she knew or should have known that there was no probable cause to proceed with the prosecution and that while her acts were not "purposefully evil or intended to harm," malice can be readily inferred and is inferred from her "reckless [and] grossly negligent disregard" of Patrick Smith's rights.

This was especially troubling for me for several reasons. It makes me cringe when thinking of what Patrick Smith's life would have been like, locked-up in that juvenile detention center if the SIU investigators hadn't been interested in what their suspect had to say. For all we know, he could still be locked up. Patrick was fortunate, but I often wonder how many other 'Patrick Smiths' may have fallen prey to or may still be suffering from any of Mulvey's egregious behavior. For those less fortunate, they're likely experiencing what Judge Hanifin described in his decision as Patrick's Kafkaesque[2] experience. From my perspective, Mulvey's conduct in the Patrick Smith case was not only 'egregious' as described by Judge Hanifin but grossly unprofessional and shameful as well. It should have been a 'red flag' for the SP upper echelon to take notice and action. Perhaps, a little closer monitoring of her work would be in order. To the best of my knowledge, that never happened.

As I turned back to Cal's case, my concern now was obvious. Mulvey's self-serving actions and decisions in the Patrick Smith case had nearly cost a young man his life of freedom. She may very well have explained it away to her superiors as an 'aberration' or a simple 'mistake,' but I tend to agree with Judge Hanifin. Most assuredly, this was no mistake nor aberration. From my perspective, this was just 'business as usual' and another example of Mulvey's corrupted ideology and methodology. Her only objective was to make herself look good while "justice be damned."

Even after being judicially rebuked by the Court of Claims, Mulvey scoffed at the decision, only to continue down the destructive path leading to her self-righteous form of justice. In her mind, she could do no wrong. Again, 'business as usual.' In-as-much, she readily justified her wrongful means along the way. In my view, Mulvey's integrity and ability to make professional, ethical, and responsible decisions were so severely damaged that it was beyond repair – never to be recovered. As such, she was no longer deserving of any trust in her leadership role with the SP.

So, what happened to Mulvey after the Patrick Smith case? Was she ever disciplined, reprimanded, censured, or even counseled for her actions? Was her *Letter of Commendation* removed from her personnel file? Apparently, none of the above. In fact, it was just the opposite. Not long after her misconduct in the Patrick Smith case, the hierarchy of the SP, following 'Peter's Principle,' promoted her to the rank of Senior Investigator. Then transferred her to her new position as the Sr. Investigator in charge of the Troop 'C' Zone III Station in Owego, NY – a position with even greater authority and responsibility. Scary, isn't it?

> Author's Note: The rank of Sr. Investigator is a very prestigious position. Authority is rarely challenged. It's important to note that at this time in SP history, there was a shortage of minorities, including women, that held leadership ranks, especially the rank of Sr. Investigator. In an effort to fill these positions, normal promotion protocols were expedited by relaxing or abbreviating the stricter qualification and credentialing requirements.

---

1. SIU: Special Investigations Unit
2. Kafkaesque: oppressive or nightmarish

13

FURTHER INVESTIGATION

Not long after Cal had been indicted, he gave me the name of a former sales representative who had worked for him at Royal Ford before Michele went missing. Ed Baldwin had previously worked at the Simmons-Rockwell dealership before Cal hired him. At that time, Nikki Burdick was still working at Royal Ford as the finance and insurance manager. Baldwin was Cal's sales manager, and Burdick worked directly for him. Cal informed me that Burdick was responsible for getting Baldwin fired. Later, he realized it was Burdick that should have been fired. After Baldwin left, he returned to Simmons-Rockwell, and Burdick received a promotion.

After Michele filed for divorce, Burdick quit and took a job at Simmons-Rockwell. A few months after Michele went missing, Cal realized how he'd been misled by Burdick. After that, Cal reached out to Baldwin and offered him his job back. He graciously accepted and returned to Royal Ford in February 2002. According to Cal, Baldwin was glad to distance himself from Nikki Burdick.

Baldwin had since left Royal Ford to accept a new position in North Carolina, but I was able to interview him by telephone. He confirmed what Cal told me earlier about having worked for him previously, before getting fired and later returning in February 2002. He also confirmed and explained how Burdick was responsible for him getting fired. He said, "She couldn't be trusted," then added, "She was a real bitch and nothing but a conniving scum-bag." Later, when she came to Simmons-Rockwell, he did his best to avoid her.

Baldwin was very familiar with most of the people I'd already talked to. As soon as I mentioned the name Ken (KC) Carrigan, the first thing he said was, "He was always bragging about his many sexual escapades with Michele, which included everything short of intercourse." He also added that Carrigan had bragged to many others at work as well. "Everybody knew. It was common knowledge among all the managers, even Nikki Burdick," he said.

So, it would seem my perception of Mr. Carrigan may have been accurate after all. But it also seemed as though KC shared the same definition of sex as President Bill. Whenever speaking with me or the SP, he'd adamantly denied ever having sex with Michele. But apparently, as long as you use the 'new' definition of sex, it must be okay to say, "I did not have sex with Ms. Harris." Okay, Bubba, I mean KC, whatever you say.

Baldwin also recalled that after Michele had her 'boob job,' she proudly waltzed into Carrigan's office and teasingly put them on full display. He said, "And she enjoyed every minute of it." Then added, "But it wasn't just Carrigan." She'd done the same for many others as well, including several of the guys at Simmons-Rockwell.

Continuing, he advised that when Burdick quit her job at Royal and came to Simmons-Rockwell, he started seeing Michele hanging out at the dealership with Nikki. She and Michele were going out with some of the managers at night, including Carrigan. He also believed Michele might have been dating one of the guys at Simmons-Rockwell by the name of Tom Nabinger. When asked about drug use, he said, "It was common knowledge that the guys at Simmons-Rockwell were notorious drug-users." Yet he had no direct knowledge of drug use by Michele but did say, "I'd be shocked if she wasn't using."

———

Linda Hyatt had been on my interview list for quite some time. Even though she was close to Michele, Cal was quite confident she would be willing to speak with me.

It was now July 2006. I located Linda Hyatt at her residence. She started by telling me how she was "on-the-fence" and was maintaining a neutral position in this matter and agreed to speak with me. She'd known Cal and Michele for several years, and her biggest concern now was the children. She really liked both Cal and Michele and loved their children. Unfortunately, ever since Cal found out that she had disclosed information to Pam Brock that he didn't like, he's denied her the opportunity to see the kids. That was about two years ago.

Hyatt told me that Michele thought she was taking sides with Cal. She'd attempted to convince Michele she was not taking sides but was just trying to do what was in the best interest of the children. Hyatt knew about Michele's boyfriend, and that his name was Brian. But she didn't know anything more about him. She recalled a telephone conversation she had with Michele on Labor Day when Michele told her the relationship with Brian had 'run-its-course' and wasn't likely to go anywhere or words to that effect.

She spoke briefly about Pam Brock, having worked for Cal but was rather sure she was now living out of the area. Probably in Florida. Continuing, she explained how Michele loved to shop and described her as kind of a 'shopaholic.' Michele enjoyed shopping and did so quite often. "Loved to spend Cal's money," she said. Then added, "She could drop $300-400 in a heart-beat." When she first learned about the divorce, Michele had never said anything about taking Cal to the cleaners. She just wanted to get things settled and get on with her life. Michele had often told her how great Cal was with the kids and didn't want to take that away from him. Regarding Cal, she recalled that sometime after the divorce was announced, he came to her house one night after work by himself. He claimed he wanted to work things out with Michele and didn't want their relationship to end.

Hyatt said she had never seen them fight, never saw Michele with injuries, and she never spoke to her about being physically injured by Cal. In her opinion, she had spent a considerable amount of time at the Harris residence with Cal, Michele, and the kids. When asked, she not aware of the March 2001 incident Michele had described in her divorce affidavit. Continuing, I asked if she knew anything about Michele buying a house? Michele had told her about putting a down payment on a house in Owego and talked positively about the house and how it would work well in keeping things smooth with Cal regarding the kids.

Michele did not confide in her like a girlfriend, but rather more like an Aunt or mother figure. "Nikki Burdick," she said, was a close friend of Michele, and she would more likely confide in her. Because Hyatt had chosen to remain neutral, or like she said, "on-the-fence," the Taylor family viewed it as her siding with Cal. As a result, she has not had any contact with them in over five years. As I was leaving, she told me that not long after Michele went missing, she and her husband had accompanied Cal on a trip to Disney World in Florida to help with the children.

Early in the SP investigation, their background check on Michael Kasper revealed that in June 2001, he had been involved in a domestic incident with his then-girlfriend Margie Quinn. If this was correct, it would have been during the same timeframe he was having his brief little tryst with Michele Harris. I was interested in learning the details of what happened.

I located Margie Quinn at her residence in Sayre, PA. Quinn confirmed the incident that was reported to the Waverly Police Department when Kasper had refused to leave her apartment. She also confirmed that when the police arrived, they spoke with Kasper, and he did end up going. He was not arrested.

I also learned that Kasper was dating her at the time Michele Harris went missing. Furthermore, Quinn had actually met Michele on one or more occasions at the Guthrie Inn, when she'd gone there with Kasper. She only learned from a friend after the fact that Kasper had been having sex with her. Continuing, Quinn told me about another incident involving her and Kasper when they dated. They had both been drinking and arguing about drugs when he pushed her backward, and she fell into a brick wall, splitting the base of her skull open. She said, "He took me to the hospital emergency room, where I received 37 stitches. We didn't want the police involved, so we told the hospital staff it was an accident."

Barb Thayer hated Cal's guts; however, she continued to work for him for the better part of a year before she finally gave him her notice. In mid-July 2002, she told him that her last day would be August 9, 2002. Within the next few days, Cal hired a new babysitter, Denise Kirby. She'd been working as an aide at St. Patrick's School in Owego, where the Harris children attended and knew both Cal and Michele. Denise started right away and worked side-by-side with Thayer for a few days to learn the routine. Even though Pam Brock continued to babysit, Denise Kirby, who was older and more mature, took over the lead role.

I'd learned from the SP leads they interviewed Kirby on several occasions. Initially, her only relationship with Cal was strictly business as a babysitter and Nanny. Over time, as I would learn from Cal, the business relationship with Kirby gradually evolved into an intimate relationship. Kirby was already on my list to interview. With Thayer out of the picture and Cal involved in a new intimate relationship with Kirby, I thought this would be a good time to re-visit the Harris home.

Thayer had been telling the SP, and anybody else who would listen, that Cal was removing and getting rid of anything and everything that belonged to Michele, including her photographs. According to Fran Harris, Thayer had told her, "It's like Michele never existed." When I questioned Cal about this, he admitted removing some of Michele's things that ended up going to the garage sale. He said, "Initially, I was just going to store her things in the basement, and Barb was helping me. Thayer asked if she could have some of Michele's clothes for her daughter. She later approached me with the idea of the garage sale. But now she's telling everybody it was my idea, and that's a bunch of crap."

Cal further advised that many of Michele's belongings were still there, just as they were in 2001. Before I could make my suggestion, Cal said, "I'll take you out there, I want you to go out there and see for yourself, and bring your camera, this is bullshit." I said, "That's exactly what I had in mind." I wanted to interview Kirby anyway. Hopefully, while I was there, I would take some new pictures to refute Thayer's claim of, "It's like Michele never existed."

I suggested it would be best if he were not present during my interview with Kirby. He understood and agreed. I also asked if Kirby would be able to direct me to where Michele's belongings were. He assured me she could. Before leaving, he called Kirby to let her know I was coming, and I spoke to her briefly, as well. She was anxious to meet with me and would be awaiting my arrival.

On October 14, 2005, I drove back to the Harris residence, where I met and interviewed Denise Kirby. Denise had a petite build and stood about five-feet-four inches tall. She was very attractive with medium length blonde hair, blue eyes, and a cute smile. At the time, she was 31-

years old. After a brief introduction, she invited me in, and we sat on the bar stools along the kitchen counter. The same bar stools Cal and I sat on when I was there four years earlier. As I glanced around, everything appeared nearly identical to what I recalled from the last time I was there.

In starting what would become a lengthy interview, I had her begin by laying out the history of her relationship with Cal. At the time, she'd known Cal for about seven years. She told me Michele had been missing about a year when Cal approached her and asked if she was interested in taking on the role of Nanny for his children. Cal's regular babysitter Barb Thayer had recently informed him that she would no longer be available to babysit. Initially, Kirby accepted on a part-time basis. She started immediately while keeping her part-time position at the school. She worked a few days with Thayer, who had agreed to stay on to help her learn the routine with the children. Then, over the next few years, her business relationship with Cal gradually evolved into an intimate relationship.

I knew Kirby had been interviewed on several occasions by the SP because I'd read all their interview summaries. I was now anxious to hear directly from her what her take was on those interviews. She said there were times when the SP came to interview her there at Cal's house, or at the school. They were concerned for her welfare and asked if she had a cell phone out here. They frequently tried to convince her that Cal had killed Michele. Furthermore, that she could be in danger because Cal was manipulative, controlling, and had anger issues. When explicitly asked, she advised that Cal had neither been violent nor acted inappropriately with her.

The interview then shifted to the topic of Michele's belongings. She started to describe many of Michele's belongings that were still in the house. I briefly interrupted and said, "This is great, keep talking, but I'd like you to show me what you're talking about." As she guided me through the house, the interview continued. She started pointing out all the things she was referring to. Throughout the entire house, there were signs of Michele everywhere. In the formal dining-room hutch, and on the dining-room and kitchen shelves, there were numerous hand-made ceramic plates, pottery, and figurines, all of which had been hand-made by Michele.

Upstairs, in the master bedroom, Michele's fleecy white bathrobe still hung in the walk-in closet. Michele's side of the closet was still full of fashion designer clothing, including a variety of dresses, pants, and jackets. Many of her Carlisle-labeled jackets were still hanging on fancy hangers with an additional label bearing the name, 'Michele Harris.'

All these things appeared as though they had been there all along, just as they were four years earlier. As we walked into the master bedroom, there was a large beautiful quilt Michele had made, which was framed and hanging on the wall near the bed. Moving through the house, I looked at numerous family photo albums, including Cal and Michele's wedding, and a variety of other special occasions, all of which included pictures of Michele. As we walked through each of the children's bedrooms, one or more photographs of Michele were framed and displayed on their dressers.

Later, as I was driving home, I was thinking about all I'd seen and learned during my interview with Kirby. My thoughts went back to what Thayer was saying. About how Cal was getting rid of anything and everything belonging to Michele and saying, "It's like Michele never existed." She even testified in the grand jury, saying, "He got rid of everything that was Michele's." Later, she improved on that saying, "After September 11th, it was like she never existed." What a bunch of crap. I'd become suspicious of Thayer long ago. Considering what I just learned, it was no longer just a suspicion. Earlier, she seemed like such a sweet lady, but now, as far as I was concerned, she could no longer be trusted to tell the truth. As for the SP, they would continue to embrace anything she had to offer.

14

GARAGE SALE

C ontrary to what Thayer told the SP, it was *not* Cal's idea for the garage sale. It was hers. Cal had, in fact, gathered up some of Michele's belongings for storage in the basement. But it was Thayer who first asked if she could have some of Michele's clothes for her daughter. Then later, she asked to store Michele's belongings at her house and offered to hold a garage sale in the spring, suggesting they could split the profits. All Cal did was grant permission for her to do so.

On June 8, 2002, Barb Thayer and Shannon Taylor held a very organized and well-planned garage sale. Part of their plan was to notify Mulvey, and according to plan, she hustled right over to attend. According to Thayer, she would have you believe that *everything* that was removed from the Harris residence for the garage sale was Michele's 'personal' belongings. And Mulvey's lead narrative about the garage sale was tailored to be consistent with Thayer. She wrote that she'd attended the garage sale of Michele Harris's 'personal' effects. Her narrative also included how Cal had arranged for Thayer to hold the garage sale, and the two of them would split the profits. She also wrote that she'd purchased two tablecloths at the sale for her personal use. As a professional, that struck me as a bit strange, but it became even more bizarre.

Mulvey wrote how she had asked Barb and Shannon to select an item that belonged to Michele that she could take back to the

Command Post. Keep in mind, there were literally hundreds of items, and she was right there. Why couldn't she make her own selection? But at least according to her narrative, Barb and Shannon carefully made their selection by choosing a beautifully handmade, blue and cream-colored, ceramic 'wedding plate' and handed it to Mulvey. Written on the plate: *"Cal and Michele August 25, 1990."*

A personalized wedding plate at a garage sale? That seemed a bit strange. Perhaps I'm wrong, but other than family or friends, I wouldn't think too many garage sale hunters would be interested in purchasing wedding memorabilia. Especially with someone else's names on it.

Attached to Mulvey's lead narrative was a hand-written, itemized list of every item in the sale, including its price. It was also noted that Thayer had taken photographs of all the items before the sale started. This was likely prompted by Mulvey. She later turned them over to Mulvey. There were literally hundreds of items. Without question, many of the items were, in fact, Michele's 'personal' effects. However, as I read through the list and looked at the photographs, it was evident what Thayer and Mulvey were saying was only half-the-truth.

Was I surprised? No. Because I'd already learned about the garage sale from Cal, who told me all about it. So, I already had an idea of what really happened. I was already of the opinion that this whole matter was a bunch of nonsense, masterminded, and augmented by Thayer's tailored lies, readily endorsed by Mulvey.

So here we had Barb and Shannon at Mulvey's request, 'selecting' Cal and Michele's 'wedding plate' and giving it to Mulvey. As proof of what? Or was she just looking for a souvenir? Does the line "If it looks like a rat and smells like a rat, it must be a rat" sound about right? It did to me. Perhaps three rats. Whew!

> Author's Note: Later, the wedding plate was used as evidence and shown to the jury at trial, with the sole purpose of portraying Cal's character as a cold-hearted scumbag who was deliberately trying to erase Michele from his life and the lives of his children.

After reviewing Mulvey's narrative and the garage sale list, I was even more confident. But now that I had the 'list,' I was anxious to learn what Cal had to say. Before offering my opinion or showing him the list, I wanted him to explain once more how the whole garage sale thing developed, and what more he could tell me about it. Cal's explanation was consistent with what he'd told me previously. The SP had just released his house back to him after completing their week-long search. Shortly after that, he started gathering up a few of Michele's belongings, placing them in bags, with plans to store them in the basement.

Thayer, who had been helping him, asked if she could store Michele's things in her barn until spring, and then hold a garage sale. She'd even asked if she could have some of Michele's clothes for her daughter. Barb had told him that she and Shannon would be willing to handle the garage sale and agreed to split the profits with him. Cal added, "If Barb hadn't suggested the garage sale, I never would have thought of it myself. Besides, I didn't have the time, and it wasn't like I needed the money. That was the furthest thing from my mind. But I did tell her if she was willing to do the work, that it would be fine. The only thing I asked was for her to let me know what she wanted to include and clear it with me first. She agreed. Then, shortly after she started taking stuff over to her place."

I told Cal I had recently reviewed a lead Mulvey had done regarding the garage sale, and there was a list attached, which included all the items that were included. When he asked if he could see the list, I said, "Of course, but before I do that, I wanted to ask you, besides the 'personal' effects that belonged to Michele, were there other things Thayer took for the garage sale?"

"Oh, hell yeah. There was a ton of stuff."

"Like what?" I asked.

"You name it. Just about anything you can think of. I would never have done it myself, but once Barb said she was willing to hold a garage sale, I saw it as a good opportunity to go through and get rid of a lot of stuff that accumulated since we first moved in. Stuff we hadn't used in years. Stuff from the whole family, not just Michele."

I said, "Ok, that's good to know and exactly what I thought after looking at this list." I then pulled out the list and showed it to Cal.

He perused through the list rather quickly running his finger down the list, nodding his head when recognizing many of the things on the list that he'd approved. He recognized several things, many of which had belonged to the children – items like baby pajamas, children's coats, and shoes. There were also other articles of children's clothing, along with a crib and mattress set. He also recognized several other household items, not specifically belonging to Michele. A few of the things included some old holiday ornaments and decorations. Other items included lamps, lanterns, picture frames, Venetian blinds, books, a popcorn maker, a sandwich maker, coasters, candle holders, a bird-house, wind chimes, and a set of roller skates. And the list goes on. After reviewing the list, he said, "Yeah, I remember most of this stuff, but not everything. Barb must have snuck some of these in without clearing them with me. But to be honest, I wasn't paying that close attention, I just wanted to get rid of some of that stuff, and there were times when I wasn't even there when she was working on it."

I then reviewed Mulvey's narrative with Cal. I was anxious to hear what he had to say about the wedding plate. Before I could even ask, he spotted it himself and said, "What the hell? This is bullshit. I didn't know that was in there. I never approved that. Barb must have snuck it in because I know she never cleared it with me. Besides, who the hell would want to buy our wedding plate?"

"Well, apparently Mulvey did," I said sarcastically. "She's probably got it hanging on her office wall."

With a rather disgusted look on his face, Cal just shook his head in disbelief – not smiling.

I was troubled as to how far Thayer was willing to go to make Cal look bad. Even more troubling was Mulvey, who continued to embrace Thayer's half-truths. After all, she had attended and personally observed first-hand the numerous items at the garage sale that were obviously *not* the 'personal' effects of Michele. Yet, she tailored her narrative to mirror Thayer by saying the sale only involved Michele's 'personal' effects. Even to the casual observer, her omissions were misleading.

I knew from early on that Mulvey had a personal bias against Cal. My fear was if that bias would control the direction of her investiga-tion, or would it be the professional integrity of her position as the lead Sr. Investigator with the SP? Unfortunately, I already knew the answer. I could no longer pretend to ignore her lack of professional integrity, as demonstrated by her self-righteous attitude, combined with her child-ish, self-serving, and disgraceful behavior. How far was she willing to go? I also realized that my long-held admiration and respect for the SP was jeopardized by the conduct of one individual. And this became very alarming for me. I had to often remind myself of the many good cops out there. Unfortunately, they weren't the ones calling the shots.

15

THE TRIAL

Trial Prep

In the weeks and months following Cal's indictment, the defense would continue to receive periodic new discovery material from the DA. There were already over 900 leads. This included, but was not limited to, thousands of telephone, bank and financial records, photographs, photo logs, videotapes, evidence logs, lab submissions, chain of custody, FIU and lab reports, legal documents, news articles, and the list goes on. On top of this, we were also provided the grand jury minutes, which included the court transcripts of each grand jury witness that testified. Needless to say, we had our work cut out for us.

During the initial SP interviews with Nikki Burdick, she had mentioned the name, Kent Cramer. Telling investigators that Cramer had once worked for Cal as a salesman at Royal Ford, and he and Michele would flirt with each other. In 2005, Cramer's name was finally pulled from the file, and Investigator Mike Young was assigned to interview him. Cramer was now living near Ithaca, NY, where he worked as a compliance analyst at a medical center. Cramer advised that after graduating from Owego Free Academy in 1997, he went to work for Cal Harris at Royal Ford in August of 1998 at the age of 19. He worked for Royal for about a year before leaving to attend Ithaca College.

When asked about Michele, Cramer said he had met her at the dealership and had gone out drinking with her and Nikki Burdick several times. During that year at Royal Ford, he admitted to having sexual intercourse with Michele on at least three occasions, all taking place in either his or her vehicle. Until now, he had not told anyone but was uncertain whether Michele had or not. During his interactions with Michele, he became aware that she was not happy with Cal and was contemplating divorce. She said to him, "I'm tired of taking care of the kids alone." Michele was interested in his opinion because he was the child of divorced parents. When asked, he advised that Michele had never mentioned any violence in her marriage to Cal and never mentioned ever being afraid of him.

Evidence Review

By the end of 2005, we were ready to examine the physical evidence. We knew what the evidence was, and now we wanted to see it for ourselves. After that, Joe called DA Keene to make the request. Within the next few days, Keene called back to advise that a physical review of the evidence had been scheduled at the SP barracks in Owego. He further advised that due to the volume of evidence, we should plan to allow 2 to 3 days to complete the review.

In early January 2006, Joe, Sue, Cal and I, traveled to the SP barracks in Owego, where we were met by Sr. Investigator Sue Mulvey and FIU Investigator Steve Andersen, who was now Sr. Investigator Andersen. Shortly after walking into the barracks, Mulvey, upon seeing Cal was with us, looked straight at Joe and said firmly, "Mr. Harris is not welcome here."

Joe politely replied, "I believe he has a right to be here, but if you want to take a moment to call Mr. Keene, we'll wait."

Mulvey scowled but said nothing, then turned quickly and stomped away in a huff, disappearing into an office, slamming the door behind her. I leaned and whispered to Joe, "She knows he has a right to be here." He nodded.

A couple of minutes passed before Mulvey re-appeared. She did not look happy, and the scowl was still there. She mentioned nothing about speaking with Keene or anyone else. With that distinctive scowl still on her face, she said snottily, "Ok, let's just do this." At that point, Andersen took over as Mulvey backed away and disappeared down the hall.

Several boxes of neatly labeled evidence sat in organized rows along the wall. Andersen was working off an alphabetical listing of all the evidence and provided us a copy to follow along. Over the next three days, under Andersen's watchful eye and following his strict examination protocol, each item of evidence was checked-off, opened, examined, photographed, and then resealed. We now had a much better understanding of what the evidence was and what it looked like. And with the 200-plus photographs I took, we could later scrutinize and discuss the evidence in more detail at our leisure.

We knew the blood issue was going to be a crucial element in the case. In preparation for trial, we had visited the scene, consulted with Dr. DeForest, and reviewed all the SP photographs and documents related to the alleged crime scene. With the poor quality of the SP photographs concerning the color and size, Joe was concerned that the prosecution's portrayal of many of the photos could be misleading to the jury. Accordingly, he wanted to consult with an illustration expert to try and create a more accurate representation of the blood evidence.

After that, we consulted and retained Karl Williams of Endicott, NY. Williams had come highly recommended as a qualified graphic illustrator and photography expert. After discussing what we were interested in having him do, he confidently said he could help. Later, while using SP photographs, measurements, and diagrams, Karl was able to re-create the exact size and location of the bloodstains on life-size colored exhibits that were identical to the scene. The exhibits were taken to the Harris residence and placed in their exact positions on the garage floor and in the entryway. They were then photographed. Later, when the police photographs were superimposed over the charted locations, they lined up perfectly.

We had been preparing for Cal's trial, which had initially been scheduled to start in September 2006. With the voluminous amount of discovery materials involved, staying on top of the investigative and factual matters was a full-time job. On top of that, when you add in all the respective legal requirements involved, Joe Cawley's volume of work had become overwhelming. His paralegal, Sue Mertens, was doing a phenomenal job, not only keeping up to speed on the investigation but conducting the legal research as well. Her knowledge of the case, as well as her legal and organizational skills, were truly amazing. However, you wouldn't think so if you saw her office. It reminded me of my own. But if we needed something, she knew right where to look. At least most of the time.

Joe decided it was time to seek someone willing to take the second chair as co-counsel. After conferring with Cal, who agreed, Joe placed a call to attorney William 'Bill' Easton in Rochester, NY. We had all worked together previously. Bill's legal mind and knowledge of the law was impressive, to say the least. When Joe called, Bill accepted and agreed to sign on as Joe's co-counsel and was able to start working immediately.

With less than six weeks to go, trial preparation was our top priority. Just when we thought we had a pretty good grasp on everything, one of Keene's delegates dropped off another big box of discovery material on Joe's doorstep. Actually, a huge box was more like it – more than twelve-thousand pages. Joe was furious. Keene had been sitting on this material for nearly six years. And he's just turning it over now? Joe immediately called Keene to complain and then to Judge Squeglia, requesting the trial be postponed, to allow enough time to review the new discovery. Surprisingly, Keene offered little objection.

As a result, Squeglia granted the postponement, and the trial was rescheduled for January 2007. Now, with a little breathing room, the defense had adequate time to review the new material. During our preliminary review of the new material, we noticed that Keene had included a copy of the grand jury proceeding. Joe and Bill latched onto that right away while I started diving into everything else.

Collectively, Joe and Bill discovered what they believed were some serious, if not fatal, flaws in the grand jury proceedings. Accordingly, they began the process of preparing a motion to the Court seeking dismissal of the murder indictment. Once the motion was completed and proof-read three times, it was formally filed with the Court and copied to Keene. A previous motion seeking dismissal of the indictment had been filed earlier but was denied. However, considering the newly discovered 'flaws,' we were confident that a much more compelling argument could be made this time.

On December 15, 2006, just before the trial was scheduled to start, Judge Squeglia called to informally announce that he would be dismissing the murder indictment against Cal Harris after reviewing the defense motion. Less than three days later, in a 50-page written motion, Keene asked Squeglia to recuse himself, alleging favoritism toward Cal Harris and Joe Cawley. Bill Easton would later argue, "Keene's motion was littered with factual misrepresentations including the 'bizarre contention' that the court (Squeglia) was a close friend of defense counsel Joseph Cawley's father and spoke at his funeral."

In response, Squeglia said, "I don't even know Mr. Cawley's father, much less speak at his funeral." He then forcefully disputed the factual basis of Keene's motion saying, "Mr. Keene, there is no foundation to your belief." Squeglia recused himself, albeit reluctantly, but emphasized he did so not because of any allegation in the motion, which he deemed baseless. Instead, by the very act of bringing the motion, Keene, he said, had "put the integrity of his office against the integrity of my office." The very next day, state court officials appointed the Honorable Martin E. Smith, a County Court Judge from neighboring Broome County, NY, to preside. Obviously, the trial would have to be postponed once again.

Judge Smith knew what Keene was doing. By asking Squeglia to recuse himself, he had engaged in a tactical misuse of his authority by attempting to manipulate the law to his advantage. Keene was trying to prevent or at least delay the murder indictment against Cal Harris from being thrown out. Now that Smith was presiding, he too would have to review the grand jury indictment proceeding and rule on Cawley's motion.

By Monday, January 29, 2007, Smith completed his review and was prepared to announce his decision. Unlike Squeglia, he did not pre-announce his decision. Instead, he summoned respective counsel to the open courtroom, where he formally announced his decision that he was throwing out the murder indictment against Cal Harris. After Smith's announcement, Keene was left with two options – appeal Smith's decision through the appellate court or make an application to re-present the case to the grand jury.

The next day, the headline in *Binghamton's Press & Sun-Bulletin* read, *"Harris murder charge tossed,"* with the sub-headline, *"Judge says Tioga DA gave grand jury inadmissible evidence."* Since I was unable to attend Monday's court proceeding, I was anxious to read the coverage by press reporter Nancy Dooling, who got right to the point.

Dooling referred to Judge Smith's written decision to throw out the murder indictment on the grounds that the grand jury proceeding was conducted improperly by the prosecutor. In Smith's decision, he said that the Tioga County District Attorney, Gerald Keene, *"intentionally presented inadmissible evidence"* during the 2005 proceedings. In Smith's decision, he also said that another of Keene's actions warranted dismissal of the indictment on its own.

Keene told members of the grand jury he would share a 'story' with them at the conclusion of the case after a grand juror had asked whether Harris had taken a lie-detector test. *"This alone,"* Smith said, *"in the Court's view, is an error of such proportion as to require dismissal of the indictment by itself, even if no other errors had occurred in the presentation."*

Then, Smith wrote about the number of other errors involving the inadmissibility of hearsay evidence as *overwhelming*, including statements made by Michele's divorce lawyer. During his announcement to throw out the indictment, Dooling said that Smith also had some harsh words for Keene while addressing his conduct in his accusations against Judge Squeglia. Smith said, *"It would appear that the recusal motion was made only to forestall the court from issuing its decision dismissing the indictment."* Then wrote, *"Such tactics should not be tolerated."*

Keene had obviously not started out on good terms with Smith. He knew Smith's 'radar' would be tracking his every move and that Smith would not tolerate any of his deceptive tactics or legal shenanigans. So, Keene chose to move forward cautiously, making sure to stay within the established legal boundaries. At least for now, it seemed he had learned his lesson.

Rather than appeal Smith's decision, he chose to re-present the case to a new grand jury. Less than a month later, Keene got his second murder indictment against Cal Harris, and a new trial date was set for May 21, 2007.

We didn't know at the time, but not long after Cal was indicted in September 2005, a joint, pre-trial meeting was held to discuss the blood evidence with Dr. Henry Lee in his Connecticut office. In attendance were District Attorney Jerry Keene, as well as senior members of the SP, including BCI Captain Mark Lester and Sr. Investigators Sue Mulvey and Steve Andersen. What we also didn't know was that this meeting had been videotaped. Not by the SP but rather, a national television news magazine. The significance and startling result of what we learned and when will be revealed in a later chapter.

With the trial date rapidly approaching, our trial preparations were actively underway. The blood evidence was going to be a crucial part of the People's case. Accordingly, we spent a great deal of our time addressing that issue. Without any formal report from the prosecutions blood expert, Dr. Henry Lee, we could not be certain of what he would testify. Part of our preparation involved regular communication with our expert, Dr. DeForest. It was still undecided whether we would call Dr. DeForest as a witness, or simply use his expertise to prepare cross-examination questions for Dr. Lee. If necessary, we also had the option of calling him as a rebuttal witness. But it was much too early to make a definitive decision.

The age and volume of blood were controversial. We were concerned the prosecution would use Dr. Lee and any other means available to lower the age of the blood and bolster its volume. Our greatest fear was not knowing what Dr. Lee would testify regarding the alleged assault theory, as opposed to an innocent scenario. Soon, however, we would have an answer.

Jerry Keene called Joe to advise him that he just learned that Dr. Lee had a conflicting schedule and would not be available during the trial as scheduled. Neither Joe nor Jerry wanted to postpone the trial any further. The suggestion was made to bring Dr. Lee to the court before trial to elicit his direct and cross-examination testimony, which would be videotaped. During the trial, when called to testify, his videotaped testimony would be played for the jury. With both sides agreeing and Judge Smith's approval, Dr. Lee appeared in a closed proceeding in Tioga County Court a week before the trial to offer his videotaped testimony.

Under direct examination by Keene, Dr. Lee briefly described his education, training, experience, and qualifications as an expert. He also testified about a few of some other high-profile cases he had been involved in, such as O. J. Simpson, JonBenét Ramsey, and the pending Phil Spector murder case in Los Angeles.

Keene then began showing Dr. Lee a series of police photographs of the blood found on the garage floor and in the kitchen entryway he had examined. Lee admitted that his assessment of the blood-stain evidence was limited since he had never been to the scene and could only rely on the two-dimensional photographs provided.

Using the photographs, Lee described seeing blood in the cracks and grooves of the chipped and peeling paint on the garage floor. He said some type of moving action, such as mopping, wiping, or brushing, could explain how the blood got into the grooves but also admitted there could be other possibilities. While describing the appearance of the blood as depicted in the photographs, he said some appeared heavier, while others were lighter, showing different degrees of dilution. Overall, the stains appeared to be reddish-brown in color, but the blood in the grooves appeared to be more consistent with whole blood rather than diluted. They appeared to be more fresh than old, probably not months or years old. After testifying that there were several drops, Keene asked if there were more than ten? Lee answered, "maybe, maybe not."

In his further review of the blood-stain photos from the kitchen entryway, it was his opinion that they appeared to be consistent with medium-velocity blood spatter. He could not, however, offer any explanation as to the amount of force, or type of force used to cause the spatter. He was then shown the throw rug. He confirmed having examined it and described finding numerous bloodstains on the rug that was also consistent with medium-velocity blood spatter. He also identified the square blood-transfer stain on the rug but could not offer any explanation as to what may have caused the stain, or how long it had been there.

Having consulted with our own expert, Bill Easton went right to work on his cross-examination of Dr. Lee. Using the same photos, Lee acknowledged there were brightness, contrast, and coloration problems, caused by various flash and exposure issues. He also admitted that those problems made it more difficult, especially in trying to determine the age of the blood. When explicitly asked about the difficulty, he answered, "Well, it's very difficult to determine anyway, to determine the age of blood. What we can do is estimate ... so basically, this is not fresh, not old. It's a couple of days, a few days. I cannot determine how many days exactly, how many weeks exactly ... I can eliminate it's not fresh, not a couple of hours old."

Following up, Bill asked, "And then that's where we lie in between those two extremes, is that correct?"

Lee answered, "Yes."

His cross-examination then shifted to medium velocity bloodstains. Again, he admitted there was no way of determining how much force was used. To address the innocent explanation theory, Bill asked, "There could be numerous explanations for medium-impact in a kitchen area that don't involve the commission of a crime, is that correct?"

"Yes," Lee said.

Lee was firm in his opinion that some of the photographs of the garage bloodstains showed evidence of dilution. Lee was asked if he knew whether any cleaning agent or solution had been found. He was not aware of any but had suggested to the SP that a chemical test for the presence of a cleaning agent could be performed. But he didn't know whether it was ever done.

Regarding the medium-velocity stains on the rug, Bill asked if they could be aspirated blood from the mouth? Lee said, "It could be," but he didn't know.

During Lee's re-direct testimony, Keene got him to back off on the range he testified to earlier between a couple of days and a year. Now, he would say, "more likely, a few days."

Bill still had another shot with Lee. He re-addressed the issue of aspirated blood by asking him about something he'd mentioned previously about an amylase[1] test. Lee explained how he'd suggested to the SP that they could do an amylase test, which can detect the enzymes present in saliva. A positive amylase test could confirm the presence of aspirated blood. But again, he didn't know whether that test had been done or not.

Going back to the age of the blood, Bill asked, "A few days. Can you testify to a reasonable degree of scientific certainty?" Lee simply replied, "A few days." That didn't sound very 'scientific' to me. He never really answered Bill's question. What was the scientific basis for his answer? There was none. It was merely a guess. A few days? How many is a few anyway? We probably haven't heard the end of this issue. From our perspective, the weight of this evidence was far from compelling and could not support a conviction.

> Author's Note: As you may recall, Capt. Tom Kelly had previously prepared a list of five questions for Dr. Lee in his Requested Analysis (Ch 7). Notably, other than his controversial opinion relative to an attempted clean-up, Dr. Lee was unable to offer a conclusive answer to any of the questions.

Michele had been missing for nearly six years now. Neither her body nor a murder weapon has ever been found. Yet Cal Harris, indicted and charged with her murder, was about to go on trial.

The Trial

The trial for Cal Harris was held in the Tioga County Court House, which is centrally located in the Village Square in Owego. The New Court House, as it was called, was designed by a local architect, then built and completed in 1872. For the past century, it's been a notable landmark of the community. The Court House is two-stories in height with four, three-story towers with one on each corner. Its design is symmetrical, with identical facades facing all four directions. The exterior consists of a smooth, hard-burned brick of a reddish-orange color, trimmed in limestone. The interior is noted for its detailed woodwork and classic examples of nineteenth-century craftsmanship. The courtroom itself is wainscoted with chestnut up to about three feet in height, then capped with heavy black walnut. The Judge's platform is made of chestnut with raised panels, carved in black walnut. The elevated galleries with five-foot projections are made of chestnut and decorative parapets. The galleries have elevated seats, made of chestnut and trimmed in black walnut, as do the benches in the courtroom. A dozen or more circular windows allow for natural light into the courtroom. Written on the wall above the Judge's bench were the words, IN GOD WE TRUST, adorned with raised gold letters.

On Sunday, the day before the trial was to start, the morning headlines in the *Press & Sun-Bulletin* read, *"Harris trial begins without body,"* with the sub-headline, *"Prosecutor faces uphill challenge,"* followed by an article authored by Nancy Dooling, one of their crime-reporters. Dooling's article was a complete summary and timeline of all that had taken place since Michele went missing.

On the first day of the trial, I arrived at the courthouse early. When I first walked into the courtroom, the memories and emotions of my own trial thirteen years earlier came rushing back. It was in this same courtroom where I sat as a defendant on trial, falsely accused of multiple charges related to my work as a police officer. Thinking back, I froze momentarily, and then a chill went down my spine as I recalled that final day …

Closing arguments had just been made, and jurors were given their instructions and commenced their deliberations. All-day long, it had been dark and gloomy with a heavy overcast. So much so that the high circular windows in the back of the courtroom were darkened.

The presiding judge, in the presence of the jury, had just rebuked special prosecutor Nelson Roth, for prosecutorial misconduct involving his withholding of evidence (Brady material) favorable to my defense. In-as-much, the case against me had fallen apart rather quickly. Therefore, I was confident in a favorable verdict. But that did not diminish the anxiety of having to wait. Then, the knock on the door. The jury had reached a verdict. After everyone reassembled into the packed courtroom, the jury came out and took their seats in the jury box. When the judge asked the foreperson if the jury had reached a unanimous verdict on all the charges, she answered, "Yes, your Honor, we have." When queried for their verdict on each respective charge, the answer was the same on all counts, "Not-Guilty." There was a loud eruption of cheers and applause from my supporters who had packed the courtroom. For me, came instant relief and elation.

I've always been a man of faith, but what was about to happen next would leave me awestruck. The words, 'Not Guilty,' were still echoing in my ears. The jury was still seated, and the loud cheers from my supporters were just starting to subside. The Judge lightly tapped his gavel and called for 'order in the court.' Complete silence overtook the courtroom. Suddenly, from a lofted window behind me, and before the judge could speak, a near laser-like beam of sunlight streaked across the courtroom, emblazoning the golden words "IN GOD WE TRUST" right in front of me. Still standing, I became motionless, as a chill ran down my spine.

In the brief period it took for me to regain my composure, I don't even remember what the judge said to the jury before excusing them. At least for me, and my witnessing family would agree, our mysterious God had just reaffirmed the jury's Not Guilty verdict ... That experience later played a major role in my decision to become a private investigator and continue the work I do today.

It was 9:00 a.m. on day one of the trial, Monday, May 21, 2007. Dressed sharply in a tan business suit, Cal sat at the defense table with Joe to his right and Bill to his left. Sue Mertens sat to the far left. Jerry Keene sat on the left side of the prosecution's table. Assisting and seated to his right was assistant counselor Christopher Belling.

One-hundred-and-ten prospective jurors had been summoned and were now filing into the courtroom behind the counsel tables. Court officials were prepared to call as many as four-hundred-and-fifty. Given all the pre-trial publicity and high-profile nature of the case, jury selection was anticipated to take several days. I already knew from personal experience that presiding judge, Martin (Marty) Smith always maintained complete control of his courtroom and ran a tight ship. In-as-much, he liked to keep things moving and had little tolerance for anything he perceived as a stall tactic. Oh, the Marty Smith stories I could tell.

Back to jury selection, despite a few hardships and dismissals for cause, jury selection moved along rather quickly. To everyone's surprise, including the media, a complete jury of six men and six women, plus four alternates, was seated the first day.

Dooling's headline article the next day read *"Harris jury selected on first day,"* with the sub-headline, *"Process had been expected to last at least until Wednesday."* Due to the rapid jury selection, no court was held on Tuesday, because witnesses had not been scheduled to testify until Wednesday. So, we all had another 24-hours of prep time.

Trial Summary

The prosecution was prepared and expected to call as many as seventy witnesses. Jurors had been told that the trial could take up to four weeks. As it turned out, the prosecution abbreviated their case by calling less than fifty, and the trial was over in about two-and-half weeks. After less than four hours of deliberations, the jury reached its verdict and returned to the courtroom to announce that they had found Cal Harris 'guilty' of murdering of his wife, Michele.

Since we already know the end result, I will not spend a great deal of time re-telling, or re-hashing what we've already learned. For the most part, there were no real surprises, and witnesses simply formalized what they had to say before the jury. However, there were some interesting highlights that took place during the trial, which I will briefly summarize.

Wednesday morning, after opening arguments, Keene called his first witnesses, starting with Barb Thayer. As expected, Thayer detailed the events that unfolded on the morning of September 12, 2001, involving the disappearance of Michele and her interactions with Cal. Although she had never previously reported placing a call to Michele's cell phone at 7:13 a.m. after arriving at the Harris home, she now claimed that she did call her, but did not leave a message. She also testified about Cal getting rid of everything that belonged to Michele and that it was his idea for the garage sale.

Under aggressive cross-examination by Cawley, Thayer was confronted with numerous photographs showing many of Michele's belongings still present in the Harris home, including pictures of Michele in the children's bedrooms. After reviewing the photographs, Thayer had to admit those things were still there. She was also questioned about the 7:13 a.m. phone call and continued to insist that she had made the call despite evidence to the contrary. Her own phone records showed she made a call to her neighbor and could not have left her house before 7:09 a.m. By the time she got into her car and drove the four-and-a-half to five-minute drive to the end of the Harris driveway, she stopped to look and search through Michele's van before continuing into the house. The 7:13 a.m. phone call had already been made by Cal, not her. When asked why she'd never left a message, she just shrugged her shoulders and offered no answer.

When I learned that Brian Earley was being called, I was anxious to hear what he had to say and how he said it. At the time, he was at the top of our suspect list. He was reportedly the last one known to have seen Michele alive. He had no verifiable alibi, hadn't been searched, and it was only his word that Michele left his apartment when he said she did. We theorized from information found in the discovery materials that the relationship between Brian and Michele had 'run its course,' and Michele had gone to his apartment that night to end it.

We also knew that Brian was totally smitten with Michele. In his anticipation of a prolonged relationship with Michele, including marriage, he moved to NY. He sacrificed his job and current girlfriend in Philadelphia to be with her. Furthermore, he had just given Michele $5,000 from his savings to help with the down-payment on the house he believed he would be living in with her. So, if Michele had gone over that night to end it all, he would have been devastated. One could only guess what his initial reaction might be. Likely, at least momentarily, he would have been stunned and emotionally distraught. Once the reality of her announcement sunk in, his thoughts would have turned to the sacrifices he'd made, including the $5,000 he'd given her. It would only make sense that he would have asked for his money back, which of course, she didn't have. It's possible that he, in the belief his money was long gone once she walked out the door, demanded her jewelry as payment. Sounds like a motive to me.

Unfortunately, I was unable to be in the courtroom when Nikki Burdick testified. She testified about calling the Harris residence and learning from Thayer that Michele was missing. She described how she called Michele's cell phone and left this message: "Where the hell are you? You need to call me as soon as freaking possible. I am worried to death about you. You need to call me on my cell phone. Goodbye." From my perspective, leaving a message is what you would expect a friend to do. Therefore, I thought it was interesting to note that even though Thayer claimed to have called Michele, she never left a message.

In Nancy Dooling's continuing coverage of the trial, her next headline in the *Press & Sun-Bulletin* read, *"Trial paints 2 pictures of missing woman. Testimony portrays Michele Harris as loving mother, bar-hopper."* In her article, Dooling described how different witnesses described two radically different lifestyles that Michele was living. While a few described Michele as a loving, caring mother of four, a majority of witnesses, both friends, and family, were describing Michele's wild side, including her free-spirited relationships with other men as well as her more recent late-night drinking and bar-hopping activities.

During the second day of testimony, an *Associated Press* news article arrived from Los Angeles, CA. According to the article, the judge in the Phil Spector murder case in Los Angeles County, CA, ruled that blood expert, Dr. Henry Lee, who was working for the defense, had removed and hidden a piece of evidence from the prosecution. Dr. Lee's testimony had already been videotaped earlier and was expected to be played for the Harris jury within the next few days. It was uncertain what effect this ruling might have on Dr. Lee's testimony and credibility in the Harris case.

Shortly after reading the article, Joe assigned me the task of obtaining a transcript of Dr. Lee's testimony and the Judge's ruling in the case. I quickly located a PI in Los Angeles County who said he could help. After a few minor snags, I was able to obtain Dr. Lee's testimony and the judges, ruling in the Spector matter. With that in hand, I rushed back to the courthouse where Joe and Bill were anxiously waiting to make their argument for its use in challenging Dr. Lee's credibility.

The issue regarding Dr. Lee had not gone unnoticed by *Press & Sun-Bulletin* reporter Nancy Dooling. Following the matter, she wrote another article under the headline, *"Fight over key witness expected today."* In her article, Dooling laid out the issue concerning Dr. Lee in the Phil Spector case. She also wrote that Harris's defense attorneys would be asking Judge Smith to throw out Lee's previously videotaped testimony, and order Keene to produce Lee in person, at trial, so his credibility could be examined.

Later, I learned that once the transcript was produced, the issue involving Dr. Lee was put on hold to allow Judge Smith time to read it. He would later hear opposing arguments outside the presence of the jury.

As the trial resumed, various family members and others were called to testify about alleged threats Cal had made to Michele. Both of Cal's sisters-in-law, Mary Jo, and Francine Harris testified about hearsay statements claimed to have been made by Michele. Francine testified that at Cal's mother's funeral, which was in March 2001, Michele told her Cal once said, "If I was going to kill you, I wouldn't use a gun. They would not find your body, and there's no way they will pin it on me." She also said that when Cal was in Cooperstown that weekend, she confronted him about his comment. At first, he denied it, but later admitted he might have said it but didn't mean it.

Mary Jo testified about having received a call from Michele one time from inside a closet, telling her that Cal was downstairs, racking a shotgun. An emotional Mary Jo also said she could hear "the desperation" in Michele's voice and that, "I was helpless to help her." Under cross-examination, she admitted to never having called the police or followed-up to help Michele. She then said, "And I regret it." Later, when Francine was cross-examined, she admitted there was a lot of 'bad blood' in the family. Including an ongoing and bitter family feud involving several lawsuits between Cal and his brothers.

Michele's hairdresser, Jerry Wilczynski, was up next. As expected, he testified about overhearing Cal's alleged death threat to Michele over the phone. Under cross-examination, he claimed the reason he waited until 2005 to talk about it, right after Cal was indicted, was because he did not trust the troopers who interviewed him in 2001. He said they were prejudiced against him because he was gay.

Sr. Investigator Les Hyman testified about the negative results associated with the GPS on Cal's truck, and the covert surveillance of Cal after announcing the new search of the Harris property that November. Under cross-examination, Cawley had him explain all that was done regarding the physical surveillances conducted. He described the covert operations carried out under the authority of a court order and how investigators, dressed in camouflage and sporting night-vision equipment, watched Cal from the woods outside his home. And how they had secretly installed a GPS device on his pick-up truck. He then explained how police were hoping that Cal would either move his wife's body or lead them to evidence that would incriminate him. He then told the jury, "That didn't happen." Cal had not done what they thought he might, and no evidence was ever found during any of their prolonged efforts.

When asked about the 'surveillance' at the Syracuse airport, Hyman was asked under cross, "Exactly what evidence did you hope to get by sitting in the airport terminal while Mr. Harris was there with his four children, his babysitter, and her husband?" He answered, "We wanted to see who Cal was with and who he would contact after seeing us at the airport."

Sr. Investigator Steve Andersen from the FIU was a major prosecution witness. His direct testimony alone would make him the sole witness on day four of the trial, followed by the second day of an aggressive cross-examination by Cawley. As expected, Andersen testified about all that was done at the Harris residence and the respective evidence that he discovered. Obviously, the primary focus of his testimony centered around the tiny specks of blood found in the garage, kitchen entryway, and the small throw rug. For the most part, Andersen's testimony was consistent with the findings, as written in his report.

Under cross-examination, Andersen admitted that some of the areas he tested for blood at the scene tested positive for blood but were later ruled out as blood by the crime lab. He also testified that no blood was found in Cal's truck, Michele's minivan, the couple's boat, all-terrain vehicles, or canoe.

Andersen himself had pawed through Cal and Michele's dirty laundry, looking for bloodstains. Nothing was found.

Cawley then asked Andersen specifically, "Was there any evidence of splatters or smears, anything that would suggest an assault?"

"No," he replied. Even though he hadn't taken the photos, he admitted during questioning there had been some flash issues with the camera that caused varying contrasts in the coloring.

During Andersen's testimony, Cawley made it clear that he wasn't as concerned with what the state police *did* do as opposed to what they *didn't* do. Andersen had to admit there was never any forensic examination of the person, property, or home of Brian Earley, nor two of Michele's co-workers who were suspects.

Cawley also questioned him about his finding that the end of the Harris driveway where Michele's van was found had been compromised. He admitted it had not been properly secured as a crime-scene.

Keene knew the SP had dropped the ball by not examining the scene at the end of the driveway. But in his attempt to minimize the damage under re-direct questioning of Andersen, asked if the driveway scene had initially been considered a crime scene? Even though this wasn't his screw-up, Andersen, being the team-player he was, tried to explain it away by claiming the scene was originally only considered to be part of a missing person case. Adding that it was not until the blood was spotted in the Harris residence that the direction of the investigation changed.

Author's Note: Oh, really? So, was he trying to say that before the discovery of the blood, there was no need to preserve the driveway scene, because there was no suspicion of foul play? That's what it sounded like. But we know that was not true because there was a suspicion of foul-play right from the get-go. Otherwise, he would not have been asked to do a forensic examination of Michele's van or be sent out to forensically examine the scene at the end of the driveway.

Both of which took place before the discovery of the blood. This was just a lousy excuse for not preserving the driveway scene sooner. If there was enough reasonable suspicion to impound and forensically examine Michele's van, that should have automatically included the area at the end of the driveway as well.

On Friday, June 1, 2007, a hearing was held outside the presence of the jury. Judge Smith listened as opposing counsel made their arguments in the matter involving Dr. Henry Lee. Cawley read from the official transcript in the Phil Spector case in California, which included the judicial ruling that Dr. Henry Lee had hidden evidence. He demanded that Dr. Lee's prior videotaped testimony be thrown out. And that Lee should be required to appear in person to allow the defense an opportunity to question him regarding the matter.

I was pre-occupied at the time and unable to attend the hearing, thereby missed many of the heated exchanges that had taken place. After court, I learned about what happened after speaking with Joe and Bill. Additionally, Nancy Dooling had been covering the hearing for the *Press & Sun-Bulletin*. She summed it up well when the next day's headline read, *"Judge rules on blood expert in Harris trial,"* with the sub-headline, *"Prosecution testimony in jeopardy."*

After speaking with Joe and Bill and reading Dooling's article, I learned that during some of those heated exchanges, Judge Smith told Keene he must try and bring his blood expert, Dr. Henry Lee, in to testify. Otherwise, he would risk having his crucial videotaped testimony thrown out. Smith told Keene that if Lee had hidden evidence in the Phil Spector case in New York state as a California judge said he did, then he would have been charged with a felony. "It's tampering with physical evidence," Smith said of Lee's conduct in California. "If it occurred here, that's what he'd be charged with." After Smith's ruling, Keene said his office would attempt to reach Lee, who was currently out of the country. Later, when addressing the matter further, Smith said, "We're simply not going to let this happen – not in this court."

We knew the 'Dr. Lee matter' was not a done deal. However, it certainly seemed as though Judge Smith's ruling supported the defense position. For now, the hearing was closed, and the decision whether Dr. Lee's videotaped testimony would be allowed was put on hold while the prosecution tried to track him down. Meanwhile, the jury was summoned back into the courtroom, and the trial resumed.

Later, in a surprise decision, Judge Smith did a complete '180' from his earlier ruling regarding Dr. Lee and was now allowing his videotaped testimony to be played for the jury. As justification for his flipped decision, Smith said that he'd allow the Lee testimony because, in California, the prosecution and defense are required by statute to exchange evidence. "That's not the law in New York," he said. I struggled to accept Smith's rationale. According to the transcript and the judge's ruling in California, Dr. Lee had broken California law by hiding evidence from the prosecution. How is that not relevant to his credibility in any court?

Needless to say, we were devastated by Smith's decision. His earlier opinion was clearly the right one. Despite our best arguments, Dr. Lee's testimony could now be used, but his credibility would go unchallenged. The jury would never hear about Lee's misconduct in California. Dr. Lee was called to the stand, and his prior videotaped testimony was played for the jury.

Jerry Keene rested his case after calling fewer than 50 of the 70 witnesses he had on his list. Several witnesses who we assumed would testify never did. Including registered sex-offender Michael Hakes. Also, on the list but never called were Cal's father Dwight, brothers Kevin and Steve, and his two oldest children, Taylor and Cayla. But most notably missing was lead investigator, Sue Mulvey.

The People had rested, at which time the defense made their standard motion to dismiss the case for lack of evidence. As expected, it was denied by Judge Smith. Then, after the jury was excused, Cawley advised the court that he expected the Harris defense testimony to last about a half-a-day or so.

The Defense

Our consults with Dr. Peter DeForest provided some valuable information that was used during the cross-examination of Dr. Henry Lee during his videotaped testimony. Before the trial, it was undecided whether to have him testify or not. During one of these consults, the topic of DNA was discussed. Afterward, he provided the name of one of his colleagues by the name of Dr. Lawrence Kobilinsky. He said, "If there's anything you need know about DNA, you should talk to

Kobilinsky." Kobilinsky was the Chairman of the Department of Science at John Jay College with very impressive credentials in the field of forensic science. A few weeks before the trial, after meeting and consulting with Dr. Kobilinsky, we were all impressed with his superior intellect, knowledge, and expertise in forensic science.

Without having to exaggerate, this guy was brilliant. His combined expertise as both a blood expert and DNA analyst, a last-minute decision was made to have him testify for the defense. When Joe called, he apologized for the short notice and asked Dr. Kobilinsky if he was available to testify. Due to the serious nature of the case, he agreed to testify and said he would make himself available. The night before his scheduled testimony, he drove up from NYC. Later, Joe, Bill, and I met with him at his hotel and prepped him for his testimony. The next morning Joe and Bill arrived at the courthouse early and began finalizing their preparations for starting the defense. Meanwhile, I was picking up Dr. Kobilinsky at his hotel for the short trip to the Owego courthouse.

Since most of the key defense points had been made through the cross-examination of the prosecution's witnesses, the Harris defense would be relatively brief.

Joe called Dr. Lawrence Kobilinsky to the stand. After establishing his qualifying credentials as a forensic scientist with expertise as a blood expert and DNA analyst, Joe began his questioning regarding the DNA and blood evidence. There were a few collateral issues concerning the DNA work that was done by the SP forensic scientists, but for the most part, the defense was not aggressively challenging the DNA results. However, Kobilinsky did clear up some of the collateral DNA issues that involved dog blood found on the garage wall and some unidentified male DNA found in a mop bucket. But the most crucial part of Kobilinsky's testimony came when he disagreed with the testimony of Dr. Henry Lee that it was possible to date the age of the blood and that the blood had been there for only a few days. It was his professional opinion that there was no scientific basis to conclusively make that determination.

Closing Arguments

After ten days of testimony that included more than 50 witnesses and close to 250 exhibits that were entered into evidence, both sides were about to offer radically different pictures of Cal, Michele, and the evidence. Cawley was up first for the defense.

Briefly, Jerry Keene had argued throughout the trial that Cal was a control freak. But Michele's recent activities were causing him to lose control over her, the children, his money, and his business. So, in his closing, Joe countered Keene's argument by telling the jury Michele had a lot of freedom from Cal in the nine months between the time she asked for a divorce and when she disappeared. He told the jury that Michele had a housekeeper and a babysitter as often as she wanted, a boyfriend she spent time with in the Pocono's, and friends she was free to go out with several times a week. She enjoyed $120 haircuts. Joe added, "Cal Harris had no more control over Michele Harris than you or I had."

Joe then hammered away at the police investigation that only focused on Cal, without ever looking at Brian Earley as a suspect. He said, "They crawled into Cal Harris' shorts, and they never crawled out." Then, as expected, he addressed the lack of any direct evidence by saying, "There's no ear-witness nor eyewitness to this event." Then added, "There's no confession, no weapon, no cause of death, and more importantly, no body." As for the tiny specks of blood found, Joe blasted and ridiculed Keene's characterization of the Harris home being a murder-scene and told the jury, "I'll bet every man on this jury has cut himself shaving and bled more than this."

Jerry Keene would have the last word. Of course, his argument and interpretation of the evidence was the polar opposite. In his interpretation, he described how Cal was losing control over Michele as she was enjoying her newfound freedom and said, "It's driving him crazy." After describing Michele's newfound freedom, he said, "She was on her way up. She was buying a house in Owego and planned to start her life over after ending her 11-year marriage." Then, he described how Cal's life was "on its way down" because of the money he would lose in the divorce settlement and the cost of child support. "Turning money over to someone you hate – that's not a bright future," Keene said. Because of that, he said, "Cal was jealous, he was angry, and he's the only person who had a motive to kill Michele."

As expected, Keene bolstered the blood evidence by showing the jury the enlarged blood photos, which made it appear much greater than it was. As a continuous reminder, he left the enlarged blood photos on the big screen for the jury to see as he continued. Cal Harris, he said, hit Michele once or twice in the kitchen and then took her into the garage where she died. He admitted he couldn't prove it – without a weapon or body. Yet he argued that Cal then cleaned up Michele's blood and took her where no one could find her. He said the blood evidence proved Cal Harris was the killer and that, "It couldn't be any other way."

Closing arguments took all morning and most of the afternoon. The jury then received their 'charge to the jury' (instructions), which was read to them by Judge Smith. By 3:00 p.m., the case was in the hands of the jury as they entered the jury room, closed the door, and started their deliberations. The wait began.

Deliberations

All eyes were on the jury as they stood and walked to the jury room. Until the door closed behind them, there was hardly a sound in the courtroom. The quiet atmosphere gradually changed, as people could be heard whispering. Others could be seen standing or milling around quietly. I walked over and joined Cal and the defense team, who was still sitting at the defense table. Keene and his assistant had also remained seated. Judge Smith spoke informally, advising both sides that they were free to leave the courtroom but to let the clerk know how to reach them if there was a verdict, or if the jury had any questions. We chatted quietly at the defense table for a few minutes, then moved into a private room in the back of the courtroom that was designated for the defense team. Keene and his assistant also went to a private office on the first floor.

As we waited, we discussed the various aspects of the trial. We were optimistic that the prosecution had not met its burden of proof and that the weight of the evidence, as presented, was insufficient to support a conviction. I'm not sure how long we had been talking when a court officer knocked on the door to inform us that the jury sent out a note. The jury requested to have the testimony of Brian Earley and his landlord, Nancy Miller, re-read. They were also asking for Judge Smith to clarify 'reasonable doubt.'

After having the requested testimony read back, Judge Smith re-defined reasonable doubt and sent the jurors back to deliberate. Considering what just took place so soon into deliberations, we thought the jury might be close to a verdict. Because there was so much for them to talk about, and since it had been less than three hours, we felt confident that it would be an acquittal.

Around 6:00 p.m., Judge Smith called everyone back into the courtroom, including the jury, to announce that court was in recess for the day. After reminding the jury of their responsibility not to discuss the case during the overnight recess, they were excused with instructions to return in the morning to resume their deliberations.

The next morning, everyone gathered back in the courtroom. As soon as all the jurors were present, they resumed their deliberations. Less than an hour passed when came the knock on the door. There was a verdict.

Verdict

Wow! That was fast. They must have been very close yesterday. Just under four hours in total. From our perspective, without a body, a murder weapon, and only those few specks of blood, a great deal more time would have been required for a guilty verdict. We were cautiously, yet nervously optimistic for a favorable verdict. But at the same time, we knew that juries could be unpredictable. We all re-entered the courtroom and calmly took our seats, trying not to show our nervous anxiety of the unknown. The word that a verdict had been reached spread rapidly and the courtroom quickly filled to capacity, with spectators and supporters packed in on both sides. Once everyone was in place, Judge Smith called for the jury. All eyes, including mine, were on the jury as they marched from the jury room and took their seats in the jury box. I was closely watching the jury, but I could not get a read on any of them from any expressions or mannerisms. From what I could see, none of them were making eye contact with anyone in the courtroom, and the looks on their faces appeared stone-faced and expressionless. Once they were all seated, Judge Smith said, "I understand you have reached a verdict." Most nodded and said, "yes, your honor." Smith then asked the jury foreman to rise. Then, in response to the court clerk's query as to the jury's verdict, he announced with a firm, clear voice, "Guilty."

Aftermath

I was stunned. We were all stunned. I could not believe what I just heard. My eyes were on Cal. Cupping his head in his hands, I watched as his head dropped onto the table in front of him. He buried his face into the photographs of his four children he had spread out in front of him throughout the trial. He began openly sobbing and was heard saying, "Oh God, Oh God, No." Joe, Bill, and Sue were trying their best to console him. When he finally looked up, the color had drained from his now chalk-white face, and I couldn't describe the look on his face, other than one of total shock. Near zombie-like. My own shock of what just happened paled by comparison. For quite some time, the courtroom remained quiet, and no one moved or made a sound. Other than Cal's open sobbing, there was no clapping, cheering, or any other open sobbing or crying.

A little later, right behind me, in a quiet voice, I heard Gary Taylor (Michele's father) say, "Arrogant bastard. Thought his rich daddy was going to buy his way out of this." Cal's sobbing and cries seemed endless but probably only lasted a few minutes. Before I had a chance to console him myself, court officers were already moving in to take him into custody. I caught another glimpse of him briefly a few minutes later in the basement. By then, he was heavily shackled and being escorted out of the building and into a waiting Sheriff's vehicle.

The huge headline in the next day's *Press & Sun-Bulletin* read, *"Oh God, Oh God, No. Tioga millionaire sobs as murder verdict is read; defense considers appeal."*

Interestingly, in the Viewpoints section of the *Press & Sun-Bulletin*, another headline read, *"Readers' reactions to the Calvin Harris verdict."* A few of those responses read:

Sayre, PA: *"This case shouldn't have even made trial. It shows the society we live in, where someone can be convicted on who they are, and the publicity they carry."*

Apalachin, NY: *"It is completely inexplicable to me that 12 clear-thinking individuals could return a guilty verdict."*

Endicott, NY: *"I don't believe you can successfully prove intent or motive without a body. I believe the aspect of 'personal opinion' is what is behind his verdict."*

Chenango Forks, NY: *"From what was portrayed to the public, there isn't a single thing pointing to him. As for the blood, I just cut my finger in the kitchen. I'm sure if we looked as hard as they did, we could find blood in each and every person's kitchen."*

Obviously, it was not just the defense team who had these thoughts, but I couldn't help wondering why no one on the jury had.

---

1. Amylase: an enzyme found chiefly in saliva and pancreatic fluid, that converts starch and glycogen into simple sugars.

PART III

IT'S NOT OVER

16

A NEW WITNESS

The defense team was stunned and still in shock as we slowly composed ourselves and left the courtroom. Meanwhile, Cal had already been shackled and hauled away to jail. Later, we all regrouped at Joe's house to try and make sense of what just happened. Joe and Bill both agreed that from a legal perspective, what we just witnessed never should have happened. As feared, the jury ignored the lack of evidence and returned a guilty verdict based on the prosecutions demonic portrayal of Cal's character. Thereby finding him guilty. Not for anything he had done, but rather, for who he was.

Understanding this did not make it any easier to accept what just happened. We had all just witnessed a huge miscarriage of justice, but other than filing the obvious notice of appeal, we didn't know where else to turn.

Surprisingly, what we didn't know but were all about to learn was that startling new evidence was about to be revealed. Evidence that would not only throw Cal a new lifeline but also unravel the entire case against him. Moreover, it would forge a new case dynamic and prompt a renewed investigation that included a whole new cast of characters. A renewed investigation that that would ultimately prolong the case for several more years.

Only a couple of hours had passed since the verdict had been announced. We were all together at Joe's house, still reeling from the impact of the verdict when a call came into Joe's office. The caller identified himself as Kevin Tubbs and left a message, requesting to speak with Joe Cawley. He claimed to have important information about the Harris case. We had all left Joe's house, but he'd gone back to his office where he listened to Tubbs' message. There was also a second message from a news reporter in Towanda, PA, who also claimed to have information about the Harris case. By the time Joe got to his office, it was after working hours, so he waited and called Tubbs the next morning, and they spoke briefly.

Tubbs explained how he did not think Cal Harris was guilty because he had just read a recent newspaper article from a reporter who was covering the trial. It was not until he read the article that he realized Michele Harris was reported missing on September 12th and not the 11th, as he previously thought. Tubbs believed he had seen her in the early morning hours of September 12th near the end of her driveway. He went on to explain that he was driving up Hagadorn Hill Road in the pre-dawn hours of September 12th, pulling a hay wagon, when he saw two vehicles at the end of the Harris driveway. He described seeing a blonde-haired woman and a younger man standing near the vehicles. It appeared the woman, who looked like Michele Harris, was crying. The man he said was younger, mid-20s, he thought, with short dark brown hair.

After hanging up with Tubbs, Joe also called the number left by the reporter in Towanda but was unable to make contact at the time. Joe then called to tell me about the two calls and filled me in on what Tubbs said. Joe said, "He certainly sounds credible to me." We both agreed we needed to follow-up. When I called Tubbs back, he reiterated the same scenario, along with some additional details. He was also willing to meet with us, and we scheduled a meeting at his house in Owego on Monday, June 11.

While speaking with Joe in anticipation of our meeting with Tubbs, we discussed the potential ramifications his information could have on the case against Cal if it were true. Most notably, if Michele were still alive around 6:00 a.m., the alleged six-hour window of opportunity that Cal had would be destroyed. It could literally eliminate him as the killer. We also knew that if what Tubbs was saying was true, then it would not be received favorably by the SP. Especially this late in the game after Cal's conviction or when they learned that he contacted the defense first. To avoid any perception of impropriety or collusion between the defense and Kevin Tubbs, I suggested we retain the services of an unbiased third-party to witness the Tubbs interview, and if necessary, take his statement. Joe agreed.

Lawrence L. 'Larry' Brown had recently retired as an investigator from the SP. Shortly after, he obtained his PI License and started working in the private sector under the business name, Security Services Plus. Previously, we had joined forces to assist each other in a few other cases. I gave him a call. After catching up a bit, I explained the situation. He understood and agreed with the idea of having a third-party witness. He was available to meet with Joe and me first thing Monday morning. We all met at Joe's office on Monday morning for a quick briefing and then drove to Owego to meet with Tubbs.

Tubbs was standing in his front yard, waiting as we pulled in his driveway, and he walked out to greet us. I introduced everybody and invited him to sit in the car. He climbed in the back with Larry. Before we had a chance to say anything, Kevin said, "I've given this whole matter a great deal of thought and really didn't want to get involved, but then decided it was too important not to." He decided he needed to do the right thing by telling someone. I asked, "Why did you decide to call Joe Cawley with this rather than the police?" He explained that due to prior bad experience with the SP, they did not like him, and he did not trust them to do the right thing. He then added, "But it troubles me to say that because my own brother is a police officer."

At the time, Tubbs was 33-years old, married, and had a young son. He was a mountain of a man, barrel-chested, stood over six-feet tall, with short dirty-blonde hair and weighing in well over 300 pounds. He was also well-tanned, and at a glance, you could tell he was rugged and strong as an ox. He could have been a lineman for the NFL. Tubbs came from a large farm family and grew up working on the farm. Currently, he was employed working a dual-role as both a hay-farmer and cattle-hauler.

During our drive to Owego to meet with him, we had briefed Larry and brought him up to speed on what Tubbs told us on the phone. If Tubbs was willing, we all felt it would be beneficial during the interview to physically visit the specific places he would be referring to in his description. Once we got acquainted with some small talk and a few preliminary questions, it was time to let him tell his story.

We had already decided that Larry would take the lead during the interview. For the most part, Joe and I just listened. But occasionally, due to our knowledge of the case, we might interject with a question or two. Kevin was extremely cooperative and more than willing to accompany us and point out all the physical locations involved and provide a detailed description of all that happened. Of everything he had done and seen, including when and where.

Kevin had already described what he'd seen at the foot of the Harris driveway in the pre-dawn hours of September 12, 2001. But since nearly six years had passed, we asked how he could be sure of the date? He said, "That's easy because 9/11 just happened the day before. Like everyone else, I knew where I was and what I was doing that day." Due to the amount of time that had passed, we knew it would be important to establish the certainty of his recollection as to what he saw that day. In-as-much, we couldn't have asked for a better memory trigger than the events of 9/11. To further corroborate what he had seen and when we took him back to where he was and what he was doing on September 11th. He said, "September 11th started out almost the same as the 12th."

We learned that Kevin and his family owned a farm on Straits Corners Road in Candor, NY, which was about six-and-a-half miles from the Harris property. Having worked in the area for many years, he'd learned where the Harris property was and would pass by the Harris driveway frequently. On occasion, he'd seen a blonde-haired woman mowing the lawn near the end of the driveway and assumed it was Mrs. Harris.

At the time, Kevin and his parents, Richard and Gloria Tubbs, were actively involved in hay-farming and had been cutting and baling hay at several locations across the Towns of Candor and Spencer. Kevin, who was living alone at the family farm on September 11th, got up around 4:30 a.m. and drove his truck to the hayfield where they had already completed some cutting and baling. The specific hayfield was on a remote hillside, about a third-of-a mile off Forstrom Road or about one mile from the Harris driveway off Hagadorn Hill. He described the property as part of the old Shappy Farm but was currently owned by a man named Stan Walsh, who lived in the NYC area. With Walsh's permission, the Tubbs family had been haying the property for the past several years.

It was still dark when he first arrived at the hayfield. A large empty hay-wagon and loading tractor were already on-site. Working for about an hour-and-a-half, he loaded the huge round hay bales onto the wagon. On account of another commitment, he didn't have time to haul the wagon out of the field and back to the farm that day. So, he left the loaded hay-wagon in the field and drove his truck, on schedule, to the Valley-Hollow Deer Farm in nearby Willseyville, NY. From there, he picked up some deer and transported them to a butcher shop specializing in exotic meats, out towards Albany, NY. During his trip, he listened to the unfolding events of 9/11 on the radio and, upon returning to Owego, went to his parent's house and watched the continued coverage on their TV throughout the evening. Adding that, "The TV reception at the farm was lousy." Later, he returned to the farm to sleep.

Kevin explained all of this during our trip as we drove from his house in Owego to the Tubbs farm on Straits Corners Road in Candor. The farm was the logical starting point. We wanted him to start at the farm and then pick up his story from there. We stopped at the farm momentarily, and then he directed us along the same route he had taken that day to get to the hayfield. As we drove, Kevin continued with his story.

On September 12th, he again woke up around 4:30 a.m. Once he was dressed and ready, he drove his new 2000, red Chevrolet, heavy-duty, flatbed pickup truck back to the hayfield. Along the way, he drove past the Harris driveway. At that time, he didn't notice anything out of the ordinary. He continued down Hagadorn and then turned left onto Forstrom Road. From there, it was just a couple hundred yards before he turned right, going off-road onto a rough, grass-covered, narrow path. He drove slowly uphill along the tree-line to the hayfield. Arriving in the hayfield, he said, "It was still dark." By the time he arrived, it was after 5:00 a.m. and may have been closer to 5:30. "I was trying to time it so that by the time I got back out to the main road, it would be light enough for other drivers to better see my hay-wagon," he said.

By the time he reached this part of his story, we were sitting on Forstrom Road, where he identified and pointed out the open hayfield on the hillside. While there, we all got out of the car momentarily and found it helpful while listening to him tell his story. He used the physical location to help explain what he was talking about. After we piled back in the car and headed up Hagadorn Hill, he continued his story.

Since the hay-wagon had been loaded the day before, all he had to do was hook it up to his truck. Being alone, he said, "was a bit of a challenge when trying to line up the hitch," but something he had done many times before. Once the trailer was hooked up, he decided to load another four bales onto the flatbed of his pick-up truck. Then, his task was to slowly maneuver his wide heavy load back down the same rough, narrow path in the dark.

According to Kevin, his hay-wagon was about nine feet wide, and he estimated there was somewhere between 20 to 24 bales, each weighing in around 700-800 pounds. He said, "My best guess would be around 7 or 8 tons." Then added, "With that kind of weight coming down that hill, there's only one way to do it, and that's real slow and steady. A little too fast, and you're going to have a major problem on your hands."

His descent down the hill took several minutes before finally reaching the bottom where it flattened out just before turning onto Forstrom Road, but it was still slow going. He continued slowly out Forstrom Road, turned right, and started up Hagadorn. From there, it was another three-quarters of a mile to the Harris driveway. At the time, Hagadorn Hill was a narrow, unpaved dirt road with open drainage ditches running along both sides. As he slowly ascended up Hagadorn, the earliest signs of civil twilight were just starting to appear as he neared the Harris driveway. As he got closer, he noticed a vehicle was stopped and parked cock-eyed in the roadway. He said, "The front of the vehicle was nosed into the end of the Harris driveway, but the rear was extending right out into the roadway at an angle, partially blocking the road."

As we drove up Hagadorn Hill, without any prompting from us, he directed me where to stop. We were right in front of the Harris drive-way. Of course, Joe and I both knew where Michele's van had been found, but we were anxious to learn what Kevin would say. Notably, he pointed out the exact location. None of us had interjected many ques-tions of Kevin. We let him do most of the talking. He obviously had a story to tell, and we were giving him leeway to do just that. I parked the car at the end of the Harris driveway, and we all got out, continuing to listen to Kevin.

He had a very precise recollection of the vehicle he saw and said, "It was a newer model, Chevrolet pick-up truck, either dark blue or black." Later, he told me, "I've been around trucks all my life, and I own a Chevy truck. I'm positive it was a Chevy truck." He added that even though his focus was on the truck sticking out into the road, he believed there was another lighter colored vehicle, possibly an SUV, parked in front of the dark pickup. The position of the dark pick-up truck made him unsure whether he could safely pass by with his wide hay-wagon. He feared he might slide into the ditch on the far side. Continuing, he said, "I slowed way down and was just trying to creep by." Then, just as he was about to pass the truck, he looked over and observed two people standing outside the truck.

The first one he saw was a blonde woman who looked like the woman he had seen previously at the Harris property. He said, "She was leaning on the box of the pick-up truck and appeared to have been crying, but she didn't look at me while I was looking at her." The other person he described as a young white male who was tanned and estimated to be in his early to mid-20s. About five-feet-eight to five-feet-ten inches tall with a muscular build and short, dark brown hair. He said, "The guy was wearing a white T-shirt and blue jeans, but the shirt the woman was wearing was darker." Then added, "This guy was staring right at me as I was going by. He looked angry and was glaring right at me. I remember him very well. I was struck by his angry look, which I took to be directed at me. But I couldn't understand why he would be angry with me when it was his truck that was blocking the road." Later, during a follow-up interview, he said, "This guy was really glaring at me. I was almost hoping he'd say something because I would've stopped and beat the snot out of him."

"Too bad you didn't," I said.

Continuing on, he explained that after barely squeezing by the truck in the road, he continued to the farm and un-hooked the hay-wagon. Shortly after, he drove to his parents' house in Owego and joined them for breakfast. While there, he told them about his unusual experience at the end of the Harris driveway.

As we finished up in front of the Harris driveway, we started our return trip to Owego. Along the way, he was asked to explain again about what prompted him to call Joe's office. He said that when he first learned of Michele's disappearance, it was his understanding that she'd gone missing on September 11th. Recalling what he'd seen on September 12th, he thought it must not have been Michele Harris but perhaps a sister, crying over Michele's disappearance. He didn't realize the significance or importance of what he had seen until reading a recent newspaper account of the trial. It was only then that he realized she was reported missing on the 12th and not the 11th as he previously believed. And that her van was found in the very location where he had seen the two vehicles. He admitted that he was unaware of any of this until he'd read the recent article. He added further that he called Cawley's office because of prior bad experience with the SP and fear of coming forward because so much time had passed.

He was then asked to tell us about this bad experience he had with the SP. He explained that it was several years earlier when his stepson was little. There had been a minor accident, and his stepson had some bruises from his car-seat. When the state police investigated, they thought he had caused the injuries while disciplining the child and was arrested. When he tried to explain how he was injured, they didn't believe him. They never did any further investigation, just arrested him. He added, "There were people who knew what really happened." Explaining further that pictures had been taken of his stepson's injuries.

He then explained how he'd taken the photographs and had them reviewed by a forensic medical examiner. The medical examiner concluded that the injuries had, in fact, been caused by the car-seat restraints and were not the result of abuse. He added, "Eventually, the charges against me were dropped, but Keene was not very happy, and neither were the state police. So that's why I didn't feel comfortable going to them with this information." Continuing, he added, "One of the reasons I decided to come forward, in this case, was because other people, who didn't have to, stepped up for me when I was accused of something I didn't do. If they hadn't done that for me, I would probably not be talking to you right now. I'm just trying to do the right thing."

During our ride back, Kevin was asked if he knew either Cal or Michele Harris. Other than knowing who they were and where they lived, he had no relationship whatsoever. When asked if he had ever been contacted in any manner by Cal Harris or anyone acting as a third party on his behalf, he said, "No, never. Absolutely not."

Before dropping him back off at his house, we told Kevin we were very interested in his story, and we would be getting back to him soon. He agreed to make himself available as needed. During our trip back to Binghamton, our only topic of conversation was Kevin Tubbs and his story. After having spent the last several hours listening to Tubbs tell his story, we all agreed that he and the information he had provided was indeed credible. We also agreed that more needed to be done, and we would be following up with Tubbs again real soon.

I had tried calling the number that came into Joe's office from the reporter in Towanda, PA, but there was no answer and no voicemail to leave a message. I'd try again later.

Back in my office, I couldn't stop thinking about everything we had learned from Tubbs. I realized that conceivably, it could undermine the entire case against Cal. But before there was any chance of that happening, I had a lot of work to do.

After meeting and spending a considerable amount of time with Tubbs, I'd found nothing to suggest that he would have any reason or motive to make up a story like this, especially one that contained so many details. It was certainly worthy of pursuing further. Of particular interest to me was Tubbs' description of the young man and dark pick-up truck he'd seen. Brian Earley came to mind immediately. His physical age, height, build, and hair all matched Tubbs' description. My next step was to try and learn whether Earley owned or had access to a dark blue or black pickup truck. Accordingly, I searched through motor vehicle records in both NY and PA, including his parents and former girlfriend. Other than his own 1983 Jeep CJ7, color blue with a white top, nothing more was found. Knowing that Earley lived within walking distance of Greg and Shannon Taylor and may have had access to one of their vehicles, I checked records in both of their names as well. Nothing. I then checked records on his brother Mark Earley who lived nearby in Waverly. Although I found nothing registered to him, I knew he worked as a salesman at the Simmons-Rockwell dealership. What I didn't know was whether he had access to any dealership vehicles. I couldn't eliminate Brian Earley just yet.

I continued on with motor vehicle searches for the next two days. I checked on other known suspects as well as other men known to have been involved in Michele's life, including, but not limited to, Mike Kasper, Mike Hakes, and KC Carrigan. Other than Kasper's bright red pick-up truck, I found nothing further. Hakes didn't own his own vehicle, and the one he did drive, which was an old white Cougar, belonged to his father. But I checked for additional vehicles registered to his parents, as well as his girlfriend at the time. Nothing close to a dark pick-up truck was found. Carrigan had no pick-up truck registered to him. However, like Mark Earley, he may have had access to vehicles from the dealership. Of all the men involved, Brian Earley best fit the physical description, but I was never able to connect a dark blue or black pick-up truck to any of them. If I was to believe Kevin Tubbs, who the hell was at the end of the driveway with Michele Harris? I was stumped, not knowing where to turn from here. I needed something more.

I decided to take a break from the office work and called Larry Brown. Later, we got together and returned to the area Tubbs had shown us. We retraced his route of travel, documenting the time and distance between specific points along the way. We also documented the target locations with photographs. After we'd finished, I called Tubbs and arranged to meet and re-interview him. He articulated his story again with remarkable consistency to what he had told us two days earlier. After re-telling his story, Larry wrote it up in a three-page written statement. Once completed, Kevin read it carefully in its entirety. As a licensed Notary Public, I took his oath, which he swore to and then signed his statement, which was followed by my own witnessing signature.

Before leaving, I had prepared a hand-drawn diagram depicting Hagadorn Hill Road and the intersection of the Harris driveway. After showing it to Kevin, I asked him, from the best of his recollection, to draw the respective positions of the two vehicles he had seen on the morning of September 12, 2001. Kevin complied by drawing their locations on the diagram, followed by the date (6/13/07) and his initials.

17

ANOTHER CALL TO THE DEFENSE

I returned to my office the next morning and decided to try and contact the other caller with the number provided by the news reporter from Towanda. A male answered, and I identified myself and who I was working for. "I was expecting your call," he said. He identified himself as Steven Greene of Gillett, PA, and confirmed that he was the one who had called the reporter in Towanda. Greene had been following the Harris case and was surprised to learn that Harris had been convicted. He said, "I would have called sooner, but I never thought Harris would be convicted." Now that he had been, he felt it was important to make the defense aware of his concerns.

In 2001, Greene was working as a maintenance supervisor at the NUCOR steel plant. Shortly after Michele Harris was reported missing, and over the next several days, there were repeated and ongoing rumors circulating around NUCOR that two or more employees had been with Michele Harris the night she disappeared. He could no longer remember their names but was certain he would recognize them if he heard them. He also recalled the police coming to NUCOR and asking questions. At least two of the employees rumored to be with Michele Harris the night she went missing were originally from Texas and not long after, moved back there.

I hung up with Greene and called Joe right away to fill him in. He was interested in learning more and wanted to meet Greene himself. I called back, and he agreed to meet with us the next morning.

Joe and I left early and drove just over an hour to Gillett, PA. We met Greene at the Café-14, a small diner that he currently owned and operated. It was mid-morning, and the Café was not very busy. Greene offered us some coffee, and we sat at a small table in the back corner to talk. At the time, Greene was in his mid-40s. He'd retired early with a disability due to a back problem. He and his wife had been following the Harris case and were both certain he would have been acquitted. But when he wasn't, he felt obligated to disclose his concerns about two men from Texas.

Greene explained that shortly after Michele Harris went missing, he overheard some co-workers talking in the break room about two other employees being with Michele the night she went missing. They were steelworkers working on a big project and making about $70-80K a year. Not long after Michele went missing, these same two somewhat abruptly moved back to Texas. He thought one of them might have driven a black SUV. He could no longer recall their names but was certain he would recognize them if he heard them. He also provided some additional information, including the names of others who worked for or may still work for NUCOR, that could provide additional information. When asked if he could describe the two, he said, "Well, it's been a long time, but they were both in their early to mid-20s. One was taller and heavier than the other, about six-foot-one with short dirty-blond hair, muscular and tanned. The other one was smaller, maybe five-foot-nine, with darker hair. He was also muscular and tanned." Before leaving, I told Greene that if I could learn the names, I would be back in touch with him.

During our drive back to Binghamton, I told Joe that there could perhaps be a connection between what Tubbs saw and the two guys from Texas. Right after that, it hit me, and I said, "You know, I think I remember reading a lead early-on where the assignment was to interview steelworkers." Joe nodded as if he remembered it too. I said, "As soon as I get back to my office, I'm going to find that lead."

Fortunately, all the 900-plus leads we had at that time were now well organized and documented into an Excel database file. I'd sorted the leads both numerically and alphabetically by lead number and witness names. I also included a brief description of what the lead pertained to. While scrolling through the alpha list, it didn't take me long before I found a lead with the entry, 'steelworkers' in the name column. Investigator's Mike Telfer and Scott Pauley had been assigned. As I read through the lead, even though it had been nearly two years, I recalled having read it before. It was all coming back to me. Previously, I mentioned this lead in an earlier chapter (Lefty's) and how new developments would bring me back to take a closer look. Indeed.

As I went back over the lead in more detail, I remembered from my original review, how vague and incomplete it seemed to be, with minimal information and only a few sketchy notes, far from what I would typically find in other leads. It was all coming back to me. Telfer and Pauly had identified and interviewed two steelworkers by the names of Doug Nagle and Stacy Stewart. Both admitted knowing Michele Harris and having seen her at Lefty's and out socially at other establishments in the area. They both claimed it had been several weeks since they had last seen her. Notably missing were any notes or details of any specific interactions they may have had with Michele. In the limited notes that were taken, the names of Wright Childers, Christopher Thomason, and Kari Cavanaugh had been included. But there was nothing to suggest that they had ever been interviewed.

As mentioned previously, investigators Telfer and Pauly returned to NUCOR later, after receiving a call from the office secretary, Jessica Hunsinger, about Stacy Stewart calling in sick around the time Michele went missing. She had also reported that shortly after interviewing him the first time, he was acting nervous and asking questions.

Before returning to re-interview Stewart, something had prompted them to run his motor-vehicle and criminal history. Although Telfer and Pauly conducted Stewart's first interview, it was not clear from the lead who re-interviewed him a week later. Initially, I'd assumed it was Telfer and Pauly but then found a reason to believe it was done by Investigator Mike Myers. Like before, Stewart claimed he had no contact with Michele for the past several weeks. He claimed that after leaving work on September 11, 2001, he went straight home where he remained until returning to work the next morning between 4:00-5:00 a.m. Notably, during this same interview, for some mysterious reason(s), Stewart was asked to take a polygraph. Troubling, was the fact that there was absolutely nothing in the lead that explained why. Obviously, Stewart had been singled out. But for what reason? As an experienced investigator, Myers undoubtedly learned or suspected something about Stewart. Was he lying about something? Did he have a relationship with Michele? You don't just randomly ask someone to submit to a polygraph. What was it? Why wasn't it included in the lead? I needed to know more.

As previously mentioned, there were obvious reasons why other 'suspects' in this case took polygraphs. But what was it about Stewart? For now, the mystery remains. But interestingly, as noted in the last line of the lead, Stewart was scheduled for a polygraph on October 10, 2001, to be conducted by none other than Investigator Mike Myers.

I already reviewed the leads about the polygraphs of the other 'suspects,' so I was especially anxious to review the results of Stewart's polygraph. It should have revealed not only the results but hopefully the reason he was taking it in the first place. I had no memory of reviewing a polygraph lead on Stewart before, so I quickly scanned through the lead log but found nothing. My first thought was, perhaps he'd changed his mind and never took it. Or, perhaps he'd taken it and failed. Either way, there should have been something in the lead. There was nothing.

After finding the names in the lead, I placed another call to Greene. He immediately recognized the names and was able to provide some additional information. He knew and described Stacy Stewart and Chris Thomason as best friends who had both been recruited and came up from Texas to work at NUCOR. "They were the ones rumored to have been with Michele Harris the night she went missing and not long after, both returned to Texas," he said. He described Stewart as the shorter of the two. Both were professional welders and lead-riggers but worked for different supervisors on different lines. At the time, the welding line-workers were working 12-hour days, six days a week, from 6:00 a.m. to 6:00 p.m.

Greene also recognized the names of Doug Nagle and Wright Childers. Nagle was believed to be in his early to mid-30s, married, and worked in a different department. He thought he might have been recruited from the state of Utah. Admittedly, Greene did not know Nagle very well but described him as being over six-foot-tall with a slender build. Other than perhaps sharing a meal together, he did not believe Nagle had otherwise socialized with Stewart and Thomason. Greene also knew Wright Childers, who was in his mid-30s. He was single and worked there as an engineer. He'd been recruited from Tennessee. He described Childers as a big man and health-nut who was into weightlifting. He was over six-foot-tall, bald, barrel-chested with broad, muscular shoulders. He also had a couple of distinctive moles on his face. He then added, "Childers loved his time-off and frequently hung out with Stewart and Thomason."

After speaking with Greene, I went back to review earlier leads where Michele's co-workers at Lefty's offered information about some young guys from the steel plant. Two or more had mentioned the name 'Stacy,' and another thought she remembered the name 'Doug,' yet her physical description was more consistent with Wright Childers. I knew from my previous review of the 'steelworkers' lead that Stacy Stewart had been arrested in Houston County, Texas, by the Crockett, Texas Police Department in June of 1999 for DWI. Lead records also revealed that Stewart was five-foot-ten-inches tall, 160 pounds, with hazel eyes and brown hair. He was born in October 1975, so at the time, he had just turned 26.

Stewart had pled guilty to the DWI and was sentenced to probation, and his driver's license was suspended. Subsequently, his probation was transferred to Tioga County, NY. At the time his record was run in September 2001, the status of his driver's license was still listed as 'suspended.' However, and this is where it gets interesting, records also showed that on June 28, 2001, Stewart transferred the registration for his 2000, black, Chevrolet pick-up truck, from Crockett, Texas to Chemung, New York.

Coincidence? Considering what we learned from Kevin Tubbs and what I just discovered, Stacy Stewart just leaped to the top of my suspect leaderboard, even ahead of Brian Earley. The preliminary indicators were self-evident.

So, what do we know so far? Stewart frequented Lefty's and knew Michele Harris. We already know of several suspicious characters and activities at Lefty's, including a couple of 'steelworkers.' The request for a polygraph would clearly suggest he knew something and/or had some type of relationship with Michele. It was also unclear as to whether he ever took the polygraph, or what the results were. Stewart's physical description, as well as that of his vehicle, both matched what Tubbs had seen at the foot of the Harris driveway. Anything else?

Remember the time of day when Tubbs saw what he saw? Although he didn't know the exact time, his description placed it at pre-dawn, during the earliest stage of civil twilight. The best estimate would be somewhere between 5:50 and 6:00 a.m., give or take a few minutes. Even though Greene said the work hours for steelworkers were between 6:00 a.m. and 6:00 p.m., Stewart told investigators that on September 12, 2001, he had gone to work between 4:00 and 5:00 a.m.

At the time, this 4:00 to 5:00 a.m. timeframe would not have been significant to the SP. Why? Because their theory was that Michele had been killed around midnight. If what Tubbs had seen was true and Michele was still alive in the 6:00 a.m. timeframe, it became very significant with respect to Stewart's claim about the time he went to work.

Let's say Stewart was, in fact, the person seen at the end of the Harris driveway with Michele around 6:00 a.m. He would have known that he had been seen by and made eye contact with a farmer slowing driving by while hauling a big hay-wagon. Therefore, without knowing what the SP knew at the time, he attempted to distance himself from the scene with an alibi, by placing himself at work between 4:00 and 5:00 a.m. Stewart was clearly on my radar, and my suspicions were growing, but I had a lot more work to do.

At this juncture, we had not yet told Cal or the SP about the new information from Tubbs. We needed more time to check-out Tubbs and further develop the information on what he had seen. With the recent conviction of Cal, the SP investigation was officially closed. Therefore, we were under no legal obligation, nor in any hurry to disclose the new information. We wanted to be sure and satisfied through our own investigation that the credibility of Kevin Tubbs and his information could withstand the scrutiny of the court. Only then would we disclose the information.

At the time, as a licensed investigator, I had a business subscription through a paid service-provider known as AutoTrack. AutoTrack can provide a variety of information including, but not limited to, witness and suspect addresses and address histories, phone numbers, employment, civil, criminal, motor-vehicle, real property records, professional licenses, and more. As the system improved, it also included e-mail addresses and social media information.

I already had the 2001 information on Stewart that was in the SP lead, but six years had passed. I wanted to see what more I could find. Accordingly, I entered Stewart's pedigree information into the Auto-Track system. The report I received back confirmed that his current primary address was in Crockett, Texas. Some of his former addresses were also listed, including his last known address when he lived in NY, which was 343 Edgecomb Hill Road in Lockwood, NY.

Lockwood is a small Hamlet in Tioga County, about nine miles north of Waverly. Records showed that Stewart had purchased the Edgecomb Hill property on August 17, 2001. Since then, the property had been sold to a man named Jeffery Gennarelli on March 30, 2004. AutoTrack records also revealed the registration of Stewart's 2000, black, Chevrolet pick-up truck that he registered in NY on June 29, 2001.

18

AN EARLY LOOK AT STACY STEWART

F rank Roney was a long-time friend and colleague of mine who had recently retired from the SP after having worked there for several years as an investigator. We had attended the SP Academy together and were assigned the same duty station when we graduated. We became friends and worked together for about two years before I was re-assigned to another duty station. Later, we worked together again in the Narcotics Unit. After retiring, Frank obtained his PI License and was just setting up shop. Like myself, he had a great deal of experience in working major-crime investigations. He'd spent the last several years before his retirement working the lead-desk during several major criminal investigations. He knew I was working on the Cal Harris case, but for confidentiality reasons, I had never shared any details with him.

Considering the bizarre new developments in the case and the additional work I had before me, I thought I could use some help. Frank lived in Tioga County and was much more familiar with the area than I was. Like everyone else, he knew Cal had just been convicted. When I called, he said he'd been following the case on the news. From what little he knew, he was surprised that Cal had been convicted. I said, "There's no one more surprised than me." I explained that there were some interesting new developments in the case since the conviction, with the potential of unraveling the entire case against Cal. But developing the information would require a lot more work. I knew he was interested when he said, "Ooh, tell me more."

I said, "I'd love to, but I can't do that unless..."

Interrupting, he said, "Could you use some help?"

I said, "You didn't let me finish. That's why I called. You must have been reading my mind. So, you're interested?"

"You bet," he said, "When do you want to get started?"

I said, "I already have, but let's get together, and I'll bring you up to speed on everything, and thanks. It'll be good working together again. But I'd like to get started as soon as possible. How soon can you get here?"

"Right now, if you'd like," he said.

"Great, I'll put the coffee on. See you when you get here, thanks."

At the time, I had only been in my commercial location for about a year. When I first started, I worked out of a small bedroom in my home, but quickly outgrew it. My new location had two office rooms and a separate storage room across the hall. I often referred to my back-office area as my 'war-room.' To the casual observer, it may not have looked well organized, but I knew where everything was and where to find it, somewhat like Sue Merten's office at Joe's office. Multiple files were neatly stacked and spread out across two long work-tables, while others laid in separate piles on the floor. I also had a large 'white-board' for notes, photographs, and reminders that were constantly being updated. It may have looked confusing but made perfect sense to me.

Shortly after Frank arrived, I walked him into the war-room to get started. I summarized the facts of the case against Cal and how things had progressed from the beginning right up through the trial. He agreed that the facts of the case were too weak to support a conviction. I then brought him up to speed on the post-conviction developments, including the specific details of what we had learned from Tubbs and Greene. I also briefed him on the preliminary results of my investigation into Stacy Stewart. He again agreed that if what Tubbs had seen was true, the case against Cal was in jeopardy. He said, "This is good stuff. Where do we want to start?" I told him that, according to Greene, Stewart had a couple of side-kicks by the names of Chris Thomason and Wright Childers. Supposedly, Thomason and Stewart were best friends and had come to NY together to work for NUCOR, but both suddenly quit and moved back to Texas. Although Childers was from Tennessee and a bit older than the others, he was known to socialize with them. So, besides Stewart, I wanted to learn more and take a closer look at both Thomason and Childers.

To further get him up to speed, I put him to work reviewing the documentation we had so far from Tubbs and Greene. Meanwhile, I turned back to AutoTrack to see what more I could learn about Thomason and Childers. I started with Thomason. Interestingly, Thomason had a more colorful criminal history than Stewart. Records showed that Thomason stood six-foot-tall, weighed 230 pounds, and had dirty-blond hair. Greene's description seemed to be right-on. I've seen lengthier rap sheets before, but Thomason had a history that included convictions for driving with a suspended drivers' license, grand thefts, making false reports, and more seriously, two separate felony convictions for intoxicated vehicular assaults in 2003 and 2005. He was currently serving a concurrent, ten-year sentence in Texas state prison.

I then turned to Wright Childers. The report on Childers revealed a current address in Tennessee and an address history showing former addresses in Alabama and Tennessee, as well as a former address when he was living in New York. It also revealed some of his motor vehicle records and his previous employment at NUCOR. No criminal records were found.

Getting back together with Frank, we decided that at least initially, we would concentrate on seeing what more we could learn about Stewart and Thomason. To start with, the next day, we traveled to NUCOR in Chemung and met with HR manager Kelsey Hammond. Other than confirming that both Stewart and Thomason had worked for NUCOR, then quit and returned to Texas, Hammond would not allow us to speak with anyone else or release any further information without a subpoena. We tried both tactfully and politely, to assure Hammond that we were not there to investigate NUCOR but rather only interested in some basic background information about some former employees that could help in a criminal investigation. He still wouldn't budge.

Trying to understand and rationalize with HR can be a challenge, but this was not my first experience of being denied. As we were leaving, I said to Frank, "Welcome to my world, but I've been through this before. We'll just have to go to plan B."

While we were still in the area, I wanted to get a peek at Stewart's former property on Edgecomb Hill Road. Frank was familiar with the area, and it was only a few minutes away. While driving up Edgecomb Hill Road, we spotted the name Gennarelli and the number "343" on a mailbox on the north side of the road. The property was remotely separated and isolated from neighboring homes. But there were no apparent boundaries, so we had no idea what the size of the property was.

As we pulled into the dirt driveway, there was a small log cabin slightly offset to the left at the top of the driveway. There was also a small pond to our immediate left, just below the cabin. The surrounding area was neatly groomed and mowed. The areas beyond the cabin and pond were wooded. A couple of hundred feet to our right, we saw a two-story, gray, steel-sided garage, with a small garden and open burn-pit nearby. We also noticed an old-style outhouse tucked in the woods not far from the garage. There was no answer after knocking on the door twice. But it was late afternoon, so we continued looking around for a few minutes, hoping someone would either answer the door or pull into the driveway.

07/25/2007

| *Stacy Stewart's Cabin and Pond*

Following a path through the woods behind the cabin for a few hundred feet led to a huge clearing, which turned out to be a right-of-way for a huge electrical transmission line. Before leaving, we snapped a few pictures of what we had seen and decided to return later to try and contact the current owner.

In further discussions with Frank, we both agreed that being able to put faces with names would be helpful in moving forward, especially with Stewart and Thomason. Knowing they both had arrest histories, we were certain their photographs would be on file. The challenge was, without being law-enforcement, how do we go about getting them from Texas?

In my office the next day, I tapped into my PI Network and found Pamela Sanders, a licensed PI in New Waverly, TX, which was about 60 miles from Crockett, TX. After explaining who I was, what I was looking for, and why, Sanders said she could easily help me with that. She then explained that she had access to Texas DMV driver's license photographs.

"Perfect, that should work fine," I said. I'd also asked if she could do a little more digging to see if she could find anything more on our two boys.

"I can do that too," she said. Then she asked that I put my request into an e-mail, which I did right away. After quoting her retainer fee, Joe cut and sent her a check right away.

Later, when meeting with Joe, I explained the roadblock we hit at NUCOR. But with the names we got from Greene, we would still be able to reach out to them, but trying to speak to them at work was not an option. I would have to find out where they lived and go from there. I then pointed out the work start-time discrepancies between what we had learned from Greene and what Stewart had told the police. I didn't need to explain any further. Joe was already on the same page and said, "So you think Stewart was trying to alibi himself?"

I said, "Well, it certainly looks that way. Why would he tell the police he went in at 4 or 5 if they didn't start until 6? We need to try and get his timecards, and if we think Thomason might be involved, we should look at his also."

Joe agreed and turned to Sue Mertens, who was sitting in on the briefing and said, "Let's do that and Beers, stick around, I want you to take it with you and get it served today."

"Works for me," I said. I knew it wouldn't take Sue long to hammer out the subpoena, so I said, "As long as I still have your ear for a moment, let's do a quick recap of what we have so far that points to Mr. Stewart. I'll start, but feel free to jump in whenever." I backed up to just a few days earlier and how everything had started with the revelations from Tubbs. His detailed descriptions of both the person and the vehicle he'd seen were remarkably consistent with Stewart. We also knew Stewart had at least been an early 'suspect' due to some unknown relationship with Michele. Then, Greene tells us of rumors floating around NUCOR about two employees being with Michele the night she went missing. And not long after she goes missing, these two guys suddenly quit and moved back to Texas.

Furthermore, an office secretary told police that Stewart called in sick around the time Michele went missing. The secretary also mentioned that after he was interviewed, he was acting nervous and asking questions.

Joe then added, "And don't forget the polygraph. We still don't know if he took it or not because it's not in the leads."

"Yep, that too. Good point," I said. There was likely much more to be learned about Stewart, and I was already working on that. Clearly, the evidence we had on Stewart was growing, but in getting back to the matter at hand, we certainly had a good faith basis for seeking his work records, including his timecards. We also decided to include Chris Thomason and Doug Nagle in the subpoena since they had been included in the SP lead as well.

With subpoena in hand, I traveled back to NUCOR and personally served it on the General Manager. The subpoena, more officially known as a Subpoena duces tecum[1] directed the person named to produce the requested documents to the issuing court (Judge Smith) on or before the return date. After explaining how to comply with the subpoena, I left it with the GM and drove over to Frank's office to give him an update and assign some leads to follow-up on.

I knew it could be several days before hearing back from PI Sanders about the photographs or the court regarding the subpoena, so I turned my attention to the telephone records. Before going to the jail to inform Cal about the newest developments, I wanted to examine the phone records to see if there was any evidence of phone contact between Kevin Tubbs and Cal Harris, or any recognizable third party on his behalf. I already had Cal's phone records. And Kevin Tubbs and members of his family had already made their home phone records available to me as well. All the phone records were downloaded into a searchable database, making it easy to search for the respective numbers. We needed to be certain, so I spent a considerable amount of time checking, cross-referencing, and re-checking all available records. There was no contact between them.

From what I'd learned so far, I wasn't seriously considering Doug Nagle as a person-of-interest. I had reason to believe that Nagle had been misidentified by one of the waitresses at Lefty's. Her description seemed to be much more consistent with that of Wright Childers. But since Nagle's name appeared in the lead, I decided to run his name through AutoTrack as well. He was originally from Warren, Utah, six years older than Stewart, married and was currently living in Sayre, PA. He had no criminal record.

It had been about two weeks since we first spoke with Kevin Tubbs. I'd asked Frank to try and contact the current owner of the Edgecomb Hill property, who we had previously identified as Jeff Gennarelli. I also asked him to interview a girl by the name of Kari Cavanaugh, whose name appeared in the notes of the NUCOR lead to see if she knew anything about Stewart and/or Thomason. During my interview with Steve Greene, he'd also given me the name of Cary Edwards, as another NUCOR employee that knew Stewart and Thomason. Frank took that lead as well.

Frank went right to work. He located Kari Cavanaugh at her residence. Kari, who was born in 1977, was two years younger than Stewart. She stood about five-foot-six, with a medium build and long pinkish-red hair. She had a multitude of tattoos covering both arms and legs. She dressed like a man, and her rugged tomboy appearance would give you the impression she could easily hold her own in a bar fight. She was currently employed as an electrician and living at home with her parents. She was acquainted with both Stewart and Thomason. She'd once worked part-time as a bartender at the Trackside Bar & Restaurant in Chemung, NY, right across from NUCOR. It was there she met both Chris and Stacy. They would frequent the Trackside at lunchtime and, at times, after work. She also knew they were both from Texas and worked at NUCOR. She'd also seen both of them out socially, at other bars in the area. When asked if she'd ever had any problems with either of them, she said no.

Frank went back to the Edgecomb Hill property a few times but never found anyone home. Finally, when checking back later in the evening, he saw a different vehicle in the driveway and lights were on inside the cabin. As Gennarelli opened the door, Frank introduced himself and explained why he was there. Gennarelli was very cooperative and told how he bought the place as abandoned property working through a realtor by the name of Melody Fairfield in Elmira, NY. He then retrieved a copy of his mortgage and showed it to Frank. The mortgage records showed that the previous owner was Stacy Stewart, who had purchased the property, which was recorded on August 17, 2001. Gennarelli had closed on the property in the spring of 2004.

When asked, Gennarelli claimed that he'd never had any contact with Stewart. When asked if he'd seen anything unusual or noticed anything that may have been left behind by Stewart, he said no. Outside, however, he had noticed an unusual, large slab of concrete, lying in the woods near a new lean-to he had built. He thought it was very odd. Frank told him that we might be interested in taking a closer look around the property and asked his permission. He graciously granted permission and offered us full access to his property anytime as needed.

Frank returned to the property the next day to take another quick look around and snap a few more photos. He then called me to fill me in on his interview with Gennarelli. I told him, "That's great work. Let's get together soon and take a closer look around the property. In the meantime, see if you can find Hunsinger, she could be very helpful."

I'd just hung up from speaking with Frank when an e-mail came in from Pam Sanders. The Texas driver's license photographs of Stewart and Thomason were attached, along with a brief notation that she'd been unable to find any other pertinent information. I quickly replied, thanking her for her fast response. This was perfect timing because we were just starting to speak with those who knew Stewart and Thomason. Now, with the photos, we would have better confirmation.

Frank knew he wouldn't be able to contact Hunsinger at NUCOR, so he waited until after business hours and started checking her residence. He finally drove by around 7:00 p.m. and found her home. After a brief introduction, Frank asked if she knew why he wanted to interview her. She said promptly, "It's probably about Stacy Stewart." Word must have spread quickly after our brief visit to NUCOR. One of the first things she said was that she'd always been a little 'creeped out' by Stewart. She then confirmed that she still worked for NUCOR as a secretary and was working there at the time Michele Harris went missing. She knew Stewart and Thomason were both steelworkers at NUCOR and were both from

Texas. When asked if she remembered the disappearance of Michele Harris, she replied, "Oh yeah." Then added, "Shortly after she disappeared, the talk around NUCOR was that Stacy, Chris, and one other guy were with her the night she disappeared. It was the talk all-around work."

When explicitly asked if she knew who was talking about it, she said, "Wright Childers talked about it a lot." Continuing, she advised that a man by the name of Scott Sanford was Stacy's supervisor. She then said, "One of the important things I remember most about Stacy was that he called in sick a couple of times around the time Michele went missing." Then added, "I remember that because I was the one who took the calls." She'd also noted and said, "After talking with the police, he was a nervous wreck and wanted out of there." She'd also heard that Stacy had taken and passed a polygraph test but couldn't say who she heard it from. When asked if she could recall what kind of vehicle he drove, she replied, "A dark-colored newer pick-up truck."

Hunsinger was also aware that when Stacy was in NY, he dated a girl by the name of Lisa Demtrak, who worked at the hospital in Sayre. Before the interview ended, she described a time during the late summer of 2001 when Stacy invited her to his cabin to go four-wheeling. She accepted and went with him. As soon as they arrived at his residence, he wanted to show her the new concrete he'd just had poured in his garage. Later, as they were pulling away from the house on his ATV, they had not gone very far before Stacy pulled off the road along the edge of a pond. She remembered the water in the pond as being a 'funny color.' Stacy said, "Look at that water. What do you think made it that color?" She said, "Stacy had this real weird grin on his face, and it really, 'creeped' me out." When asked if she had ever gone riding with him after that, she said no. When asked if her ride with Stewart was before or after Michele went missing, she said, "I believe it was after."

Cary Edwards was another name we learned from Steve Greene, and he still worked at NUCOR. Frank caught up with him at home after work. Edwards knew both Stewart and Thomason. He also knew they had been recruited from another NUCOR plant in Grapeland, Texas. He said, "They were 'lead-riggers' who worked as welders on assembly-lines manufacturing steel trusses for commercial and industrial buildings." Edwards had heard the same rumors around work that, "two or three guys from NUCOR were with her the night she went missing." Two of the names he heard were Stewart and Thomason.

He could not say specifically who he heard it from, but did say, "It was common knowledge throughout the plant." He was also aware that Stewart had recently purchased a new home but later heard he never made a payment on it. According to Edwards, Stewart and Thomason were best friends that frequently socialized together. Although Edwards worked on a different line, he did the same kind of work. Therefore, he was familiar with the work schedule and how line-workers check-in for work each day. He said, "The business was just getting started, and there were no time-clocks. Check-in was on the 'honor system.' Everyone managed and filled out their own timecards." Without any prompting, he added, "Some supervisors were stricter than others, while others would look-the-other-way and didn't care as much.

They gave their better guys a lot of slack if they were late, as long as the work got done in the end." He also explained that Stewart's supervisor was a man by the name of Scott Sanford. He had since retired and moved back to Nebraska. The other supervisor he knew was James Brent, who was Thomason's supervisor, who was also married to Stacy's first cousin Angela. He, too, had retired and moved back to Texas.

According to Edwards, Michele's brother Greg Taylor was now working at NUCOR as an inspector, which might explain why NUCOR was not very helpful in this matter. When asked about their work hours, Edwards said, "At that time we were all working six-days-a-week on 12-hour shifts from 6:00 a.m. to 6:00 p.m. Occasionally, we might go home early on Saturday." Following up, Frank asked if work would ever start any earlier? He said, "No, never. Other than a supervisor, maybe, coming in a few minutes early." Pressing further, Frank asked, "Would there ever be a reason for a line-worker to go in between 4:00-5:00 a.m.? He kind of chuckled and said, "No way. Nobody would ever go in that early. There would be no reason to because there would be nothing to do unless the whole line was there."

Later, Frank called and briefed me on the results of his interviews. When I asked him to document his interviews and prepare a written narrative, he said, "Already done, check your email."

"Thanks, you da man, but we'll have more to do soon," I said. I quickly forwarded his interview narratives to Joe, then sat down and started reading them for myself.

I became very curious about this 'abandoned' property Gennarelli mentioned. With a little help from Google, I tracked down the real-estate listings and learned that Melody Fairfield, with Dubois Realty, was the one I needed to speak to. I spoke with Melody at her office in Elmira. She checked her file, which confirmed the Edgecomb Hill property had apparently been abandoned by Stewart. She then advised that one of her associates handled the original listing and may have more information. I moved down the hall and spoke to her associate. She recalled the property had, in fact, been abandoned by Stewart with records showing the property being foreclosed on and re-claimed by Citi-Mortgage. She said, "You can probably get more details at the County Clerk's Office." I thanked her and said, "That'll be my next stop."

After leaving Elmira, I stopped at the County Clerk's office in Owego to check on the real-property and foreclosure records regarding Stewart. It didn't take me long to find what I was looking for. The more I read, the more interesting it became. Documents revealed that Stewart did abandon the property, which resulted in its ultimate fore-closure. A tax map in the file showed that the property was 4.1 acres in size.

Records further showed that on August 10, 2001, Stewart signed a thirty-year mortgage agreement with Citi-Mortgage for $57,545.00, with an affordable monthly payment of $402.36. The closing was on August 17, 2001, with his first payment due on September 15, 2001 – 3-days after Michele went missing. Records further revealed that no mortgage payments were ever made. Foreclosure proceedings were commenced in late February 2002 and completed in July 2002. In the interim, attempts were made to serve notice on Stewart. Process-servers made a note of the property having been vacated and the electric meter being red-tagged. After that, I obtained copies of everything in the file and had them certified.

Frank was continuing to follow-up with leads in the Waverly area. Jessica Hunsinger had given us the name of Lisa Demtrak, a girlfriend Stewart dated when he was in NY. Frank located Demtrak at her home in Waverly. She acknowledged knowing both Stewart and Thomason and recognized both from their photographs. She had first met the two one night at Alliger's House of Wings in Sayre, PA. Later, she learned they were from Texas and came up to help start-up the new NUCOR plant. Later, she and Stewart began dating, and by late summer of 2001, their relationship had become intimate. She added, "When they first came up from Texas in the spring, NUCOR put them up at the Guthrie Inn, which is now the Best Western in Sayre."

Sometime after they started dating, Stewart bought his own place, a little cabin in the woods on Edgecomb Hill Road in Lockwood, NY. She'd spent a considerable amount of time there. Before that, he would spend all his time hanging out "all-over-the-place" in the valley (Waverly/Sayre area). However, after acquiring the property, he would mostly hang out there working and making improvements. She had often seen him working around the pond, trimming trees, mowing the lawn, and sprucing up the place. "It seemed like he really loved the place," she said.

She also recalled the two-story garage on the property and was quite sure it was already there when he bought the place. She said Stacy and Chris were close and did a lot of things together. Later, when she learned that Stacy had decided to leave the area and move back to Texas, she wasn't surprised to learn that Chris had decided to go with him.

Continuing, she added, "Stacy never said anything specific, and I can't say why I'm saying this, but I felt something was wrong, and he may have been leaving over some criminal matter. And then Chris stopped paying his rent in Horseheads and moved in with Stacy." When asked, she described the vehicle Stewart drove as a newer model, black, Chevrolet pick-up truck – adding that it had a bumper sticker on the back with something about a 'redneck' on it. Later, she'd heard that his vehicle was repossessed shortly after his return to Texas. She described Stewart as a real 'momma's boy' and how his mother had once flown up to visit him at his cabin. She also recalled him having a big, green, four-wheeler he'd purchased while living at the cabin. She had never ridden with him but knew he kept it in the garage.

Demtrak knew that Stewart had been interviewed by the SP after Michele Harris went missing. When Frank asked, "Did you know Michele personally? She said, "No, I didn't. But Stacy did. He was a regular at Lefty's where she worked, and he talked about her all the time. He even told me he'd been out drinking with her." Later, when speaking with him after his police interview, he'd told her the police had him on videotape with Michele at the Guthrie Inn. He'd also told her that the police searched his property, and he had to take a polygraph test. She also knew from talking with him after Michele went missing, that he'd been interviewed by Investigator Mike Myers. And it was Myers that knew he and Chris had been out drinking with Michele afterward. "I can still remember him telling me that he wanted to take the test just to get it over with," she said. And she remembered being at the cabin the night he went for his polygraph.

Demtrak then advised that another woman from NUCOR by the name of Yolanda Lewis had picked up Stewart to take him for his polygraph because his license was suspended. When he returned later that night, he told her he'd passed, but other than that didn't want to talk about it. Furthermore, she added, "He was unusually quiet and had a very concerned look on his face." She then recalled how they'd quit their jobs at NUCOR and moved back to Texas in February 2002. And the reason Stacy used was that his boss was always 'ragging' on him and harassing him. "But I'm not sure if that was the real reason," she said. Then added, "Because I know he wasn't getting up for work a lot. He was late quite often. And even more so after Michele Harris went missing." She and Stacy stayed in touch for a few months, but no longer had any contact.

Frank found Yolanda Lewis at her apartment in Waverly. Lewis was still working as the Safety Director at NUCOR. When shown the photographs, she recognized both Stewart and Thomason – recalling that both had worked at the Grapeland, Texas NUCOR plant before coming to NY in 2001.

Lewis remembered when Michele Harris went missing, both Stewart and Thomason were interviewed by the SP. A few days after Stewart's interview, she took him for a polygraph at the SP barracks in Owego. She said, "I remember waiting, but it didn't seem to take very long." Then estimated it being about half to three-quarters-of-an-hour. "An hour tops," she said. She'd taken him for his exam because he'd lost his driver's license in Texas for a DWI. Afterward, during their return trip, Stewart told her he'd passed the test, but she said, "He seemed unusually quiet, kind of stone-faced and looked very concerned." She also remembered being at a party one night at Stewart's cabin when there had been a big bonfire. Later, when Stewart and Thomason both returned to Texas, she thought it was because Chris was in trouble with drugs, and Stacy was a 'momma's boy,' and both were homesick. She described both as a couple of 'roughnecks' from Texas.

As Safety Director, Lewis knew that Stewart's boss was Scott Sanford. He was from Nebraska, where he had since returned. Lewis then advised that all the guys who came in from out-of-state were initially housed at the Guthrie Inn until they could find their own places. She said, "They were all working 12-hour shifts that started at 6:00 a.m." When asked about the 4:00-5:00 a.m. start time, she confirmed what Cary Edwards told us earlier. She said, "There would be nothing to do if you went in that early. It was line-work that couldn't start until the whole line was there. The very soonest would be 6:00 a.m., but normally it was well after that because guys would often wander in late." Lewis also knew that while Stewart was staying at the Guthrie Inn, he became a frequent customer at Lefty's.

Frank had just finished his interview with Lewis when Lisa Demtrak called him back. After Frank left, she recalled that Stewart had poured a cement floor in the garage. She was not present when it was done, but only recalled the weather was on the brisk side at the time.

Jessica Hunsinger and Lisa Demtrak had both told us about a new concrete floor being poured in the garage on Stewart's property around the time Michele went missing. Our curious and suspicious minds wanted to learn more. With the six years that had passed, we wanted to be as sure as we could. With Gennarelli's permission, I asked Frank to take a closer look at the garage to see if we could determine whether the cement floor was poured before or after the building was erected. While Frank was doing that, I was trying to locate Ken Turnbull, who owned the property before selling it to Stewart. After some searching and a couple of phone calls, I spoke with a Lee Turnbull, who said he was Ken's brother. I explained what I was interested in, and he said he would have his brother call me.

Less than an hour later, Ken Turnbull called me. He was now living in Georgia. Turnbull said he had purchased the property from his younger brother and then sold it to Stewart in 2001. He referred to the garage as a gray pole-barn that was already on the property when he bought it. His brother had it built to replace an older barn that had collapsed. He said, "The pole-barn only had a dirt floor at the time I sold it in 2001." His brother had also put in the pond that was there. When asked about the slab of concrete lying on the ground west of the cabin, it had been used to cover an old well, but he could no longer recall where it was.

We were now certain that Stewart had poured the concrete floor in the garage. Our objective now was to try and determine *when* he poured it. He had only owned the property just shy of four weeks before Michele went missing. We learned from the foreclosure documents that he never made the first payment on his mortgage and then abandoned the property and moved back to Texas. The big question we wanted to try and answer was, did he pour the concrete before or after Michele went missing?

Preliminary indications were, it was after. Considering the mounting evidence that Stewart may be responsible for Michele's disappearance, the pouring on this concrete floor became very suspect. Which raised the question, if he was responsible, had he buried her in or under the new concrete?

Because it had been six years, we knew it might be a long-shot trying to find out where Stewart acquired the concrete. But we decided to make a list and start checking with local contractors and concrete dealers. We were able to estimate that approximately 7.5 cubic yards of concrete would be required. With this, we started contacting local contractors and concrete dealers in the area. We made inquiries with no less than a dozen over several days. Some of the well-established dealers had excellent records, and we were quickly able to scratch them off the list. Unfortunately, that wasn't the case with some of the smaller outfits. Some had no records at all. Others looked and couldn't find anything. Several told us they would check and to get back with them later, only to come up empty.

After striking out with the concrete dealers, we decided to pay Lisa Demtrak another visit. This time, Frank and I went together. Lisa was attractive and stood about five-foot-five inches tall, with a medium build and blonde hair. She was ten years older than Stewart. We asked if she could remember anything further about Stewart's interview with the police? She replied, "I know that Stacy, Chris, and Wright were all interviewed about where they were that night, how well they knew Michele, and how often they ate at Lefty's. But Stacy never told me how he'd answered those questions."

She recalled that when Stacy first bought the cabin, he became like a hermit. Before that, she said, "He was out partying all the time. But after he bought the cabin, he spent much more time there." She remembered him trimming trees and fixing the place up. "He was really proud of the place," she said. She remembered the night of his polygraph. She was at the cabin, waiting for him to return. She thought it might have been around 10:00 p.m. when he got back. "He had a very concerned look on his face but, other than saying he passed, didn't want to talk about it," she said. She continued seeing him through December of 2001. After that, she thought he'd started seeing someone else but didn't know who. Continuing, we asked, "Can you tell us anything more about Thomason or anyone he may have been seeing or dating?" She said, "Well, the only thing I can say is, I heard Chris got one of the girls at NUCOR pregnant."

Demtrak also recalled that about two weeks before Stacy and Chris moved back to Texas, Chris came to live with Stacy. He drove a newer model, white, Chevrolet pick-up truck. When they left to go back to Texas, they both drove their separate vehicles. When asked whether Stacy owned any guns, she said he had several. He kept them in a cabinet at the cabin. She seemed to think all his guns were shotguns and rifles. She'd never seen any handguns. We also learned that Stewart was a frequent customer of the Trackside for lunch, but after eating at Lefty's, his usual evening hang-out was the Night-Train Lounge at the Guthrie Inn. As we were leaving, she suggested we might want to speak with Stacy's old boss, Scott Sanford. She said, "Stacy was always butting heads with him."

Stacy Stewart

| Christopher Thomason

Later, I switched gears and headed out to Willseyville, NY, where I located the Valley-Hollow Deer Farm and interviewed Joyce Henderson. She confirmed that she and her husband owned the deer farm, and they had frequently used the hauling services of Kevin Tubbs and his family on several occasions to transport animals to their clients. She was certain they would still have records from 2001 in the attic but would need some time to locate them. She said she would check and get back to me. The following day, she called me back. She'd located the records which she advised, confirmed Kevin Tubbs' arrival, and pick up at their deer farm on the morning of September 11, 2001. Three days later, I received her records in the mail.

By this time, Cal had been made aware of the Tubbs sighting and the information we had so far in our efforts to corroborate what he'd seen. Joe had been meeting with Cal and Dwight regularly to keep them apprised of the new developments. Dwight called and asked to meet with me for a personal update on the situation and status of my investigation. After briefing him on all the evidence pointing towards Stewart and the pouring of the concrete floor, I had his full attention. He wanted me to continue my pursuit of anything and everything regarding Stacy Stewart.

While I was meeting with Dwight, Frank went back to reinterview Jessica Hunsinger. She was asked if she knew anything about a girl at NUCOR becoming pregnant by Chris Thomason. We learned that Lydia Monico, who still worked there, did get pregnant through her association with Thomason. Then later, after he moved back to Texas, she had a son. Monico told her she never told Chris and didn't want him to know because she was certain he would deny being the father anyway. Hunsinger said, "If you want to talk to her, you better do it soon because she's making plans to move out of state." Before ending the interview, she reiterated her four-wheeling experience with Stewart. When asked again whether it was before or after Michele went missing, she again thought it was after.

After learning from Hunsinger about Monico's relationship with Thomason, Frank wanted to try and catch up with her before she left the area. Monico was at her home in Athens, PA. She was shown the color photographs of Stewart and Thomason and recognized both as being former employees who worked at NUCOR in 2001. She said, "They were both friends and came to NY from Texas. Initially, they were both staying at the Guthrie Inn." Advising further that NUCOR placed all the out-of-state employees there and gave them up to four months to find their own place to live. She admitted dating Thomason and having slept with him twice between July and August of 2001. Later, she admitted that she did become pregnant by Thomason, and after he returned to TX, she had his son.

Regarding Stewart, she said, "He always creeped me out" but couldn't explain why. She thought it might have been just his mannerisms or the way he looked at her, then said, "It felt like he was undressing me with his eyes." She claimed she'd never been to Stacy's house in the country but did know about it. Then added, "When he first bought the place, he seemed really excited about it, and he shared his excitement with everybody."

Monico was working at the front desk when the police came to interview Stacy, Chris, and Wright. She knew from speaking with them almost daily that all three were frequent customers at Lefty's, and Michele was their favorite waitress. She added, "They always hung out together after work. And Chris and Wright used to moonlight as bouncers at a night club in Elmira, NY." When asked what kind of vehicles they drove, she recalled that Stacy drove a black pick-up, and Chris drove a big white pick-up. She knew Chris had done some time in prison in Texas but thought he was currently back working for NUCOR at their Texas plant.

When asked how it came about that they quit and went back to Texas, she said, "When they left, it came down quickly. One quit one day and the other the next." She couldn't recall who was first. She'd also heard the rumor of them breaking into another NUCOR employee's house, stealing cash and jewelry. And that they had been down to the guy's house a couple of times before that. She was quite sure the guy who was burglarized still works at NUCOR but couldn't think of his name.

During one of Frank's many interviews of people who knew or worked with Stewart, we learned a man by the name of Scott Sanford was Stewart's supervisor when he worked at NUCOR. After putting out some feelers seeking contact information about Sanford, Frank got a call back with an e-mail address for him. I drafted and sent a short e-mail message to Sanford explaining who I was and why I wanted to speak with him. Later that same day, he called me.

Sanford confirmed that he worked at NUCOR from 2001 until February of 2007. He acknowledged that Stewart was one of the workers he'd supervised. He recalled Stewart having come up from Texas with James Brent and Chris Thomason and later buying property in Lockwood. Sanford was several years older than Stewart and didn't usually socialize with him much, although he had been to his cabin a few times. Sanford stated that Stewart was, by far, his best welder and lead-rigger on his line. He claimed there were no conflicts between them other than him coming in late many times. Then he added, "Stacy was habitually late." Continuing, he explained that there were several occasions when Stewart came in as late as 9 or 10 a.m. Sanford believed his tardiness was directly related to his heavy drinking and partying lifestyle. He recalled having to call him on several occasions when he didn't show up, and he wouldn't answer his phone. Then added, "When Stacy finally showed up, he did a great job. So, as long as we got our work done and the boss was happy, I gave him a lot of slack." When asked if he'd ever 'butted heads' with him, he said, "I know what you mean, but I wouldn't call it that. Like I said, he was my best welder, and I was pretty easy going and just wanted to get the job done. At most, I may have asked him to try and get in a little earlier, but I wouldn't say we butted heads."

Sanford had always felt it strange that Stewart just up-and-quit suddenly and moved back to Texas. Then added, "Now that I think about it, there was something else I felt was pretty strange about Stacy. He would often brag about shooting and killing some guy in TX. I heard him say it a few times. He never said it directly to me, but I'd hear him say it to others." Elaborating, he said Stacy's comment was often followed by him saying, "So, don't be fuckin with me or, you better not fuck with me." Then he added, "I have no idea what it was all about, but I do remember him saying that a few times. Usually to someone who'd been giving him a hard time about something."

Later, when asked, he denied ever knowingly covering for Stewart but then admitted he didn't always look over his shoulder to see what was entered on his timecard. Then added, "These were hand-picked guys by the company. We were all on the honor system. I didn't find it necessary to be checking up on them." He did admit, however, that there may have been some cheating at times. But added, "It would be risky if you got caught because you could get fired." He, too, had heard about the NUCOR employee whose home was burglarized and that Stewart and Thomason were suspects but couldn't offer anything further.

In keeping Joe and Dwight updated with all that we were learning about Stewart and his property, they were both anxious to see the property for themselves. After getting renewed permission from Gennarelli, arrangements were made, and I drove Joe and Dwight to the Edgecomb Hill property. Frank met us there, and we led them around to see for themselves, all that we had been telling and describing to them. Gennarelli had given us permission to go inside the garage, where Joe and Dwight got their first look at the concrete floor. I explained we hadn't yet been able to confirm a date as to when the concrete was poured. However, Lisa Demtrak seemed to think it was poured after Michele went missing, and in two separate interviews with Jessica Hunsinger, she also believed that the concrete had been poured after Michele went missing.

Although the early consensus was to tear up the concrete, I suggested that there was a less invasive procedure we could do first that, depending on the results, may provide a more solid justification for tearing up the concrete. From previous experience, I had witnessed the successful use of GPR[2] scanning that was used to detect electrical conduits buried beneath the surface of finished concrete. I also knew from my research that GPR scanning had the capability of detecting other foreign objects below the surface, including human remains. We all agreed that it was a logical starting point. Joe asked me to follow-up on it.

---

1. Subpoena duces tecum: a writ ordering a person to attend a court and bring relevant documents.
2. GPR: Ground Penetrating Radar

19

CHECKING OUT KEVIN TUBBS

During a prior interview with Kevin Tubbs, he told me he and his family had permission and a contract with a man by the name of Stan Walsh, who owned the haying property. He'd also told me that Walsh lived in and ran a building supply business somewhere on Long Island. Earlier, Kevin had checked for a copy of the contract or some of their canceled checks but couldn't find any. I needed to find Walsh.

I checked the real property records at the County Clerk's Office, looking for ownership information of the haying property off Forstrom Road. Records revealed two adjoining properties totaling 170 plus acres surrounding the area described by Tubbs. Both were owned by Stan L. Walsh of Glen Oaks, NY. I was also able to identify Walsh's business as Walco-Supply in Hempstead, NY, along with a phone number. I called the listed 800 number, and Walsh answered.

Walsh confirmed that he was the owner of both Walco-Supply and the properties in Spencer, NY. He also confirmed that he knew both Kevin Tubbs and his family and that there was a signed lease granting them permission to harvest the hay crop on his property. He also advised that the Tubbs family had been harvesting hay on that same property for about two years before he owned it and then for another three years after. When asked, Walsh later found and mailed me a copy of the lease agreement.

I had been anxious to follow-up with Kevin Tubbs' story by interviewing his parents. I finally caught up to his mom, Gloria Tubbs, at her home in Candor, NY. Gloria was a pleasant middle-aged woman in her late fifties with light brown, greying hair. After laying out the Tubbs family history, the interview shifted to her son Kevin. At the time, Kevin and his son were living with her and her husband due to problems he was having with his wife, Ashley. Explaining that he had several ongoing issues with Ashley, who she believed to be mentally unstable but uncertain if there had ever been an official diagnosis. Ashley had called the police on numerous occasions, but as far as she knew, they were all unfounded.

Together with Kevin and her husband, they had been harvesting hay throughout the towns of Spencer and Candor for several years. She said, "It was a family operation. My husband Richard did the cutting, I did the raking, and Kevin did the baling and hauling. Kevin was really good with mechanical things and could operate the loader better than Richard, so that became his job."

Gloria confirmed that in 2001, Kevin was living and working out of their family's farmhouse on Straits Corners Road, while she and her husband were living on Glen Mary Drive in Owego. She said, "Originally, I was the one scheduled to haul the deer from the Valley-Hollow Deer Farm that day, but something came up, and Kevin had to do it." She was at home with her husband when 9/11 happened. She knew Kevin was traveling out of the area and called to tell him what was going on. "He told me he'd been listening on the radio," she said. When he returned around 3-4 p.m., he came to their home where he remained the rest of the afternoon and evening watching the continuing coverage of 9/11 on television.

Gloria said their family had been harvesting hay off the Walsh property for several years, including the fall of 2001. She remembered Kevin coming to her house for breakfast the next morning and the conversation they had about an incident he'd observed earlier. He'd told her about a pick-up truck sticking out into the road near the Harris property and how tight it was getting his hay-wagon passed the truck. He also mentioned seeing a young man by the pick-up with the Harris woman. "He told me the two appeared to have been having a dispute," she said. Gloria, like Kevin, didn't know Michele Harris personally. But from working in the area, on occasion, she had seen a woman wearing a bikini and riding a lawn-tractor. She learned from other neighbors that it was Michele Harris.

Just as I was finishing up with Gloria, her husband Richard came home, and I was able to speak with him for a few minutes. His story was the same, which re-affirmed what Gloria told me. He, too, heard Kevin telling the story at breakfast about his experience on Hagadorn Hill.

As I was leaving, Gloria stopped me and said, "Kevin would probably never tell you this, but I want to because it goes to his character and type of person he is."

"Please, tell me," I said.

She said, "Not long ago, there was a man here in town who was in debt to Kevin for several thousand dollars. He'd been diagnosed with an aggressive form of cancer and only had a few weeks to live. A few days later, he went into hospice care and was bedridden. When Kevin heard about it, he went to the man's bedside and told him his debt had been forgiven – the man died the next day."

I said, "Oh, wow! That does say a lot about his character, thanks for telling me."

"I just wanted you to know," she said.

20

TEAR UP THE CONCRETE

Although we could never confirm a definitive date for the pouring of concrete in Stewart's garage, our source had provided a good faith basis to believe it had been done *after* Michele went missing. Therefore, we decided it was too important to ignore, and we needed to move forward. A good way to get started was to see if we could have the floor scanned by GPR.

In that effort, I contacted and later retained the services of Geo-Rad Survey's, a GPR scanning service in Ithaca, NY. Then, with permission from current property owner Jeff Gennarelli, Frank and I cleared out the garage and prepped it for scanning. After that, Geo-Rad president William 'Bill' Perks and business partner, using their GPR scanning equipment, scanned and recorded the sub-surface imagery beneath the garage floor.

The subsequent analysis of the imagery revealed the presence of a layer of concrete reinforcing rebar about eight inches below the surface. Further down, a sizeable mass was observed that appeared to have a distinctive contrast from that of the surrounding area. Its shape was non-definitive and could not be readily explained.

After reviewing the imagery with Geo-Rad and later with Joe Cawley and Bill Easton, more discussion was held with Cal and Dwight. In a unanimous decision, we decided to move forward and tear up the concrete.

Not wanting to get too many others involved, Frank and I decided to take on the project ourselves. Frank had some prior experience with heavy equipment and made the arrangements to rent the equipment we would need. We also hired another trusted friend to help with the grunt work.

It was mid-August, and the day we chose to start was brutally hot. Frank went right to work with the jackhammer while us two grunts picked up the pieces. We examined each one carefully, before tossing them in the front-end loader to be hauled down and dumped onto a huge tarp in the side yard, to undergo further examination. We continued this process for the next few days until all the concrete had been removed from the floor.

Nothing was found in the concrete itself.

Our next step was to examine and then remove the dirt floor underneath. During the surface examination of the dirt floor, we noticed an area near the rear of the garage where the soil appeared to have been disturbed at one time. That's where we decided to start digging. We dug down manually to a depth of about thirty inches and didn't discover anything. Then, the digging started getting more difficult as we began to hit hardened deposits of clay. From there, we started to systematically dig up the remaining dirt floor. Some areas seemed to dig much easier than others, but then we started striking more hard clay deposits. When comparing the orientation of the clay deposits with the GPR imagery, we began to realize that the clay deposits were the likely source of the contrasting imagery.

After going down three feet and finding nothing, we were disappointed and discouraged but decided, if the job was worth doing, it was worth doing right. So, we dug up the entire area to a depth of six feet. Because the digging was getting progressively more difficult, we became completely satisfied that Michele had not been buried under the concrete.

As part of our written agreement with Gennarelli, we had a contractor come in to haul away the material we removed. Then, they refilled the area and poured a new concrete floor. Later, when signing the satisfaction agreement, Gennarelli said, "It's better than before."

In the weeks and months that followed, my investigation would take us back to the Edgecomb Hill property several more times. We conducted additional searches in our effort to find Michele's remains. This included that small pond in front of the cabin. I called on another

PI colleague by the name of Pat Whelan, who was a certified diver. He volunteered his services to check the pond. Other than briefly getting tangled in a few cattails, the only thing found on the bottom was some mud, a few stones, and some water-logged branches. Later efforts included digging the area under and around the old outhouse and old well.

Still nothing.

21

'330' HEARING

With the post-conviction discovery of new evidence, based on the eye-witness account of Kevin Tubbs, Joe Cawley and Bill Easton was working to prepare a new motion to file with the court. Under the provisions of the NYS Criminal Procedure Law, a motion can be made to the court under Article 330 (commonly referred to as a '330' motion) to set aside a verdict. Applicable in this matter, the provisions under Section 330.30-3 read as follows

At any time after rendition of a verdict of guilty and before sentence, the court may, upon motion of the defendant, set aside or modify the verdict or any part thereof upon the following grounds:

Sub 3: That new evidence has been discovered since the trial which could not have been produced by the defendant at the trial even with due diligence on his part and which is of such character as to create a probability that had such evidence been received at the trial the verdict would have been more favorable to the defendant.

In support of the '330' motion, they wanted to include formal affidavits from Kevin, Gloria, and Richard Tubbs. Using Kevin's previous written statement and the information from my interviews with Gloria, and Richard Tubbs, paralegal Sue Mertens drafted their tentative affidavits. After each read and reviewed their respective affidavits, only a few minor changes were necessary and made. With their final approval, I took their oaths and had them sign their affidavits. Together, they would provide the key exhibits to be attached to the motion.

I explained how their affidavits were going to be used and how it would be filed with the court very soon, which would include a copy to Keene. I gave Kevin a heads-up that a visit from the SP would be imminent. He said he understood but then asked, "Do I have to talk with them?"

I said, "No, you don't have to, but I would encourage you to do so. Just tell them what you've been telling us all along." I also told him they would probably be asking to speak to him alone and likely insist on it. I then suggested he may want to have someone with him to witness the interview. Then added, "If you'd like, I'd be more than happy to be your witness."

He said, "Good, I'd like that. I'll let you know when I hear from them."

A little over a week later, the '330' motion was finalized and filed with the court with a copy sent to Keene. I knew it wouldn't take long before things started happening. Behind the scene, in a panic, Keene would likely be on the phone with Mulvey even before he finished reading the motion. Together, they knew something would need to be done if there was any hope of salvaging Cal's conviction. Initially, they would suspect and start looking for any type of association, contact, or connection between Cal Harris and Kevin Tubbs that might point to some conspiracy of sorts. In-as-much, they would be carefully scrutinizing Tubbs' telephone, business and financial records and comparing them with Cal's. If nothing was found there, the second phase of their investigation would, or should involve a two-prong approach. First, to conduct a background investigation on Kevin Tubbs. Second, to investigate what he saw.

About one week after the '330' motion was filed, Keene filed a scathing response motion that included some vicious and libelous accusations attacking the credibility of Kevin Tubbs. In his attempt, he improperly, unprofessionally and unethically presented to the court, records that had been 'sealed' by the court regarding criminal charges against Tubbs that had been previously dismissed. He also improperly included records of another criminal matter that was still pending, knowing there were rules against doing so.

Notably, Keene admits that Kevin Tubbs, "may have developed some animosity toward the SP over the years..." He also admits that the information asserted by Tubbs "could have shed tremendous light on the investigation of this case," but added that because Tubbs sat on the information for six years and never told anyone until now, it was not credible. Interestingly, Keene also wrote, "no one from the defense team notified me or anyone in the state police of this important witness over the past two months so that we could attempt to find the 'real killer.' No, we did not. And the reason? Because of all the things he just alluded to in his attempt to discredit Tubbs.

Keene's only interest was to destroy Tubbs' credibility. With absolutely no interest in pursuing the real killer. But Keene's comment about this 'important witness' got me thinking. What if Tubbs had seen something slightly different that morning that actually supported the police theory? He would have been more than just an 'important witness' – he'd be a hero.

So briefly, let's back up to the pre-dawn hours of September 12, 2001. Tubbs is hauling his hay-wagon up Hagadorn Hill just like he said. As he approaches the Harris driveway, instead of seeing a dark pick-up truck partially blocking the road, he sees a middle-aged bald guy jumping out of a light-colored mini-van and running down the Harris driveway. Need I say more?

But as we know, that's not what happened. Because this eyewitness (Tubbs) saw something and someone other than Cal Harris, their theory would fall apart, and the only way to salvage their conviction was to turn Tubbs into a pugnacious liar. Afterward, Kevin Tubbs, along with other members of his family, were placed under the investigative microscope of the SP. Nary a single other witness, including other suspects, came remotely close to undergoing the same tyrannical level of investigative scrutiny by the SP more than Kevin Tubbs.

Here we have a young man who's trying to do the right thing. Instead of pursuing what he had seen, their only pursuit was of him, as if he was the one who killed somebody. Perhaps Shakespeare was right when he said, *"Don't like the news, then kill the messenger."*

We were grateful that Kevin Tubbs decided to make his revelations known to the defense first. If he had gone to the SP first, they would have likely shown him the door. Rather quickly too. But not before calling him a liar, telling him to keep his mouth shut and threatening him with arrest. After that, the defense and the rest of the world would never have heard the likes of Kevin Tubbs.

Judge Smith, having received and reviewed the motions, ordered a hearing on the matter with instructions for both sides to have witnesses available to offer testimony. With less than two days' notice before the hearing, we had to scramble to subpoena and prepare our witnesses. Accordingly, the night before the hearing, Bill Easton and I met with Kevin Tubbs and his parents to prep them for their testimony. Kevin, knowing that Bill and I would be there, scheduled his interview with Investigator Myers and asked us to be present.

We had just finished preparing our witnesses when Myers arrived to interview Kevin. He appeared somewhat surprised when he saw that Bill and I were there, and as expected, asked to interview Kevin alone. Kevin quickly spoke up on his own and said, "I would prefer that they be present." Not ready to relinquish control, Myers repeated his request to interview Kevin alone two more times. Each time, Kevin politely yet firmly continued his refusal and would only agree to the interview in our presence. Myers had no choice but to cave-in and conduct the interview in our presence. Albeit reluctantly, he did take Kevin's written statement, which was entirely consistent with what he'd been telling us all along.

The following morning, an open-court hearing was held before Judge Smith to address the '330' motion. I met Kevin and his parents as they arrived at the courthouse and escorted them into the witness waiting room. Since none of them had ever testified in court before, I gave them a brief heads-up as to what to expect. I then stayed with them until they had each been called in separately to offer their testimony. Kevin was up first, followed by Gloria, then Richard.

After Kevin completed his testimony, he returned to the waiting area, and Gloria was called right in. I took the opportunity to speak with him. He'd repeated his story the same way he told us all along and said, "But Keene was trying to discredit me by trying to use things from my past he shouldn't have."

"Like what?" I asked.

"Like some of the stuff I'd been charged with but were later dismissed, but the judge stopped him and told him he couldn't use that stuff. The judge said what he was doing was inappropriate."

I said, "Well, it was inappropriate, but remember, Keene's desperate, and he'll use any means available to try and discredit you. But I'm glad the judge sees it that way too." I really wanted to be in the court-room myself, but I knew it was vital for me to remain with our witnesses to ensure there was no outside influence or intimidation before they testified. I could get the details from Joe and Bill later. Gloria and Richard completed their testimony without too much fanfare, and both had helped to corroborate their son.

I never got to see Cal who had been brought to the hearing in his orange jail jump-suit and quickly whisked away right after.

But I caught up with Joe and Bill outside, and we spoke briefly. They both felt Kevin and his parents had done exceptionally well. They explained how Smith admonished Keene for trying to use sealed court records against Kevin, calling Keene's actions "egregious."

"Keene was fumbling badly," Joe said. More importantly, they added, Smith didn't see any motive for them (Tubbs') to fabricate evidence and found their testimony "entirely credible."

"We feel good about that," Joe said. Then added, "Smith is reserving his decision and giving both sides time to submit final written arguments, but with the way it went today, we're feeling confident."

Not surprisingly, *Binghamton Press & Sun-Bulletin* reporter Nancy Dooling had covered the hearing, and the next day's headline read, *"Harris case Judge: New Testimony 'entirely credible'"* with the sub-headline, *"Slaying sentencing postponed indefinitely."* In her article, Dooling reiterated what I learned from Joe and Bill. Under direct examination, Kevin Tubbs had laid out his entire story. Dooling described how Smith prohibited Keene from using any criminal information against Tubbs that had been illegally obtained from court records previously sealed by a judge. Then Dooling quoted Judge Smith when he said, "That's pretty egregious – as you know. There are very few things that can be more inappropriate than that."

Dooling also described how Tubbs explained the reason he told Joe Cawley his information was with the hope he could use it or pass it along to someone else in the case. He didn't want to get involved or have to be in a courtroom. Then, when questioned by Keene said, "Do you think I want to be here? Do you think I want my name in today's paper?" She then described how Tubbs explained why he didn't intend to tell the state police what he saw. Claiming their only response to him would be, "shut up," because he'd filed a civil suit against them previously. Dooling also reiterated what Joe told me about Smith's ruling that Tubbs' testimony was "entirely credible." She went on to say that

Smith added, "I don't see a motive for their fabricating evidence." He also pointed out that Tubbs' testimony was the only piece of direct evidence in the case. All the evidence presented at trial against Calvin Harris had been circumstantial. She ended her article by saying Judge Smith must now decide whether today's testimony would have changed the verdict had it been presented during the Harris murder trial.

22

CONTINUING CONFLICT

A little over two weeks after the '330' hearing, a Letter to the Editor appeared in the Viewpoints section of the *Press & Sun-Bulletin*, under the title, *"Credible Judgment."* I read the letter initially but never paid much attention to it. It had obviously been written by someone who was not pleased with Judge Smith's decision after the hearing. It was signed by a woman from Vestal, NY, by the name of Candi Phelps. Like all other case-related articles that appeared in the news, I copied the letter and filed it away. It read as follows:

On the day of the Tioga County businessman Calvin Harris sentencing for the murder of his wife, Michelle, Judge Martin Smith allowed defense attorney Joseph Cawley to present a surprise witness, one Kevin Tubbs. Tubbs claimed to have seen Michelle Harris the morning after she disappeared. Following this testimony, Judge Smith, in a TV interview, declared Tubbs was an "entirely credible" witness.

Calvin Harris was convicted after a trial with testimony from several law enforcement personnel, expert witnesses, and family members of the accused and deceased. Never once during or after that trial did Judge Smith ever declare anyone of those witnesses "entirely credible."

A few weeks later, Dwight Harris called me after receiving a call and speaking to a family friend by the name of Lexi Hunter. According to Dwight, Hunter explained how she was close friends with a woman by the name of Sheila Mosher, who was the mother of the letter writer, Candi Phelps. Hunter told Dwight that while speaking with Mosher, she learned that her daughter Candi, had signed the letter that appeared in the *Press & Sun-Bulletin,* but she was *not* the author. When Dwight inquired if she knew who the author was, she said, "Well, that's why I'm calling you. She told me it was John Andrews."

Dwight provided Hunter's contact information, and I told him I would check into it. I called Hunter right away, and she confirmed everything she told Dwight. Prior to calling Hunter, she had spoken to her friend Sheila Mosher again, who had told her she was concerned about what happened and was willing to speak to me about it.

I wanted to do a face-to-face with Mosher, so I drove right to her house and found her home. She was expecting me and invited me in. She confirmed her friendship and conversations with Lexi Hunter and that Candi Phelps was her daughter. Continuing, she explained how her daughter Candi had been approached by John Andrews with a letter he had written and asked her to submit it using her name. Wanting to be helpful but without giving it much thought, Candi signed it and sent it. Later, she became concerned and realized it wasn't right. Mosher had only learned of this after the fact when she saw her daughter's name in the paper and questioned her about it. She said, "I knew something wasn't right because it didn't sound like anything Candi would have written. Then, about three weeks later, Candi brought home a second letter written by Andrews. Candi showed it to me but said she felt uncomfortable signing another one and asked me if I would sign it. I refused."

Learning that John Andrews had authored the Viewpoints letter then cowardly conned Candi Phelps into signing and submitting it for him came as no real surprise. But why? He was undoubtedly entitled to offer his opinion in a letter to the editor. And the letter itself made it rather obvious that the author was interested in and had been following the Harris case very closely.

However, as we've already learned, there was some mutual and long-standing bad blood between John Andrews and Cal Harris. Considering his animus towards Cal, and the fact that his own daughter, Sue 'Andrews' Mulvey, was the lead investigator, he knew there was a conflict. However, he couldn't resist the urge to be heard. So much so, that he authored a second letter. But it was rather quickly shut down by the same young girl he'd conned into signing his first letter. She refused to do it again. Good for her.

Considering John Andrews' ongoing and continued backdoor involvement, I couldn't help wondering whether the letter-writing was of his own volition? Or, was it being orchestrated behind the scenes by his daughter, Sue Mulvey? It would have been no real surprise to me if I were to learn that she was the one writing the letters. Perhaps, it's true, "The apple doesn't fall far from the tree."

23

KEVIN TUBBS – CONTINUED

By now, the SP, under the direction of Mulvey and Keene, was scrambling behind the scenes to dig up anything and everything they could on Kevin Tubbs or his family in their ongoing effort to discredit them. In time, I was sure I would learn more about their efforts. My concern was whether they would ever stop investigating Kevin Tubbs and start investigating what he saw. Disappointed but not surprised, I'd soon learn that my fear was valid.

Less than three days after the '330' hearing, Keene filed with the court, his request for a 30-day extension to investigate 'numerous issues' raised during the hearing. Ostensibly, this could lay the ground-work for Keene to request a re-opening of the hearing. Moreover, this was above and beyond the original one week granted by Judge Smith for the submission of final arguments. After receiving and reviewing Keene's request, Joe and Bill responded with their own letter to Smith, respectfully objecting to any extension or potential re-opening of the hearing. In Keene's request, no reference was made as to what the 'numerous issues' were, which he contended would justify the extension.

Briefly, Joe reiterated what transpired during the hearing and that Keene had initially taken the position that no hearing was necessary, and the motion could be decided on the papers. Furthermore, when the court indicated it was going to proceed with the hearing, Keene made neither a request for an adjournment nor a protest that he didn't have adequate opportunity to investigate either the witness or his claims. Joe also pointed out that Keene had the opportunity to call witnesses during the hearing but elected not to, even after the court painstakingly advised him of that opportunity. Then, once the proof was declared by the court to be closed, Keene offered no objection. In further support of denying the extension, Joe argued, "It is painfully transparent that Mr. Keene's planned 'investigation' has little to do with the evidence offered by the witness, but instead is directed at discrediting the witness himself."

Later, when referring to Keene's improper use of Tubbs' sealed court records during the hearing, Joe added,

> He (Keene) was apparently confident that he could destroy the witness' credibility by libelous attacks on his character and by furnishing the court with sealed court records regarding criminal charges which were dismissed. Only now, after the court has properly rejected that evidence and found the witnesses to be credible, does Mr. Keene suddenly need additional time to investigate.

24

RE-VISIT HAGADORN HILL

T he sixth-anniversary of Michele's disappearance was almost here. I met with Dwight Harris and Frank Roney to finalize our plans to revisit the scene at the end of the Harris driveway. We had previously discussed our intent to revisit the end of the driveway on Hagadorn Hill Road in the pre-dawn hours, on/or about September 12th, to document the scene around the same time as described by Kevin Tubbs.

Ideally, I would have preferred doing this right on September 12th. However, knowing that the SP would likely be doing the same thing, I had no interest in butting heads with them. Besides, for our purpose, the exact day was not essential. Therefore, in the alternative, to avoid any conflict, we decided to do our thing the next day.

Well before daylight, we all met in Smithboro on September 13th and completed our plans. I mounted my video camera on the dashboard of Frank's pick-up truck. Dwight was interested in knowing what he would be able to see once he got to the driveway, so he rode with Frank. I left first and drove to the end of the driveway, and positioned my vehicle in the approximate location of where Tubbs observed the dark pick-up truck jutting out into the road. Kevin had also described a young man wearing blue jeans and a white T-shirt standing near the right-rear fender of the truck. Dressed similarly, I positioned myself accordingly.

I notified Frank by two-way radio when I was ready. Then instructed him to start video-recording once he reached Forstrom Road. I also reminded him that once my vehicle was in sight, to start slowing down and just before reaching my vehicle, slow to a crawl as he drove by, to try and simulate what Tubbs had done. Frank followed my instructions, and we repeated the process four times between 5:30 and 6:00 a.m. During the final segment, the first signs of civil twilight could be seen in the East. Speaking briefly with Frank and Dwight between each segment, both said they could clearly see me and easily recognize my features as they drove by. Later, when re-playing the video segments, I could clearly recognize myself and the vehicle. Interestingly, both Frank and Dwight said that viewing it with their own eyes was even clearer than the video.

25

KEENE'S NEW MOTION

Judge Smith was growing tired of Keene's whining and continued legal manipulation of the court and the law to try and gain the advantage. But to avoid the possibility of any legal fallout, he reluctantly approved Keene's request for the 30-day extension. Then three weeks later, it was no real surprise to learn that Keene had filed a formal motion to reopen the hearing.

One of his many bizarre claims was to challenge Tubbs' ability to see. He said that because of the limited, pre-dawn lighting conditions, Tubbs would not have been unable to see what he claims to have seen. He wrote the following

> *On the morning of September 12, 2007, the New York State Police videotaped the amount of daylight on Hagadorn Hill Road from 4:15 a.m. until 6:30 a.m. which clearly shows the lighting at 5:30 a.m. was not sufficient for the witness to make the detailed observations he claims to have made on September 12, 2001.*

He also said he would offer the video for the court's review if the hearing was reopened.

After reading this, my first thoughts went immediately to my own video, and I asked myself, "How can that be? Why would their video be any different than mine?" If anything, with their resources and equipment, it should be better. I was anxious to see this video Keene said he would make available, and a bit dumbfounded in my attempt to understand the discrepancies between the two videos. I assumed they had done their video the same way we had, by positioning a vehicle and a person at the end of the driveway, and videotaping it as they drove by.

Then it hit me. What if they had not done that but instead just videotaped the natural lighting conditions without the use of head-lights? Nah – that wouldn't make any sense. Why would they do that? It was not like Tubbs would have been driving up a remote dirt road in the dark without his headlights on. Again, it made no sense. I would soon have an answer.

When their video was finally turned over, I anxiously reviewed it. I couldn't believe what I saw as I rolled my eyes and shook my head in disbelief. I didn't know whether to laugh, cry, or pound my fist on the table. I may have done all three. Moreover, I was more disappointed than angry. A proper re-enactment would have either confirmed or disputed Tubbs' scenario. Apparently, that was a risk they were not willing to take. There was a conscious decision not to do that. They dumped the more logical and intelligent plan by replacing it with a rather dumb plan that served no legitimate purpose whatsoever. The video showed that for more than two hours, they sat in a van across from the Harris driveway, videotaping the dark night.

Did they even realize how ridiculous that was? They may as well have left the lens cap on the camera. For all I know, that's what they did. If this was their way of trying to discredit what Tubbs saw, they should be ashamed of themselves. Was this the professional and responsible thing to do? And do I really need to ask the question? Whose idea was this anyway? As I stated before, this was not the SP that I knew.

Joe had written another scathing response to Keene's motion. Tearing it apart by stating it was filled with multiple inaccuracies and mischar-acterizations of the facts. He pointed out once again how Keene had not utilized the considerable resources available to him to develop any further leads from the newly discovered evidence offered by Kevin Tubbs, but rather to investigate Mr. Tubbs himself. Joe slammed Keene when reminding the court of his attempt to 'poison this court's opinion of Kevin Tubbs by introducing documents about an unrelated civil dispute, and implying that Tubbs' actions were criminal in nature.

In summing up with the court, Joe made some final points. With respect to Kevin Tubbs, he said, "I cannot help but wonder how many of us could undergo that kind of scrutiny and not come out looking worse for it." Then added, "So thorough was their investigation, that it appears to have exceeded the investigation undertaken by the same agency with respect to certain potential suspects in the case. One would think that Mr. Tubbs was a suspect, rather than a disinterested witness." Then, in conclusion, his words read as if he's raising his voice saying, "Notwithstanding the investigative efforts put forth by the state police and the prosecutor, not a single shred of evidence has been offered which would suggest any motive on the part of Kevin Tubbs to fabricate this story."

After the original hearing, Smith had given both sides three days to file their final arguments with a plan to make his decision within a week. However, with all the back-and-forth letters and motions, it was now a month later. But everything was in the hands of Smith for his review and ultimate decision. Considering all the new information, we had no idea how long it would take for his decision this time. In the meantime, there was still more work to do.

STACY STEWART – CONTINUED

During some of our interviews with those who knew or had worked with Stacy Stewart and Chris Thomason, we were given the names Nick and Nancy Gilbert, who were husband and wife. We learned Nick worked at NUCOR and knew both Stewart and Thomason. His wife, Nancy, worked at the Candlelite Lounge and knew them also. Our information was that the Gilbert's home had been burglarized. Cash and jewelry had been taken, and Stewart and Thomason were the believed suspects. Obviously, we wanted to learn more about this, so I asked Frank to interview the Gilberts. Before doing that, I wanted him to re-interview Stewart's ex-girlfriend, Lisa Demtrak, to see what, if anything, she knew about the Gilberts or the burglary. I was also interested whether Demtrak had been contacted by the SP since the 'horse was out of the barn,' so to speak.

Frank re-interviewed Demtrak at her apartment. She had recently read the news article about the hearing and recognized Stacy Stewart's name. She also advised that she had been contacted by telephone three times by Investigator Mike Myers. She informed Myers of her interviews with us, then said, "He was very interested to learn what I was asked during my interview." According to Demtrak, Myers said, "Those guys are just private investigators trying to throw a wrench into the case. We're the police." She then asked Frank what she could tell

Myers. He encouraged her to tell him everything she knew that could help them.

As the interview shifted to any knowledge of the Gilbert burglary, she recognized the names of Nick and Nancy Gilbert because Stacy had mentioned and talked about them. She said, "Nick worked at NUCOR with Stacy, and Nancy had befriended him at the Candlelite bar in Athens." Stacy had often talked about Nancy as somewhat of a mother-like figure he would go to for advice. She also recalled hearing the rumor of the Gilbert burglary and that Stacy and Chris may have done it.

After his interview with Demtrak, Frank headed down to Ulster, PA, to find the Gilberts. It was early evening when he found them at home. After identifying himself and his purpose, the Gilberts both agreed to be interviewed. Frank started by showing them the photographs of Stewart and Thomason. They readily recognized both.

Nancy spoke about her relationship with Stewart. She'd first met him at the Candlelite Lounge, where she worked as a bartender. She learned from her husband Nick, that Stewart worked with him at NUCOR. Nick jumped in and said, "I've worked there since they first started." According to Nancy, Stacy would call her almost every day. Other times, he would often show up at the Candlelite just to talk or ask for her advice. Nancy said, "I liked the kid, so I kind of took him under my wing to help him out with some of his personal and financial matters." Nick added that both he and Stacy were welders at NUCOR. Then recalled how several men had been recruited from around the country to help start up the new NUCOR plant. He specifically recalled Stewart and Thomason coming up from Texas.

Shortly into the interview, Nick made it clear that he was not fond of either of them, believing they were the ones responsible for burglar-izing his home. Nancy jumped in and said, "It was our elderly neighbor (now deceased) who witnessed the burglary." He'd described the pair and Stacy's pick-up truck, including a bumper sticker on the driver's side rear with red lettering and white background that read, *"You are Folloween a Red Neck."* Continuing on, Nancy described her jewelry that had been taken, which was worth approximately $200 to $300. A small amount of US currency ($60 to $70) had also been taken.

From the neighbor's description, they knew immediately it was Stewart and Thomason with Stewart's truck. He'd also seen an ATV in the back of the truck − a green one, he thought. He watched them back-kick the front door and then heard a loud snapping sound as the door swung open, and they went inside. Nick said, "The door wasn't even locked. They didn't need to kick it in."

Nancy added, "The most bizarre thing was when one of the pieces of my stolen jewelry turned up in a mail package that was delivered to the Candlelite Lounge." At work one day, her boss handed her an envelope that was addressed to her, in care of the Candlelite. It had a Texas postmark. Opening the package, she immediately recognized the jewelry inside. It was her gold bracelet that had been stolen. It had great sentimental value since it was the only gift her brother, now in prison, had ever given her. She further added, "After the burglary, I let everyone know how pissed I was about the theft, especially my bracelet." In anger, she got on the phone and called Stewart's cousin Angela Brent and girlfriend, Lisa Demtrak, to tell them what happened and how pissed she was. Then added, "One of them must have called to tell him how pissed I was and convinced him to return it."

Nick said, "I called the state police to report the burglary, but no one ever responded to investigate." They explained that the reason police ignored their complaint was that Nancy's brother was in state prison on charges of burglary and possession of stolen property. Nancy explained further that during the investigation of her brother, police had accused her of harboring him as a fugitive, which she adamantly denied.

When asked, Nancy knew about Stacy's house on Edgecomb Hill Road, and she'd been there a few times. She described it as a small log cabin with a fireplace. Then added, "There was an outbuilding (barn), where Stacy and Chris stored their four-wheelers." She was quite sure that Chris had a red one, and Stacy's was green. They often rode on extended trails behind Stacy's property.

Before ending the interview, Frank asked if either of them could think of anything else that might be helpful for us to know? Nancy said, "I almost forgot to tell you. There was one other thing taken during the burglary. Stacy had trouble managing his money, and I'd been trying to help him with his finances. So, I was keeping a small folder with his name on it that contained most, if not all, his financial dealings. His phone and electric bills were in there, and I think a bill for some furniture he bought. That folder was also taken."

As a final question, Frank asked, "How would Stacy and Chris have known where you lived?" Both answering at once advised that Chris and Stacy had been to their home on at least two occasions. They specifically recalled inviting and having them over for Thanksgiving dinner. There had also been at least one other time but could not recall the specific occasion. Later, Nancy added, "I'm thinking it was either Christmas or New Years. One of those." Nick said, "Yeah, and we felt sorry for these guys because they were single and far away from their families, so we invited them to share Thanksgiving dinner with us, and they turn around and steal from us. Go figure."

27

ASHLEY TUBBS

During one of my many interviews with Kevin Tubbs, he had learned and told me that the SP had been interviewing his wife, Ashley. He said, "I have no idea what she might be telling them, but whatever it is, it's probably not the truth." He further added that Ashley was not well educated, was easily influenced, and could break into a wild tirade in a heartbeat. He described the prior as well as ongoing issues he was having with her, including several false accusations against him in her effort to gain custody of their son. He explained how she'd lost custody of her other two children from a previous marriage due to her mental health issues. She had also made false accusations against her ex-husband. He said, "There's a ton of records on file about all this. Not just unfounded accusations but her lack of credibility as well." Then added, "You should pull the records and see for yourself." Even though Ashley's mental health issues were readily apparent, he did not believe she had ever been officially diagnosed.

Before attempting to speak with Ashley, I wanted to learn more about these issues Kevin was telling me about. I traveled to Windham, PA, and interviewed her ex-husband. After explaining the situation, he said, "Come on in. I'll tell you about the ten-years of hell Ashley put me through." Like Kevin, he, too, described Ashley as having serious mental health and credibility issues. Many of which involved numerous false accusations during the custody battle over their two children. He said, "You really need to go and look at the Family Court records at the County Clerk's Office to see for yourself." Then added, "It's nearly unprecedented for a father to win custody over a mother around here, but I now have full custody of my two sons. Ashley's only allowed supervised visitation." I left him my card and asked him to call if he could think of anything further. As I was leaving, he stopped me and said, "Just so you know, I'm not a big fan of Kevin Tubbs, but I do feel sorry for him because I know what he's going through."

Since I was already in PA, I decided to check to see what records I could find at the Bradford County Clerk's Office. Having little experience with Family Court records in PA, I didn't know what to expect. Surprisingly, the records I sought and requested were public and freely provided for my review. And it didn't take me long to find what I was looking for. There were numerous records of various court proceedings involving the custody battles between Ashley and her ex. Just as he had told me, several court records were documenting her unfounded complaints against her ex. But more importantly, there was a single court document signed by the presiding judge, who made specific and undeniable reference to Ashley's lack of credibility. Pay-dirt. I selected the pertinent documents from the file and had them copied and certified.

Meanwhile, Ashley had asked Kevin to come to her house to discuss visitation for their son. When he arrived, there was an alleged argument followed by an accusation of assault. Ashely had called the police and had Kevin arrested. Later, I identified and interviewed a teenage girl by the name of Brandi Sprague, who had witnessed everything. Ashley's accusations against Kevin were once again false. More on this later.

28

A STEWART CONFIDANT

I asked Frank to set up another interview with Nancy Gilbert because I wanted to meet her myself to learn what more she could tell us about Stewart and Thomason. We already knew she was somewhat of a confidant, who claimed to have taken Stewart under her wing – taking an almost mother-like role. Nancy usually worked evenings at the Candlelite Lounge, but her mornings were typically free, so she agreed to meet with us mid-morning, at a nearby restaurant in Sayre. Nancy was several years older than Stacy. She was about five-foot-seven, heavy-set, with medium-length brown curly hair. She had worked as a bartender for several years. It was no surprise when we met that she came across as being 'street-smart' and a no-nonsense type of woman.

To start, we talked a little more about Stacy's cabin in the woods and her knowledge of the four-wheelers. She remembered that both Stacy and Chris kept their four-wheelers in the detached garage. She also remembered that one of them had a yellow dirt bike. As we talked about the house, she recalled that all of Stacy's furniture was green, and she had been with him when he purchased it from a wholesale furniture outlet. She said, "I don't think he ever paid for the furniture." Then added, "Stacy was making good money, but he had lousy credit, and I was trying to help him with that. I remember him trying to get cable TV but was denied. So, most of the time, he'd just rent porno movies from Blockbuster Video." When asked if he had a hunting license, she said, "I think maybe, because I do know he had several guns."

I then re-opened the matter about the burglary of their home and the return of the jewelry. She explained that the burglary occurred on the same day Stacy and Chris moved back to Texas. According to their neighbor, it was sometime between 10 and 10:30 a.m. Shortly after that, she had seen Stacy and Chris drive by the Candlelite Lounge. She said, "Chris was driving a U-Haul truck towing his white pick-up, and Stacy was following in his own pick-up. I saw his green four-wheeler in the back. But I guess we now know why they never even stopped in to say good-bye." She'd learned of the burglary from her husband Nick, who'd discovered the busted front-door frame and that things were stolen when he arrived home from work.

We discussed the rumor that Stacy, Chris, and Wright Childers were with Michele Harris on the night she disappeared. Wanting to learn a little more about Wright Childers, we asked, "What can you tell us about Wright?" Nancy said, "Wright was a big body-builder, a big guy, about six-foot-four and probably weighed about 260. He was bald and had a couple of moles on his face. He was a little older and wasn't really like Stacy or Chris, but he did hang out with them." She thought he was originally from Alabama and returned there after having a bad accident with his Jeep. She'd never seen him after his accident but heard he might have suffered a brain injury and experienced some memory loss.

Nancy recalled that at times, she would see Stacy out socially at other bars, recalling specifically having seen him in the Night-Train Lounge at the Guthrie Inn several times. She remembered one night in particular when he'd pointed out Michele, who she only knew at the time as the 'cute blonde' from Lefty's. She said, "I can still remember when I first saw her. I'd cautioned Stacy, telling him he'd better be careful. She looked like high-maintenance." Later, she added, "You know, now that I think about it before Michele Harris went missing, Stacy's 'cute blonde' from Lefty's was a fairly frequent topic of conversation. That's all he ever wanted to talk about. I mean, I knew he was attracted to her, but over time it seemed like his attraction had grown into an obsession. But after she went missing, whenever her name came up, his expression would change, and he'd quickly change the subject – didn't want to talk about her."

We also learned that Stacy and Chris spent a lot of time at Bare Facts, an adult gentleman's club that featured totally nude dancers. Nancy thought Wright might have gone there also. They would take the girls (strip-dancers) from Bare Facts to Stacy's cabin in the woods to party. She felt the owner of Bare Facts might remember them and possibly identify the girls who were working there at that time. Continuing, we asked if Stacy had ever talked about killing anyone? She said, "It's funny you say that, because I do remember sometime between Thanksgiving and Christmas that year, him saying he had shot and killed someone in Texas." She also remembered his follow-up comment right after when he said, "So, you better not fuck with me." Believing he was just joking around, she simply brushed it off as some macho tough-guy talk.

> Author's Note: Later, it was learned that Stewart had, in fact, shot and killed a man in TX when he was a juvenile, which he claimed was later ruled to be self-defense.

Nancy told us more about Stacy's financial problems and learned that he was in danger of having his truck re-possessed as of January of 2002. We then turned to Lisa Demtrak and what more she could tell us about her. She knew Stacy was dating her because he would talk about her often, as well. But most times, it was to complain about her trying to be too possessive. "He'd even asked me one time if me or some of my friends could go and beat her up," she said. Stacy had also talked about one of the dancers at Bare Facts he identified as Sheena Reynolds, who used the stage name of "Chastity." He'd been taking her up to his cabin. Furthermore, his cousin Angela and another girl who cuts his hair were meeting and bringing guys to party at the cabin.

After our first couple of interviews with Nancy Gilbert, it was apparent we had generated some renewed interest in Stacy Stewart, and she was trying to help. We didn't know it at the time, but after our interviews with her, she had been giving a lot more thought about what she knew about Stewart and Thomason and began writing things down. Our talks about Stewart's cabin in the woods had also prompted her to draw a diagram of the cabin from memory. During one of our final interviews, she turned over her notes and diagram. Even after more than five years, her diagram of Stewart's cabin was remarkably accurate.

In her notes, she described being at an anniversary party at The Barge in Athens, PA, and remembered Thomason being there. She noted that Chris had always given her the creeps and she never liked the way he looked at her. "It was like his eyes always looked as if they had no soul, and it seemed like he was undressing me with his eyes," she wrote. Where have we heard that before? It gave her the chills that would cause her to back away from him. She recalled Stewart showing up that night as well.

There was another time she felt was right after Halloween, when she and her husband had gone out with Stacy and ended up spending the night at his cabin. She remembered the guys grilling steaks and later watching a movie. She had also attended a Christmas gathering at James and Angela Brent's house, and Stacy was there. He and James had a falling out earlier, but by Christmas, they had made up. She remembered the guys shot craps all night and Wright Childers being there playing with the kids. That following week, Stacy went out with her and Nick for New Year's Eve, and he (Stacy) spent the night at their house.

At the end of her notes, Nancy included some of her personal thoughts, where she described Stacy as quiet, troubled, and ball-less. Whereas Chris was loud, showy, creepy, and enough balls for both him and Stacy. Her notes ended by describing Lisa Demtrak as being possessive, and a stalker looking for a 'sugar daddy,' who liked younger guys but was very jealous of other women.

29

PRESS INTEREST IN STEWART

Precisely four months had passed since Cal's conviction. When I opened my copy of the *Press & Sun-Bulletin* newspaper, I was surprised to read the headline, *"Texas man fits witness' description in Harris case,"* with the sub-headline, *"Steelworker, vehicle match claim of roadside sighting."* In the article, co-authored by Nancy Dooling and Brian Liberatore, they described how a steelworker, identified as Stacy Stewart, had initially been treated as a 'person of interest,' but had been cleared by the SP six years earlier. It was evident that Dooling and Liberatore had been doing their homework regarding Stewart. Certainly, much more than the SP were doing.

Several things they discovered during their investigation, mirrored those of my own. For the article, Dooling had interviewed SP Captain Mark Lester, who told her that Stewart had been eliminated as a suspect early in the investigation. Interestingly, when asked whether state police investigators ever searched Stewart's property in 2001 or more recently due to the recent revelations, Lester declined to comment. Can't comment? Why? Either you did or you didn't. That was a legitimate question. Dooling had also been reviewing court records and found one of Joe Cawley's documents where he referred to Keene's withholding of Stewart's polygraph, claiming it was a violation of trial procedure. Also, in the article, reference was made of a phone call Dooling placed to Stewart in Texas. She spoke with a woman who identified herself as Stewart's mother, who refused to let her speak with Stacy.

Interestingly, she did tell Dooling that her son had willfully taken and passed a polygraph test, as did ten of his co-workers. He'd also told her that the police set up surveillance around his house. According to the police leads and what I had learned so far, none of this was true. Near the end of the article, they wrote how Cawley had accused Keene in court papers of failing to pursue the new leads offered by Tubbs. Keene, in response, said the state police exhaustively investigated Tubbs' lead. He said, "There didn't seem to be a motive" for Stewart to have killed Michele Harris. I just rolled my eyes and shook my head in disgust. Finding it hard to believe he just said that. An 'exhaustive' investigation? 'Didn't seem to be a motive?' Indeed.

30

MEETING WITH SP

E ven though my investigation into Stacy Stewart and Chris Thomason was still in its infancy and a work in progress, evidence of their possible involvement was mounting. Both Stewart and his vehicle fit Tubbs' description, and Stewart had been an early suspect in the case due to his relationship with Michele at Lefty's and elsewhere. From my perspective, that was not just a coincidence. Moreover, when Stewart was first questioned by the SP, he lied about what time he went to work on September 12th. The fact that he purchased his cabin shortly before Michele went missing, never made the first payment, and later abandoned it altogether, was clearly a red-flag. Also, his friends and coworkers had described his close relationship with Thomason, his heavy drinking, and habitual tardiness at work.

We had also learned from Jessica Hunsinger that Stewart began asking questions and was acting nervous after his interview with the police. He had called in sick a couple of times around the time Michele went missing. Yet notably, there were no entries on any of Stewart's self-written timecards, indicating that he'd called in sick. Nor were there any entries of him starting work at 4-5:00 a.m.

Frank and I had already learned a great deal about Stewart and Thomason from our interviews with Lisa Demtrak and Nancy Gilbert. With their continued cooperation, I was confident we would learn even more. When considering everything collectively, including the recent revelation from Nancy Gilbert about the burglary of her home and the subsequent return of a sentimental piece of jewelry, Stewart and Thomason had officially jumped well ahead of Brian Earley on my suspect leaderboard.

Shortly after first making the connection between Stewart and what Tubbs had seen, I was tempted to alert the SP. I thought back to what Sr. Investigator Skinner told me during the early part of the investigation – that if I were to develop any information about a suspect, they would take the lead to follow-up on it. What was preventing me now was the fact that Cal had already been convicted. I feared that presenting them with the information now would not be well received. So, before deciding whether I wanted to do that, I would first conduct my own investigation to learn more.

Though, as I continued my investigation and the more I learned about Stewart, the more tempted I became to share my information with the SP. Since Tubbs first came forward with his revelation, I'd spent the next four months investigating anything and everything related to Stewart. With all the lies and other noteworthy revelations discovered regarding Stewart, my suspicion that he was somehow involved or responsible for Michele's disappearance, was growing rapidly. Yet, I was still struggling with whether to go to the SP or not. Why? Because there was a serious clash between my optimism and pessimism while wondering, "Will they do the right thing and take the lead to follow-up on Stewart? Or will everything fall on deaf ears?"

When speaking with Joe, I expressed my interest and my concerns about sharing the results of my investigation into Stewart with the SP. Joe's first response was, "You know these guys better than I do, what do you think they'll do?"

I said, "That's just it, I don't know for sure. On the one hand, I want to believe they'll take the lead on this, but on the other hand, they could show me the door."

Joe then made a good point that none of the information I had regarding Stewart pertained to Cal in any way. So, if I limited my information to only what I learned about Stewart, there would be no potential harm to Cal.

I said, "Well, there's no reason to include Cal in any of this. It's all about Stewart."

Joe said, "As long as that's understood, I don't have a problem with you talking to them about Stewart. I'll leave that up to you, but if you decide to do that, let me know how it goes."

"Absolutely, you'll be the first to know," I said.

I pondered my dilemma for several more days before making my decision. I remained skeptical but decided I really didn't have anything to lose. Besides, there may be an advantage in this for me as well. I might just get a better feel for or understanding of their thought process. If I were going to do this, I would need to speak with one of the senior Investigators. I would have preferred talking to Skinner, but he had since retired. My other choices were Sue Mulvey or Les Hyman. Since I had no interest in speaking with Mulvey, my only option was Hyman. We had worked several years together as uniform troopers and later, for several more years in the Narcotics Unit. We'd always had a good working rapport. I contacted the major crimes unit and spoke with Hyman, expressing my desire to meet and speak with him. When he inquired about my purpose, I briefly summarized some of my concerns about Stewart. He agreed to meet with me, and arrangements were made to talk with him the next day at the SP Owego barracks.

When I arrived at the barracks the next morning, I was met at the door by Hyman. We briefly greeted each other, and he invited me in. I assumed we would have an informal discussion in the BCI office, but instead, he escorted me into the polygraph room, which is also used for interrogation. Upon entering, Mulvey was sitting there waiting. I thought, "Oh, no, this is not going to go well." My first thought after that was to just turn around and walk out. But then decided, "No, I want to see how this plays out." But if things didn't go well, I could always leave whenever.

As we sat down in the polygraph room, we started to engage in some small talk, at which time I asked if our conversation was being recorded? I was told no. But I'm thinking, "Ok, they must think I'm a fool." I knew damn well they were recording; otherwise, we would have met in the BCI office. For my limited purpose, I was not at all concerned about being recorded, but knowing I'd just been lied to was troubling, putting me on alert.

Hyman and I did most of the talking for the next few minutes as we reminisced a bit before turning to the matter at hand. I explained in detail how I had taken the information revealed by Tubbs and made the connection to Stacy Stewart through one of their own early leads. I further explained that other than Stewart, I was unable to link any of the other suspects to the dark-colored pick-up truck described by Tubbs. I went on to disclose all the concerning issues about Stewart that I'd developed over the past four months. Continuing on, I explained how we learned that Stewart had taken a polygraph, yet there was no lead, and when we finally did get the lead, it was incomplete.

I told them how we had spoken with NUCOR's Safety Director, who had taken Stewart for his polygraph, and only waited about forty-five minutes to an hour. Mulvey quickly jumped in and said, "No, it was a lot longer," then attempted to reassure me that the reason no lead was taken was the result of a 'clerical error' on her part. She then threw Investigator Myers under the bus by claiming, "he made it a lead in the 'regular lead thing' instead of a lead in here, and I didn't catch it."

Knowing how the lead system works during a major investigation, this made absolutely no sense to me whatsoever. I hope the rolling of my eyes wasn't too noticeable. Myers had been assigned to the Harris case since day one. So, why would he, knowing that Stewart was coming in for a *scheduled* polygraph on the Harris case, adopt some other type of lead? He wouldn't. Myers would have had prior knowledge of Stewart, and he needed to prepare his questions for the polygraph. But wait, it gets worse. Mulvey goes on to say, "…it was so 100 percent truthful and so innocuous. He (Myers) mistakenly makes it a 'regular lead' in how he regularly adopts his lead instead of a lead here."

This time I nearly gagged, thinking to myself, "what 'regular lead' thing is she talking about?" Okay. I realize there may have been other BCI cases going on simultaneously with the Harris case. However, it would make no sense, nor does it explain why Myers would adopt a lead on Stewart in some unrelated case, especially when he knew why he was coming in. Even with the remote chance that did happen, the 'mistaken' lead or case number should have appeared on Stewart's polygraph documents. There was no 'mistaken' lead or case number. In fact, there was no number. Period.

This was an insult. Again, Mulvey must have taken me for a fool. For someone who didn't know better, she may have been able to weasel her way out with this type of BS explanation. But I wasn't buying it. Not for a second. The bottom line was she'd been caught red-handed trying to hide Stewart's polygraph and was now trying to cover it up with this bogus explanation. Besides, if it were true, she could have easily convinced me by simply showing me the 'other lead thing' she claimed existed just down the hall in her office.

The pieces were starting to come together as I began recalling how vague the original Stewart lead was as well as that related bar lead with nothing in it. Remember? The one where no one was interviewed and no camera footage. I was troubled, thinking, "something's not right here." It made me wonder. What else do they know about Stewart? What else may have been hidden or withheld? Stick with me because we haven't heard the last of this.

The temptation was great, and I came 'this-close' to challenging Mulvey about the missing polygraph lead. Instead, I opted to restrain myself by using my poker-face. In so doing, I forgot to ask her why Stewart was asked to take a polygraph in the first place. It's not likely I would have gotten a truthful answer anyway, but I kicked myself later for not asking. For now, the mystery would remain.

Hyman may have recognized Mulvey's bogus explanation about Stewart's poly and quickly changed the subject. He asked if the other polygraph information that was turned over was any different. I explained that the other four we received all contained the same information, but what we finally received regarding Stewart was incomplete. Specifically, the two conclusion pages were still missing. I explained that all we had on Stewart was the preliminary questionnaire and history sheet. They both agreed to provide the missing documents. I assumed they would have, or at least could have, provided them before I left that day, but they never did. Again, it was just down the hall in their office.

Other than explaining what documents were missing, I hadn't otherwise challenged or suggested any impropriety. In-as-much, I was somewhat taken back when Hyman commented, "Yea, it was not like, oh my god, this was not like the hiding of a suspect or anything like that." Those were his words, not mine. But in restraining myself further, I said, "No, I never actually thought that." Yet, I was actually thinking to myself, "why would he say something like that? Because that's what I was thinking and what it certainly seemed to be." I went on to explain, with the lack of documentation, we questioned whether Stewart had actually completed the polygraph. Mulvey quickly jumped in again to say that Stewart had not only taken it, but he'd also aced it with flying colors.

Ok then, if that's the case – convince me. But the most troubling and disturbing part for me was the fact that the only missing pages just happened to be Myers' conclusion pages. What are the chances of that? And how would they have gotten separated from the rest of the report? Moreover, there was an effortless way of reconciling the matter to clear up any confusion or misunderstanding. Simply walk to their office, pull out the missing pages, and show me; matter closed. I was right there, so the perfect opportunity presented itself to do just that. And they should have been anxious to do so. Yet, it never happened. As a result, my level of suspicion just jumped another notch.

As we continued, from the nature of their questions, I was getting the impression they were expecting me to offer some 'smoking gun' type evidence against Stewart. That, I didn't have. Hyman kept hitting me with questions like, "Did anyone have any direct knowledge of a transgression that day?" Then adding, "Are you aware of any ties between Stewart and Hagadorn Hill Road?" Later, in respect to Stewart and Michele, he asked, "Do you have anybody that indicates they had physical contact together?" When I explained that I did not have the answers to those questions, Hyman followed up with, "Yet, as you come to us today, you say that Stacy Stewart is a suspect?" In response, I said, "Yes. I still think Stacy Stewart is a viable suspect, with everything else I know. I think if you pursued Stacy Stewart and/or Chris Thomason, I think there is a strong possibility that you would find out who actually did it with a good potential of recovering the body." Hyman replied, "I've got to really understand. You think there's potential for us to find her remains? That's everyone's objective here. The facts that you bring are interesting, but nothing indicates that he had contact with Michele." Growing more frustrated, I said, "Well, that's what needs to be pursued," while thinking to myself, "I just painted you the picture. What part of it, can't you see? You're just going to completely ignore this, aren't you?"

As we continued, we started talking about Kevin Tubbs. Their criticism of Tubbs made it painfully obvious they did not believe him, or at least, didn't want to believe him. They brought up the domestic issues with his wife, his animosity towards the police and DA, and really took exception to the fact he had not called them first. My response could have been much harsher, but I was deliberately trying to avoid a confrontation. Those things had no bearing whatsoever on his credibility as a witness. It was also apparent from their questioning that due to the limited lighting conditions, they believed Tubbs would not have been unable to see what he described on that specific day. Instead, they believed what he saw must have occurred on some prior or later date.

Mulvey said, "I don't doubt he saw something, but I really think it's August 24th..." I simply replied, "I would have to disagree." Hyman then referred to yet a later date in September that he claimed fit better than the 12th. Attempting to support his argument, he claimed they had talked to the property owner, who claimed to know 'exactly' when things were hayed and weren't. I had to chuckle a little at this. I'd spoken with the owner as well, who was living and working on Long Island. Therefore, there was no way for him to know 'exactly' when the fields were being hayed. Next.

The topic of the lighting conditions came up again when Mulvey said, "It's pitch black at 5:30 and not getting light like he describes..." That statement was not accurate. Tubbs had never said it was 5:30 and could not offer a specific time, other than it was just starting to get light. I couldn't understand why they were trying to make such a big deal of the lighting conditions anyway. I then told them about the video work we had done at the scene, and despite the exact lighting conditions, there was no reason to believe Tubbs would have been driving up Hagadorn Hill without his headlights on. They both looked confused as if they'd never thought of that. Hyman then tried to strengthen his argument further by claiming that 'some people' were telling them that, "farmers just don't take a hay-wagon those hours of the day." I must have rolled my eyes this time. I knew from my own personal experience from working on a farm as a teenager, that was not true. I also knew from talking with the Tubbs family and others that hauling hay out of the field in the predawn hours was a regular part of their routine. So, who are these 'people' telling them that?

Hyman once again brought up the animosity issue when he said, "I still see a back-drop of such animosity towards certain people in the justice system in this county from Kevin." In response, I said, "But I don't think that's motive behind coming forward about this." Hyman said, "Which comes to what would be a motive for Kevin to do this?" I said, "I don't think it is motive. I think it was more of a responsibility." Explaining further that Kevin had this knowledge and needed to tell somebody. Speaking from Kevin's perspective, I said, "Why would I want to put myself through all this abuse if this didn't happen? I know what I saw and when I saw it." There was no response.

As we shifted back to Stewart, Hyman said, "People have come to you with their opinions of him that you think we should interview." In response, I said, "I'd like to see you take the lead on this. I'll continue regardless, but you have the resources, you have the authority, and if I thought you were really sincere about taking the lead, I could share all of this with you because there's some good stuff here that I think needs to be pursued. And there are certainly people out there that have suggested to me that Stewart could very well be responsible for this."

Hyman seemed to be, or perhaps pretended to be interested in the matter involving the Gilbert burglary, and I reminded him of the connection between Stewart and the Gilberts. He said, "Yeah, maybe, that would get us to the same place, which is, who is..." Interrupting, I said, "That's kind of what I'm interested in. You know, like I said, I would really like to see you take the lead and pursue this at least see where it goes."

Earlier in the interview, I told them about having photographs of Stewart and Thomason, but I had not yet shown them to Kevin Tubbs. I also told them that when I first interviewed Tubbs, he told me he got a good look at the guy because they glared at each other. And he could easily identify the guy if he saw him again. Later, Hyman asked, "Are you going to show this picture to Tubbs?" I said, "I'd rather you did that – in a line-up."

Hyman then hit me with a zinger when he said, "And then we have Mr. Tubbs seeing a pick-up truck that kind-of-fits the description similar to what he had. Did you provide him the description of that truck?" This really pissed me off. Now they're accusing me or at least thinking that I had fed the description to Kevin Tubbs. I came close to walking out on the spot, but my disciplined, cooler-self prevailed and firmly responded, "Absolutely not." I then re-explained how I had only obtained the description of Stewart's truck *after* Kevin had already described it.

This was a major turning point for me. From my experience, I was able to read through their feigned interest in what I was telling them. It was now evident that their only real interest was in finding out what I knew and how they might use it to their advantage. Whether they realized it or not, I was doing the same thing with them.

I was totally confused with their contradictory arguments in respect to Kevin Tubbs. First, they argue that Kevin is not credible because of his animosity towards the police and DA. Then, they claim that farmers don't pull hay-wagons at that time of day. The implication being – he's lying. Yet in contrast, Mulvey just said she had no doubt Kevin saw what he saw, but it must have been on a different day. Therefore, when considering their perspective, it was my understanding that, if what Kevin saw had been on any day other than September 12th, there would be no problem – even if pulling a hay-wagon in the dark. But, if what he saw was on the 12th, he's not only mistaken – he's a liar. Am I missing something here? Or are they trying to argue this both ways?

When hearing for the first time of their belief that Kevin actually saw what he saw, even if it was a different day, reminded me of my purpose in speaking with them in the first place. I was trying to generate interest for them to investigate what Kevin had seen, as opposed to just investigating Kevin himself. Trying to learn who it was that Kevin saw that morning should have been paramount to either confirm or refute what he had seen. I did not like the way this was going.

Throughout the interview, we jumped around and often spoke about topics where the only thing we could agree on was to disagree. Mulvey probably said it best when she said, "We're not going to convince each other."

No argument there, but I was still struggling to understand their rationale. Hyman then brought up Stewart again when he said, "He maybe did, he maybe didn't have contact with her, (Michele) or maybe had contact with her in bars, where is the motive?"

Before answering, I was thinking to myself, and at least virtually shaking my head saying, *"You've got to be kidding. Take your reality-blinders off. With all that was happening with Michele, you really need to ask me that question? What can't you see?"* I finally said, "How about a sex or robbery motive, or even rejection, or any combination."

There was no response.

As the interview was ending, Hyman, being somewhat condescending, said, "Let's evaluate and let me see what's what to assist in the Tubbs sightings." As we walked out of the polygraph room, he escorted me to the exit door. Before leaving, he asked if I would provide copies of all I had done, including my notes. I told him I could do that, but it would take a few days to get things organized and copied but would get it to him soon. Just as I was about to walk out the door, I watched as he proudly pumped-up his chest, grasped the lapels of his sport-coat, and said, "Well, it looks like we'll be taking a trip to Texas." As I was walking back to my car, my thoughts drifted back to my original fear and concern, that everything I just told them had fallen on deaf ears. So, they're taking a trip to Texas? Yeah, we'll see.

31

ASHLEY TUBBS INTERVIEW

Returning to my car after my meeting with Mulvey and Hyman, I checked my cell phone and noticed I had a voicemail. It was from Ashley Tubbs. She wanted to talk to me. Considering she'd just had Kevin arrested for assaulting her a few days earlier, I was surprised she wanted to speak with me. I called her back and told her I was in the area now, and she agreed to meet with me. We decided to meet at Hickories Park, on the east side of town.

Ashley was sitting on a picnic table in an empty pavilion as I pulled into the park. She was anxious to speak with me. She started by explaining how she'd been at the SP barracks earlier, attempting to withdraw a prior written statement but was told she couldn't do that. Claiming that the statement she gave was mostly truthful, but some things were 'twisted' or taken out of context, and she wanted to withdraw it.

She further advised that the SP had threatened her by saying if she did this, things would not go well for her or Kevin, and she may never see her son again. Adding further that, when I was done talking with her, she was going to return to the barracks to make another attempt at withdrawing her statement.

I was still curious and asked, "Why did you want to speak with me?"

She said, "I heard you've been talking to Brandi Sprague."

I said, "I have, but how do you know?"

"Brandi called me. She said she told you and her mom what really happened the other day between me and Kevin."

"And?" I asked.

"I was mad at Kevin because he was fighting me for custody of our son, and I was trying to get him to fight with me, so he'd get in trouble."

"Yeah, that's kind of what I figured, but tell me about this statement you're talking about."

A female investigator had talked with her after Kevin was arrested and wanted to know what he was saying about the Harris case. She told her a couple of things she'd heard from Kevin, but when she wrote up the statement, she 'twisted' things. Although she couldn't specifically recall what she'd told the investigator, when she read her statement, it sounded different from what she told her. But the investigator told her it would be fine, so she just signed it. I got the impression that Ashley knew more about what was in the statement, but didn't want to elaborate, and I didn't want to push the issue at the time. I already had some good information.

Continuing, she said, "If they won't let me withdraw it this time, I'm going to call that reporter at the newspaper."

I then asked if she could remember how long ago she'd given her statement?

"About a week ago," she said.

Following up, I asked, "Was it around the same time you had Kevin arrested?"

She said, "Yea, but how did you know? It was later that same day, that same investigator came to get me."

Now I was starting to see the bigger picture, thinking to myself, "This has to be Mulvey." She likely learned of Ashley having Kevin arrested for assault and was taking advantage of her anger against him as an opportunity to elicit information about him. Ordinarily, this would have been a good strategy, but knowing that Ashley had a known history of credibility and mental health issues, anything gleaned from her would require some solid corroboration. Before leaving the park, I asked her if she would let me know how things go in her new attempt to withdraw her statement. She agreed.

I had just finished speaking with Ashley and was headed back to Binghamton when Joe called. He wanted to see me in his office right away. I could tell by the sound of his voice it was something important. I told him I'd be there in a few minutes since I was already on my way to brief him regarding my meetings with the SP and Ashley Tubbs.

Joe had an angry look on his face and was pacing around the front office as I walked in. I asked, "What's up? What's wrong?" He said, "You need to see this," as he handed me a copy of Keene's newest motion, which had just been filed with the court with his request to re-open the '330' hearing. Attached to his motion was a copy of a statement from Ashley Tubbs taken by none other than Sue Mulvey. "Oh no, here it comes," I said to myself. After quickly reading Keene's two-page motion, which included Ashley's one-page statement, I understood Joe's anger. I was angry as well. Mulvey had been taking the low road all along, but I found it hard to believe she was willing to stoop to this level of unprofessional and unethical conduct. On second thought, knowing that Mulvey was behind it, I did believe it.

Briefly, in the statement prepared by Mulvey, Ashley Tubbs was alleging that during conversations with her estranged husband, Kevin Tubbs, he told her the Cal Harris defense team had told him about the suspect and provided him with his description. We knew that was nonsense. She also claimed that he told her someone from the defense told him they would take good care of him, and he would find a 'brown paper sack' full of money on the seat of his truck. Wow! The claptrap continues. In her statement, Ashley also claimed that Kevin told her about all the money he was going to get after speaking with Cal's lawyers. I could understand Joe's fury. In reading Ashley's statement, it was rather easy to discern that they were not Ashley's words but rather, a clever mischaracterization of her words, drafted by Mulvey. Perhaps 'clever' is being too kind. Malicious was more like it.

The more obvious part that jumped out at me was near the end of her statement, which read, *"There is a newspaper reporter, Nancy Dooling, who is trying to smear the District Attorney and the New York State Police."* I knew instantly that these were not Ashley's words. Notably, she never said she'd learned this from Kevin, or that it had anything to do with the alleged payoff conspiracy. So, where is this coming from? Furthermore, Ashley could have cared less whether Dooling was smearing the DA or and SP. Therefore, she would have had no interest or reason to include that in her statement. On the other hand, Mulvey was upset with Dooling, hearing that some of her articles had been critical of the DA and the SP. Mulvey's desperation was making her look foolish.

I was still fuming from the accusations, but it was now painfully clear where they were trying to go with this. Joe was furious and still pacing around, talking to himself, speaking out loud. In all the years I had worked with him, I had never seen him like this. With his integrity and credibility on-the-line, I knew he wasn't going to take this lying down. When he finally calmed down a bit, I was able to fill him in on my meeting with the SP. I explained how they wanted me to turn over copies of my investigative reports, and notes and I agreed to do that. Joe, who was obviously still upset, with somewhat of a puzzled look on his face, said, "You told them you would do that?"

I said, "I did, but I just changed my mind. I actually thought I could convince them to do the right thing, but I was wrong. Now they accuse us. I think it's safe to say they're never going to pursue any of this. They'll get nothing from me now." I then filled him in on what I'd learned from Ashley. I said, "If Ashley tries but isn't allowed to withdraw or change her statement, she may very well go to press like she said. And I think Dooling would be very receptive to anything Ashley has to say. So, we may not have heard the last from Ashley."

32

MORE GOOD PRESS

I spoke with news reporter Nancy Dooling on several occasions during my investigation. She had taken a particular interest in the case, and some of her articles were somewhat favorable to the defense. As a result, she had taken some heat from the SP over some of her work. But her interest in the case perked up even more after the revelations of Kevin Tubbs. Nancy and her colleagues, as experienced crime reporters, knew there would be an abundance of back-and-forth motions being filed by both sides. Not wanting to miss any in or out-of-court action, they arranged with the Court Clerks to be notified when motions had been filed.

> Author's Note: Once motions are filed with the Court unless sealed, they become public record and are made available on request.

Keene's newest motion with Ashley's statement was no exception, and the press obtained a copy from the court. When reaching out to Joe for a comment, he agreed but wanted to do so in an open press conference. It was scheduled for the next day.

Press & Sun-Bulletin reporter Brian Libertore, covered the press conference and the following day's headline read, *"Attorney: Talk of payoff in Harris case is 'absolutely ridiculous,'"* with the sub-headline, *"Wife of witness claims money was offered by defense."* In his article, Libertore

304 | REIGN OF INJUSTICE

described an angered Joe Cawley shaking his fist while accusing the prosecution of supporting a wild accusation and attacking his integrity. Keene was quoted saying, "It's up to the court to decide" if Ashley Tubbs' statement has any merit. Cawley, on the other hand, said the money bag accusation was "absolutely ridiculous," and her story is a complete fabrication.

Cawley continued, "Never at any time, in any way did anyone ever suggest to Mr. Tubbs that he would receive or get anything for his testimony. I consider this to be an attack on me personally. I'm not going to stand for it." The article also mentioned Keene admitting that he had prior dealings with Ashley Tubbs and had his own personal opinions of her. He also admitted that he didn't know who was telling the truth, and the court should decide by re-opening the hearing. Cawley had the final word saying, "To be honest, I resent this personally as an officer of the court."

Keene's admission to having his own personal opinions about the credibility of Ashley Tubbs was clearly revealing that he knew she was an unreliable witness. He purposely attached her statement and fed it to the press, knowing it would inflame the passions of the community and smear the name of Kevin Tubbs and the defense team. However, Keene's strategy was about to backfire.

After being arrested for allegedly assaulting Ashley, Kevin Tubbs had since retained the services of Binghamton attorney Tom Saitta. After his arrest, he was released on his own recognizance, but the judge had issued an Order of Protection (OP), which prohibited him from having any contact with Ashley.

Through Nancy Dooling and attorney Saitta, we learned that Ashley had been calling Kevin repeatedly, trying to get him to talk to her. Kevin knew she was recording the calls in her attempt to have him arrested for violating the OP.

Dooling had also interviewed Ashley Tubbs, who confirmed the SP had provided her with a recording device. They were coaching her in what to say when she called Kevin, trying to get him to violate the OP. After learning of this, Saitta called the SP to caution them that Kevin was represented by counsel, and the calls and recordings had to stop. Despite his warning, the calls continued.

After receiving Keene's motion, Judge Smith ordered a hearing the very next day. I picked up Kevin Tubbs and brought him to the courthouse in anticipation of his possible testimony. As it turned out, Smith only asked to hear oral arguments. I was sitting in the waiting room with Kevin, unable to witness the debacle taking place inside the courtroom. When it was over, Joe and Bill filled me in, but Dooling summed it up well under the next day's *Press & Sun-Bulletin* headline that read, *"Judge in Harris case lashed D.A., state police,"* with the sub-headline, *"Fight over recordings 'starting to have an ugly air,'"* judge says.

Dooling described how the defense laid out the scenario of how Ashely, under the control of the SP, made repeated controlled and recorded phone calls to Kevin Tubbs to try and get him to violate the OP. The defense alleged that even after the SP was warned to stop the control calls, the calls continued. In response, Smith said, "This is starting to have an ugly air to it." Dooling pointed out that the original purpose of the hearing was to address the issue of whether to re-open the original hearing. Instead, it turned into an examination of the conduct of the Tioga County District Attorney and state police after Kevin Tubbs testified at the original hearing.

Joe Cawley, addressing the court, said, "…she acted as an agent of the state police by trying to get her husband to violate the order, which, if successful, would have led to another arrest of Kevin Tubbs." Saitta then addressed the court and explained how he had personally told Investigator Mike Myers in a phone call that he was representing Tubbs, and the calls Ashley was making to him needed to stop. However, he added, "The calls continued." Several days later, learning that the calls were continuing, this time in a letter to the court, Saitta said he called the SP again and spoke with Mulvey. She denied that Ashley was making any calls to her husband on behalf of the state police. Judge Smith again said, "This is getting worse by the second." In addressing the phone calls and Keene's conduct throughout the proceedings against Harris, Smith added, "Troubling at best. I have a real problem with some of the things in this case." After oral arguments, Smith agreed to a limited re-opening of the hearing and adjourned the matter for one week.

Two days before the scheduled re-opening of the hearing, another article appeared in the *Press & Sun-Bulletin* by Brian Liberatore under the headline, *"Woman in Harris case: No payoff was offered,"* with the sub-headline, *"Ashley Tubbs: Statement about witness 'twisted.'"* Ashley had obviously followed through about going to press if she wasn't allowed to withdraw her statement. In her interview with Liberatore, she said, Kevin Tubbs "never said that the defense promised him money. Rather, he had said he would never take a dime from anybody for his testimony." Ashley explained to Liberatore how the state police (Myers & Mulvey) had come to her home shortly after she had Kevin arrested. They wanted to talk to her about Kevin. She also explained how they had given her a recording device and wanted her to get Kevin to confirm his statement about the alleged 'bag of money.' *"They told me what he needed to say and to try and get him to say it if I could,"* she said. Ashley also explained about going to the SP looking for help with her custody matter and how she'd poured her heart out to Mulvey, telling her everything she knew about Kevin. Then added, *"I know they used me to their advantage, and I've taken advantage of any help they could give me. They took advantage of me, but my statement was the truth twisted in a minor way with major consequences."*

33

'330' HEARING – RE-OPENED

As expected, Ashley Tubbs was called to testify about the information in her statement. Under cross-examination, Cawley went on the offense, attacking her credibility. The prosecution had also called a couple of collateral witnesses. Neither one offered anything of significant value to the issue involved. After that, in a decision by Judge Smith, Ashley's alleged 'payoff' statement was sealed and ruled inadmissible. At the close of the hearing, Smith said he would be making a written decision within a few days.

Six days later, on November 2, 2007, Smith's office called to advise that he had made and prepared a written decision. He would be making his formal announcement in open-court tomorrow afternoon. The next day, Cal was seated at the defense table with Joe and Bill on either side. He was handcuffed and wearing his orange jump-suit. Smith announced his decision in front of a packed courtroom. After reading several segments from his written decision, Smith formally announced that he was vacating the verdict against Cal Harris and ordering a new trial.

There were obviously a variety of mixed reactions, but my eyes were on Cal. I watched as he placed his hands over his face and openly wept while being comforted on both sides by Joe and Bill. Keene, who showed little reaction, asked Smith to raise the bail to $1 million – it was quickly denied. While still at the bench, Smith looked at Cal, then turned to Keene and said, "Remove his cuffs," and ordered that Cal be released from custody as soon as possible. His original $500 thousand dollar bail would remain in effect. After five months in jail, Cal was back home with his children before the end of the day.

Albeit temporary, this was undoubtedly a significant victory for Cal and the defense team. We all knew there was still a long road ahead, but for now, it was a victory worth celebrating. We let Cal enjoy some time with his family, as the rest of us gathered briefly at Joe's house to reflect on everything that happened. Even though we knew it would be short-lived and that we would have to do it all over again in a second trial, it felt good knowing that Cal was home enjoying his freedom with his children. In a few days, we'll all re-group and gear-up for the next battle.

The next day's headline in the *Press & Sun-Bulletin* said it all, *"Harris verdict dismissed,"* with the sub-headline, *"Judge orders retrial in murder case: defendant released on $500,000 bail."* Another headline read, *"Tubbs credibility proved key in Smith's decision."* A separate back-page article read, *"Decision could spur investigation, Police mum on next step."* There was even an op-ed article under the heading, *"Back to Court, Harris verdict thrown out after new testimony surfaces."* In the lead article, written by Nancy Dooling, she described Cal's emotional reaction very similar to what I observed. In her interview with Keene, he said he intended to appeal Smith's decision, "I still have a hard time accepting someone would come forward after six years and make these allegations." Keene also insisted that Tubbs' testimony was "completely implausible."

Judge Smith, reading from his written decision, disagreed, saying,

> The evidence at the trial in this case was entirely circumstantial. The proof of guilt, although legally sufficient, and establishing guilt to the jury's satisfaction beyond a reasonable doubt, was far from overwhelming.

Continuing, he added,

> The direct evidence (Tubbs' account) offered at the hearing, credited by this court, would serve to establish the victim was alive, and in the company of another man many hours after the People alleged and proved at trial that she was murdered by her husband.

Smith had also addressed the issue of the alleged 'payoff' by

Kevin's estranged wife, Ashley, by saying she was not credible. He also addressed the secret recordings made by Ashley under control and at the direction of the state police when he said, "nothing in the tapes remotely suggested that Kevin Tubbs sought, expected or was offered anything in exchange for his testimony, which the Court found, and continues to find credible."

In the back-page article written by Eric Reinagel, police say it's too soon to say how their investigation might proceed in the wake of the judge's decision. He interviewed Captain Mark Lester, who said, "We're still working on the case. There's still a missing person out there, and we'll continue that case as long as necessary." Interestingly, Lester also said that police don't have any new specific leads to investigate. When explicitly asked if the police would be searching the property of Stacy Stewart, the Texas steelworker, Lester said, "If we feel another search is appropriate, we'll do it."

The Back to Court op-ed described the Hollywood-movie fashion and dramatic nature of the Harris case, which had polarized Tioga County. Then it posed this question, *"Is a retrial possible within a community where most of the residents have firm opinions already on Harris' guilt or innocence?"* The article continued by saying, *"This case has had more twists and turns than the Cyclone at Coney Island, more drama than a TV soap opera during sweeps month."* But more importantly, it said, *"...if there is evidence that can cast some doubt authentically on the verdict, a retrial is absolutely warranted. Obviously, Judge Smith believes there is."* They ended with this final question, *"If there is the possibility that she died at the hands of another, though, shouldn't that be investigated as thoroughly as Mr. Harris himself was?"* Exactly. I couldn't have said it better myself.

For Joe Cawley, this was one of his last official functions as Cal's attorney. Several months before the May trial, he had decided to run for an open position as Broome County Court Judge. He'd announced his decision to seek the position back in February of 2007, about four months before the trial. When he asked, I graciously accepted his request and joined his campaign committee. With the trial starting in May and the election not until early November, we didn't anticipate any conflict. We had plenty of time to prepare for the trial and still organize his campaign run for County Court Judge. Once the trial was over in early June, we thought it would be clear sailing into the November election. Little did we know that the end of the trial would not be the end of our involvement.

Enter, Kevin Tubbs, and the introduction of surprising new evidence that would propel the case well beyond the end of the trial. Fortunately, Bill Easton, who had been actively involved as co-counsel, was in a position to take the helm as Cal's lead attorney. Even though the election was only a few days away, Joe remained on-board and stayed actively involved as we made the transition over to Bill as lead counsel for the defense.

So, Judge Smith had made his decision to set aside the verdict. Cal had been released from jail but was still under indictment. Until there was a second trial, he would remain free on bail. Keene was expected to appeal Smith's decision. But according to Bill Easton, the appeal process could take several months. If Smith's decision is upheld, and he was confident it would be, the case would eventually come back to Smith to be rescheduled for a second trial.

As expected, Keene filed a lengthy appeal of Judge Smith's decision to vacate the guilty verdict as a result of the '330' hearing. After the defense filed a firm and lengthy response, the matter was placed in the hands of a five-member panel of New York appellate judges to decide. In short, all five appellate judges voted unanimously to uphold Smith's decision to vacate the conviction and to re-affirm the credibility of Kevin Tubbs and his parents. Cal Harris would be getting a new trial.

34

ANOTHER NEW WITNESS

Four days after Judge Smith's decision to vacate Cal's conviction, Joe Cawley won the election for the Broome County Court Judge – a prestigious position that was well-earned and well deserved. Did that mean I'd have to start calling him 'Your Honor' instead of 'Joe'? I supposed it did, but maybe not all the time. He would continue his involvement with the Harris case until mid-December when he would officially turn over the reins to Bill Easton before being sworn in to his new position the first of the year.

A few days later, I met with Joe, Bill, and Sue for a defense meeting. Not knowing whether the SP was going to follow-up with Stacy Stewart or not, we discussed the possibility of sending me to Texas. I'd already proposed and discussed the idea with Frank Roney. He thought it would be a good idea and was willing to go with me. Later, when speaking with Cal and Dwight, Joe ran the idea by them. They both agreed and wanted to see it happen sooner than later. That same day I met with Frank and started making tentative plans for the week after Thanksgiving.

We were still in the early stage of our planning when Joe called. When I answered, he said, "You're not going to believe this." I said, "The suspense is killing me, just tell me." He'd just received a letter in the mail, which was a copy of an original that had been sent to Tioga County Court Judge Vincent Squeglia. Briefly, in the letter addressed to

Judge Squeglia, a man identified himself as John Steele, from Waverly, NY. After explaining that he was faced with a moral dilemma, he described driving with a companion on Hagadorn Hill Road during the early morning hours of September 12, 2001, witnessing a scene "very similar to the account given by Mr. Tubbs." In-as-much, he had observed a man and a woman arguing with each other alongside the road. He then explained the reason he had not come forward sooner was due to his fear of causing embarrassment to both himself and his companion, which would likely jeopardize his marriage. He also did not want to place himself or his friend in Keene's gunsights and wrote, *"MR. KEENE HAS PROVEN HIMSELF A POWERFUL MAN AND I DON'T WANT TO BRING HIS WRATH DOWN ON ME."* He ended his letter by saying he would be more than happy to discuss the matter privately.

As soon as I hung up with Joe, I immediately contacted Steele, and after explaining who I was and that we had just received a copy of his letter, I arranged for a personal interview. He said I could come over right away. Frank was still with me, and I said, "Come on, this could get interesting, and I may need you as a witness." Steele greeted us at the door of his garage workshop, where we agreed to meet and invited us in. What we were about to learn would add a strong and corroborative new element to Kevin Tubbs' story.

John Steele was a life-long resident of Waverly. He was semi-retired and ran his own small, general contracting business. He had his own shop set up in a garage along state route 17C just East of Waverly, about one-quarter mile from his home on Ellis Creek Road. At the time, Steele was 62-years old, five-foot-ten inches tall, with gray hair, and weighed about 200 pounds. His garage office was comfortable, yet unkempt and cluttered with things that had obviously accumulated over many years. After confirming that he was the one who wrote the letter to Judge Squeglia, and then later sent a copy to Joe Cawley, he agreed to be interviewed. I said, "I know what you said in your letter, but I know there's more to the story so, why don't you start right from the beginning." Then adding, "But before you get started, first tell me about the letter you wrote to Judge Squeglia."

Steele explained how he had witnessed certain things but didn't want to come forward initially. After learning from the news what Kevin Tubbs had seen, his conscience started bothering him, and he needed to do something. So, he decided to write a letter to Judge Squeglia. He said, "I knew Judge Squeglia was a good man, and I trusted him." He then explained how the judge had called him after receiving his letter. The judge told him he wished he could but could not offer him any advice whatsoever and couldn't discuss it. He told the judge he understood and that if Judge Smith wanted to contact him, he could. So, he assumed Squeglia would forward the letter to Smith, but after waiting over a week and not hearing anything, he decided to send a copy of his letter directly to Joe Cawley.

I then asked Steele to start by taking us back to the beginning and lay out his whole story. We just listened as he laid out the details of his entire story and asked if he was willing to show us the area where he made his observations.

He said, "Well, it's been a long time, and I haven't been up there since, but I think I would still recognize the area." We had Frank's truck, so I had John sit up front with Frank, and I sat in the middle in the back, so we could all talk.

Frank drove to Tioga Center and then turned and went up Halsey Valley Road. When we arrived at the intersection of Hagadorn Hill Road, I asked Frank to stop. Then I asked John if he knew where he was.

Pointing, he said, "Yep, I was coming down Halsey Valley and turned right here to go up Hagadorn."

I said, "Okay, were going to start up Hagadorn. If you see anything that looks familiar, let us know."

We drove up Hagadorn about a mile before he said, "I remember that barn there on the left, just because it sits so close to the edge of the road."

"Anything else?" I asked.

"Nope, let's keep going. It's up further," he said. We continued up and then passed Forstrom Road. As we were approaching the end of the Harris driveway, I began to wonder whether he would still recognize the area after all these years.

Frank maintained a steady speed as we drove past the Harris driveway. We went right past the driveway and continued for another two or three hundred feet, thinking to myself, "He doesn't remember."

No sooner than having that thought, John yelled, "Stop! Back up. This is it. It's right here."

Following his directions, Frank stopped, backed up, and then stopped again right at the end of the Harris driveway.

I said, "What is it about this spot that you recognize?"

He said, "Like I told you earlier, it was kind of a funny area, because it looks like somebody's front lawn, but there's no house. This is it. It was right here."

Neither Frank nor I had prompted or provided him with any information about the exact location. An important element in corroborating his story, was to have him point out the location on his own, which he did. We never told him whether he'd pointed out the right spot or not. We then drove back to his office and had him retell his story. But this time, with his permission, I turned on my recorder.

To get started, I said, "In your letter, you indicated that you had seen certain things that you thought were important, so to start, let's go back to September 11th, 2001. What were you doing that day?"

He explained that he wasn't doing much of anything that day other than watching TV that morning when, as he said, "The shit-hit-the-fan." He sat in his office glued to the TV, watching the coverage for a good part of the day before going home for dinner around 6:00 p.m. Then, right after dinner, he returned to and continued watching TV. Later that evening, around 11:00 p.m., he had a visitor. Prompted by that day's events, a female acquaintance who he knew from back in high school had been driving by, saw his lights on, and stopped in to see him. After exchanging a few pleasantries, they began talking about the day's events, which later turned into reminiscing about yesteryear.

Afterward, they decided to go for a drive and continued to reminisce about, "what could have been, what should have been, and what might have been." While slowly meandering over the back roads, they decided to drive up to Spencer Lake, which had been a popular hangout when they were teenagers. Not having been there in many years, he didn't know the area was no longer accessible. It had been blocked off. So instead, they just drifted around from place to place, stopping from time to time to talk. "We talked for hours," he said.

They didn't stay in any one place for very long. Steele said, "We spent the entire night talking, wishing this and that and you know, that kind of crap." Continuing, he said, "It was probably around 6:00 a.m. when we decided we'd better get our butts home because daylight was just breaking." He added, "I didn't want to drive back down Ellis Creek Road because that was my daily bailiwick,[1] and I didn't want anybody to see me with my female companion."

John wanted to make it clear that even though his companion had since died, he did not want to besmirch her name. He said, "The only reason I'm telling you this now is that she has died. I would have said something sooner, but I didn't want to cause her or her family any embarrassment." Other than talk, he said, "we did nothing to be ashamed of, but others may not have seen it that way."

Getting back to his story, they started drifting slowly down Halsey Valley Road. He intentionally avoided Ellis Creek Road by turning up Hagadorn Hill. As they headed up Hagadorn, he was still driving slowly, and they'd traveled about two, maybe three miles. He then described seeing two people standing right out next to the road arguing with each other. He could clearly see that it was a man and a woman because they came very close to them as they drove by. He added that the passenger window was down in his truck because his friend was smoking. Then, as they drove by, he thought he heard the man say, "get in the car, just get in the damn car," or something like that. He wasn't exactly sure. Continuing, he explained that he'd seen what he believed to be two vehicles right close to the road. The closest one he described as a dark truck but couldn't describe the other one. He said, "I was paying more attention to the two people." In describing the area, he said, "It was kind of a funny area that looked like somebody's front lawn, but there was no house there."

When I asked if he could remember anything more about the people, he said, at first, he figured it may have been a husband and wife arguing, yet the guy looked much younger than the woman. Describing him as very average looking and nothing spectacular. He recalled talking with his companion about what they had seen. They both agreed that the man looked too old to be the woman's son, yet too young to be her husband. He remembered telling her, "I don't know what the hell the deal is there." He then explained that even though he had witnessed them arguing, the woman never waved her hands or indicated that she needed help, so, "I just minded my own business and continued on our way, eventually arriving back at my office around 7:30 a.m."

I then asked if he could recall anything about their hair or clothing. He said, "I couldn't tell you what they were wearing, but the woman definitely had light hair, and I know the man had hair, but there was nothing spectacular about it. I do know it wasn't very long, and he wasn't bald, but that's the best I can do."

When asked, Steele replied that he did not know Cal Harris, Kevin Tubbs, or any of their family members. He added that he had never been involved with any of them whatsoever. We talked a little more about his companion and how they had been friends since high school. He again reiterated his desire to keep her name out of it, if possible. He went on to explain that the relationship between him and his wife was not good, so he wasn't really concerned about himself. He then explained how his companion had died from diabetes. Then added that he was suffering from the same disease and would likely die the same way.

Continuing, Frank asked, "When did you realize that the information you had was important?"

He said, "I didn't realize it at all until after Mr. Tubbs came forward. But after he came forward and said what he said, you know, that's the same thing I saw." Continuing on, he said, "At the time it didn't seem important at all, it was just a couple of people fighting, but when Mr. Tubbs came forward, I knew I'd seen the same thing and needed to tell someone."

When we finished, I asked John if he was willing to let me use my recording to help prepare a formal written statement for him to later read and sign. With his permission, I returned to my office and prepared his statement. Before taking it back for his signature, I ran it by Joe and Bill. Both agreed it was good to go. The next day I returned to Steele's office to have him read his statement. After his approval, I took his oath, which he swore to and then signed his statement. Which I then notarized and witnessed with my own signature.

This wasn't just powerful new information. It was dynamite. With only subtle differences, there were now two eyewitnesses who were describing the same exact scenario, at the same time and place. In-as-much, they were unknowingly yet independently corroborating one another. Furthermore, the new eyewitness, fearing the wrath of Jerry Keene, as demonstrated in his treatment of Kevin Tubbs, had also chosen to disclose his revelations to the defense.

In my view, the subtle differences in their respective sightings helped to authenticate their stories. Too many similarities or exact like-nesses would have been suspect. As with Kevin Tubbs, the defense was under no obligation to disclose this new information or the identity of its source to the prosecution. Since Cal's conviction had already been vacated, there would be no need for another '330' hearing. Conceivably, Steele's revelations and identity could be withheld until trial. Unlike Tubbs, a background check on Steele revealed nothing more than a traffic ticket and no apparent issues with law enforcement. With Steele's info, we were feeling a lot better as we moved closer toward a second trial.

Just before our scheduled trip to Texas, Frank returned and re-interviewed Nancy Gilbert to see what more he could learn. When asked, Nancy had never known Stacy to use any type of illegal drugs. However, he was on a high blood-pressure medication that he needed to take two-or-three times daily. Adding that his blood pressure was extremely high, and he'd received treatment at the Guthrie Clinic in Sayre, PA.

Frank asked, "If Stacy was responsible for the death of Michele Harris, what would his motive have been. Without hesitation, Nancy quickly replied, "Rejection. He does not take rejection well."

According to Nancy, Stacy had slept with Michele on two or three occasions, back when he was still staying at the Guthrie Inn. Telling Frank, she knew this because Stacy had proudly told her, more than once, that he had 'scored' with his 'cute little blonde' from Lefty's. Frank then asked about Stacy's financial situation, and she said, "Stacy was being paid very well, but he never had any money because he'd spend it as fast as he got it." Then added, "Yet he would tip his 'cute blonde' (Michele) with hundred-dollar bills at Lefty's." Frank asked, "How do you know that?" She said, "Because he'd call and tell me that dinner had just cost him $130. When I asked why so much, he told me he'd just tipped her a hundred bucks." Later, she added, "and he bragged about the hundred-dollar tips at least three times that I know of."

---

1. Bailiwick: Familiar territory or particular area of interest.

35
___

OFF TO TEXAS

F rank and I went back to work, planning our trip to Texas. We had no idea what to expect regarding anything the SP may have done concerning Stewart or the information I had shared with them. If they'd gone to Texas, we could very well run into another of their roadblocks, like my experience at Lefty's early on. However, the overwhelming consensus among the defense team was that we needed to go. So, moving forward, we booked our flight, then made a list of what we wanted to accomplish, along with a tentative yet flexible itinerary and timeline to get it done. Part of our game-plan was to try and talk with Wright Childers in Tennessee before approaching Stewart and Thomason in Texas. However, knowing that Childers had been seriously injured in an automobile accident and not knowing his current mental condition, we had no clue what to expect.

On the Monday after Thanksgiving, we flew out of Binghamton Regional Airport to Chattanooga, TN, with stops in Detroit and Atlanta. Like myself, Frank shared the same passion in our pursuit of the truth. Therefore, he was willing to fly, even though he was not fond of doing so. In fact, he was somewhat fearful, and the intermediate stops didn't help. He especially disliked the sound of the landing gear going up or down and was often heard saying, "Oooh, Frankie, don't like that."

Finally, I couldn't resist and said, "Frankie, relax, not to worry. If the landing gear doesn't work, they can always do a belly-landing."

"You're an asshole, Beers," he replied.

After arriving in Chattanooga around dinner time, we picked up the one-way rental car we would be using until our return flight home out of Houston. I'd arranged for an economy mid-sized sedan, but when we checked in, we were upgraded to a black Cadillac Escalade, at no additional charge. The rental agency needed it in Houston. Nice. We were at least going to go in style and look official. As an added perk, it had a built-in GPS unit.

First thing in the morning, we drove directly to Wright Childers residence in nearby Hixson, TN. While pulling into the driveway, I noticed a large kennel nearby that was home to three huge Rottweilers. I remember saying, "Oh man, I sure hope that gate is locked." I certainly didn't want to get caught sprinting back to my car, yelling, "who let the dogs out." As it turned out, we didn't even have to knock on the door. The Rots had announced our arrival. An older woman came to the door, and after identifying ourselves and our purpose, she invited us in. Introductions were made as we greeted each other. Present were Wright's mother, Linda Rogers, and his stepdad, Walter 'Dub' Rogers, and Wright Childers himself.

Wright appeared to be physically stable, but we weren't yet sure about his memory. During our conversation, we learned that Wright had been seriously injured in a January 27, 2002 automobile accident in Chemung County, NY. While he appeared to be fully recovered from his injuries, according to Wright and his family, his memory of the past is 'clouded' at times. And some memories were said to be totally lost. We also learned that he was unable to hear on his left side. Wright and his parents were more than willing to participate in the interview. However, it wasn't long into the interview before his mother demonstrated some caution when she stated she would not let investigators 'pin' anything on her son.

Wright remembered NUCOR and working there, as well as his duties as a structural engineer. He'd been recruited and arrived there in early April of 2001. He remembered the names of James Brent and Scott Sanford as two of the supervisors at the plant.

Initially, he didn't readily remember Stacy Stewart or Chris Thomason. Later, however, he did remember them and said they were always out late drinking and chasing women. He added, "They were doing some wild and crazy things." Initially, he did not remember or admit knowing Michele Harris. However, later, when asking him about Lefty's, he remembered liking their 'gravy fries.' Then he remembered Michele. His memory seemed to improve further as he went on to describe Michele as being, "blondish, not heavy-set but more than thin with a B breast size and a nice rounded butt." He thought she was probably in her mid-30s. He then added, "She was nice. Not a trollop." That was a pretty good description. It sounded like his memory wasn't too bad, after all.

He remembered Stacy telling him at a going-away party that he (Stacy) had "found religion" and was going back to Texas.

He claimed that the conversation took place just before his accident. I asked if he knew anything about another woman who had gone missing in the Waverly area when he was up there. "That would have been Tammi Leonard," he said. She lived nearby his place on Chemung Street in Waverly. He further described her as a "quasi-girl-friend" he'd met at a local strip club. She was one of the nude dancers at the club who used the stage name, 'Delilah.' According to Wright's mom Linda, Tammi showed up at the hospital after Wright's accident, while he was still in a coma, telling her that Wright had asked her to marry him. Linda felt Tammi was just looking for money and wanted to go back to TN with Wright.

As the interview shifted back to Stacy Stewart, I described the cabin he had owned in Lockwood. Wright remembered the cabin and started to describe it further as being "in a hilly area with a pond in front." Suddenly, his whole demeanor and entire expression on his face changed rather abruptly. Appearing fearful, as if he'd just remembered something that frightened him. He quickly backed off his recollection of the cabin by saying that it sounded familiar, but, "I only drove by once and never went inside."

Of course, we knew from speaking with others that he'd been to Stacy's house on several occasions. And he was doing so well. But he just lied to us. Until now, his memory had served him well. What was it about Stewart's cabin that caused him to back away so abruptly? Without confrontation, I continued the interview.

I certainly didn't want him to clam up on me entirely or worse yet, have his mama show us the door. I still wanted to see what more we could learn. Staying on the topic of Stacy Stewart, I asked if he had ever done any four-wheeling with him. He'd done a lot of four-wheeling, but never in NY and never with Stewart. When asked if he knew why Stacy left the area, he thought it was more of a transfer back to the NUCOR plant in Texas, rather than quitting or being fired.

As the interview continued, Wright explained how he was into bodybuilding and motorcycles. He recalled working-out at a place called New Image in Waverly. He also spoke about his Harley-Davidson motorcycle he referred to as a "fat-boy." While in NY, he also had a BMW and a Jeep. It was the Jeep he was driving when he had his accident. When asked about the accident, he had no memory of it whatsoever.

Just before ending the interview, I asked Wright if I could get his picture. He agreed, and I took a quick snapshot of him in the kitchen. Mom was quick to question why we needed his picture. I fibbed a little and told her we were going to be speaking with several others who knew and had worked with Wright and how they would be interested in knowing he's doing so well after his accident. She was fine with that.

We were almost done when I remembered to ask if he knew who Yolanda Lewis was. Yep. He remembered her as the Safety Director at NUCOR. His memory was still there but was now more selective. Mom then piped in and said that Yolanda had come all the way down to see Wright in TN while he was in rehab and was concerned by the way she tried to kiss him on the mouth. She didn't care for her and didn't want her visiting her son. We were a bit surprised to learn this because she'd never mentioned it during her interview with Frank. But I wasn't surprised that mom didn't want her around Wright. It was evident throughout the interview that Linda was very protective of her son. What more she may have known that could have caused her to go into her parental protect mode remains a mystery.

Just as we were finishing, Wright's stepdad, Walter, who remained silent throughout the interview, said, "That Stacy Stewart guy? I remember seeing him at the Guthrie Inn. He had a lot of whores around him." I asked if he could remember anything more, and he said, "No, not really. It was a long time ago when we were up there, visiting Wright, long before his accident." After thanking them for their time, we handed them our business cards and asked them to call if they thought of anything further that might help.

As we pulled out of the driveway, we both started sharing our thoughts about our interview with Wright. Frank had also noticed how Wright's demeanor and expression had changed so quickly as he tried to distance himself from knowing anything more about Stacy's cabin. Claiming all he'd done was drive by and had never gone inside. Neither one of us were buying that. Frank said, "We know he's been there. Everybody we've talked to told us that. He knows something. What's he hiding? And why would he lie about being there if nothing ever happened?"

I said, "My thoughts exactly. We're on the same page. And my suspicion of his involvement just went up a notch."

"Mine too," Frank said.

I added, "Oh, and did you notice how protective momma was?"

Frank said, "Oh yeah, she thought we were there to 'pin' something on her baby boy. Why would she be thinking that? Unless she fears or knows something too."

"Good point, but it does make you wonder," I said.

| Wright Childers

Frank had taken notes during the interview and agreed to write up the interview summary. He worked on that as I drove. We were now headed towards central Louisiana to the small town of Natchez, about 600 miles away. What's in Natchez?

During our investigation, we learned that Stewart's pick-up truck had been repossessed shortly after his return to Texas in 2002. It had since been resold at auction to a new owner we identified as Salvatore Tearpock, who lived in Natchez, LA. Our mission was to try and locate the new owner and seek permission to either purchase the truck, or in the alternative, conduct an on-site forensic examination. Knowing that six years had passed, it was a long shot, but the presence of trace evidence was still a possibility. If we had the opportunity and needed to conduct an exam on-site, I was equipped to do so. I had carefully selected the items and equipment I might need and brought them along in my forensic 'black bag' just in case.

We didn't pull into Natchez until after 10:00 p.m., but before checking into our motel, we decided to at least try and locate the address we had for the new owner. We located the address along Highway 484, but unfortunately, all we found was an open field and no buildings. Tired from driving all day, we checked into the motel for a few hours' sleep. The next morning, we returned to the same area and started interviewing nearby neighbors. Several of those we talked to were familiar with the name Sal Tearpock, but nobody seemed to know where he was currently living. We spoke with a few more neighbors, checked with the local utility company, and looked through the local telephone book. We still couldn't find him. We spent almost half the day trying to find Tearpock without success. Due to our time schedule, with more important leads to follow in Texas, we decided to abandon our efforts in Natchez for now and start heading for Texas. If need be, we could follow-up with this later.

Crockett, Texas, is a small town a little more than a two-hour drive north of Houston. It was late afternoon on Wednesday by the time we pulled into Crockett. While there, we hoped to find and talk to James and Angela Brent, Chris Thomason, and of course, Stacy Stewart. After checking into our hotel, we traveled to the last known address we had for the Brents. The current owner said they were no longer living there, but he knew Angela and said she worked at a nearby nursing center. The receptionist at the Oakwood Nursing Center told us that Angela had left for the day, but she would try and contact her and have her call us. Before we left, the receptionist called Angela and left her a voicemail to call her. She also provided us with a more current address for Angela and her phone number. We had also learned that James Brent recently started his own construction business in Crockett by the name of JB Construction.

While we were attempting to locate their new address, Angela called and spoke with Frank. She'd received the message to call us. Frank explained who we were, why we were in Texas, and asked if she and her husband would be willing to meet with us. Angela said she was aware of the trial of Cal Harris and knew he had been convicted. She'd also been following the case and knew about the new witness who had come forward after six years. She was very interested in what we had to say and would contact us with a place to meet after her husband returned home from work.

After hanging up, Frank told me what she said about following the case. We were both curious about her knowledge and interest in the Cal Harris case and why she'd been following it all this time. As far as we knew, she wouldn't have known Cal or Michele. So why the interest? Our suspicious minds thought perhaps, Angela had learned something about Michele from her cousin Stacy.

About an hour later, Angela called back. Frank put her on speakerphone, and we could tell from the sound of her voice that her attitude and interest in speaking with us had done a complete flip-flop. She claimed to have talked with her husband and decided they weren't going to meet with us. She said firmly, "I know everything that's going on with the case, and if I find out anything more, I will contact the New York State Police." Where have I heard that before? Oh yeah, Nikki Burdick, six years ago. She then asked, "Who are you working for?" Frank had already explained that earlier but explained it again. She said, "Well, you're not the police, so anything I have to report, I will report to the New York State Police." Before she hung up, Frank said, "You know, we've already talked to Wright Childers." She said, "Well, you can't believe anything he says, he's just a vegetable." Before he could explain further, 'click.' She hung up.

I turned to Frank, but before I could say anything, he said, "Who the hell's she been talking to?" I said, "Well, she obviously called somebody. Maybe she called Stacy or even the state police. It sounds an awful lot like what I ran into at Lefty's." Surprisingly, a few minutes later, James Brent called. Frank again explained who we were and the purpose of our visit to Texas and our interest in interviewing Stacy Stewart and Chris Thomason. James was familiar with both subjects as they came out as a group to New York to build the new NUCOR plant in Chemung. He was familiar with Scott Sanford, who was Stacy's supervisor, and he (James) was the line-supervisor for Chris Thomason. James advised that he was married with children and he did not hang out with Stacy or Chris while he was in New York. At the end of the workday, he went home to his wife and children while Stacy and Chris went out-on-the-town. He had no idea where Stacy was living now. He thought Chris might have gotten his job back at the local NUCOR plant. After that, he said, "I really don't like talking on the phone with people I didn't know." Frank offered to meet with him face-to-face, so we could show him our credentials, but he declined. He then apologized for not being able to help more but still declined our repeated request to meet.

After speaking with Angela, we couldn't help wondering whether the SP was, or had been in town, or had simply called her and asked her not to speak with us. We also wondered whether they had also talked with Stewart or Thomason to put up more roadblocks.

Moving forward, we decided to try and find Thomason. We had a couple of different addresses, but we weren't having much success. There didn't appear to be any numerical consistency with the house numbers, which seemed to be random. We knocked on a few doors, but nobody recognized his name. Finally, we shot over to the NUCOR plant and spoke with a receptionist at the main desk. She was very helpful. She confirmed that Chris was working there, but he was currently working the second shift and wasn't in yet. She also confirmed his physical address, which was one we already had. We explained our difficulty in locating his address. She said she knew where he lived and gave us directions to a small convenience store and said it was right across the street.

We returned to the area and found the convenience store, but we still weren't sure which house was Thomason's. We learned from speaking with the clerk at the store that she knew Chris because he worked with her husband. She said, "Chris doesn't drive. Someone picks him up for work." She then walked us to the front door and pointed out his house.

We knocked on the door several times before Chris finally answered it. Even though it was almost 11:00 a.m., it was obvious he just woke up. After explaining who we were and our purpose, Chris agreed to be interviewed and invited us in. He looked just like his photograph. In a quick look around, it appeared as though Chris lived alone. I've seen my share of bachelor pads. We all sat down at a small round table in his kitchen. I asked Chris about his association with Stacy Stewart, Wright Childers, and others he was working with him at the NUCOR in Chemung, NY. Chris said, "I haven't seen Stacy in over six months. The last I heard, he was working for James Brent and living in Lake Jackson, Texas."

Chris said he'd lived with Stacy at his house in Lockwood, NY, during the final two weeks they were in New York. He explained how they'd utilized a moving van to move their belongings back and that as far as he knew, Stacy still had his (Chris') belongings. When asked about Wright Childers, he said, "Wright was my best friend up there." When they first went up, they all stayed at the Guthrie Inn and became friends. He'd probably spent more time with Wright than Stacy. He recalled Wright's accident and how seriously injured he was. He claimed to have visited him in the hospital and helped his mother clean out Wright's apartment. That's strange, because neither Wright's mom nor stepdad, ever mentioned that. Chris said Wright's accident was one of the reasons he decided to come back to Texas. After showing him Wright's picture and telling him that we had just recently spoken to him, he seemed pleased to know that Wright had recovered rather well from his accident.

When the interview turned to Michele Harris, he said he didn't really know her but said, "The SP came to the Trackside and inter-viewed Stacy and me." Frank and I just looked at each other. Surprisingly, this was the first we'd ever heard this. None of the leads we'd reviewed earlier, revealed anything about either Thomason or Stewart being interviewed at the Trackside. In fact, there was nothing about Thomason ever being questioned.

Continuing, he said, "We were sitting at the bar when the police came in. The first thing they told us was, we were in violation of our probation by being in a bar, but that was not why they wanted to talk to us." He said, "They separated us, and one of them interviewed me for a short time. But they kept Stacy a lot longer. What they were feeding us is there was this videotape of us at some nightclub and that we (Stacy and I) got separated, and Stacy had danced with the girl and knew her."

After the police left, Stacy told him that some waitress had told the police that he and Stacy had danced with her. Stacy also told him about taking a polygraph but never told him the results. Chris said, "I was never asked to take a polygraph." According to Thomason, when asked, he admitted that he, Stacy, and Wright would all frequently eat at Lefty's. He also admitted that the three of them frequented several of the area bars, including a strip-club just outside of town. Then added, "Wright dated one of the strippers for a while." And remembered her stage name was 'Delilah.' Together, the three of them had invited some of the dancers up to Stacy's cabin to party. Adding further, "When Stacy first got the place, we would spend a lot of time up there, riding four-wheelers, drinking beer and partying with the girls." We also learned that Stacy had a blonde girlfriend named Lisa, who worked at the hospital and was older than Stacy. Chris added, "Stacy preferred older women."

When asked what he could remember about September 11, 2001, he replied, "I was working. Got off work and went to the Trackside with Stacy." He claimed to have left the Trackside before Stacy but could not say what time. He said, "I can't vouch for Stacy's whereabouts after that." He was asked about their timecards and whether it would have been unusual for Stacy to go into work early? He answered, "We filled out our own timecards. It was kind of like the honor system, but as far as Stacy going in early, I never remember him going in early. If anything, he was probably late." I asked, "Do you know whether Stacy was fired or just quit?" He replied, "I got fired for not showing up for work, but as far as I know, Stacy just quit, but I can't say for sure."

When asked what more he could tell us about Stacy, he talked a little about the cabin he bought in the woods. He said, "I looked at that place before Stacy did but decided not to buy it because it only had one bedroom." Later, he learned that Stacy bought it and used to have some big party's up there. He mentioned further that Stacy had chronic high blood pressure and had to take medication daily. When asked, he confirmed that Stacy, at that time, was driving a black Chevrolet pick-up truck, and he was driving a white Chevrolet pick-up truck. We then asked if Stacy had ever told him about being with or arguing with a woman (Michele) on a backroad in the early morning hours and seeing a farmer pulling a hay-wagon drive by? "Nope. Never heard nothin' like that from Stacy." He was also asked if he knew anything about Stacy breaking into and burglarizing the house of one of his co-workers on his way back to Texas? "Nope. Don't know nothin about that either," he said.

As we were driving back to Crockett, we discussed our interview with Thomason. We both agreed he most likely knew who Michele was, and there was much more he wasn't telling us. No surprise there. I mentioned to Frank what I thought was very interesting was our learning of the SP interviews of Chris and Stacy at the Trackside. Frank said, "They didn't give us everything. They have something they don't want us to know."

"My thoughts exactly," I said. Then added, "Oh, and do you remember how vague the information was in that original lead, with no notes?"

Frank replied, "Yep. If they asked Stewart to take a poly, they know something we don't. That should've been in there."

"Right again. Agreed. I'm glad it's not just me thinking that," I said. Then added, "But It's good to know we're on the same page here." After a quick fist-bump, we were on our way back to Crockett.

We traveled back to Crockett to make another attempt at finding Betty or Stacy Stewart. The AutoTrack address history I had listed another address to try. The house we found appeared vacant. Neighbors we spoke to knew who they were but had not seen them in months and had no idea where they were now. We were running out of options when Frank suggested going back to the nursing center and try to speak with Angela Brent face-to-face.

The receptionist we had spoken to previously called Angela to the front desk. Since Frank had talked to her on the phone, I let him take the lead. Frank introduced us and again explained our purpose and asked if she could help us find Stacy. Frank said, "You know we're not the police. We just want to talk to him." Angela refused to provide any address or contact number for the Stewarts. Instead, she said she would call Stacy and provide him with our contact information. Frank said, "We're not here to accuse him of anything, we just want to talk to him. If he hasn't done anything wrong, why won't he talk to us to help clear his name?" Angela said she'd been researching our names on the internet. She wanted to discuss the Harris case and the judge's decision after the conviction. It was her understanding that Wright, Chris, and Stacy had all taken polygraphs and was surprised to learn that Stacy was the only one.

Frank explained the so-called 'clerical error' that prevented us from getting the results of his polygraph, and that was one of the reasons we wanted to speak with him. He also explained that others had taken polygraphs, and we had those results. Angela mentioned she had been following the case in the newspaper and had seen her cousin Stacy's name. She also knew that the eyewitness had seen a black or navy-blue pick-up truck. She felt the witness would never have been able to tell whether the truck was black or navy blue. It was also her opinion that when the farmer swerved into the other lane and could have been hit head-on by oncoming traffic but was still able to see what he says he saw was not believable. Obviously, Angela was not familiar with Hagadorn Hill. Suddenly, she could not talk anymore and had to get back to work. As she walked away, Frank said, "Tell Stacy we just want to clear up a few things. Have him call us." There was no reply.

We were now sure that Angela, too, knew something more. Why was she so protective of Stacy, and why was she taking such an interest in the case if she had no reason to believe Stacy was involved?

We were certain Stewart knew we were trying to locate him, and he was either deliberately avoiding us on his own or had been told not to talk to us. We were obviously disappointed that we had to leave Texas without being able to speak with him, but we were still encouraged with what information we did learn. For now, it was time to get back to NY and continue our investigation there.

36

BACK IN NEW YORK

After returning to NY, updating the attorney work product, and briefing Joe and Bill of our investigation in Texas, we went back to work to pick up where we'd left off. During our briefing, Bill said he'd read Steele's letter to the Judge, the statement he had given us, and had listened to the recording of his interview. Now, he wanted to meet with John Steele in person. I called Steele, made the arrangements, and took Bill to meet with him. After that, Bill said he was impressed with Steele and believed he would be a valuable and credible witness in the upcoming trial.

It was now December 28, 2007. For Cal's defense, there were some changes. As his last official function as Cal's attorney before stepping aside to become the next Broome County Court Judge, Joe Cawley wrote a letter to Jerry Keene and sent a copy to Judge Smith. In his letter, Joe referenced the matter of the 'new witness' and the letter he had written to the court and later receiving a copy himself.

Author's Note: Somehow, Keene learned of the new witness's letter to the court and made several written requests to the court (Judge Smith) demanding that the letter and identity of the new witness be turned over to him. Smith denied all of his requests.

As a professional courtesy, although under no obligation to do so, Joe decided to release the contents of Steele's letter and statement, but not his identity, in a two-page letter. As previously mentioned, with Joe stepping aside, Bill Easton would be taking over the role of lead defense counsel. Another significant change came when Dwight announced that Bill's new co-counsel was a highly qualified and respected defense attorney from Albany, NY, by the name of Terence 'Terry' Kindlon. He was now on-board and was already getting up to speed on the case.

The following day, I attended Joe's swearing-in ceremony as Broome County Court Judge at the Supreme Court Building in Binghamton. After congratulating him, I told him that the selfish me would miss working for him, but I was happy for him, and he was certainly the right man for the job. After taking a couple of days off for New Year's, it was time to get back to work.

Frank and I got back together and went to see Lisa Demtrak again. She was interested in what we had learned in Texas, and we were able to share a few things with her. We asked her what she knew about Wright Childers and a possible girlfriend he had by the name of Tammi. She knew Wright, but not all that well. Like Stewart, she knew he first lived at the Guthrie Inn when he first came to town but then later purchased a house on Chemung Street in Waverly. We explained that Tammi was possibly a 'pole dancer' at a strip club. She recommended we talk to Sue Nash, who she said was the owner of the Bare Facts strip-club.

Lisa confirmed what we had learned from Chris Thomason, about him staying with Stacy for a couple of weeks before they moved back to Texas. She also recalled seeing Nancy Gilbert at Stacy's house in December of that year. By then, her relationship with Stacy had become more of an "on-and-off thing." Where they would go for weeks without talking or seeing each other, and then he'd just show up. She added, "Now that I think about it when he did show up, it was just for sex." She admitted her relationship with Stacy was a bit strange. Surprisingly, without being asked, she said, "I think Stacy was involved in something and had something to hide, but I can't explain why I think that." A little female intuition, perhaps?

Being older than Stacy, I asked why she thought Stacy was attracted to her. She thought it might have been because she was a mature woman and mother with a steady job. We also learned that before she started dating Stacy, he had another girlfriend named Terra, who he brought up from Texas. She'd learned from Stacy that Terra got bored after a couple of weeks and moved back to Texas. She also remembered that Thomason had a girlfriend and thought she might have worked at the local convenience store. She was a little younger than Chris, maybe 18 to 20, with short blonde hair. When asked, she was not aware of Stacy's high blood pressure but did know he was taking medication for something. Before finishing up, we learned that several other girls had frequented Stacy's cabin in Lockwood, including Nancy Gilbert, Yolanda Lewis, and some of the strip-dancers from Bare Facts. She also confirmed what Nancy Gilbert told us that Stacy had bad credit and couldn't get cable TV, so he would rent and watch porno films.

> Author's Note: According to Stewart's pre-polygraph questionnaire, he was taking the prescription drug Diovan for the treatment of hypertension and high blood pressure.

I learned from Frank that he already knew Bare Facts owner Sue Nash, having interviewed her several years earlier during another investigation. He agreed to follow-up with her to see what we could learn about our trio's involvement with any of her nude dancers. Frank located Nash at home, and after explaining what we were interested in, she agreed to be interviewed. She confirmed that she and her husband were the owners of Bare Facts. After she offered a little history of the club, Frank showed her the color photographs of Stewart, Thomason, and Childers. Although she didn't know them by name, she immediately recognized all three as "regular customers" who came to her club. She then identified several of the dancers that would have been working back in 2001. She kept excellent employee records on all the girls, with dossiers that included their real names, stage names, photographs, and other pedigree information. Anxious to help us with our investigation, she voluntarily turned over all her records.

In a follow-up phone call with Nancy Gilbert, Frank learned the reason no one at NUCOR was willing to speak with us was that Michele's brother, Greg Taylor, was now working there as an inspector. During the call, Frank asked Nancy how she obtained the information about Stacy Stewart and Michele Harris having a sexual relationship? She explained that on Thanksgiving 2001, when Stacy was at her home for dinner, he'd told her that he'd been sleeping with Michele. She also added, "Whenever I mentioned her to Stacy after she went missing, he would just shut down." When asked to clarify 'shutdown,' she said, "He just didn't want to talk about her."

For the next several months, things had quieted down considerably, which gave me some time to catch up on a few other things that needed to be done. It wasn't until August 20, 2008, that things started to pick-up again. Our first demand for a complete copy of Stewart's polygraph report had been provided earlier, but a quick review revealed that it was incomplete. At least two significant pages were missing – specifically, the conclusion pages. After my meeting with the SP, we were supposed to be provided with the remaining documents. Now, almost a year later, we were receiving what was supposedly the missing pages, yet the conclusion pages were still missing. Notably, during my review of the pages we received, I noticed some discrepancies when comparing them to the other polygraphs.

The two polygraphs conducted by Investigator Bill McEvoy were those of Brian Earley and Michael Hakes. The duration of each was just shy of three hours. In contrast, the polygraphs of Mike Kasper and Stacy Stewart, conducted by Investigator Mike Myers, were slightly over an hour-and-a-half. In other words, nearly half the time.

Admittedly, I'm no polygraph examiner, but something wasn't right. I knew from personal experience that a completed polygraph takes much more than an hour-and-a-half. I also knew that McEvoy and Myers, as members of the same agency, had received the same training and supposedly followed the same examination protocols. So, why such a significant discrepancy in exam times? Why were the polys taken by McEvoy nearly twice as long? So, it would seem, that the shortened versions by Myers, is all that was necessary to make it official. Does any of this sound familiar? I was starting to see an ugly theme developing, which was markedly similar to what I had seen earlier. This looked suspiciously similar to some of the short-cuts they used to eliminate suspects earlier. It was also Myers who conducted that early bar lead. Remember? The one that revealed little or nothing. Was he just being lazy? Or was something else going on?

Finally, after another slow couple of months went by, there was a pre-trial scheduling conference held on October 22, 2008, to set a new trial date. With Judge Smith presiding, along with opposing counsel, a new trial date was set for February 17, 2009. The scheduling conference had only taken a few minutes. New attorney, Terry Kindlon, along with Bill and I, gathered after for a little chat over lunch. We had just started eating when Frank called to inform us that John Steele, our new witness, had passed away a few days earlier.

Not to trivialize his death but, talk about bad timing – or bad luck. This was another stunning blow and indeed the last thing we wanted to hear. I remembered Steele telling me he had diabetes, that he thought it would eventually take his life, but that was less than a year ago. I never dreamed it would be so quickly. Even though we had his sworn statement, which was backed up with a recorded interview, we knew his information would now fall under the legal classification of 'hearsay.' Bill and Terry said they would do some research to see if there was any way to legally salvage Steele's information for use at trial. With the likelihood that Steele's info could be denied, they asked me to continue my investigation to tighten up our defense, including my pursuit of Stacy Stewart.

In early December, Bill filed a 36-page motion regarding our now-deceased witness, John Steele, making arguments to support using his sworn statement at trial. Additionally, we had learned that John Steele had died on October 1, 2008. It was now two months later when Bill asked me to reach out to Steele's widow to see if she would speak with us. Since she lived in Waverly, I called Frank and asked him to accompany me. We found Sandra Steele, John's widow, at her home on Ellis Creek Road, and she agreed to speak with us. We learned that her late husband John had never said anything to her about writing a letter to a judge or speaking with Private Investigators. When asked, she described the details and circumstances surrounding his death, which involved having a heart attack and later dying at the hospital. She said, "The doctors believed his heart-attack was directly related to his diabetes."

After sharing the general contents of his statement, she was not surprised John had never said anything to her and admitted they didn't have a great relationship. We asked if she could recall where she was on

9/11. She remembered being home watching TV, and as far as she knew, John was at his office doing the same. She wondered whether his companion was male or female. We told her it was a female friend he had known back in high school, but she didn't recognize her name. Continuing, she added, "It wasn't unusual for John to drive the back roads." When we told her he had witnessed something important in a pending criminal matter, she immediately said, "Is it the Harris case?" At that time, we provided her with a few additional details about what John had seen.

After hearing the details, she said, "That sounds like John, he would never have told me anything about that." Notably, she was not demonstrating any animosity towards John and did not appear at all concerned that he had been with another woman. She remembered the post-trial information she heard about Kevin Tubbs and said, "I can understand why John would have been reluctant to say anything at the time." Then she added, "But if his conscience was bothering him, I could also understand him coming forth eventually. That just sounds so much like him."

Jerry Keene had learned the identity of John Steele from Bill's motion and immediately filed an opposing motion. Even in his death, Keene and the SP went on the attack to discredit Steele just as they had done with Kevin Tubbs. Hauntingly, Steele's fear of Keene's wrath would hold true even in death. Although there were now two independent witnesses, both describing similar scenarios, their only interest was to attack the witness's credibility. They had no interest whatsoever in investigating what either Steele or Tubbs had seen.

Other than a traffic ticket, Steele had no criminal history, nor any other issues involving law-enforcement. Not having found anything, they turned instead to the estranged relationship he had with his son, John Steele Jr. I had already learned about this from an earlier interview I had with Steele's sister, Dona Saltzgiver, in Elmira, NY. According to Dona, father-and-son had a major falling out over a substantial financial debt John Jr. had with his father. She'd cautioned me that if I were to speak with him, he would have nothing good to say about his father.

Not surprisingly, John Jr. was tracked down in Minnesota and provided the SP with a written statement. Subsequently, Keene prepared and filed an affidavit signed by John Jr., who was claiming that his father was not only a liar but also had poor eyesight. Of course, Keene could not resist turning over Jr.'s affidavit to the press, just like he'd done with Ashley Tubbs. In his affidavit, other than his own biased opinion, John Jr. offered nothing in support of his allegations.

Calling his father, a liar was one thing, but I couldn't let the eyesight issue go unchallenged. I had personal knowledge during my interview with John Steele that he had no problems with his eyesight, and that was six years after the fact. Furthermore, I checked motor vehicle records to learn that John Steele had successfully renewed his driver's license in 2003, with no restrictions for corrective lenses. In other words, he had passed the required eye-test two years *after* his 2001 sighting. Upon sharing John Jr.'s affidavit with Dona Saltzgiver, she said, "There was nothing wrong with John's eyes, and the only one lying here is John Jr."

With the trial only about a month away, we began re-interviewing our witnesses and tightening up any loose ends we could find. For those that might be called to testify, we reviewed their prior statements or testimony to prepare them for trial. I met with Kevin Tubbs and his family several times, reviewing and explaining what to expect at trial for their direct testimony, and more importantly, what to expect under cross-examination.

In mid-January, with the trial about a month out, Judge Smith made his two-part ruling. One, on our deceased witness, John Steele, and two, whether Dr. Henry Lee would be allowed to testify about the age of the blood. The next morning's headlines in the *Binghamton Press & Sun-Bulletin* read *"Man's statement barred from Harris trial,"* with the sub-headline, *"Judge also blocks testimony of blood samples."* In the article written by Nancy Dooling, her very first paragraph summed it up well. *"There will be no evidence from a dead man and no expert testimony on the precise age of blood during the second trial of Calvin Harris."* Having Steele's statement barred from being used at trial was a massive blow to the defense. Obviously, his account would have helped to corroborate Kevin Tubbs. This was a huge disappointment, but from a legal perspective, it was considered 'hearsay.' Therefore, it was not totally unexpected. On a more positive note, Smith's ruling also precluded Dr. Lee from testifying that the age of the blood was "a few days," as he did in the first trial. There was no scientific basis to support his opinion.

We didn't know if we would be calling Nancy Gilbert to testify at trial or not or if she would even be willing to do so. Until now, both Frank and I had established a good rapport with her. We decided to meet with her again to review everything and to see if she could add anything further. We learned that Stewart had never explicitly mentioned or referred to Michele Harris by name. He'd only referred to her as his 'cute little blonde' at Lefty's. Nancy only learned it was Michele Harris after she went missing. But whenever she brought up her (Michele's) name with Stewart, he would shut down, refuse to talk about it, and change the subject.

Nancy explained that Stewart would call her frequently, asking for advice or just to talk. She described herself as somewhat of a mother-like figure to him. He would often call, complaining about another girlfriend she knew to be Lisa Demtrak. At times, Demtrak used to show up at the Candlelite and pump her for information about Stacy. She added, "Lisa knows more than she's telling about Stacy."

When we showed her Stewart's photo, she said, "Yep looks just like him." When asked about the facial hair, she said, "It would vary from time-to-time from clean-shaven to a few days of growth, to neatly trimmed lines."

She also recognized the photos of Chris Thomason and Wright Childers, who were co-workers and friends of Stewart's. For her, there was always something suspicious about Thomason as well. She recalled, "He had to vacate his apartment shortly after Michele disappeared, but I never knew why." She then explained that all three of them would frequent the Bare Facts strip-club and invite the dancers up to Stewart's house in Lockwood to party.

Later, she told us that she had been interviewed by a tall male SP investigator (Myers) she believed in May or June of 2008. He said he was just following up some loose-ends and knew she had talked with a couple of the defense investigators. She told him everything she told us. Then said, "But he showed no interest and didn't like what I had to say."

During her interview with Myers, he told her they were convinced Cal was the killer, and they had "no reason to believe Stewart had anything to do with this." Then added, "We convicted him once, and we'll do it again." Nancy was unsure whether Stacy ever had Michele up to his cabin but believed it was very likely.

She recalled asking Stewart on many occasions, "How are things going with the 'cute blonde' at Lefty's?" Stewart would just smile, give her a thumbs up and say, "I scored."

In 1992, as part of my SP training, I attended the Institute on the Physical Significance of Bloodstain Evidence in Corning, NY. There, I trained under the expert instruction of Dr. Herb MacDonell and his skilled associate, Paul Kish.

In preparation for the second trial, Bill had expressed an interest in using a different blood expert and asked if I knew of anyone. I suggested Paul Kish, who had since started his own consulting business in blood-stain analysis and interpretation. When I called Kish, he still remembered me. He was interested but wanted to learn more. I told him I would have Bill get in touch with him. Later, Bill called me and said that Kish had agreed to take the case. He asked me to gather up and send him the pertinent photographs and other documentation he would need. Over the next two days, I made copies of everything and delivered them to Kish. About a week later, Bill and I consulted with Kish at his office in Corning, NY, to prepare for trial.

The trial was only two weeks out when Bill received notice that the newest discovery materials that included nearly 200 leads were available for pick-up at the DA's office. Frank picked it up and brought it to my office. We quickly made copies of everything and forwarded them to Bill and Terry, who were anxious to review the new material.

During my preliminary review, I realized there were leads in the file about interviews in Texas, which included Stacy Stewart and Chris Thomason. I said to myself, "Oh, this is going to be good. I can't wait to see what they have to say." I then noticed that it was *not* the SP who had done the interviews, but rather, a Texas Ranger by the name of Rudy Flores. His official title: Sgt. William Rodolfo 'Rudy' Flores – Texas Ranger. I was a bit confused as to why a Texas Ranger was doing the interviews and not the SP, but I was still very anxious to start reading.

Over the next few days, I spent a considerable amount of time reviewing the new material. I was especially interested in anything having to do with Stewart and/or Thomson. It didn't take long to realize that both Stewart and Thomason were obviously lying. It was also apparent that Ranger Flores, who was not really familiar with the case, had not been provided with enough information to ask the right questions.

Author's Note: Interestingly, it was noted that Stewart had been interviewed by Ranger Flores around the same time that Frank and I were in TN interviewing Wright Childers. Furthermore, Thomason had also been interviewed by Flores, shortly after our interview with him.

In a quick review of the lead log, I noted that Flores had interviewed Rachel Stewart, Stacy Stewart's ex-wife. Collectively, these interviews revealed a great deal of valuable information. I thought I should save the best for last, so, before I got to Stacy Stewart, I started with the Ranger interviews of Chris Thomason and Rachael Stewart.

In his interview of Thomason, Flores noted that the request to interview him had come from Sr. Investigator Les Hyman. Yet there was no info about when he had been contacted, what information had been provided, or any instructions about what questions to ask. During the discussion, it was apparent that the limited and incomplete information Flores had impeded his ability to conduct a thorough interview. Don't get me wrong. His conversation was not without value, but Flores' limited knowledge of the case prevented him from asking some pertinent questions. I was still a bit baffled as to why the SP, the ones with the most significant knowledge of the case, were not the ones doing the interview.

Thomason told Flores he had just been interviewed by two private investigators from New York and showed Flores the business cards we had given him. Flores was interested in what we had asked him. He just said we were asking many of the same questions he was. Flores included our questioning of whether he had any knowledge of Stacy doing a burglary. Even though we had never implied that Chris was involved in the burglary with

Stewart, he tells Flores, "…we didn't have the time, you know. We were at work the whole time." Obviously, Flores was unaware or had not been informed the alleged burglary took place *after* Thomason and Stewart had quit their jobs at NUCOR and were on their way back to Texas.

When Thomason was asked if he had ever frequented Lefty's, he replied, "I may have only been there once or twice, maybe three times."

That's *not* what he'd just told us hours earlier. Flores then asked, "Do you know the lady we're talking about?"

"I have no idea," he said.

Flores then asked, "If I told you her name, would you recognize it?"

"No. I don't have any idea who she is. I didn't know she worked there."

Really? As the interview shifted to Stacy Stewart, he told Flores that Stacy had dated a woman by the name of Lisa. Then added, "Stacy had an attraction to older women."

Flores asked a couple of work-related questions but nothing about their work hours, timecards, or going in early. The interview shifted to Stacy's cabin in the woods. After admitting he knew about the cabin and had been there with Stacy and Wright, Flores asked, "Did you all ever travel out there, take any gals with you, or anything like that?" Thomason's response was confusing and didn't seem to make much sense. He replied, "No. I mean, I had a couple of my girlfriends out there, but I mean he had his girlfriends out there too, but we never took anybody out there, no." Flores just left it at that.

Continuing, he told Flores that he had dated a couple of girls while he was up in New York. One was a girl with a lot of tattoo's that worked at the Trackside. But he claimed he could no longer remember her name. He'd also dated another girl by the name of 'Sapphire' who worked as a dancer at the Bare Facts strip-club. But couldn't remember her real name. He also told Flores a little about Wright Childers and how they hung out together. But he had "never seen Wright with a woman the whole time he was up there." Wow! How quickly he forgets. He'd just told us that Wright dated a strip-club dancer by the name of 'Delilah.' Wright told us the same thing.

With Thomason, it was nearly if not completely impossible to separate the truth from the lies. There may have been some bits of truth mixed in, with what he was telling Flores and us, but in my view, he knew a lot more and was not being entirely truthful. Also, notably missing from Flores' interview with Thomason were any questions about what he and Stacy were doing on 9/11 and 9/12.

From what I could tell, Flores had not been assigned a lead to interview Angela Brent. But shortly after our interview with her, she called him, and they spoke over the phone. Presumably, Angela had learned of Flores' involvement from Stacy Stewart, who we just learned had just been interviewed by Flores two days earlier. Although it appears this call happened after we had spoken with Angela at her workplace, it also indicated that she had spoken to Flores earlier. This may also explain why Stacy may have been deliberately avoiding us after being told not to speak with us. That being said, what did Angela have to say to Flores?

In Angela's call to Flores, she told him that we were asking several questions about Stacy. She told him that, in her opinion, we were trying to get info to incriminate him. And we'd told her about Stacy's time-cards, that showed him at work at 6:00 a.m. but how we suspect it may have been altered. She also mentioned us telling her about a witness who had seen a young man fitting Stacy's description with the girl after she was reported missing. Furthermore, the witness also described Stacy's truck and picked him out of a line-up.

Well, we did have Stacy's photograph, but there was no line-up, and we had not yet shown it to Kevin Tubbs. She'd also told Flores that we thought Stacy's polygraph was questionable. For the most part, with some minor exceptions, Angela's account of our interview that she shared with Flores was reasonably accurate. Interestingly, after his interview with Angela, Flores included a note at the end of his narrative which read; she claims to have read all the info on the web. She is very protective of Stewart. Even though I asked her not to talk to the PIs, she did. My impression was that she was too inquisitive to resist the chance to be involved in this.

Next up was Rachel Stewart, Stacy's ex-wife. This should be good. The day after Flores spoke with Angela, he also called and had a brief interview with Rachel Stewart by telephone. He learned from Rachel that she had known Stacy for about four years, but they had only been married for twenty-two months and were currently going through a divorce. She added that things were not going well because Stacy was refusing to sign the papers.

Continuing, she tells Flores that they do not communicate well at all. Stacy hadn't even called to let her know that Flores would be calling. She and Stacy had talked about the Harris case several times in the past, but he told her very little and tended to change the subject whenever it came up. That sounded familiar.

When she asked Stacy directly, whether he had anything to do with her disappearance, he said no. He'd told her that he never really knew Harris and that it was Chris Thomason who dated her. Continuing, she described Stacy as nothing but a 'drunk and a liar' who was also 'shady and secretive.' She advised there were many reasons for their break-up, but mostly it was because of his drinking, lying, and cheating. She also commented to Flores about his sketchy work history and how he'd left NUCOR on bad terms. He had tried getting his job back at the NUCOR plant in Grapeland, TX, but they wouldn't re-hire him. Later, she claimed Stacy's reason for leaving NY was to take care of his mother, who had bad alcohol and prescription drug problems. Describing her as "a freaking nut job" and blaming her for many of their marital woes. When asked, she had not yet been contacted by the PIs from New York then added, "But if I am, I'm going to talk to them."

Shortly after reading this, I got right on the phone and called Rachel. I wanted to learn what more she could tell me. She reaffirmed what she told Flores about Stacy being a drunk, a liar, and very secretive. She'd kicked him out of her house on November 17, 2007 (just days before we were there). She claimed that Stacy told her we had followed him home from work one day. Of course, that never happened. But it would seem that he did know we were in town looking for him. As far as she knew, he was now living with his mother in Crockett. But she also heard that he recently remarried and was living somewhere with his new wife. She had also learned that his mother, Betty, was no longer living in Crockett. Then added, "Betty has a major prescription drug and alcohol problem." Before I could ask, she offered further, "Stacy likes and is attracted to older women. He claims they are less complicated and easier to deal with." I had reached Rachel at her place of employment, and she had to get back to work. I told her she might be hearing from me again soon. "Any time," she said.

Even at this early stage, there was reason to believe that Wright Childers and Chris Thomason were both lying, which suggested they knew and were hiding something. With nothing to hide, there would have been no reason to lie. At this point, I had little doubt that a review of Stacy Stewart's interview would reveal even more lies. However, I was still concerned that Ranger Flores was not equipped with enough knowledge of the facts to conduct an effective interview. We're about to find out. But first, there were some exciting new developments taking place before the second trial.

PART IV

TRIAL #2

37

NEW JUDGE – NEW TRIAL DATE

A s the second trial date drew closer, we continued our preparation, including that brand-new batch of discovery material. The trial was now only four days away. We were in our final stage of trial prep and had just finished our review of the new discovery material we had received.

Judge Smith made some favorable post-conviction decisions on behalf of the defense, so Bill discussed with Cal about waiving his right to a trial by jury. Instead, opting for a 'bench trial' where Judge Smith alone, would be the sole trier of the facts. Ordinarily, a 'bench trial' is extremely risky, especially in a high-profile murder case. The analogy being, you're putting 'all your eggs in one basket.' After discussing the pros-and-cons, Cal decided that was what he wanted to do. After that, Bill filed a formal non-jury waiver with the court, which was subsequently granted.

However, within hours of the court's approval in granting the non-jury waiver, Keene filed a motion asking Judge Smith to recuse himself, once again alleging defense favoritism. Here we go again. Obviously, Smith was not happy, but on the day the trial was supposed to start, he recused himself, albeit reluctantly, and stepped aside. But not before blasting Keene once again for his ludicrous and unfounded reasons. As a result, the trial was postponed once again.

The day after Smith's recusal, another Nancy Dooling article appeared in the *Press & Sun-Bulletin* under the headline, *"Harris case judge steps aside."* After reviewing court papers, Dooling noted that Smith wrote, *"after examining his conscience, he could not have convicted Harris of murder 'beyond a reasonable doubt.'"* She also wrote that in Smith's decision, he made specific reference to the reasons Keene had cited for his removal and called them baseless. He also added, *"The District Attorney has yet again sought to take the low-road to accomplish his mission."*

I'd spent most of the day before the original start date of the trial doing prep with Bill, who had moved into a local motel in anticipation of a lengthy trial. The entire case file had been organized and stacked in plainly labeled boxes in his room, easily accessible for our review, and later transported to the courthouse. With the trial postponed, I took possession of the entire case file, except for a few documents retained by Bill. I stored them until a new trial date was set, and we were ready to start gearing up again.

Only one day after Smith's recusal, the Honorable James Hayden, a County Court Judge from neighboring Chemung County, NY, was appointed to preside over the Harris case as Smith's replacement. Hayden was a long-time prosecutor, who also had several years' experience on the bench. But within the local defense community, he had a well-known reputation as being a 'prosecutor's judge.' It was not a difficult decision for Bill to withdraw the non-jury waiver and proceed with a jury trial knowing this. The very next day, during a scheduling conference, with Judge Hayden presiding, a new trial date was set for July 13, 2009. We now had five months to absorb the new discovery and better prepare for the jury trial.

As District Attorney, Jerry Keene had been engaging in a recognizable and troubling pattern of prosecutorial misconduct, which was tantamount to unethical behavior. Much of which had already drawn judicial rebuke. Accordingly, Bill Easton prepared and filed a 28-page motion with the court, asking that the murder indictment against Cal be dismissed. He claimed that Cal's right to due process had already been violated and would continue to be violated. Or, as an alternative, Keene be dismissed from his role as prosecutor, and a 'Special Prosecutor' be appointed to replace him. Bill's motion outlined and detailed all the specific issues previously mentioned and more. I have little doubt, had Judge Smith been the one to rule on this motion, that it would have been granted. Unfortunately, Judge Hayden didn't see it that way, and he denied everything. The indictment would stand, and Keene would remain the prosecutor. The trial would continue as scheduled.

If you recall, shortly after Kevin Tubbs came forward after the first trial in June 2007, Frank Roney had interviewed a NUCOR employee, Lydia Monico. She admitted to having a relationship with Chris Thomason.

In reviewing the latest discovery material, we learned that the SP had interviewed Monico a few months later, in October 2007. Interestingly, during that interview, she told them something rather tangible that she'd never mentioned to Frank. Monico had been out with Chris Thomason one night when he'd become very drunk. They were walking out of the Best Western (former Guthrie Inn) towards their vehicles. Out-of-the-blue, he commented that he had gone up to Stacy Stewart's house one night to help him burn a bloody shirt he was wearing. Monico said, "It kind of freaked me out," but being fearful, had not asked Thomason for any details. I sent Frank back to re-interview Monico.

Monico was adamant that what Chris had said was absolutely true. She remembered it very vividly. She didn't know why she'd never told Frank about it earlier. She recalled being interviewed by the SP and telling them what Chris said but at the time, couldn't remember if it was before or after 9/11. However, having given the matter more thought since then, she had a much better recollection of when Chris made his comment. She said, "I had just learned that I was pregnant and knew there was a strong possibility Chris was the father. It was also the last time I ever saw Chris, and that was just after Thanksgiving. I'm positive."

38

THE STACY STEWART INTERVIEWS

I had already reviewed Ranger Flores' first interview with Stacy Stewart. But the latest discovery material also included a second interview. Ordinarily, I don't get too excited about things. But learning there was a second Stewart interview made me more than anxiously curious. I was excited and couldn't wait to see what else he had to say.

This time, the new discovery material included some of the back-and-forth e-mail correspondence between the SP and Ranger Flores, which finally provided some insight about when and what Flores was asked to do. According to the e-mails, Flores had first been in contact with Sr. Investigator Les Hyman, who was coordinating and requesting who he wanted to be interviewed in Texas. In his original e-mail to Flores, dated November 9, 2007, Hyman referred to a prior discussion he had with Flores and was now requesting he attempt to locate and interview Stewart.

Hyman had also asked Flores to try and determine whether Frank and I had been to Texas looking for Stewart. Continuing, he described Stewart as a suspect, whose vehicle was ostensibly seen by a witness at the end of the Harris driveway on the morning of her disappearance. He attached what little intelligence they had on Stewart and advised Flores that he could do an internet search for 'Cal Harris' to find a summary of the case. Hyman then wrote, *"Please advise when you've located him."*

Author's Note: I found it rather bizarre that Flores would have to rely on his own internet search for information on the case. But if it's on the internet, it must be true, right?

On November 26, 2007, Flores replied in an e-mail to Hyman, advising that after speaking with 'some folks in the know,' he'd been unable to locate Stewart. He also wrote, *"Rumor has it that he joined the military. Have ya'll received any info of this sort?"* There was no reply. However, even though there was no email that Stewart had been located, it became clear from Hyman's next e-mail that he had been. He was now e-mailing Flores with his request for what to include in the interview. Hyman's lead sentence to Flores jumped right off the page. I immediately highlighted where he wrote, *"Thanks. This is the request. Low-key and friendly."*

My first thought was, wait a minute. In his earlier e-mail, he'd just identified Stewart as a 'suspect.' Why on earth would he be asking Flores to keep it 'low-key and friendly' if he's a suspect? I'd known and worked with Hyman for over 12-years. He would be the last person I would expect to ever use a 'low-key and friendly' approach with any suspect. I've seen him in action many times. This just reaffirmed my belief that the SP feared that digging too deeply into Stewart could result in a total unraveling of their case against Cal. So, to avoid or eliminate that from happening, they would instead, strictly limit their investigation. In so doing, it would enable them to salvage their earlier elimination of Stewart as a suspect. Clearly, they had no interest in pursuing him as an actual suspect. Further support of that was found in reviewing the minimal requests made of Flores when interviewing Stewart. In the e-mail to Flores, his only request was that Stewart was asked the following:

- *Is he aware of the Harris trial?*
- *Last time he saw Michele?*
- *Ever to her house?*
- *Was she in his car?*
- *What was his vehicle – hers?*
- *Did he mention his attraction for her to others?*
- *Contact with anyone from NUCOR or New York? – Is he aware of any jewelry taken from New York?*

With all they knew about Stewart, that was it? No questions about his work hours or timecards. No questions about going in at 4:00 or 5:00 a.m. Nothing about his relationship with Lisa Demtrak or Nancy Gilbert. No questions about where he was, who he was with, or what he was doing on September 11th and 12th. Nothing about being at the base of the Harris driveway with Michele, his cabin in the woods, abandoning his property, or never making his first mortgage payment. No questions about Lefty's or Michele selling her jewelry. How about some questions about Thomason and Childers? These were just *some* of the elementary (no-brainer) questions that needed to be asked. Then, depending on his answers, there would likely be follow-up ones. Oh, and don't forget the 'burning of the bloody shirt.' Another no-brainer.

They must have thought we were deaf, dumb, and blind. Therefore, we would never recognize the true intent behind their irresponsible and unprofessional behavior or total lack of interest in pursuing the truth. With prideful egos and self-serving interests on-the-line, I understood why they were doing this. However, in the interest of justice, especially with a man's life at stake, there was an ethical, professional, and responsible obligation to do the right thing. But apparently, that only happens in the movies.

On November 27, 2007, Stewart had been located and was interviewed by Ranger Flores, at the office of the County Attorney at the Houston County Courthouse. Flores' narrative did not reveal how or where Stewart had been located. However, it did reveal that he was currently, and for the past five years, employed as a correctional supervisor (Sergeant) by the Texas Department of Criminal Justice, at the Ferguson Prison Unit in nearby Midway, Texas.

Stewart acknowledged that he had been in New York in 2001 and had worked at NUCOR. He also confirmed that he had initially resided in a hotel in Sayre, PA.

In explaining to Flores how it all started, a couple of police officers came to NUCOR and pulled him off the line and started asking him questions.

Continuing, he then described himself as the 'quiet' type, but detectives had told him he 'fit the profile.'

Flores asked, "The profile of what?"

Stewart replied, "Whatever, I didn't even know what happened, I mean, I do know the girl, or I knew her."

Then, when Flores asked if he knew the young lady they were

talking about, he denied knowing her name but knew who she was. When asked how well he knew her, he said he didn't know her as a friend, but more like a casual acquaintance.

Flores continued his questioning by asking him to describe the circumstances of the casual acquaintance. He claimed to have met her where she worked at this little burger joint named Lefty's, having met her through his friends, Wright Childers and Chris Thomason. He also added that Wright and Chris were more into talking with her then he was. Yet he knew she had a bunch of kids but claimed to have only learned that from Wright and Chris.

Flores asked, "Was she a good-looking young lady?"

"She wasn't ugly," he said.

Stewart knew his name had appeared in the newspaper and explained how he'd learned from his cousin Angela that the case had appeared on television. When asked, he denied following the case himself. Flores, in response, made a good point when he said, "You hadn't? I know if my name had been brought up in connection with some unsolved crime, I might still be curious about it and want to look into it as tracking what's going on just morbid curiosity."

Stewart replied, "I had too many other things going on in my life to worry about it."

The interview then shifted back to his knowledge of Michele. He asked, "When was the last time that you saw this lady that we're talking about, Michele?"

Stewart replied, "I want to say down there in the bar in that hotel. That was the last time I'd seen her, and then I know Chris and Wright, these other two guys that I hung out with, they actually went out with um."

Flores continued, "Were they kind of hustling her?"

Stewart said, "From what I was told, now I don't know for sure, but I'm not a nosy person. I heard them talk about it that maybe Chris had slept with her."

So, now he's trying to throw his so-called friend, under the bus.

They then talk a little about his relationship with Thomason and Childers and how they'd hang out together, including there at Lefty's. Flores asked, "Did this gal Michele and her girlfriend and other friends from work, did you all wind-up kind of interacting and visiting there at Lefty's?"

Stewart replied, "No, never had, never."

Personally, I think Flores knew Stewart was lying to him, but he'd continue to obey his instructions to keep it 'low-key and friendly.'

In his own 'friendly' way of confronting Stewart, he follows up with, "I mean you know it just becomes like this group and that group see each other and visit when they run into each other."

In his continued effort to distance himself from Michele, Stewart says, "No. I wouldn't say that. It was more like ah ... hey how ya doin ... but it was the other two who would always do the talking, you know."

What a line of crap. I was sure Flores wasn't buying it because I knew I wasn't. Sure enough, in his attempt to pursue the matter further, he tells Stewart how he knows how young single guys are around women and how they talk about them.

In response, Stewart said, "Well, he (Chris) had his share of women up there, and I had a, I was with an older woman but like I said that was pretty much, that was the only thing I did." He then denied ever having talks or conversations with Chris about women but only over-heard him talking. Come on! I was young and single once. And like Flores said, "I know how young single guys are, and what they like to talk about." More lies.

Continuing, Stewart told Flores about the house he bought in the woods. His friends would come and hang out there on the weekends. Flores asked, "Did he (Chris) ever bring her to your house?"

Responding quickly, Stewart said, "No, no sir, never. She was never out there."

Flores asked similar questions about whether he and Chris had ever been to her (Michele's) house, or whether she had ever been in either of their vehicles. Stewart sturdily denied everything.

Following up, Flores asked, "Did you even know what kind of vehicle she drove?"

Interestingly, Stewart answered, "I think she had a mini-van. A ragged mini-van and I want to say she had a bunch of kids." But he was then quick to clarify that he'd only learned that from his conversations with Wright and Chris. Indeed.

When Flores was talking to him about his cabin, I found it interesting that he had not asked why he'd abandoned it and moved back to Texas without ever making his first mortgage payment or trying to sell it. Perhaps, the SP just 'forgot' to include those little details.

In my interpretation of his next question, it appeared he was setting the groundwork for an important question to ask Stewart. "I know that a lot of us place ourselves or relate to things in our lives by significant dates and events." He then asks, "For instance, do you remember when the Columbia Shuttle disaster happened, and the pieces of it started falling on East Texas?"

Stewart replied, "Right, yes sir, I was lying on the couch with the sonic boom. You could feel it." I was quite certain I knew where Flores was going with this. Sure enough. With the stage set, even though he had not been instructed to do so, he follows up by reminding Stewart that this case happened back around 9/11. To start, Stewart confirmed that he was in NY at the time.

Flores asks, "Can you remember where you were at on 9/11?"

Stewart dodged the question and replied, "9/11. That weekend I went to New York City, the first time I'd ever been there. I think we left on Friday evening, and we all took off work on Saturday, me, and Wright and Chris." Then went on to explain how the three of them spent the weekend before 9/11 in New York City and then started heading back late Sunday night. When asked, he said that while they were in New York City, they had done some sightseeing and barhopping, but other than that, he did not elaborate further. Notably, Flores had not asked him where he was *before* 9/11 but rather where he was when it happened. It's still a mystery as to why Stewart answered that way, and what we'll learn shortly will only add to the mystery.

As the interview continued, Stewart explained how they had returned home late Sunday evening and into the early morning hours of Monday. During the interview, Flores indicated that he was following along with a calendar.

In finishing his story to Flores, he said, "Monday morning, I got up late for work. I was tired, and I can still remember getting in my truck on the way to work, and it came over the radio. The first one had done hit, and then by the time I got to the parking lot at work, the second one done hit. I still remember that very, very vividly."

Unfortunately, Flores had not been provided with Stewart's time-cards. Otherwise, he would have realized that Stewart was either mistaken or lying about his trip to NYC and his account of what happened on Monday. Why? Because 9/11 didn't happen on Monday, it was Tuesday. His timecards would have also shown that he worked a full day on the same Saturday he claimed to have gone to NYC. With the right information, Flores could have given Stewart the opportunity to either correct himself or sink himself further.

When questioned about the older girlfriend he had in NY, Stewart confirmed he had been seeing a woman by the name of Lisa but could no longer remember her last name.

Flores then switched gears and resumed his questioning about the day he was questioned by the NY investigators who had told him he 'fit the profile.' He asks, "Were they trying to make you a suspect or pull you into this deal somehow or what?"

Stewart, in somewhat of a muddled response replied, "Cause me knowing that Chris, they had hung out before with these guys and they didn't say a word to them, and you know, and the guys are like well really, we've got people in town say you're the quiet one, you'd fit the profile for somebody coming up missing or somebody getting killed and all this. I'm like...it took me for a loop right there. It scared me. I mean cause, I don't know, I don't know the law, I don't know, I know I ain't done nothing, but then again you know things can get turned around. So, I was, I didn't figure out how they came out with that profile."

Flores then, in another 'low-key and friendly' manner, questioned Stewart about the jewelry burglary. He softened his approach by telling him, "Look, you're not in any trouble for anything, but I had a bunch of questions that I wanted to ask based on the guys up there that are asking, talking to me." Flores then informs Stewart and asks him about the jewelry that was taken and how some of it had later been returned. Stewart quickly denied knowing anything at all.

When Flores asked if he was aware of it at all, he said, "I'm not. That's the first I've heard."

Flores tries to soften it further by saying, "I'm not saying you were involved. I'm saying maybe somebody else was involved and you said, that's BS guys, we gotta send that back, I'm taking it, and I'm sending it for you."

Stewart didn't quite take the bait. Instead, he tries to imply that Chris may have done something when he says, "I don't know. Chris never said anything about it, but Chris kind of got off on a, and I'm not telling on the guy, he got off on the beaten path up there. I think they started what do you call this stuff, methamphetamines or something maybe."

Switching back to the topic of Michele, Flores continues with, "Well, let me ask you this. You said that girl wasn't ugly, and maybe that is being polite, maybe it is just a little gentlemanly but without remarking on her looks, was she an attractive girl? Did you find her attractive?"

"Yea, it would have been somebody you could have probably went out with, you know, but I didn't. I just, she didn't strike me as that type or didn't get my fancy."

So, she wasn't your type and didn't fit your fancy? Seriously? Come on, Stacy, other than the SP, do you really think anyone else is going to buy that? From my perspective, Flores wasn't buying any of this either and was likely on the verge of a confrontation. But when remembering his instructions to keep it 'low-key and friendly,' he just bit his lip and backed off.

Nearing the end of the interview, Stewart brought up the topic of his polygraph when he said, "You know I went up there and I had to go take a polygraph test, they had asked me." He then explained how one of the lead detectives (Myers), who was a "pretty cool guy" had given him the test. Interestingly, he added, "It kind of boiled down to there was like fourteen or fifteen of us that got subjected to this polygraph and supposedly her husband is the only one that wouldn't take it because they were going through a divorce and he was going to have to drop a nice chunk of change to her."

Fourteen or fifteen other polygraphs? Where did he come up with those figures, and who is 'us?' Was someone feeding him the information about the husband, or did he have some direct knowledge?

Flores then asked how he did with his polygraph. Stewart replied, "He said there ain't nothing for me to worry about." To me, being told you have 'nothing to worry about' is not the same as being told, 'you passed.' Considering the suspicious nature of the missing results of his polygraph, for all I knew, he'd failed. But in Myers' adamant belief that Cal killed Michele, simply told Stewart that he had 'nothing to worry about.'

Ranger Flores had audio-recorded his interview with Stewart, which he subsequently turned over to the SP. It was later transcribed word-for-word. Copies of both the audio-recording and the written transcripts were later turned over to the defense through the discovery process. Considering the limited amount of information he had to work with, Flores had done an excellent job. More importantly, had he been provided with complete information about the case, and the authority to go above-and-beyond the 'low-key and friendly' approach, the end results could have been markedly different.

Flores had done everything requested of him and more. Notably, more than a year had passed since Stewart's interview, and it was now early February of 2009. The second trial was less than two weeks away. At some point, the SP recognized some rather stark discrepancies that needed to be addressed and realized they would need to provide Flores with additional information and then ask him to interview Stewart again. I still couldn't understand why they hadn't done this in the first place. Unless, of course, they thought by keeping it simple, they could close-the-book on Stewart once and for all. Perhaps, they realized that Flores' expanded interview of Stewart had opened the door to other issues that kept the matter alive. Regardless, Flores was contacted again and provided with the additional information he would need when re-interviewing Stewart.

The new information sent to Flores included a copy of Stewart's phone records, for the cell phone he used while he was in NY. Records showed that he'd used his cell phone to call work (NUCOR) on September 12, 13, & 14 of 2001. Notably, even though he'd been working there since April, these were the *only* times he had ever used his cell phone to call work. The obvious question that needed to be asked; if he was already at work on those days, why was he calling work? Before September 12, 2001, he had never done that. Then, starting on the very day Michele was first reported missing, he called three consecutive days in a row.

The SP also wanted Flores to ask Stewart about his relationship with Nancy Gilbert since she was the one who had reported the burglary and the returned jewelry. They'd also sent him a copy of Stewart's timecards and asked to have Stewart explain and clarify his entries. Finally! Perhaps now we're getting somewhere. On February 9, 2009, in a reply e-mail, Flores notified Hyman that he was meeting with Stewart the next day, and he would record the interview and send it to him. I couldn't wait to hear what he had to say this time.

Flores conducted his second interview of Stewart at the Ferguson Prison Unit in Midway, Texas, where Stewart was still working but had since been promoted to the rank of Lieutenant. When starting his interview, Flores referred to having Stewart's timecards and a calendar in front of him. Before the interview, he'd given Stewart some lead-time to review his timecards. He started by reminding him that during his first interview, he'd talked about a trip he'd made to NYC with Childers and Thomason in September of 2001. Stewart agreed.

When asked if he could still remember the dates of his trip, Stewart replied, "Well, evidently, after looking at the records it's like I said, I could have over-shot the weekend that we took, because it's showing up the weekend of the eighth and ninth was that Saturday and Sunday. It shows that I was working. So, like I said, it could have been the prior weekend, but it seemed like it was the weekend of the 11th." Obviously, Stewart hadn't looked at his work records for the prior weekend, either. Or for that matter, the week before that. His records indicated he had worked all three weekends prior to 9/11. So, were his own records wrong, or was he lying? And if he was lying, why lie about something like that?

Under continued questioning, Stewart insisted that the trip was in September and again reiterated that Chris and Wright had gone with him. With the questions that followed, it seemed rather evident that Flores didn't believe what he was saying and was looking for some type of corroboration when he asks, "Anybody else that you went with that could maybe give a better date or time on the trip, or where you stayed at, what hotel, or motel?" These were great questions. I was surprised he hadn't asked these during his first interview. He even asked him about any credit card or other receipts he may have filed away. Stewart said he didn't keep those kinds of records. And couldn't even remember where they had stayed.

Flores abandoned his effort to corroborate Stewart's NYC trip and shifted the interview back to the timecards. Systematically going through the timecards and having Stewart explain all the entries, which were all handwritten. Later, Stewart admitted and confirmed that all the entries on his timecards were in his own handwriting and had been personally made by him. The only exception was the signature of his supervisor, who signed the bottom of the card at the end of each week before going to payroll. He further admitted that because it was a new business just getting started, they did not use punch-cards and added, "We just managed our own time."

Flores asked, "Could you be running late and have one of your buddies sign in or something like that?"

"Never was late. If I was late, I called in to my supervisor."

That was certainly not the story we heard from those who knew and worked with him, including his supervisor. A review of his time-cards revealed multiple 'late' entries. Flores then referred to his calendar to show Stewart that 9/11 was on a Tuesday and not Monday, as he'd claimed during his first interview. He also pointed out that according to his timecard, he was late for work by three hours on Tuesday, not Monday. He then admitted that he was late that day and that he had personally made the 'late' notation on his card. But when asked, he couldn't remember why he was late that day.

Flores then brought Stewart's cell phone records into the interview. After a few lead-in questions, Stewart finally admitted they were his records. Flores was interested in a number he had called that had been identified as the main number for the office at NUCOR. He admitted that if his records showed any calls to NUCOR, it would have been him making the calls. Flores then hit Stewart with the question I'd been waiting for; "If you were at work, why would you need to call work?"

He attempted to dodge the question initially by answering, "Well, it was a big facility. It was nothing to walk around with a cell phone." Then added, "We all had cell phones on us. There were no rules says we couldn't."

He had not answered the question.

Flores then zeroed in on the calls he made to NUCOR while supposedly, he was already at work on the 12th, 13th, and 14th of September. Flores asked, "Can you recollect if you had any reason to call the office that day for anything that stands out in your mind?"

I didn't like his bogus answer, and I doubt Flores did either. Stewart said, "Well, the only reason I would have called back is to talk to my supervisor or one of the other supervisors. Letting them know that I had a lot of running around to do. You know what I'm saying? Still trying to get settled in. Or, I called and said, hey, I may be a few minutes late coming from lunch."

Seriously? Still trying to get 'settled in?' What does that mean? He'd been working there for six months. More importantly, the only calls he ever made to the office from his cell phone, just happened to start on the very day Michele went missing and the two days that immediately followed. He'd been working there since April. Nary once, prior to September 12th, had he ever called his office using his cell phone. Coincidence? Indeed.

As instructed, Flores re-questioned Stewart about the jewelry burglary. He remained steadfast in his denial that he had anything to do with it and didn't know of anyone else that was. Flores shifted back to the timecards and explicitly asked if he could recall actually being at work on that Wednesday, September 12th. Stewart said if the record shows he was there Wednesday, then he was there.

Flores switched back to his cell phone records and the calls he made to the office on those three days (12th, 13th & 14th) using his cell phone and asked, "Do you remember, or do you have a clear recollection of the calls you made on those days when you called the front office at the NUCOR facility?"

"I don't have recollection of it, but it is very possible I did because it was not uncommon to call the office."

Not uncommon? If it was not 'uncommon,' why were there no other calls other than those three consecutive days, right after Michele went missing?

Flores wasn't buying his explanation and followed-up with, "When you do call the front office, what various reasons could you have for doing that?"

Again, he said it could have been that he was late returning from lunch or had to stop at the post office to pay bills, or perhaps go to a Doctor's appointment.

Interestingly, the one explanation I was expecting him to offer that he never did, was calling in sick. Remember the office secretary, Jessica Hunsinger? She said Stewart had called in sick a couple of days around the time Michele went missing. Although she had not made a note of it and was unable to recall an exact date(s), she was sure it was within a day or two. Notably, on Stewart's timecards, that he filled in himself, there were no 'sick' entries noted during the entire week *before* or *after* Michele went missing. So much for the 'honor' system. Anyway, it became obvious that the SP knew there was a problem with these calls, especially since they only took place on those key dates following Michele's disappearance. Therefore, their only hope of resolving the issue was if Stewart could provide a plausible explanation. From my perspective, that never happened.

Author's Note: Interestingly, Stewart not only had a cell phone but a landline phone as well, which was clearly documented in the original lead in 2001. Unfortunately, we'll never know what additional information may have been revealed in those records because the SP never obtained them. Or, if they did, they were never disclosed.

I found it troubling that even after more than a year and two lengthy interviews of Stacy Stewart by Ranger Flores, several of the previously mentioned pertinent questions still had never been asked. Troubling, because I knew from my own experience how thorough and aggressive the SP could be during the questioning of a suspect. From what I had just learned in my assessment of Stewart's interviews, with no other plausible explanation, the only conclusion I could draw was that there had been a conscious decision not to ask specific questions. But the most troubling part was trying to understand why. Had their rational pursuit of justice been compromised or replaced by confirmation bias,[1] self-righteous attitudes, or prideful egos? Or perhaps some combination of each? I could not even fathom how the SP could so blindly and willfully ignore the obvious.

From my perspective, the police's refusal to listen was a clear sign of ignorance or denial. Healthy skepticism is one thing. That I can accept. Denialism, on the other hand, is the cowardly way of avoiding or rejecting an 'uncomfortable truth.' In-as-much, a cognitive bias had deeply embedded itself. Potentially valuable facts that didn't coincide with their preconceived beliefs were being selectively filtered out, shoved aside, or buried. Thereby causing adverse effects on their perceptions and decision-making process, resulting in less-than-optimal choices. Whether they realized it or not, they were embracing a 'formula for injustice.' And their continued efforts to hide the truth were making them look foolish. I've said this before, but I'll say it again, "This was not the SP that I knew."

What we just learned from the Flores interviews, would strengthen the defense position and belief that Stacy Stewart, along with one or more others, were responsible for, or directly involved in the disappearance of Michele Harris. We were now equipped with new information along with a renewed motivation to continue the pursuit of our own independent investigation. The second trial is near, and preparations are underway.

---

1. Confirmation bias: a type of cognitive bias that causes people to search for, favor, interpret and recall information in a way that confirms their preexisting beliefs.

39

BACK TO TEXAS

With the new trial date set for July, we still had a great deal of work to do. After reviewing the most recent discovery material, especially that about the Texas interviews, the overwhelming consensus during our defense team briefings was for Frank and me to return to Texas. Nearly sixteen months had passed since our first trip. Since then, we had learned a great deal more. Pending final approval, Frank and I began gathering information and mapping out a plan for a return trip. Dwight and Cal were all for it, and permission was granted. Our preparations continued.

I was somewhat concerned, or perhaps even a bit paranoid that the SP might be on alert for a defense trip back to Texas. Fearing that if they found out, they might try to shut down our investigation by instructing witnesses not to cooperate with us. After all, they'd done it before. Believing that they may have flagged our names with the airlines, and/or our credit card transactions, I made an executive decision that we would drive to Texas and use cash for all our expenses. Frank agreed.

Early afternoon on Sunday, March 8, 2009, I picked up Frank, and we were on our way to Texas. We drove as far as Louisville, KY before stopping around 2:30 A.M., catching about four hours of sleep, and then hitting the road again. We pulled into Crockett, TX later that night around 10:00 p.m. We did not have a current confirmed address for Stewart, but we knew he worked at the Ferguson Prison Unit in nearby Midway, Texas. With a little help from AutoTrack, we also learned that he was currently driving a white, 2008 Toyota, Tacoma pick-up truck.

After quickly checking into our hotel in Crockett, we drove out to the prison, arriving just before 11:00 p.m. We drove around the prison campus familiarizing ourselves with the layout and looking for Stewart's vehicle in the parking areas. We didn't want to spend too much time, repeatedly driving around the campus that might arouse suspicion, so we set-up loose surveillance just off prison grounds to see if we could spot Stewart's truck either coming or going. Around midnight, we observed some activity that we thought may have been related to a shift change, but we didn't see Stewart's vehicle. We maintained our surveillance for another two hours but saw no further activity. We were still a bit tired from our trip, so we packed it in for the night and headed back to the hotel. During our drive back, Frank suggested having Stewart's old girlfriend, Lisa Demtrak, back in NY, call the prison and just ask for Stewart to see if he was working. We could have called ourselves, but we knew the call would be recorded, so Frank's idea was a better option.

From all the times Frank had interviewed Demtrak, he'd developed a much better rapport with her, and she had always been cooperative. Before we left, he'd met with Demtrak and taken her picture just in case we decided to show it to some of the people we would be talking to. The next morning, Frank called, and she agreed to make the call. Within fifteen minutes, she called back. She'd learned that Stewart worked the 6:00 a.m. to 6:00 p.m. shift but was currently off on a four-day pass.

While we were contemplating our next move in locating Stewart, we decided we would try and re-interview Chris Thomason. Frank called NUCOR and learned that he was not at work but was still working the afternoon shift, so we went directly to his house. After opening the door, Chris recognized us from before and said, "I was told not to talk to you guys." We explained how we knew he had been interviewed by Ranger Flores shortly after we left last time, but there were a few things we wanted to try and clear up. He said, "Sure, why not, come on in." I didn't bother asking who it was that told him not to speak with us because I already knew. As suspected, the SP was trying to roadblock our investigation, but why? My thought was, and Frank agreed, they likely feared that we would learn something favorable to the defense, that might further undermine their case. Therefore, in their effort to prevent anything like that from happening, they would try and shut us down any way they could.

To open-up, I asked Chris if he had learned anything during his interview with Ranger Flores about what he had learned from Stacy Stewart, who he had interviewed two days earlier. Flores had never mentioned anything about his interview with Stewart. I was curious because when I first reviewed Flores' interview with Thomason, even though he'd already interviewed Stewart, I noticed he'd never asked him anything about Stewart's claim of going to NYC with him and Childers. So, I started by asking Chris to tell us about the trip he had taken to NYC with Stewart and Childers the weekend before 9/11.

Chris, appearing somewhat dumbfounded, said, "What are you talking about? I never took a trip to New York City with Stacy. I've never been to New York City in my life."

I said, "Well, according to Stacy, you did."

"Well, I'm telling you that never happened."

Following up, I asked if Stacy had ever said anything about a trip to NYC. He seemed to think he had heard something about going for New Year's but didn't believe it ever happened. He said, "All I know is, I never went, and Stacy never said anything to me about going there with anyone."

Of course, my first thought was, a trip to NYC for New Year's should have been a lot more memorable than a generic trip to go sight-seeing and barhopping. How could Stewart be so mistaken about who he went with, what he did while he was there, and when? For now, it would have to remain a mystery.

Thomason was then asked if he knew Michele Harris.

He answered, "Never even met the girl."

We then told him that Stacy identified him as the one who was dating and involved with Michele Harris. Appearing somewhat surprised, he couldn't understand why Stacy would be saying that because "it was Stacy who was involved with her." Continuing, he said, "Stacy always went for the older girls. Every girl he ever dated was much older." He went on to say that he (Chris) always went for the younger girls and described one of the girls he was dating that worked at the Trackside. He remembered her having multiple tattoos and long red hair.

Frank asked, "Would that be Kari, Kari Cavanaugh?"

"Yep, that's the name," he said.

Moving on, I asked, "Out of all the steelworkers at NUCOR, why would Stacy be singled out to take a polygraph? Chris said, "That's easy. Because Stacy knew the girl."

I shifted the interview back to the day of 9/11 and asked what he could remember doing that day. After work, he had met up with Cavanaugh at the Trackside. Other than meeting up with her, he couldn't recall anything further.

As we continued, even though he had just told us that he "never even met the girl," he explained that Michele Harris was one of the first girls that Stacy met. He knew he was attracted to her because he talked about her all the time. He then added, "Whenever we went there (Lefty's), he'd always ask for a table in her section, and he was always saying how much he'd love to get in her pants." Later he added, "We went to Lefty's quite often." When explicitly asked whether he knew or Stacy had ever told him that he'd slept with Michele, he said, "I just assumed he had, but I can't say for sure."

As the interview continued, he said he and Stacy lost touch with each other and had not spoken in a long time. He described how they'd each driven back to TX with their own pick-up trucks. He had a white Chevy pick-up, and Stacy had a black one. About two weeks before they started back to Texas, he'd moved in with Stacy at his cabin. All their collective belongings were packed in a big Mayflower moving-van and moved back to Texas.

The interview then shifted to Lydia Monico, the girl we learned had been dating Chris when he was in NY. He admitted that he did have a relationship with her. Frank then explained what he had learned, about the two of them being at the Guthrie Inn, when he'd been drinking heavily and made a comment about going up to Stewart's house to help him burn some bloody clothes. Thomason's entire demeanor and expression changed rather abruptly. He then nervously denied having any recollection of ever saying that but added quickly, "She's probably just saying that to try and get me back to NY to pay child support."

I said, "So, I'm assuming that if you think it's possible, she had your child, you must have slept with her?"

"Yeah, a few times," he said.

I then turned the interview to the burglary of the Gilbert residence and the jewelry that was taken. To ease the tension a little, I told Chris, regardless of who may have done this, the statute of limitations on the crime was long gone. Thomason remained steadfast that he was not involved and did not know who was, then added, "I'm not a thief." He also denied that Stewart had ever said anything about stealing money, jewelry, or the 'Stewart file' from the Gilbert's.

As we continued, we spoke briefly about Wright Childers and his accident, the timecards at NUCOR and some of Stacy's old girlfriends. He told us he was good friends with Wright and how he had hung around with him and Stacy quite often, including Lefty's, the strip club, and Stacy's house. He said, "We had some big parties up there." When asked further, he admitted to some heavy beer drinking, bonfires, and lots of girls.

I then asked, "What about porno movies?"

"That too," he said.

Shifting back to NUCOR, Chris agreed that the individual workers filled out their own timecards on the honor system. If any corrections needed to be made, they were done by the supervisor. Explaining further that his supervisor was James Brent, who did everything by-the-book. Then said, "But Stacy and his supervisor had a different relationship."

"What do you mean by 'different relationship'?" I asked.

"Sanford was never one to rock-the-boat so, as long as the work got done, he'd cut Stacy a lot of slack. I could never get away with that shit with Brent."

Following up, I asked, "So, do you think Sanford would ever cover for him?"

"Well, he'd probably deny it, but yeah, it wouldn't surprise me."

Just before ending the interview, Chris admitted that he knew the Gilberts, and he and Stewart had been to their house for Thanksgiving and perhaps one other time. They had also visited Nancy Gilbert at the Candlelite Lounge, where she worked. Before leaving, we exchanged phone numbers, and he said we could call him any time if we had more questions. As we were walking out the door, I said, "You know Chris, you should call Stacy and ask him why he's pointing the finger at you." He said, "Yeah, maybe I'll do that."

It was now early afternoon. We were just leaving Thomason's and heading back to Crockett to renew our search for Stewart. Along the way, we discussed our interview with Thomason. We were both still in agreement that even though he was cooperative, he knew something more and wasn't being entirely truthful. He was still holding back and hiding something. We thought by telling him that Stewart was pointing the finger at him, he might be more forthcoming with what more he knew. Unless, of course, he was also involved, and anything he said might tend to incriminate himself as well. We also considered the likely possibility that if they both had knowledge of, or were equally involved in what happened to Michele, they may have made a pact between themselves to keep their mouths shut. Otherwise, they might both go down.

Earlier, I called and spoke with Rachel Stewart, Stacy's ex-wife. I explained that we were in the area and would like to meet with her. She was still at work but said if we came in the late afternoon, things would be quieter, and we could talk with her there. Just before 4:00 p.m., we arrived at Baker-Hughes Drilling Fluids in nearby Trinity, Texas, where she worked as a receptionist. She was anxious to speak with us and invited us into her office. Rachel was attractive and stood only about five-two, with short blonde hair, hazel eyes, petite figure, and a cute smile. I was surprised at how young she looked and then learned that she was nearly nine years younger than Stewart. Apparently, he likes them young as well.

Rachel was very forthcoming about her relationship and marriage to Stacy. In her opening comments, she quickly characterized Stacy as a 'drunken liar' and 'very secretive.' I remembered her telling me this previously. We then asked if Stacy had ever given her any jewelry. During their relationship, he had given her a diamond necklace in a silver setting that he'd purchased at a pawn shop, and she was with him when he bought it. He'd also given her a wedding ring, which she still had. After they divorced, and he left, his mother wanted her to return the jewelry, but she refused.

Rachel also knew that Betty Stewart, who had health problems due to alcohol and prescription drugs, had left Crockett to move in with her sister down near Houston. She had told me previously that she thought Stacy had remarried. Since then, she learned he had gotten remarried to a woman by the name of Crystal Thomas. Crystal had been married before and had children. She and Stacy were currently living together in a campus housing unit right on the grounds of the Ferguson Prison Unit. She advised further that an added perk of being a Lieutenant was free housing at the facility. She described Crystal as being older and a little taller than her, heavy-set, with a round face and brown curly hair. She'd also seen Chrystal's vehicle and gave us the description.

Later, Frank and I returned to the Ferguson Prison Unit and pulled into the facility just as the sun was starting to set. We located the housing area and started looking for the Stewart vehicles. It didn't take long before we spotted both vehicles sitting in front of a small house on Williamson Lane. As we were parking, we noticed in front of the house that a lawn sprinkler was running, and two women stood near-by talking. We approached and identified ourselves and asked if Stacy was home. One of the women identified herself as Stacy's wife, Crystal. She said Stacy wasn't home, but she expected him soon. After we further explained our purpose, she invited us into their home.

Crystal explained that Stacy was nearby hunting wild boar, but it was getting dark, so he would be home soon. She then called and told him we were at the house. While we waited, she told us that she'd been married to a cop for thirteen years, and her three children were from that marriage. She and Stacy had gone to High School together, then reconnected after they'd each divorced and got married. Her children refer to Stacy as 'Uncle Stewie.' We chatted for about 15 minutes before Stacy arrived, entering through the back door, into the kitchen, and on into the living room where we were waiting. He had an open Miller Lite beer in one hand and the remains of a six-pack dangling from the other. He was dressed in camouflage pants, a beige shirt, and a baseball cap. He was clean-shaven, and his dark brown hair appeared short and cropped.

After identifying ourselves and handing him our business cards, we explained why we were there. We assured him that we were not the police, but we were working for an attorney on behalf of Cal Harris. Stacy advised that he had already been interviewed by the police several times and had given them statements and was not going to give anymore. He went into defense mode rather quickly and appeared clearly agitated. We thought for sure he was about to show us the door. Instead, he started talking and saying he took exception to the money we were making and asked how we could sleep at night. He was upset that his name had appeared in the newspaper, and a reporter called his mother. He also claimed he told the police he was willing to fly up to NY for the trial and take his wife with him. Crystal, who was present during the interview, was all ears.

Once he seemed to be done venting, we told him about our interviews with Wright Childers and Chris Thomason, including our most recent interview with Chris earlier today. Unlike Thomason, he didn't seem the least bit interested to learn that Wright Childers had recovered quite well after his accident. We then told him that Chris couldn't understand why he (Stacy) was telling the police that it was Chris who was involved with Michele Harris and not himself. Telling him further that Chris denied even knowing Michele and stated that he (Stacy) was the one involved with her. Other than dead silence and a cold blank stare, there was no response.

We then explained the information from Lydia Monico, who told police about Chris being up at his house and helping him with the burning of a bloody shirt. He just continued to stare straight ahead with a strange look on his face, but again – no response.

I then switched gears and asked, "Why did you tell the police that you had gone to work between 4:00 and 5:00 a.m. on September 12, 2001?"

"Dedication," he replied. It took a conscious effort to keep my eyes from rolling and my head from shaking. Although tempting, I knew any confrontation or challenge to his answers could likely result in a very short interview. At least for now, I thought it best to just keep him talking. So, I just bit my lip and continued. I was anxious to see what more I could learn.

Continuing, I asked, "Why did the police single you out from all the other steelworkers for a polygraph exam?" I was expecting the same answer he'd given to Ranger Flores. That, "there were 14 or 15 of us who had taken the polygraph."

Instead, he replied, "I had someone downtown that hated me. I hired and fired a lot of guys."

With that answer, I really had to restrain myself, while hoping I'd been able to suppress my expression of disbelief. But then decided to pursue it just a little by asking, "Who was it downtown that hated you?"

"I don't know. There were several."

I just let it go. I knew he wasn't truthful because he'd never held a position at NUCOR where he would 'hire and fire' people. And who are all these others who supposedly took the polygraph? He was just making stuff up as we went along.

Okay, I thought, maybe just a little challenge and asked, "Do you remember telling Ranger Flores that there were several others from NUCOR who had taken polygraph tests?"

"Yeah, I remember that."

Continuing, I asked, "Do you know if Chris or Wright took polygraphs?"

"I'm not really sure. I think they may have."

I then asked, "Is there anyone you can think of that you know for sure took it?"

"It's been a long time; I really can't remember."

Okay, so out of a dozen or more of his co-workers that he claims took the polygraph, he can't remember even one. Indeed. I'd better let it go at that.

I then explained how two different witnesses both described seeing a young white male, fitting his description, along with a black Chevrolet pick-up truck near the end of the Harris driveway on the morning of September 12, 2001. He just laughed at the Tubbs story and the hay-wagon. Then also took exception to me saying it was a black truck because he had understood it to be a dark blue truck. I corrected myself and explained how the witness said it was either black or dark blue. I explained that because of the similarities in his description, the description of the truck, along with the interest the SP had shown in him earlier, including the polygraph, he was a 'person of interest' and someone to look at. I also added, "If you're really interested in clearing your name, work with us, and we may be able to find a way to eliminate you as a suspect."

Again, complete silence and that same cold glare.

I was continuously monitoring his body language throughout the interview. He appeared nervous and remained tense, agitated, and defensive. It seemed rather obvious he couldn't wait until we were gone. His cold, steady glare said it all.

We had acquired some useful information, and I didn't want to push the envelope much further. But I hadn't asked him anything about his little cabin in the woods yet. I knew he was overly anxious for us to leave, so I just asked, "Can you tell me why you bought your little house up there, then just abandoned it, without ever making the first payment?"

He replied, "I never got a payment book from the bank."

I followed up with, "Yeah, but couldn't you have sold it before moving back to Texas?"

"Didn't know how to do that," he said.

I'd noticed during the interview that Crystal was all ears and had been listening very attentively. She was obviously very interested in every word being said. After the interview, Crystal walked us to the door. Stacy had already popped another beer, turned away, and left the room.

I said quietly, "Has Stacy ever talked to you about this?"

She said, "Very little, but nothing like what I just heard. I'm going to talk to him some more."

I said, "Well, you have our numbers. If you learn anything more, let us know." She agreed, and we walked out the door back to our car.

We had no sooner closed the doors of the car when Frank and I looked at each other and almost simultaneously said, "Did you see his eyes?" Both of us found it difficult to describe the look we had seen in his eyes. Frank said, "I think he was trying to figure out a way he could kill us." I couldn't disagree. I had always heard that 'pupils never lie' and the quote from William Shakespeare, "The eyes are the window of the soul." Perhaps, 'eerily evil' might fit, but even to this day, I don't know of any words that could adequately describe the look in his eyes I had seen. All I know is, it was a look I had never seen before and hope never to see again.

All things considered, the interview with Stewart had gone about as well as we could expect. We knew there was a good possibility he could have shut us down completely. Obviously, I would like to have learned more, but without enforcement authority, we had pushed it about as far as we could go. Between the two of us, as we drove back to Crockett, we reminded each other of all we had learned during the Stewart interview as Frank took notes that would later be used to prepare our interview summary.

So far, we had accomplished our objectives ahead of schedule. We still had some time before we needed to leave Texas and head back to Tennessee to try and re-interview Wright Childers before returning to NY. We decided to see if we could find Ranger Rudy Flores. We knew from his reports that he had an office at the Texas Department of Public Safety Building on West Spring Street in Palestine, Texas. We didn't know what to expect or whether he would even be willing to speak with us. We decided not to call ahead but rather attempt a face-to-face at his office. We got lucky; he was there.

After identifying ourselves, Flores welcomed us into his office. The first thing he said was, "I know who ya'll are. I was kinda wonderin if ya'll might come and see me, nice to meet ya." If you ever had a stereotype image of what a Texas Ranger might look like, Flores would be a good match. In his mid-40s, he was neatly dressed, clean-shaven, and walked with a proud strut in his step. His surrounding office was as neat as he was. It was evident that he was a proud Texas Ranger. Without asking, he began giving us a tour of his office, which included a short dissertation of the history and heritage of the Texas Rangers along with a review of several photographs and other Ranger memorabilia proudly displayed on the walls.

After some additional police talk, including the exchange of a few short war stories, he invited us to sit down in front of his desk. After explaining how we had interviewed Chris Thomason, Stacy Stewart, and others, Flores said he had heard we were in town. We then told him we knew he had interviewed these same individuals because we had reviewed his reports. We then talked a little about some of the discrepancies between his interviews and ours.

We then asked if he had ever been asked to question Stewart or Thomason about a woman named Lydia Monico, who had told the SP of Thomason's comment about the 'burning of a bloody shirt.' He had not been provided with that information.

He then volunteered, "For me, it was like looking at the case through a key-hole." He thought it unusual for the SP not to send their own investigators to conduct the interviews themselves. Then he added, "Normally, in my experience, an agency will call, and I will meet them and assist in locating the subjects to be interviewed, but in this case, they asked me to do the interviews, so I did."

I then asked if he had ever been provided any information about Stewart buying a house, never making the first payment, and then abandoning it to move back to Texas?

"I knew he bought a house, but nothing about never making a payment or abandoning it."

I said, "Okay, so like you said, it was kind of like looking at the case through a key-hole?"

"It was," he said.

Flores had already given us his ear and a lot more time than we expected. But before leaving, I asked him if he had ever been made aware of Stewart's claim to have gone into work between 4:00 and 5:00 a.m. on the morning of September 12, 2001, when his timecards showed that it was 6:00 a.m.?

He answered, "I had his timecards because I reviewed them with him, but no, I was not aware that he'd said that. That would have been a good question."

After thanking him for his time and hospitality, we left and headed back to Crockett to get ready to leave the Lonestar state. Ranger Rudy Flores was a gentleman and a true professional. Our informal interview with him was a welcomed bonus to our trip and ongoing investigation.

It was only around lunchtime when we arrived back at our hotel in Crockett. We knew it was going to be a 12-hour arduous journey to Hixson, Tennessee, so we decided to get started and see how far we could get. We quickly packed our bags, tossed them in the car, and we were on our way. We made it as far as Tuscaloosa, Alabama, where we spent the night and then on to Hixson, Tennessee, early the next morning.

We pulled into Wright Childers' residence in mid-afternoon. I immediately noticed that those huge Rots were not in their kennel. As we started to get out of the car, I knew why. They were all in the house barking excitedly, running back-and-forth, slobbering on and shaking the front window, appearing as though they could come crashing through at any minute.

We stayed close to the car and kept our distance as Wright's mother, Linda Rogers, came and cracked open the door. She recognized us, but before we even had a chance to tell her why we were there, she said she didn't want her son to be interviewed any further. She yelled, "Wright has a global head injury and can't even remember yesterday. I don't want him bothered with any more stuff from New York, and if you don't leave right now, I'm going to let these dogs out."

Before I could finish saying, "Okay, okay were leaving, we won't bother you again," Frank was already closing the door of the car yelling, "Come on, let's get the hell out of here."

Once we were safely inside and pulling away, I said, "What the hell did you do to set her off?"

"Me? I thought it was you. I thought she liked me the last time we were here."

I said, "Yeah, me too, but I'm in no hurry to cross paths with her again anytime soon, at least not with those f...in dogs around."

Later, after our heartbeats settled back to normal, we continued our long journey home. We talked a bit more about our experience at the Childers residence and wondered why was mama so protective of her 45-year-old adult son, who we knew from our previous interview, could communicate and make his own decisions? What had caused the abrupt change in cooperation? Of course, we speculated some that perhaps Wright might have told his mother about what happened in NY, which might explain her aggressive defense. Or, that he may have said something she overheard when he was coming out of his coma after his accident. We also considered that they might have been in contact with Stewart or Thomason. Regardless, our questions were many, but answers were few. For now, it would have to remain a mystery.

We arrived back in NY on Friday, March 13, 2009, around 3:00 p.m. Bill and Terry were anxiously waiting to hear about our trip. As soon as we got back, we held a conference call to bring them up to speed and assured them that, as soon as Frank completed the written narrative, it would be forwarded to them for their file and review. They were pleased with the successful results of our trip. We knew before we left that we could have come back empty-handed, especially if nobody agreed to talk with us. Other than Wright Childers, we had done rather well. It's not as if we had expectations of getting confessions from either Stewart or Thomason admitting their involvement or developing that 'smoking gun' type of evidence that could solve the case. Ideally, that would have been great, but realistically, the information we did get strengthened our belief that Stewart, Thomason, and possibly Wright Childers, could all be involved with the disappearance of Michele Harris. We now had only four months left to prepare for the second trial.

40

TRIAL # 2

By mid-April 2009, trial preparation was moving along well. Our blood expert Paul Kish had requested some additional documents and photographs to help with his assessment. This time, wanting to consult with Kish in person, I prepared the requested materials and hand-delivered them to Kish at his office in Corning, NY.

Together, we conducted a preliminary review of the new materials and had further discussion about what he would be able to testify to. Kish said he would need more time to look at the content but gave me some early indications of what he may be able to say. Later, after returning to Binghamton, I called Bill and briefed him.

Over the next several days, we continued with our trial prep, which included getting our defense witnesses subpoenaed and prepped for trial. Kevin Tubbs, in particular, was not happy knowing he had to testify all over again. This time in front of a jury. However, he graciously accepted his subpoena and said, "I'll be anxious to just get it over with." Then added, "But I'll tell you right now, jury or no jury. I'm not going to take any more of Keene's crap." I told him, "Just tell the same story you've told all along, and you'll be fine." I then went back over his previous testimony with him.

From a defense position, retrying Cal in the same small town was arguably unfair. The high-profile nature and extensive publicity surrounding the case had polarized the community. Cal's first trial had been lost at the end of an uphill battle resulting in his conviction, followed by extensive and detailed media coverage. The entire regional community was aware of the guilty verdict. Compounding the unfairness was the fact that shortly after his conviction, his case was aired in the national spotlight on CBS *48-Hours*. How would we be able to get a fair and impartial jury? The cards were stacked against him from the beginning. But he was still trying to get a fair trial a second time around without a change of venue. It could very likely be a no-win situation. Justifiable change of venue motions had been made and denied. Even though a high number of jurors who admitted having knowledge of the case were excused, enough remained to continue jury selection. For those that remained, could they truly be fair and impartial?

By the end of day two, eleven jurors had been selected. Jury selection was completed on day three, followed immediately by opening statements. Before the completion of jury selection, Terry Kindlon filed another last-minute change-of-venue motion with the NY appellate division. It outlined the numerous issues that made a second trial in Tioga County, NY, unfair to Cal Harris.

A jury of eight men and four women had been selected along with six alternates. For the most part, the prosecution's case would be mainly a carbon-copy of the first trial. However, for the defense, there would be a few changes. Joe Cawley was gone, so Bill Easton would take on the role of lead defense counsel, assisted by Terry Kindlon. Obviously, there would be the added new testimony from Kevin and Gloria Tubbs. Then, Paul Kish would testify as our new blood expert. Then lastly, since Keene had successfully demonized Cal in the first trial, our objective now was to try to humanize him. In that effort, after lengthy discussions and preparations, with Cal in agreement, it was decided that he would testify on his own behalf.

As expected, Keene's strategy had not changed as he called the same line-up of witnesses to repeat their testimony. For the most part, both their direct and cross-examination testimony mirrored that of the first trial. This time, however, the testimony of blood expert, Dr. Henry Lee, would be in-person. That meant that when he took the stand, the defense could directly address the controversy surrounding his credibility that was discovered after his pre-recorded testimony for the first trial. Additionally, Judge Smith, before recusing himself, barred Dr. Lee from testifying again that he could date the blood to within a 'few days' by its color, as he did in the first trial. Agreeing with the defense, Smith said, "There is no scientific basis for such specific dating of blood by its color."

The testimony in the second trial was about to get underway. Rather than repeating much of what we already know, I will briefly summarize some of the trial highlights, and offer some added details about the new witnesses – including Cal.

As before, Barb Thayer took the stand to offer her testimony, which was almost the same as the first trial but not quite. Thayer once again testified that she was the one who made that 7:13 a.m. phone call to Michele's cell phone. Previously, in statements to police, Thayer said she didn't remember what time she called or where she was in the Harris house when she made the call. Then, as the years went by, her memory improved, telling the first trial jury that she was the one who made that 7:13 a.m. call. In the second trial, her memory improved even more. She testified for the first time that not only did she remember making the call, she now recalled the specific house phone she used. To further help the cause, she now claimed for the first time that Cal was nowhere in sight when she first arrived, and it was during his absence that she quickly made the call.

> Author's Note: This was not the quick call and hang-up scenario she described. Phone records revealed a call duration of one-minute and twelve seconds.

When challenging her testimony during cross, Terry Kindlon accused her of changing her story in saying, "You're just trying to get yourself to the house at a certain time." Thayer's demeanor suddenly changed as she switched into defense-mode and quickly denied that to be true.

Other 'interested' parties testifying included Nikki Burdick and Shannon Taylor. Under cross-examination, they were both asked if they knew about the relationship between Michele and Michael Kasper. Burdick flatly denied knowing anything at all going on between Michele and Kasper. Shannon Taylor's response was, "That name doesn't ring a bell. I was only told of that afterward." They were both lying.

Recall that after repeated police interviews, Burdick eventually told the police (Skinner and Hochdanner) that she *was* aware of Michele's relationship with Kasper. She also believed it ended sometime in June of 2001. She even described Kasper's jealousy when seeing Michele talking to other men and how Michele would be 'on egg-shells.' As for Shannon, shortly after

Michele went missing, she and Nikki both ran down to Lefty's. And who did they go to see? Mike Kasper. But now, "that name doesn't ring a bell."

As mentioned, Burdick had also denied knowing of Michele's relationship with Kasper during an episode broadcast on national television by CBS *48-Hours*. Keeping her lies straight wasn't working very well.

There was no hiding the fact that Cindy Turner's testimony was a clear reflection of where her interest was while claiming to be Michele's best friend. As expected, she offered her testimony about the day Cal used the description, 'bread loaf-size' when telling her about the blood the police had found. Then, she adds for the first time that she had asked Cal where the blood came from, and he told her he cut himself shaving, or maybe it was from the dog.

> Author's Note: Again, if Cal were guilty, he would have known the blood found was Michele's, and a DNA test would prove it. Therefore, implying that the blood was from himself or the dog would be inconsistent with a consciousness of guilt.

It didn't take long under Terry's cross-examination before Turner's real bias came shining through. Her whole expression and demeanor instantly changed as she switched into defense mode. She became defiant, uncooperative, and downright hostile, with an accompanying scowl on her face and a very nasty attitude. Several times throughout her cross, she attempted to dodge or avoid answering Terry's questions. He would often have to interrupt and bring her back to the question asked. Other times, she would go off-topic, trying to squeeze in something she thought might be helpful that was not part of the question. More than once, Terry challenged the veracity of her testimony about things she'd never said before or had improved upon since her previous testimony.

Dr. Henry Lee appeared in person this time to offer his testimony. For the most part, it was a rehashing of his videotaped testimony in the first trial. This time, however, based on Judge Smith's earlier court ruling that, without a supporting scientific basis, Dr. Lee was prevented from offering any testimony concerning the age of the blood. Previously, he had testified that the age of the blood could have been from a couple of days to a few days in age. Now, he was only allowed to say that it was either fresh, recent, or old. During his testimony, it was clearly established, and he agreed that none of the blood was fresh. Most of what he looked at, he described as recent but added that there was a wide range between recent and old – anywhere from days to weeks, or even months. He also described the blood on the throw rug as being older than what he had seen in the photographs of the other areas. But he admitted that, by the time he looked at the rug, it was years later. Therefore, he could not say whether the blood on the rug was deposited at the same time as the blood found in the other areas, or the sequence of the deposits.

During cross-examination, Dr. Lee approximated that the collective volume of blood that he saw was in the range of about ten drops. More or less. After that, Dr. Lee was handed a container of fake blood, along with an empty blood tube and an eyedropper. When asked, Lee counted out ten drops as he dropped them one-by-one into the tube. Bill then had him hold it up for the jury to see. It was then marked and received into evidence as a court exhibit.

Bill had researched the matter regarding Dr. Lee's testimony in the Phil Spectrum case in California, where a judge admonished him for hiding evidence. When challenged under cross-examination, Dr. Lee explained how and what had happened in that case. Then adamantly denied doing anything improper. After hearing his testimony, I believed his explanation seemed credible. I think Bill did as well because there was no further challenge to his credibility.

Remember Michele's hairdresser, Jerry Wilczynski? Well, he testified once again. He didn't do much better this time. In fact, under a little more aggressive cross-examination by Terry, some new revelations were exposed that further destroyed his already polluted credibility.

During his cross, for the first time, he admitted that he did not believe that the early SP investigators to interview him (DelGiorno and Phillips) were real police officers. Twice, he insisted that neither one of them had taken any notes during the interview. Not true. DelGiorno took several notes. Then, when asked if he assumed they were not the police, he said, "I did assume they were not." But later, after acknowledging that one of them (DelGiorno) left him his business card, he said,

"I then believed." When asked why he hadn't told them the truth at that time, he said. "I still didn't trust them."

Challenging further, Terry asked why he called DelGiorno (the one he didn't trust) three days later to offer some additional information. He said he wanted to make DelGiorno aware of an affair Cal was having because DelGiorno had only asked him about an affair Michele was having. He then admitted to withholding the information he knew about Michele's affairs, claiming that "he (DelGiorno) was just trying to make Michele look bad." With the damage done, Keene just left it at that. There was no re-direct testimony.

Jerry Keene rested his case. As expected and previously mentioned, with a few exceptions, the testimony of prosecution witnesses was close to a carbon-copy of the first trial. It was now time for the defense. And this time around, things would be markedly different. With the new testimony of Kevin Tubbs, followed by our new blood expert, Paul Kish, things should be interesting. But don't forget. Cal will also be testifying. So, how will it all play out? You already know the answer, but let's take a glimpse at what happened.

Defense

The line-up of defense witnesses was short and would start with blood expert, Paul Kish, followed by Kevin and Gloria Tubbs. Tubbs' business associate, Jim DeVita, would follow right after. The final part of the defense strategy was to have the jury hear the testimony from Cal Harris himself, before resting their case.

Paul Kish was called to the stand. After establishing his long list of credentials, he was qualified to testify as an expert. Bill then began to systematically have him testify about the examinations he performed and the subsequent results of his assessment.

Recall during my own assessment of the blood at the alleged crime scene, I remarked about the absence of evidence, where blood appeared to be missing from areas where it should have been. During Kish's testimony, he made specific reference to the absence of blood. I earlier described it as the 'neutral-zone,' the five-foot area, on top of the brown rugs, between the kitchen entryway and where the blood was found on the bare garage floor. He testified that, from his assessment, a reasonable inference could be made that blood would be found in that area but was not.

Notably, during Keene's cross-examination, Kish was asked a hypothetical question. Keene proposed this scenario: That, if a person was struck in the referenced area, started bleeding and was then struck again, there would be splatter. Then, that same person was taken out into the garage, where they continued to bleed. Keene asked, "Is there anything in the evidence that you examined that would exclude that possibility?" Kish agreed that it would be possible, but not likely. He questioned the lack of transfer staining, blood in the grout, and quantity of blood on the rug, which showed no passive drops of blood on it. I don't think Keene was prepared for that answer.

Kish was right. If Michele had been struck in that entryway, the visual results of her subsequent bleeding should have presented itself not only in the form of small specks but passive dripping as well. Continuing his answer to Keene's question, Kish added, "Using your hypothetical, when they get struck, you would see drips of blood. And we don't have any of that on the carpet, which you believe to be there at that point in time. So, that doesn't – the carpet doesn't fit because we're not seeing any drips."

From the defense perspective, Kish's answer had just blown Keene's hypothetical (actual) theory right out of the water. Our concern was whether the jury understood the significance.

Kish's testimony then shifted to the aging of blood. The first thing he said was, "There is no valid methodology by which we can determine the age of blood, based on color." Explaining further, Kish said part of the problem in trying to age blood stains is that any number of unknown and changing environmental factors could influence the drying time and aging process. My thoughts exactly.

Bill and I had spent a considerable amount of time preparing Kevin Tubbs for his testimony. Even in his earlier testimony during the '330' hearing, he had already experienced some of Keene's wrath. Ever since then, Keene and the SP, in their effort to salvage their case against Cal, launched a mammoth investigative campaign against Tubbs and his family. They were doing anything and everything within their power to destroy his credibility. While simultaneously, ignoring and doing absolutely nothing to investigate anything he had seen. Kevin, of course, knew this better than anyone.

Throughout his ordeal, despite the negative impact it was having on him and his family, friends, and business, Kevin had remained remarkably calm. At least on the outside. Inside was a different story. His frustration had grown into anger at the way he was being treated when all he was trying to do was the right thing. The collateral attacks on the other members of his family only fueled his anger. For the past two years, Kevin had suppressed his anger rather well, but at times, he would still reveal his concerns and frustrations. I was usually the first one to hear about them. Kevin's prior experience with both Keene and the SP had already created a bad-blood issue between them. With the current situation, the bad-blood issue had grown a lot worse. How would this play out during the trial?

Knowing everything that had transpired since the '330' hearing, we were sure that Keene's cross-examination attack on Kevin during the trial would be radically more aggressive. During our preparations with Kevin, we wanted to make him aware of what to expect. Kevin said, "There's no need to explain. I know Keene, and I know exactly what's coming." He then reminded us of what he had told us previously that he would "not take any of Keene's crap."

Back to the Trial

Calling his next witness, Bill said, "Your Honor, the defense calls Kevin Tubbs." Neatly dressed in shirt and tie, Kevin walked in and stood in front of the Court Clerk, and was sworn in. He then moved over and took up his position on the elevated witness stand, also known as the 'hot-seat.' For Tubbs, at least, its slang name would be more fitting. In anticipation of his testimony, both sides of the courtroom had filled to near capacity. The media area in the raised galleries above the courtroom was also filled with anxious television and newspaper reporters with their cameras focused and notebooks ready.

Before getting into his testimony, Bill had Kevin tell the jury a little about himself, his family, his background, what he did for a living, and so forth. Then his testimony turned to the issue at hand. While answering Bill's direct and detailed questions, Kevin calmly laid out his story to the jury. As expected, it was remarkably consistent with the same story he'd been telling all along.

Kevin's calm composure quickly faded during Keene's relentless grilling during his cross. Their heated exchanges were emotional and, at times, turned to anger. When Kevin told us he wasn't going to take any of Keene's crap, he was serious. And it was now playing out in true form in front of the jury. Occasionally, some of their exchanges drew audible reactions of emotional outbursts from the crowded courtroom. During one exchange, Tubbs, believing that Keene was repeatedly hammering on him about things that weren't relevant, blurted out, "this has nothing to do with the Harris's. I don't know what we're screwing around for."

One of the more notable moments of Keene's combative cross-examination came when he asked Tubbs about a conversation he had with his business associate, Jim DeVita. After he acknowledged having the conversation, Keene asked, "And one of those conversations was about getting a bag full of money in your pocket someday, wasn't it?"

Tubbs replied, "No, that's incorrect." Then he went on to explain how DeVita had made the comment jokingly. Tubbs, now smiling, said, "He was making a joke, he was joking. You know that…"

Keene responded, "No. Is there something funny about this to you? That's…"

Interrupting, Tubbs said, "It's funny that you know the difference and you're bringing in stupid stuff that doesn't have anything – why don't you care about the Taylor family or the Harris family? Instead, you're trying to protect yourself because you look like an idiot."

Oh, wow! I may not have used those exact words, but Kevin was right. Keene did know the truth because he had spoken with DeVita previously. His question to Tubbs about the brown paper bag was totally improper and was deliberately designed to plant the idea of a pay-off in the minds of the jury.

Kevin's angry response, of course, was one of those moments that drew some rather distinctive audible responses from courtroom spectators. Judge Hayden immediately halted testimony. Then, before recessing for the day, cautioned both spectators and news reporters to respect the jury's impartiality and avoid emotional outbursts.

When Court resumed the next day, Tubbs was once again lambasted with repeated nit-picking. He was growing impatient and angry. At times, he'd pound his fist on the witness stand, and more than once said, "I'm not going to play games."

In response to Tubbs' answers, for the benefit of the jury, Keene was often seen using some courtroom 'theatrics.' When he'd deliberately shake his head and roll his eyes while displaying a disgusted and distinctive look of disbelief on his face, he made sure the jury would notice.

Keene's badgering and Kevin's hot-headed responses continued throughout his remaining testimony. Later, after Keene had run out of legitimate questions, he decided to throw some nonsense questions into the mix. He tried tripping up Tubbs anyway he could think of. To the point where it was making him look desperate and foolish. At times, his questioning became laughable and so ridiculous that even some of the jurors could be seen snickering.

Keene was suggesting that Tubbs, when meeting with defense investigators, had been provided with information about the black Chevy pickup truck and the man he had seen. Kevin was adamant that nothing about the truck or any man had ever been provided to him by anyone prior to his first testimony. He said that after he first testified, is when he first learned anything about the person he had seen, but nothing about the truck.

When asked what he was shown later, he said, Dave Beers had shown him the photographs of three guys. While looking at one of the photographs, he said, "That guy right there, that picture right there, if the guy didn't have those whiskers. I'd put my money on it that that's the fellow that was there that morning."

Under the circumstances, Kevin had held up as well as could be expected. Keene had unjustly brutalized him. What the jury's perception would be was anyone's guess.

Finally, Keene finished his cross. Bill now had a chance at some re-direct. To reduce the sting and straighten out some of the confusion that surfaced during his cross-examination, Bill simply rephrased some of the same questions allowing Tubbs the opportunity to clear up any confusion.

Near the end of Bills re-direct, he asked Tubbs about the one photograph he thought looked like the fellow he had seen that morning. Tubbs said, "I'm pretty damn sure that's the fellow that was there that morning. I haven't had anybody besides Dave Beers say anything about it. I don't know how come nobody will look at it."

There had been no advance notice that Cal would be testifying on his own behalf. I think it's safe to say that no one was expecting that to happen. Keene was the first to be notified that Cal would be testifying. From there, it spread like wildfire. The few empty seats that remained in the courtroom filled up quickly, as did the media seats in the lofted gallery. There was an audible 'buzz' throughout the courtroom as anxious spectators gathered and waited.

Cal was called to the stand. Dressed sharply in a long-sleeve white dress shirt and blue tie, he stood up and walked to the Court Clerk to be sworn in. He then stepped up to the witness stand on the elevated platform next to the judge's bench. It was now Cal's turn in the 'hot-seat.' A seat he would be sitting in for several hours over the next few days.

Terry Kindlon controlled the questioning of Cal's direct testimony. Like the many witnesses before him, Cal, too, was nervous. Even more so knowing he was the defendant. Knowing that all eyes and ears are focused on you, the witness is a bit nerve-racking, to say the least. Terry knew from experience that the first thing he needed to do was start with some easy, or 'soft' questions. This would help Cal to relax and get a little more comfortable testifying. With some preliminary questions out of the way, his nervousness would ease up.

Starting from high school, Terry chronologically walked Cal through his family and business history and how he got started in the family automobile business. From there, he turned to his relationship with Michele and how it all started. How they first met, how they had lived together and later, got married and had children. Cal admitted that, when his father first started him in the business, he was just a 25-year old snot-nosed kid – starting out as a 'grunt' just washing and moving cars around the lot. Then he explained how he became the boss overnight after being thrust into the position prematurely after his father had a heart attack. He found himself trying to supervise those who were old enough to be his parents.

When he first met Michele, she was working for Dwight in the corporate office next door. And she continued working there until their first son Taylor was born. When asked about Michele as a mother, he had nothing but praise for her ability and went on to describe the numerous different things she would do for the children.

He went on to explain how various problems started developing in their marriage and some of the contributing factors that lead Michele to file for divorce. He then admitted and accepted responsibility for Michele wanting the divorce. His long work hours and petty arguments were just some of the contributing factors. He realized he was not fair to her. He also admitted that when Michele first filed, he was furious, and there had been many heated arguments. He'd also sought help from the Taylor family when trying to reconcile the marriage.

The SP had long maintained and argued that the financial part of Cal's motive stemmed from his fear of losing his multimillion-dollar business. During his testimony, Cal explained that initially, he was concerned about the business. However, after meeting with his attorney, shortly after Michele filed for the divorce, he'd been reassured that his business was safe. Having been advised that by law, because he had the business before they were married, it could not be included as part of the divorce settlement.

After getting through the preliminaries, Cal's testimony turned to the matter at hand. His testimony of the scenario surrounding all the events that happened at the time, including everything he knew at the time, was remarkably consistent with what he had been saying all along. He'd explained everything rather well – with no surprises.

Under cross-examination, as best he could, Keene hammered away at Cal's direct testimony. Throughout his cross, Cal maintained a markedly calm demeanor, while offering spontaneous and forthright answers to all of Keene's questions. He never showed any signs of animosity, anger, or contempt. Keene was working hard, trying to get under Cal's skin, asking questions he hoped would prompt a sudden outburst of anger for the jury to see. It never happened. Cal remained unflappable, and for someone who had never testified before, held up exceptionally well.

Shortly after Cal finished his lengthy testimony, both sides rested. The jury was excused for the day as the court went into recess. Before leaving, they were told to return the next morning to hear closing arguments. The attorneys met in chambers with Judge Hayden to make final motions and to approve the wording of the 'jury-charge' that would be read to the jury after closing arguments and before beginning their deliberations.

Closings – Deliberations – Verdict

Bill Easton and Terry Kindlon spent a considerable amount of time during the overnight hours, making their final additions and adjustments to their closing. At Cal's request, Terry was on tap to do the clos-ing. Presumably, Keene was doing his final prep, as well.

The next morning, by the time Judge Hayden entered the court-room and assumed his position at the bench, all parties were seated and ready to proceed. Hayden called for the jury. Once the jury was seated, he welcomed them back and briefly explained the purpose of closing arguments, how they worked, and who would go first.

Briefly, Terry Kindlon and Jerry Keene made their respective closing arguments, which were each several hours in length. It was a long trial, with numerous controversial issues that needed to be addressed. Both would argue their respective and opposing interpreta-tions of the evidence and testimony that was introduced during the trial. Once completed, the judge would give the jury their final instruc-tions, and deliberations would begin. Considering the length of the trial, as well as the closing arguments from both sides, the jury of eight men and four women had a lot to talk about. Now, for a second time, Cal's fate was once again in the hands of the jury.

On day two, after only nine hours of deliberations, the verdict was in. "GUILTY."

It's hard to find a word that would best describe what I was feeling: devastation, disappointment, disbelief, even some anger. I couldn't believe what I just heard. More troubling was the fact that Judge Smith had previously found Kevin and Gloria Tubbs to be entirely credible. Then, after Keene appealed his decision, all five appellate judges unan-imously upheld Smith's decision, finding the Tubbs' credible. How can this be happening? What we feared had just become a reality – again. Influenced by Cal's earlier conviction and a multitude of negative publicity, the second jury, whether they realized it or not, was incapable of being fair and impartial.

In a state of shock once again, Cal shook and then hung his head in disbelieve as he was handcuffed, escorted from the courtroom, and hauled off to the Tioga County jail.

The next day's headline in the *Press & Sun-Bulletin* read, *"GUILTY! Harris stoic as jury says he killed wife."* In the article, written by staff writer, Debbie Swartz, she had interviewed Keene, who was, of course, basking in the glory. Swartz had also interviewed Terry Kindlon, who said, "This is not the result we obviously expected. We're frankly, quite surprised. Cal did not commit this crime. An innocent man has been wrongfully convicted." She added that, without any prompting, Kindlon said there would be an appeal.

Two months later, Cal returned to the courtroom and was about to hear what his formal sentence would be. He was escorted into the courtroom. This time, heavily shackled and dressed in the standard orange jail jump-suit attire. He sat at the defense table with Bill and Terry. The courtroom was packed once again. After both sides made their respective sentencing recommendations, Cal was given an opportunity to make a statement.

Standing up, Cal addressed the court, saying, "I've been trying to keep my head up because I've done nothing wrong, nothing to be ashamed of." During the past eight years, he said, "I didn't run. I didn't hide. My children deserve better, your honor, and I will fight every step of the way to get our family back together again." After Cal's address, Judge Hayden paused briefly, then as expected, following Keene's recommendation, sentenced Cal to 25-years-to-life in state prison. Just before sentencing, Bill had filed Cal's notice of appeal, but that would be a long way down the road.

During Cal's sentencing, in the crowded courtroom, I noticed Cal's father Dwight, sitting about two rows behind the defense table. The look on his face was understandably somber. But sitting about two rows behind Dwight was another man I recognized. It was Mulvey's father, John Andrews. When Cal first stood up to be sentenced, he glanced over his shoulder and made brief eye contact with his dad. At the same time, John Andrews winked at Cal with a snide grin on his face, which then turned into a broad smile. I had no doubt that daughter Susan was nearby doing the same.

Cal was removed from the courtroom and returned to the County jail. There, he would await a decision from the NYS Department of Corrections as to where he would ultimately be placed to serve out his sentence. As the courtroom started to clear, Keene and company were seen doing their high-fives, handshaking, and fist-pumps. In contrast, others were seen hugging each other, including members of the Taylor family. Ordinarily, under normal circumstances, believing that justice had been served, this would be considered perfectly normal behavior. But there was nothing ordinary or normal about the circumstances surrounding Cal's case. It was anything but normal.

Aftermath

In most cases, the chances of a favorable appeal decision are slim –
50/50 at best. More often, the odds are much less. Cal's conviction was
a major blow to our pre-trial optimism of being able to exonerate an
innocent man. However, belief in Cal's innocence and determined that
we were right, Bill was confident that a strong appeal could be made on
Cal's behalf. Accordingly, Bill decided to take on the task of writing the
appeal himself. His knowledge of the case and everything that transpired during the trial made him the best man for the job. We had no
clue at the time that Cal's legal battle and fight for freedom was far
from over.

41

APPEAL

With Cal's conviction, at least for now, there was nothing left for me to do. Officially, my case was considered closed. Unofficially, however, I couldn't bring myself to type the word 'closed' in the status column. At least for now, pending the appeal, the word 'pending' would remain. Considering the miscarriage of justice, I often found myself returning to revisit the case time-after-time. I was still thinking and searching for something, anything, that I could do to help right this wrong.

After the trial, I became the official custodian of the case file. Near the end of February 2010, Bill called to tell me he was in town. He wanted to stop in and retrieve some information from the case file he needed for the appeal. Before he arrived, I pulled out the pertinent files and spread them out in my war-room. Later, as Bill searched through the file to find what he needed, we talked about the trial and miscarriage of justice we had experienced. Like myself, he, too, had some sleepless nights. But he was working diligently on the appeal and felt confident that there were some good appeal issues.

Over the next several months, up until the appeal was filed, I checked in periodically to see how the appeal was coming. It was a slow process, but he remained confident and continued to reassure me that other than moving along slowly, it was going well. Finally, in July of 2010, he called to tell me that the appeal had been filed and sent me a copy. Later, he called again to tell me that oral arguments had been made, which he felt had gone very well. But for now – the wait continued.

Appeal Denied

On July 28, 2011, one year after the appeal was filed, the Third Judicial Department of the New York State Supreme Court, Appellate Division, announced in a 3-1 decision that it was affirming the conviction of Cal Harris. Another disappointing battle lost.

Three of the four participating judges rejected the defense arguments, agreed with the People, and rubber-stamped (affirmed) the conviction. Notably, however, that was not the case with the fourth dissenting judge, Bernard J. Malone Jr. In contrast, Malone agreed with nearly every defense argument, frequently rebuking the court and District Attorney throughout. In the early part of his scathing 28-page decision, he wrote, *"I do not believe that on this body of proof, as a whole, the jury could have concluded that the People sustained its burden of proof without making impermissible inferences drawn from equivocal evidence."*

I couldn't have said it better.

Throughout his decision, Malone addressed every important aspect of the case, and then persuasively explained his rationale in support of the defense arguments. In the end, he wrote, "Although I believe the proper remedy here would be a reversal and dismissal of the indictment due to the legal insufficiency of the evidence, considering both the many pretrial and trial errors that deprived defendant of his right to a fair trial, at the very least, defendant should receive a new trial."

The Appellate Divisions' majority decision, affirming Cal's conviction, was truly devastating and a hard nut to swallow, especially after reading Malone's dissenting decision. Another battle lost. Justice for Cal, after nearly ten years, denied once again. For now, he would remain in jail to continue his sentence. But was there any way to use Malone's decision to keep Cal's battle for justice alive? After speaking with Bill, he seemed to think there was, and Cal may still have another shot. Explaining it was possible, that with Malone's dissenting decision, he had thrown Cal another lifeline. And if Malone grants his permission, Cal's case may be allowed to be heard at a higher level, before the New York Court of Appeals.

PART V

A NEW LIFELINE | TRIAL #3

42

A NEW LIFELINE

About five weeks later, on September 7, 2011, Judge Malone, after reviewing Bill's request, signed an order, recommending that the case should be heard by the Court of Appeals. Subsequently, the Court of Appeals accepted Malone's recommendation and agreed to hear the case. The appeal process would start all over again.

Fast-forwarding another year to September 9, 2012, it was now eleven years since Michele went missing. Oral arguments were held before a Court of Appeals judicial panel of six judges. Once again, Bill felt they had gone very well. The waiting game began once again.

Surprisingly, the wait this time wasn't very long. Just five weeks later, on October 18, 2012, a decision was made and written by Judge Eugene F. Pigott Jr., with all five participating judges concurring. It cited judicial errors that were made during jury selection of a woman who had a preexisting opinion of Cal's guilt. Also, there was a failure by the court to offer limiting instructions to the jury about hearsay rules. As a result, a new trial was ordered. The lower Appellate Court's decision was reversed. The Court of Appeals also agreed with the defense and strongly recommended changing the venue for the third trial. Now we were getting somewhere.

Cal was immediately released from the Auburn Correctional Facility and transported back to the Tioga County jail as arrangements were made to have him released on bail. Keene argued unsuccessfully to have Cal remanded. But the $500K lien on his property was still in effect. As a result, after more than three years in state prison, Cal was released and once again back home with his children.

———————

More than eleven years had passed, and the same ongoing battle was starting all over again. But with a third trial on the horizon, things would be much different for both sides. A lot had changed, and the dynamics would be different this time around. Jerry Keene was just elected as the new Tioga County Court Judge, and the newly elected District Attorney was a rookie prosecutor by the name of Kirk Martin. We had also heard rumblings that Judge Hayden would not be presiding over the case again. The matter about the change of venue was still to be determined. Surprisingly, I learned from Cal that Bill Easton and Terry Kindlon would no longer be defending him. Unbeknownst to me, he had chosen a new attorney by the name of Bruce Barket from Garden City, NY.

At the time, with changes in both opposing counsel as well as other matters, it seemed unlikely that a new venue or trial date could be set anytime soon. Regardless, Judge Hayden called for and presided over a scheduling conference in his chambers to set a new trial date. Kirk Martin, as the new prosecutor and Bruce Barket as the new defense attorney, were both asking for a substantial amount of time to get up to speed on the case.

Cal had told me earlier that Bruce was in town for the conference and wanted to meet me after to get a look at the case file. After the conference, he called to tell me they were on their way.

Having seen Bruce's photograph on his web page, I recognized him as he walked into my office with Cal. After some small talk, we spoke briefly about the case, and Bruce filled me in on his short meeting with Judge Hayden. Even though it wasn't likely to happen, the judge wanted to get a trial date on the calendar, so it was tentatively set for the first week in October 2013.

We spoke briefly about some of the various aspects of the case, but it was apparent at this point, he knew very little. Moving across the hall to my storage room, I opened the door, pointed to the case files, and said, "Cal told me you wanted to see this." At first, it seemed he was a bit overwhelmed by the size of the file. As he randomly opened and peeked into some of the file boxes, he asked a few questions, then turned to glance at some of the defense court exhibits. After only a few minutes, he said, "The first thing we need to do is get all of this down to my place."

Less than a week later, Cal called, and we scheduled our trip to Long Island. It was now March 28, 2013. We knew it was going to be a long day, so we decided to get an early start. Cal backed his van up to the side door of my office just before 5:00 a.m. Between the two of us, we had the van loaded within minutes, and we were on our way.

By mid-morning, we arrived in Garden City and pulled into the parking lot of a huge office building. Bruce's law firm offices were located on the 7th floor. Bruce had a conference room emptied out and designated for the exclusive use of Cal's case. As the boxes began to pile up in the room, various members of Bruce's staff, walking by, would stop to peek in and introduce themselves.

Later, Bruce stopped in and said he wanted Cal and me to meet his investigative staff that was down the hall waiting. There, we were introduced to Peter Smith and Jay Salpeter. Peter and Jay were both licensed PI's with extensive backgrounds and experience in law enforcement. Peter wore a second hat as a licensed attorney, as well.

We spoke briefly about our respective backgrounds and experience. Collectively, we had over 75-years of investigative experience. Peter and Jay had already done some preliminary work on the case and had a basic understanding of what was involved. Now that the entire case file was available to them, they would need more time to get fully up to speed. Before leaving, I told them that I welcomed their fresh eyes on the case, looked forward to working with them, and would make myself available to answer questions or assist in any way I could.

In the months that followed, I frequently spoke with both Peter and Jay, answering their questions and directing them to specific case files. On other occasions, I met with them in person at my office or to assist them in locating and interviewing various witnesses.

I was confident in my assessment of the case, especially in the matter of Texas suspects, Stacy Stewart and Chris Thomason. By the end of July 2013, both Peter and Jay were fully up to speed on the case. When sharing their independent assessments, it was good to hear that they both agreed with me that Stacy Stewart and Chris Thomason were both viable suspects. After that, Peter and Jay were on their way to Texas.

43

NEW EYES IN TEXAS

While in Texas, Peter and Jay learned that Chris Thomason was married. But he was now estranged from his wife, Melissa Devries, and they were no longer living together. Devries, who was still living in the area, agreed to speak with them. They learned that in the spring of 2013, after drinking heavily, Thomason had told her 'out of the blue,' about a woman in New York who was murdered in September of 2001. And that her body was never found. He then said to her, "Stacy probably buried her in concrete."

They also tracked down a former Stewart girlfriend by the name of Terra Wade. I'd learned her name during one of my early interviews with Lisa Demtrak. Wade was very cooperative and spoke openly. She had met and dated Stewart in 2001 when they were both in Texas. That same spring Stewart went to work in NY. Later, he flew her up to be with him. It was fun for the first few days, but then, because of Stewart's long hours at work, she became bored and lonely and went back to Texas.

She saw Stewart again much later, after he returned to Texas, and was introduced to Chris Thomason. Later, she and Thomason became friends. She recalled having a conversation with him in 2011 about why he and Stewart decided to move back to Texas after living in NY. Thomason told her the move was tied to a murder case that police were questioning them about. He told Wade the morning after she

(Michele Harris) disappeared, he and his girlfriend went over to Stacy's house and that he (Thomason) was covered in blood. He said he had killed a deer. Wade asked him, "What do you mean?" He said, "I had blood on my clothes from skinning a deer, and you can't get blood out of clothes." He then told her he wasn't worried about any of this stuff coming up because Cal Harris had already been found guilty.

Interestingly, this conversation between Wade and Thomason took place in 2011. He had already been interviewed years earlier about the bloody clothes comment he made to Lydia Monico. Of course, he denied ever making the comment, claiming that Monico was just trying to get him back to NY to pay child support. But now, when fast-forwarding a few years, he offers this interesting yet bizarre new scenario to Wade about being with his girlfriend and going to Stacy's house covered in blood. We need to learn more.

Follow-up

While Peter and Jay were in Texas, we would regularly speak to discuss what they had learned as well as the investigative strategy for the continued investigation. Later, when they returned, we reviewed everything and identified any new leads that needed to be pursued. Peter suggested a re-interview with Lydia Monico to firm up the bloody clothes comment made by Thomason. Later, he located and interviewed her in Indiana. She remembered her two previous interviews with Frank as well as the one with the SP. Her story had not changed. She re-affirmed and was still sure what she heard from Chris Thomason, was just after Thanksgiving in 2001. She'd just learned she was pregnant, and there was a strong possibility that Chris was the father. She was with Chris at the bar, and he was drunk. Out-of-the-blue, he made the comment that he had gone up to Stewart's house to help him burn a bloody shirt that Stewart was wearing. When asked, she said, "After saying it, it seemed like he was relieved to get it out."

———————

Peter was also interested in meeting and re-interviewing Nancy Gilbert. After locating Gilbert and introducing himself, she initially expressed no interest in being re-interviewed. But after explaining his interest in Michele's missing jewelry, Nancy opened-up, and they had a long talk.

Gilbert reiterated her story about the theft of jewelry from her home and how she knew that Stewart and Thomason were responsible. She also explained that some of it had been returned to her by mail at the Candlelite. It had a Texas post-mark.

Once Peter got her comfortable talking, the focus of his questioning shifted back to more information regarding Stewart and Thomason. Surprisingly, when talking about her relationship with Stewart, Gilbert described a scenario of how she had overheard a comment that was remarkably similar to that of Lydia Monico. It was Saturday after Michele went missing, September 15, 2001, and she and her husband were celebrating their anniversary that included some barhopping in the area. They had run into Stewart and Thomason at one of the bars. They'd hit several, but she thought it might have been at The Barge where she saw them. She recalled Thomason being with a girl by the name of Lydia, who had a real crush on him. Upon seeing them, she recalled saying, "What are you guys doing? Are you coming with us?" Chris then turned around and blurted out, "We've got to burn the evidence." Nancy said, "Huh?" Chris replied, "You know – got to go burn bloody clothes."

Even though there were obvious discrepancies between when and where this occurred as described by Gilbert and Monico, the 'burning of bloody clothes' comment, they both heard from Thomason, was very similar. Yet, as we just learned from Terra Wade, when Thomason spoke with her in 2011, he offered an entirely different bloody clothes scenario. What's the real story? Or could there be elements of truth in both?

By early September 2013, Bruce Barket was about to formally file his motion for the much-needed change of venue. By using the strong recommendation from the Court of Appeals' decision, having the venue motion granted this time was all but guaranteed. But pending that decision, the trial date tentatively scheduled for October would need to be changed again.

Learning More

As our investigation continued, Peter and Jay returned to Texas to speak again with Stewart and Thomason. With each subsequent interview, it became rather obvious that they'd both forgotten what they'd said previously. Their stories and recollection of people, places, and events were always changing, with little or no consistency. Most notably, for two guys who had once been best friends, each new interview drew increasing animosity between the two, demonstrated by their back-and-forth finger-pointing. Yet they were both careful to avoid making any direct accusations of one another. Without directly accusing the other, the growing suspicion was they were both involved, and neither could directly accuse the other without implicating himself. Admittedly, I'm no expert in human behavior, but I've seen this type of scenario play out many times. Where two or more suspects believed to be involved in the same crime started pointing the finger at each other when the heat came on. That certainly seemed to be the case here.

After reviewing my earlier interview with Wright Childers and learning how Frank and I had been shut-out from a reinterview, Jay and Peter expressed an interest in taking another shot at Childers. I advised them that to me, Wright had seemed very mild-mannered, and I thought there was a good chance he would talk with them. But only if mama bear wasn't around and those damn Rots were in their kennel.

Later, Jay and Peter traveled to Tennessee and staked out the Childers' residence. The Rots were in their kennel, and they only waited a few minutes before seeing mama come out and drive away. Wright invited them in, and they spoke to him briefly. Wright exaggerated what he described as the 'global' head injury he received from his accident and claimed to have no memory of anything in New York. They didn't press the issue and simply left it at that.

Interestingly, they had left him with their business cards, and about a week later, Barket's office received a formal letter from an attorney representing Childers. Barket's office was given notice that he was representing Wright Childers and insisted any further inquiries on the matter would need to be directed through him. Our suspicion that

Childers may also have been involved just raised up a notch. He knew something.

Well before the September 2014 trial date, Barket's motion for a much-needed change of venue had been granted. Cal's third trial was now going to be held about 125 miles East of Owego in Schoharie[1] County, New York. With only a few exceptions, the demographic make-up of Tioga and Schoharie was quite similar. A rural, farm and agricultural county, with a sparse population and no cities. The County Seat was in a small village bearing the same name (Schoharie). With more time needed to make the necessary adjustments for the venue change, a new trial date was set for the end of January 2015. We were anxious to get started, so hopefully, there would be no more delays.

---

1. Schoharie: Native American (Mohawk) meaning; 'floating driftwood'

44

BARKET MEETS STEWART

Bruce Barket had taken a special interest in the information we were developing relative to Stacy Stewart and Chris Thomason, but even more-so with Stewart. He'd read through all the leads and interviews that were done with Stewart and decided it was time for him to meet and interview Stewart himself.

In early August 2014, Bruce teamed up with Peter Smith and flew to Texas to try and speak with Stewart. Since his last interview with Peter and Jay, a few things had changed. Stewart was still working for the Texas Department of Corrections but had since been promoted to the rank of Captain. He'd also re-married a few months earlier and was now living with his third wife, Nadine, in Clute, Texas. Nadine was a corrections officer, and they worked at the same prison unit in Brazoria, TX.

Both Stewart and his wife were home when Bruce and Peter showed up. Albeit reluctantly, Stewart agreed to another interview. Peter was surreptitiously recording the interview. Stewart started right out, claiming that while at NUCOR, he was working 12 to 16, even 17-hour days, often going in at 3:00 or 4:00 a.m. Another lie. Then claimed he had only been in Lefty's "maybe three times" the entire time he was there. Nope, that wasn't true either. When asked, he also denied ever going to the Bare Facts strip-club himself but claimed Thomason and Childers went there often. Then described Chris as a "frequent-flyer." They've only just begun, and he had already lied three times. One lie just leads to the next. Like I mentioned before, he just makes things up as he goes along.

Later, he admitted to watching a documentary of the case on television. During which, he'd recognized Nikki Burdick as the person he had seen with Michele at the Guthrie Inn one night, and he'd talked to her. But quickly denied ever speaking with Michele and insisted it was only Nikki he'd talked to.

Throughout the interview, Stewart was continuously trying to distance himself from Michele as his finger-pointing and animosity towards Chris became more aggressive. This time he described Chris as a loose cannon, who had gone off the beaten path and was heavily into drugs, including meth. He then tried to strengthen his position that it was Chris who had the relationship with Michele, by implying that Chris had slept with her. When Bruce reminded him of what Chris said, that "you guys were all out with her that night," Stewart's only response was, "Nope." Bruce then reminded him of what Chris's girlfriend told Investigators. According to what she learned from Chris, initially, they were both with Michele that night at a dance club. Later, however, Chris claimed to have left the club, leaving Stacy behind with Michele, who seemed fine. There was no response.

Further into the interview, with every mention of the name Chris Thomason, Stewart's anger and tawdry responses were growing steadily. Keeping him angry at Chris was part of their strategy, hoping that if angered enough, he might blurt out some spontaneous remark(s) that could be useful. Later, that's what happened.

Bruce raised the topic of the bloody clothes by asking him about the allegations from others that he and Chris were joking about burning bloody clothing. Stewart replied, "No. Chris, like I told the investigators the other day, Chris and that other girl with the tattoos, they had come up there one night with blood on their clothes. I didn't think twice about it. My girl Lisa, she was out there with me at the house." Bruce followed by asking the logical question, "Where did you think the blood came from?" He replied, "I don't know. I didn't even think twice about it. Chris said, you got any clothes for me to wear, and I said yeah, get what you need, you know where it's at."

Initially, Stewart couldn't remember the girl's name but knew she had pinkish-red hair and a bunch of tattoos. After Peter told him that he had spoken with her and her name was Kari Cavanaugh, he agreed that it was probably her. Bruce continued,

"And so they just showed up with bloody clothes one night?" Stewart answered, "It was just covered in blood. You know, it looked like they might have skinned a deer or something. That's all I could think of. I didn't think much about it."

Later, Peter brought up the subject of the bloody clothes again. He informed Stewart that after speaking with Thomason, Cavanaugh, and then, Lydia Monico, their recollections of the bloody clothes matter were all different. Thomason denied it entirely, claiming that Monico was just trying to get him back to New York to try and collect child support. Cavanaugh, other than admitting that she briefly dated Thomason, denied knowing anything about the burning of bloody clothes, or Chris ever telling her anything about it. Monico, however, claimed to have been with Thomason when he blurted out the comment about going up to Stewart's place to help him (Stewart) burn a bloody shirt he was wearing. Peter said, "It scared the hell out of her." He also told him he was planning on following up with his old flame, Lisa Demtrak.

Responding, Stewart replied, "Let me tell you this much. I'll tell you what I told them. Lisa was in the house, and they came up. Like I said, I was like, what the fuck y'all been doing, you know?" Then went on to describe what they were wearing, "Chris was in jeans and his girl in a plaid shirt." Bruce jumped in, "So, what did he say to you?" Stewart replied, "What are you doing? Well, we just need to change clothes, get rid of these clothes. I didn't think much about it." Peter asks, "You didn't find it bizarre?" Followed by Bruce, "Yeah, I mean, somebody walks in your house with bloody clothes, and they burned them in your yard?" Stewart replied, "Uh-huh from what I remember, yeah. I had a little burn-pit."

I couldn't help noticing that Stewart said, "I told the investigators the other day" and "I'll tell you what I told them." What investigators? Told who? We didn't know it at the time but later learned the SP finally did interview him, and he'd told them this same bizarre story. Please, don't tell me they're buying it? But supposedly they did because it was never pursued any further.

Continuing, he explained how, after changing into some of his clothes, Thomason and his girlfriend went outside and burned the bloody clothes. Bruce, who was obviously not buying his story, said, "Is it just me, or is this straight and utterly bizarre? You walk in somebody else's house and say, I have to change clothes, give me your clothes, even if you go with the deer. What's the burning about?" Stewart answered, "I can still remember like what the fuck, you know? But I wasn't really paying attention to it."

I'd have to agree with Bruce. Was it just me, or was this scenario utterly bizarre? I think we all knew the answer to that. Considering the odd story, he just told, he would've been better off denying any knowledge of the bloody clothes. And notably, while speaking of clothes. Would Kari Cavanaugh even be able to wear Stewart's clothes? Perhaps. But Thomason? He was four inches taller than Stewart and outweighed him by more than 70 pounds.

If he was wearing Stewart's clothes, he would've looked like the Incredible Hulk.

Author's Note: I never could figure out how the Hulk kept his pants on.

Going back to Stewart's interview, he had been saying all along that it was Thomason having a fling with Michele, not him. When Bruce reminded him of what Thomason said, that he didn't know Michele, never met her, never talked to her, never went out with her. Stewart angrily replied, "That's fuckin bullshit." Bruce continued, "This is Chris. He says he didn't know Michele Harris, never dated her or anyone by the name of Michele, didn't know who she was. Vaguely aware, the case involved a missing woman but didn't know who it was." Stewart, now growing angrier, said, "He's fucking lying, the little fucker." Bruce asked, "What do you mean?" Angrier yet, and this is the part I like. Stewart nearly yelled, **"Everybody fuckin knew who she was. We all went into Lefty's. Do you know what I'm saying? We talked to her at the goddamn bar, the Guthrie Inn that night – that night I told you I actually met her. He was there fuckin with me. Do you know what I'm saying? He knew who the fuck she was. The dude's fuckin blowing smoke. This shit's gettin out of control."**

Obviously, Stewart's angry comment could be interpreted several ways, but in my view, considering everything else I knew, he had just further implicated himself and Thomason as viable suspects.

45

TRIAL # 3

Gearing up for Trial # 3

Bruce and Peter returned from Texas, and it was now mid-August 2014. Bruce called to tell me he was coming into town and wanted me to introduce him to Kevin Tubbs and Todd Mansfield. I called both, and they agreed to meet with us. As soon as Bruce arrived, I called Mansfield, who was in the middle of a golf game. He agreed to make himself available and said he would meet us behind the clubhouse. There, I introduced Bruce, and the three of us sat in his golf cart as Bruce questioned him about his relationship with Cal. Because of his friendship with Cal, Mansfield had mixed feelings about what happened. He was concerned that Cal could have had something to do with Michele's disappearance. He explained his relationship and history with Cal, as well as his involvement and interactions with him in the days following Michele's disappearance. He was also aware of and had witnessed some demonstrations of anger by Cal in the past. Bruce reassured him that if he were called to testify, other than what we just discussed, there would be no surprises. Mansfield agreed and was willing to testify.

Our interview with Mansfield had taken longer than anticipated. After we finished with him, I called Tubbs to tell him we were running late, but we were on our way. It was after dark by the time we pulled into Candor, NY. Tubbs was waiting for us at his parents' house when we arrived. As he stepped out on the porch, I introduced him to Bruce, and the interview started. A few minutes into the interview, Bruce asked Kevin if he was willing to re-trace the areas and events, and by pointing out those same areas, retell his story. Kevin agreed and said it would probably be easier if he drove. As we pulled away in his truck, the interview continued. Step-by-step, starting, and later ending at the Tubbs farm on Straights Corners Road, Kevin retold his story from beginning to end. Along the way, with some occasional questions by Bruce, he pointed out all the pertinent locations, then redescribed all the respective events he had witnessed. Bruce, like myself, having met Tubbs in person, found him to be entirely credible.

After interviewing Stewart, Peter wanted to follow-up with his former girlfriend, Lisa Demtrak. Stewart had claimed that Demtrak was present on the night Thomason and his girlfriend showed up in bloody clothes and later burned them. Investigator Tom Brennan, who was working with Peter, located and interviewed Demtrak. Initially, she had no desire to be re-interviewed and just wanted the whole mess to go away. When asked, she acknowledged having been interviewed by Frank and me as well as Investigator Mike Myers from the SP. Despite her initial reluctance, she continued to answer Brennan's questions.

In summary, although admitting having been at Stewart's cabin on several occasions, she adamantly denied being there during the 'burning of bloody clothes' event described by Stewart. She said, "That never happened. At least not while I was there." Later in the interview, she said, "But now that you mention it, I know he did have bonfires up there at times, and I did hear something about burning of clothes but nothing more. I just remembered that. But all I know is, if it did happen, I wasn't there." When questioned further, she had no clue how she remembered that or who she may have heard it from.

Meanwhile, in a further attempt to confirm or refute Stewart's story, I contacted and re-interviewed Kari Cavanaugh. She acknowledged her relationship with Thomason and advised that on a few occasions, she had been to his apartment in Horseheads, NY. Furthermore, on two or more occasions, she and Thomason had attended beer parties at Stewart's cabin. She added that the parties usually included a bonfire.

After describing Stewart's version of the burning of bloody clothes, she said, "That's ridiculous. Nothing like that ever happened. Besides, I just lived around the corner from there. If I needed a change of clothes, I would have just gone home. But I'm telling you, it never happened. And even if it did, why would I need to burn my clothes after gutting a deer?" "Good point," I said. I then asked her if she ever met Stewart's girlfriend, Lisa Demtrak. She knew he had a girlfriend because Chris had mentioned her, but she had no recollection of ever meeting her.

Cavanaugh then recalled being interviewed earlier and said, "Wasn't it, Chris, who told somebody he helped Stacy burn a bloody shirt?" I said, "Correct. Therein lies the problem. Because now we have this other version from Stewart." As I was leaving, she stopped me and added, "Well, this is stupid. Somebody's lying. Who do you believe?" I said, "Well, they're probably both lying, but I do believe something happened that involved the burning of bloody clothing. They could both be involved." As a final comment, she said, "Well, I can't speak for either one, but I can tell you this, whatever did happen, did not include me."

Third Trial Nears

Sometime between August of 2014 when Stewart was interviewed by Peter and Bruce, and mid-January of 2015, Stacy had met and started dating a new girlfriend after splitting with his third wife, Nadine. The trial was only a week away when Bruce's office received a call from a woman identified as Julie Brinkman. During her call to Bruce, she revealed some information about Stacy Stewart that she thought he should know. She'd recently met him, and he'd invited her over to his house for their first date. While there, she noticed the business card of an NYSP investigator on his refrigerator. When she inquired, he said, "They want me to testify in a murder case I had nothing to do with." Then, she told Bruce, "he seemed evasive about the subject at first, but after a few more beers, I pressed him a bit further." He then bragged to her, saying, "I know how to hide a body." Later, after more beer and pressing further yet, he said, "I was the last person seen with her (Michele) alive."

Before the trial, the defense team had been watching and reviewing the nationally televised presentation of the Cal Harris case on CBS *48-Hours.* Several key segments had been cut from the presentation, which was to be expected. However, believing that some of those cut segments could have provided crucial new information helpful to the defense, Barket filed a motion with the Honorable George Bartlett, Schoharie County Court Judge. His motion was for an order for CBS *48 Hours* to release the unedited footage to the defense. Surprisingly, Bartlett approved the motion, ordering CBS to release the footage. In response, CBS opposed Bartlett's order and refused to turn it over. After that, Barket appealed to the Third Judicial Department of the New York State Supreme Court, Appellate Division. Subsequently, Bartlett's decision was upheld, forcing CBS to release the footage. With the unedited footage now in the hands of the defense, we were about to discover, not only some startling but troubling new revelations.

I mentioned earlier that prior to the first trial, District Attorney Jerry Keene and senior members of the SP, including BCI Captain Mark Lester and Sr. Investigators Sue Mulvey and Steve Andersen, held a joint meeting in the Connecticut lab of Dr. Henry Lee to discuss the blood evidence.

Of the three raw-footage videos from CBS, the first was their coverage of this joint meeting with Dr. Lee. Only now it included the added footage that had been cut from their broadcast version. In this version, Dr. Lee was seen present as Keene and Mulvey were heard discussing the 'altering' of photographs. Keene was seen speaking with Dr. Lee and, while showing him some of the photographs, explained in his own words that they had been 'altered.' Mulvey was heard interjecting, in an attempt to clarify, when she said that the photographs had been 'corrected.'

When our own photo expert examined the photos, we learned the SP specifically targeted and augmented (altered) the bloodstains by enhancing the red hue by some twenty points. It was a significant departure from what the stains really looked like.

Later, Keene was heard questioning Dr. Lee about whether the blood could have been deposited from a cut finger. Lee admitted it could have but said, "the defense will need to prove there was a cut finger." After Keene reminded him of his burden of proof, Lee said,

"Don't worry, you say cut hand, a jury will say, show me cut hand." They all laughed. Even though Keene knew from Michele's divorce papers (prepared by his wife) that she had cut her hand, he never told Lee.

We knew from the earliest part of the SP investigation that there were significant problems with the photographs. Regardless of what word is used, be it altered, corrected, modified, or enhanced, the bottom line was – the probative value of the blood photographs had been augmented artificially, by digitally 'turning-up' the red hue. This was done, by design, to make the red look redder and therefore making the blood appear more recent than it was. As a result, the 'doctored' photos were inaccurate, misleading, and misrepresentative of the actual blood evidence. More troubling was the fact that Dr. Lee, knowing the photographs had been altered, continued to use them in his assessment before offering his testimony.

The second raw-footage video was a blood-spatter demonstration by Sr. Investigator Steve Andersen in the forensics lab of Troop 'C' Headquarters in Sidney, NY. Other than being tailored to correspond with their theory, nothing unusual was noted.

The third video segment was also interesting. Greg and Shannon Taylor had long denied knowing anything about Stacy Stewart. During the broadcast version of *48-Hours*, they only made some brief comments about the case. However, in the unedited version, they both admitted to knowing who Stacy Stewart was and that Michele had talked about him. Shannon told *48-Hours* lead correspondent, Erin Moriarty, that she not only knew who he was but also knew from speaking with Michele that he worked at Vulcraft (NUCOR). She knew that after he moved up from Texas, he stayed in a local hotel and that he was a frequent customer at Lefty's. Adding, he would visit there often. Greg also admitted knowing who Stewart was and admitted that he and Michele had talked about him and Vulcraft.

Isn't it interesting how the truth finds a way of bubbling to the surface when you least expect it? This would only help reaffirm my belief that lies have speed, but truth has endurance. Why would they withhold this type of information? I can think of at least two reasons. One, to further protect Michele's already tainted image, and two, to prevent the police from taking their focus off the man they abhorred the most and believed to have killed Michele – Cal Harris.

Fourteen years had passed. Michele was still missing. Cal's third trial was about to start. A lot had changed over the years. Witnesses have aged. Memories have faded. Investigating officers have since retired. And the third trial would be held in a new venue, with a new judge, a new DA, and a new, more aggressive defense attorney. Even the battle of the blood experts would change. Yet the evidence against Cal remained unchanged. There was still no body, no murder weapon, and only those few tiny specks of blood, totaling no more than ten drops. How would it be different this time? Hopefully, with the 125-mile separation between Tioga and Schoharie, prospective jurors would not be tainted by preconceived opinions, or otherwise influenced by any pretrial publicity.

Trial # 3

Jury selection started as prospective jurors filtered into the Schoharie County Courthouse on January 22, 2015. County Court Judge George Bartlett was presiding. Other than a few aesthetic differences, such as its blue limestone exterior, the late nineteenth-century architecture of the Schoharie County Courthouse was very much like that of Tioga County. The interior was similar as well, although in a slightly different configuration.

Judge Bartlett advised potential jurors that the trial was expected to take six to eight weeks. As it turned out, it took eleven weeks. After a full week, a full panel of twelve jurors made up of seven men and five women, along with six alternates was selected, sworn-in and seated. After opening remarks, the prosecution called its first witness.

For the most part, with few exceptions, the direct testimony of the prosecution's witnesses was presented the same as it was in the first two trials. This time, however, witnesses were facing a much more aggressive and challenging cross-examination, especially those who had a 'special interest' in the outcome.

Following the script of the first two trials, Martin presented his case with all the same witnesses and, for the most part, the same testimony. For those 'specially-interested' witnesses, it didn't take long under Bruce's challenging cross-examination, to notice how quickly their demeanor and facial expressions changed as they withdrew into defense mode. Their changing manner was like night-and-day. Their once comfortable expressions of concern and sincerity, replaced by uncomfortable nervousness, anxiety, and at times – outright hostility.

Despite the controversial and conflicting interpretations, those tiny specks of blood were still the strongest evidence against Cal. As expected, Dr. Henry Lee's testimony was notably consistent with his prior testimony. No surprise there. However, under Bruce's cross, he was challenged every step of the way. As a seasoned witness, I had never seen Dr. Lee so uncomfortable on the witness stand.

Later, the defense called Terry Laber, a new blood expert, who offered his testimony for the first time. Like Dr. Lee, Laber had conducted his own independent examination and assessment, using the same police documents and photographs. During his testimony, Laber agreed with much of Dr. Lee's testimony. However, he concluded and testified that, had the blood been caused by a fatal assault, there would have been more blood spatter and evidence of force. He also said the stains showed no signs of attempted clean-up, and there was no way to pinpoint or determine what caused them.

About six weeks into the trial, Bruce informed Judge Bartlett of his intent to introduce evidence that would exonerate Cal and implicate the two Texas residents, Stacy Stewart and Chris Thomason. This was done outside the presence of the jury. Bruce argued that the evidence would clearly establish how the two were more linked to Michele's death than Cal. In his argument, he also referred to statements made to other witnesses, such as Stewart, once saying, "I know how to hide a body." And, "I was the last person seen with her (Michele) alive." While summing up, Barket said the defense evidence might not prove who killed Michele Harris, but it would cast reasonable doubt on whether Cal Harris was guilty. He finished by adding, "If a jury were to hear this (evidence), as they should, they would acquit Mr. Harris."

Under rare circumstances, as these were, the defense was trying to argue what's known in the legal world as, 'third-party culpability.' In other words, the introduction and admissibility of evidence that has the propensity to show that someone, other than the accused, a third party, may be responsible for the crime charged. Thus, the probative value and legitimate tendency of such evidence, if permitted, may be enough to raise a reasonable doubt as to the defendant's guilt.

Two more weeks of the trial went by before Bartlett announced his decision. Jurors would *not* be allowed to hear the 'third-party' evidence.

In his decision, he said he would not allow the defense evidence because it was too weak and based largely on hearsay. Later, when speaking with reporters, Bruce said, "This may be the worse decision I've ever heard." He also added that he found it very "troubling" the jury would never hear the evidence implicating the other suspects. He claimed further that it was a grotesque injustice that ran the risk of an innocent man being convicted.

Jurors had heard the testimony of more than 60 witnesses. This time, even without Cal's testimony, the trial dragged on for eleven weeks. Throughout the entire trial, the key issues were surrounded by contrasting accounts that were riddled with differing interpretations. Even the experts couldn't agree.

Furthermore, two polar-opposite portraits of Cal had been presented. One, a controlling, emotionless, and cold-blooded killer. The other, a caring and devoted father, innocent of the crime charged – a man who was trying for his children, to keep the memory of his estranged wife's memory alive. Both sides rested their case. Closing arguments were about to begin.

Closing Arguments

Briefly, throughout his four-hour closing argument, Barket went on the offense by attacking the veracity and credibility of several of the prosecution's witnesses, who clearly demonstrated their animus towards Cal. He argued the weight of the evidence, what little evidence they had, was not supportive of a guilty verdict. If anything, it was more consistent with innocence. Near the end of his closing, he added, "Had Cal been the right person, the mystery of what happened to Michele would have been solved. But the mystery endures. It's time to look elsewhere."

Kirk Martin's closing followed. His was also four-hours in length. He laid out his case as aggressively as Barket had. He, too, addressed virtually every element of the case, offering his own perspective of what the evidence showed. He admitted that the evidence was circumstantial but said that it was strong enough to prove that Cal killed his wife on the night of September 11, 2001. Later, he added, "Her only known enemy was Cal Harris. When viewed in its entirety, the evidence against the defendant is powerful in this case."

Closing arguments had finally come to an end. Bruce asked to renew some of his objections before the jury received their instructions, and they were excused to the jury room. The courtroom was still crowded as he began renewing some of his valid objections. At times there were some rather heated exchanges between opposing counsel and the judge.

Then, one after another, despite their validity, Bartlett overruled the objections. In a sudden outburst, after hearing one of Bartlett's adverse ruling's Cal shouted out from the defense table, "It isn't fair. Twelve weeks I've been going through this, you've given every benefit to them. It's a disgrace. Shame on you." Before Bartlett could respond, Bruce hustled Cal out of the courtroom before he could say anything further. After several minutes, they returned to the courtroom. Cal offered a short apology, and the trial resumed. Later, while speaking with reporters outside the courtroom, Bruce said he was surprised an outburst like this hadn't happened sooner, considering the allegations faced by Cal for the past 14 years.

During the first two trials, guilty verdicts had been reached within a matter of a few hours. But the jury in this trial, after deliberating for more than eleven days, was unable to reach a verdict. Even after Judge Bartlett sent them back to the jury room twice during their deliberations to try and reach a verdict. Throughout most of their deliberations, they were deadlocked in an even 6/6 split. In the end, the best they could do was 7/5. The nearly 12-week trial officially came to an end as Judge Bartlett declared a mistrial.

Aftermath

Speaking positively after the mistrial was declared, Cal said, "It's been 14-years since this nightmare began. I had hoped that my children and I would finally be free to live our lives without these allegations hanging over our heads." Then added, "Still, I am thankful to be going home with my family." He also urged law enforcement to look elsewhere because "they've been pursuing the wrong man." Continuing, he said,

"We got closer to justice, but we're not there yet. We will continue to fight and find the truth of Michele's disappearance."

The mistrial was just another chapter in the ongoing saga. Like Barket had argued, after three trials and in the interest of justice, enough was enough. It should be over. Apparently, that was just wishful thinking, because, within just a few days, Martin announced his decision to move forward with a fourth trial.

PART VI

TRIAL #4

46

HERE WE GO AGAIN

A fter the mistrial, we all took some much-needed time off to reflect on all that happened and to spend time catching up on some older cases that had been put on hold. That only lasted a few months before a scheduled conference was held to map out the details for the fourth trial. The fourth trial would once again be held in Schoharie County Court. Like before, Kirk Martin would prosecute, and Bruce Barket would defend. Judge George Bartlett, however, had stepped down and would no longer be presiding.

Replacing Bartlett was the Honorable, Richard Mott, a Supreme Court Justice from the 3rd Judicial District of the Supreme Court, in Columbia County, New York. Mott brought with him over 34-years of legal experience. Before becoming a Supreme Court Justice in 2012, Mott worked in private practice and later, for about five years as an assistant public defender in Columbia County. Amongst his peers, including prosecutors as well as defense attorneys, Mott was both well-known and respected within the legal community. He also had a long-standing reputation for his impartiality, constitutional fairness, and ethical integrity. From a defense perspective, Mott had all the attributes we were looking for. All we ever wanted was someone who was unbiased, impartial, objective, and fair. Hopefully, with Judge Mott presiding, he would see the case for what it really was. Later, Mott met with the attorneys, and the fourth trial date was scheduled for the end of March 2016.

The trial was still a few months away, which gave us some time to re-group and get back up to speed on everything. By now, due to some personal matters, attorney/investigator Peter Smith had stepped down from the case. In his absence, Bruce turned to another experienced investigator by the name of William 'Bill' Flanagan. Bill had recently retired from his prestigious position as 2nd Deputy Commissioner of the Nassau County Police Department. After his retirement, Bill went back to work and joined forces with PI Natalie Beyer, an experienced forensic analyst who was working under the business name, NB Investigations Corporation, in Islip, NY. Bill had a great deal of experience in law enforcement, and together with Natalie, Bruce put them to work, getting up to speed on the case.

Later, once Bill and Natalie were up to speed, we held another long-distance defense team briefing via Skype. During the third trial, Bruce's motion to allow the introduction of third-party culpability had been denied. Knowing that a new judge would be presiding, Bruce was planning on renewing his motion. But he wanted us to look for something more that could further support his argument.

47

THE BURN-PIT

With all the hype surrounding the 'burning of bloody clothes,' including Stewart's bizarre story, we discussed the feasibility of excavating the burn-pit on his former property. The obvious drawbacks included the open burn-pit itself, having been exposed to the elements for 15 years, and also having been used by the current owner. The chances of finding anything of evidentiary value was minimal at best. Complicating matters further was the fact that is was now winter, and the ground may be frozen. Regardless, we decided to move forward to see what it would take to make it happen. We had nothing to lose.

Bill mentioned having worked with some forensic archeologists in the past. He advised there were teams out there, experienced in doing archeological digs. He'd make the necessary contact to see who was available and willing to take on the project. Meanwhile, I was to contact the current owner, Jeff Gennarelli, to let him know what we had in mind and get his permission.

As expected, after speaking with Gennarelli, permission was granted. While I had him on the phone, I asked him about his own history with the burn-pit. He only had a few fires in the pit. When I asked him what kinds of things he burned, he said, "Just scraps of wood, brush, or broken tree branches." I then asked, specifically. "Since you've been there, have you or anyone else ever burned any dead animals, clothing, footwear, household garbage, or anything like that?"

He said, "No. I'm the only one that ever burned anything, and I've never burned anything like that, never."

About two days later, Bill called. He'd contacted a forensic anthropologist by the name of Dr. Dennis Dirkmaat, at Mercyhurst University in Erie, PA. Dr. Dirkmaat was a professor of archeological studies at the university. After learning of our objective, he was willing to assist. He advised he had a group of students already experienced in archeological digs that were anxious to gain some additional experience.

With Gennarelli's permission, Bill scheduled an excavation date for January 8, 2016. Dirkmaat advised he and his team would provide all the necessary equipment. I emailed Gennarelli to let him know.

Winter can be harsh in upstate New York. But so far, the winter had been somewhat mild. Other than some light ground frost, there had not yet been a deep freeze. The forecast for January 8th, other than another light frost overnight, looked good. Arrangements were made to meet Dr. Dirkmaat and his team in Waverly and then escort them to the site.

Bill Flanagan and Natalie Beyer drove in the night before, and I met them in Waverly the next morning for a briefing. Dr. Dirkmaat, with his team of nine students and all their equipment, arrived right on schedule. After some brief introductions, Bill, Natalie, and Dirkmaat's team followed me to the remote site, about eight miles away. I greeted Gennarelli and introduced him to the others. During their trip, Dr. Dirkmaat had briefed his team about what they would be looking for. But as they were getting set up, Bill reminded them again about what we were asking them to look for.

Dirkmaat had confidence in his team members since they all had prior experience. The team quickly went to work, first, by assembling some tall tripods. Then, hanging their wood-framed sifting and screening containers from the tripods, keeping them elevated, about three feet off the ground. From there, they went to work digging and sifting through layer-by-layer of material from the burn-pit. They carefully and meticulously examined every shovel full. Any item(s) of interest found, were placed separately, just as they were found, into a clean paper bag. Dirkmaat was right. It was apparent his team knew what they were doing. Ordinarily, I'm the one getting my hands dirty, but this time, I was there strictly as an observer.

Bill was observing, too, but he was also documenting the whole process with photographs, including the items that were found, collected, and subsequently turned over to him. He was also video-taping the process using an aerial view from a small drone hovering above.

The burn-pit was not very big, but it still took the better part of the day to complete. I knew certain artifacts had been found and collected from the bottom-most layer of the burn-pit. But they were blackened and dirt-covered, so I wasn't sure exactly what they were. Bill said that he would be taking the evidence with him for closer examination and more photographs. Later, we would get together to review what was found.

Evidence vs. Garbage

So, what exactly did Dr. Dirkmaat and his Mercyhurst University team discover during their archeological dig? Considering the length of time that had passed, I wasn't overly optimistic that anything of significance would be found. Yet knowing some things were found, I was anxious to learn what they were. And whether they might be considered evidence. Or perhaps just some extraneous garbage.

When Bill finally called, he advised me what was found and forwarded the photographs. After learning what was found and seeing the photographs for myself, I immediately placed the found items in the evidence category. They were not just garbage. From the concurring perspective of the defense team, the physical evidence found corroborated the fact that two or more articles of clothing had been burned there.

The items, all of which were found in the lower-most layer of the burn-pit, included the following:

- One five-inch serrated knife blade, hunting style, rusted
- One decorative button, unique, ornate design
- One partial, navy-blue strap from woman's sports bra, w/metal adjustment clasp
- One charred fragment of fabric, navy blue
- One charred fragment of fabric, khaki
- One standard house key, rusted
- One coin, US dime, 1997

Before discovering these items, a considerable length of time (15-

years) had passed. During that time, they were not only exposed to burning but also 15-years of exposure to nature's elements. Therefore, the chances of finding any identifiable DNA was extremely remote. Despite the odds, the evidence was submitted to an accredited DNA lab for testing. Unfortunately, but not surprisingly, no DNA was found. Later, the fabric items were submitted to another lab for composition testing to identify a possible manufacturer. Due to the severe degradation of the material, test results were inconclusive. Even without proof positive that any of the items specifically belonged to Michele, their circumstantial value was significant, with enough to suggest that they may be related to her disappearance.

Based on what we already know, the significance of these items should be self-evident. However, for those in denial, they might argue that this was nothing more than everyday household garbage. And any possible connection to Michele Harris would be purely coincidental. But I would have to ask whether those same naysayers would still be in denial had this same evidence been found in a burn-pit on Cal's property? I think we all know the answer to that. But let's briefly take-a-look at the evidence and see how it does relate to Michele, and how it corresponds with the other known facts that have been developed.

To start, we know that Michele was last seen wearing her navy-blue 'Lefty's' polo-shirt and khaki-colored shorts. Both of which were consistent in color with the two fabric items found in the burn-pit. There was also a partial, navy-blue bra-strap, with a metal adjustment clasp still intact.

I've always felt a bit uncomfortable wandering around the women's apparel department. But with a little research, I was able to find what appeared to be identical adjustment clasps on the back of some of the sports bras I examined. And according to Cal, Michele was very athletic and routinely wore a sports bra. The other 'coincidence' was the coordinating navy-blue color with her Lefty's shirt.

Turning to the decorative button, house key, and coin that was found, they too had their own significance. We knew from the investigation that Michele loved and regularly shopped for fashionable items and apparel. The button with an ornate design might have been attached to a fancy handbag, gloves, hat, wallet or purse, or some other unknown article of clothing. As we've already learned, Michele's wallet and purse were never found.

There was also an interesting connection to the house key. Possibly, two connections. Police learned from Brian Earley that he had initially given Michele a key to his apartment two months earlier, but she'd lost it. Then, the day before she disappeared, he'd given her a new one. Did she just stick it in her pocket? There was also another possible explanation. The house Michele intended to purchase was vacant at the time. As such, once she made her down-payment, she may have been given a key. Unfortunately, the realtor couldn't remember. When I checked to see if the key we found might still fit at either location, I learned the locks had long since been changed. Due to the length of time, I knew it was a long shot.

And what about the coin? The 1997 dime? In-and-of-itself, not a lot of significance other than the fact that it pre-dated Michele's disappearance. But more importantly, had it post-dated her disappearance, it would likely have negated all the other evidence.

Finally, what about the rusty hunting knife blade? More likely than not, the knife blade originally had some type of grip or handle that burned or melted off in the fire. Although we don't know for sure what was used to kill Michele, we do know that some bloody clothes were burned in that burn-pit. Should we believe Stewart that these were the bloody clothes of Thomason and his girlfriend after skinning a deer? Or, should we believe Thomason's drunken comment that he'd helped burn Stewart's bloody shirt? The bizarre nature of Stewart's story was simply too far-fetched and made no sense. Therefore, I'm more inclined to go with Thomason's drunken remark, made out-of-the-blue to Lydia Monico. But even when considering what was just found in the burn-pit, it seems Thomason's revelation may have only been part of the story. He may have helped Stewart burn his own bloody shirt, but the new evidence suggests there was more involved than just Stewart's shirt.

Previously, the 'bloody clothes' stories of Stewart and Thomason, albeit conflicting, and the other known facts had already established reasonable suspicion. It suggested they were both involved in some sinister activity involving Michele Harris. With the recent discovery of the items in the burn-pit, circumstantially linked to Michele Harris, we now had supporting evidence to believe they were involved in the killing of Michele. Together, they disposed of her bloody clothing in the burn-pit, along with the knife used to kill her.

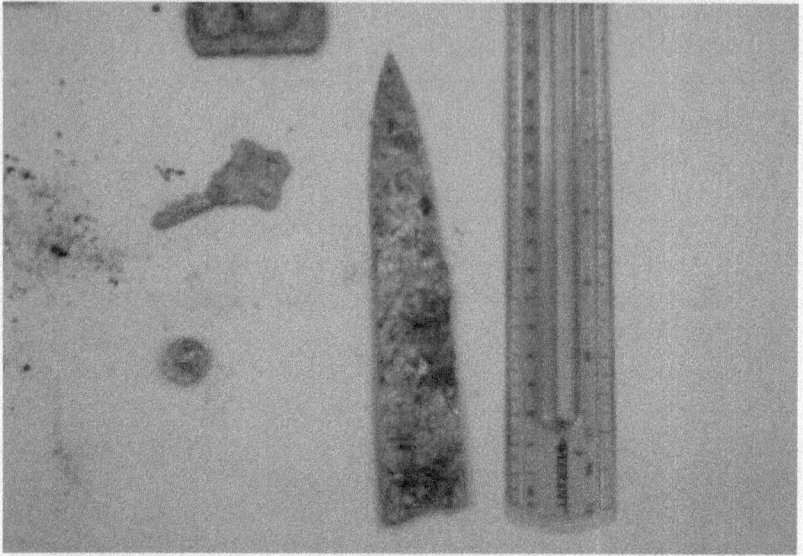

Burn-Pit Items

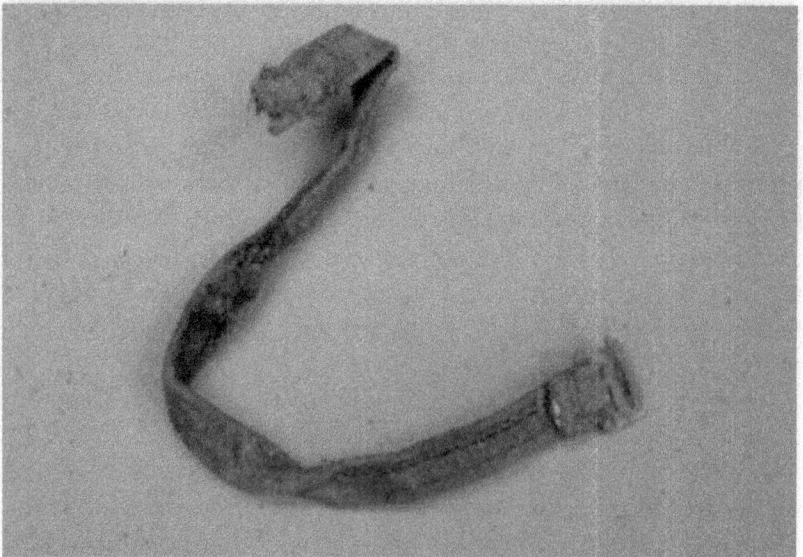

Burn-Pit Items

48

STEWART'S TRUCK

A s I mentioned earlier, during my first trip to Texas, Frank and I attempted to locate the black Chevy pick-up truck formerly owned by Stacy Stewart. However, we ran out of time.

During one of our pre-trial defense briefings, Bruce recommended we renew our effort to try and find the truck and have it examined forensically. Bill Flanagan was assigned the task.

By tracing historical vehicle records, Bill was able to track down the current registered owner by the name of Jeremiah Wilkins. He was living in one of the southern-most bayous of Louisiana. Being unable to contact Wilkins, Bill had an associate in Texas, physically go to the Wilkins address to confirm his ownership status and get a contact number. From his associate, Bill learned that Wilkins was an older African American, poorly educated, and living alone in an extremely remote area. Somewhat jokingly, his assistant added, "I wasn't sure if I was going to make it out of there alive. So, if you decide to go there, don't go alone. You may never be seen again." Later, Bill called and spoke with Wilkins.

While speaking with Wilkins, Bill also learned that he was the only one who had ever driven the truck. Initially, after explaining what we were interested in doing, Bill attempted to buy the truck. After hesitating briefly, Wilkins declined and said, "This be the best dang truck I ever did own. It ain't for sale." Bill quickly switched to plan B and negotiated a generous fee for 'renting' the truck, long enough to perform a forensic examination. Wilkins agreed, and further arrangements were made to take the vehicle to a secure mechanic's facility for the exam.

Meanwhile, the search was on to locate a forensic crime-scene specialist in southern Louisiana to actually conduct the examination. After a few phone calls, Bill made contact with Owen McDonnell, of O.M. Forensics LLC. McDonnell had retired as a Lieutenant from the local Sheriff's Office as the supervisor of the Crime Scene Investigations Division in Shreveport, LA. McDonnell, who was now working in the private sector, agreed to help and was retained.

Once the plan was finalized, Bill's business associate Natalie Beyer, also an experienced forensic examiner, flew to Louisiana and met with McDonnell. Joining forces, they conducted a forensic exam of the truck.

During their examination, areas of suspicious reddish-brown staining were found on the rear seat and within the protected areas behind the passenger door panels. After being photographed, field-tests were conducted that indicated a positive presence of blood. They were then collected and later tested by an accredited DNA lab. Although a weak presence of co-mingled DNA was found, no definitive profile could be made.

Also, during their exam, Natalie located, photographed, and recovered a diamond stud earring. Under closer examination, it was remarkably similar to a set Cal had purchased for Michele. You can see her wearing them in several of her photographs. The earring itself was sterling silver. Other than being heavily tarnished and pitted, the setting was fully intact. The earring was discovered partially hidden and wedged between the bottom of the molded plastic seatbelt stiffener and the floor along the inboard passenger side. This, too, was submitted for DNA testing. Again, there was a weak presence of co-mingled DNA found. Interestingly, even though no definitive profile could be made, the partial profile that was made, could not exclude Michele.

In a follow-up call with Jeremiah Wilkins, Bill inquired about the diamond earring. Wilkins said, "ain't no woman I ever know'd ever been in my truck, and I never know'd no woman with no diamond earring." Okay then, I guess that answers that.

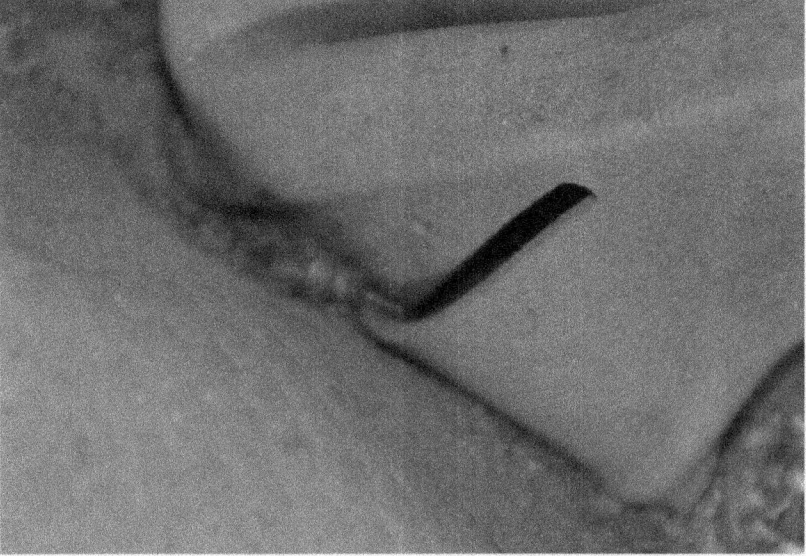

| Earring

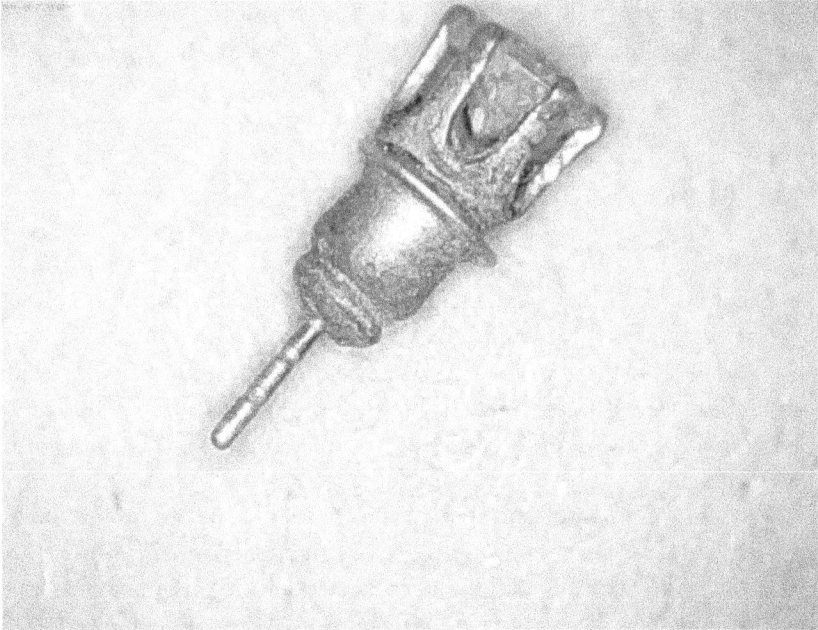

| Earring

49

TRIAL # 4

The opening day of jury selection for the fourth trial started on Monday, March 28, 2016. Prospective jurors were starting to gather in the courtroom. Before the first day of trial, Bruce, and his assistants, attorneys Donna Aldea and Aida Leisenring, were meeting privately with Cal behind closed doors, preparing and discussing their trial strategy. That was normal. What wasn't normal was an announcement that was as much a surprise to me as it was to everyone else. Before jury selection officially got started, Barket announced that Cal was waiving his right to a jury trial, electing instead, to go with a non-jury, bench-trial. Later, when explaining part of his rationale to reporters, he said, "waiving a jury trial was not a choice made lightly." Then added, "Cal seems to have fared better with the courts than with jurors. Our view is the prosecution's case is long on sympathy and short on evidence, and the judge will look for the proof. We trust him to be fair."

For Cal, the risks of a bench trial were many, but the only alternative was another jury. Considering what happened in the third trial, could we really expect a different result? Under the circumstances, the benefits seemed to be outweighing the risks. Ultimately, it was Cal's decision. After some lengthy back-and-forth discussion, he finally decided that his best option was to move forward with a bench-trial. A ballsy decision? Indeed. But under the circumstances presented, it was the right one.

When we received the prosecution's witness list for trial number four, there were only a couple of names we didn't recognize. The name Gregory Farr was on the list, and we had no idea who he was. With some quick research, I was able to learn that Farr had been convicted in 2011 of a brutal murder in Cattaraugus County, in western NY. He had been incarcerated at the Auburn Correctional Facility at the same time as Cal Harris. Presumably, in an attempt to gain some benefit for himself, he would be testifying as a jail-house snitch, claiming that Cal Harris had made incriminating admissions to him. Bruce asked me to try and get some details.

So, as the trial was getting underway, I traveled to the Cattaraugus County Courthouse in Little Valley, NY, to review the case against Farr. My review revealed some rather gruesome details of the murder he was convicted of. With the help of a Deputy Clerk, I obtained copies of Farr's case file and headed back to Schoharie County and turned them over to Bruce. Should Farr testify, knowing the details of his case would be essential in the preparation of his cross-examination.

Noticeably missing from the prosecution's witness list was the name of Dr. Henry Lee. We didn't know it at the time, but Lee had refused to testify again. As a result, Martin found himself scrambling in search of a new blood expert. Not just any blood expert, but one willing to testify in the footsteps of Dr. Lee. Considering Lee's qualifications, level of expertise, and the fact that he already testified three times, finding someone equally qualified and willing to testify would not be easy.

The name Patrick Laturnus was the other new name on the list we didn't recognize. With more research, we identified him as the new blood expert. None of us had ever heard of him before in the forensic community, which was very unusual. A little more research revealed why. Laturnus was retired from a 30-year career as a Mounty with the Royal Canadian Mounted Police in Ottawa, Ontario, Canada. He had a good reputation as a respected and experienced member in the Ottawa community, in the forensic field of blood-pattern interpretation, along with some excellent credentials. However, his scientific and educational qualifications, as well as his years of experience, paled by comparison to that of Dr. Henry Lee. Therefore, testifying in his wake would not be easy.

Since the last trial, the defense had uncovered significant new evidence supporting their theory of third-party culpability. During the early stages of the trial, armed with the new evidence, Barket renewed his argument before Judge Mott that the new evidence be allowed. If you recall, this same argument had been denied during the third trial. As expected, knowing how damaging it could be to his case, Martin aggressively argued against it. After that, their respective arguments were taken behind-closed-doors and continued in Mott's chambers. Upon returning to the courtroom, Judge Mott announced his decision, allowing the defense to argue third-party culpability.

This was a huge breakthrough for the defense, that would now open the door for witnesses to testify about statements made by Stacy Stewart and Chris Thomason. The two Texas men the defense believed had killed Michele Harris.

However, in his decision, Mott said, "I'm allowing it to a certain extent. We're not going into mini-trials." By 'to a certain extent,' I knew what he meant. Without limitations, there's a risk that the focus of the trial could shift or drift off course, creating a trial-within-a-trial, or like Mott said, a mini-trial. Something he was obviously trying to avoid. In my understanding, Mott was giving the defense some leeway but was prepared to limit or even bring it to a halt if they tried pushing it too far. This was a good decision.

Following up after Mott's decision to allow third-party testimony, Barket sought and received judicial subpoenas for several out-of-state witnesses, including Stewart and Thomason. The subpoenas would compel them to appear and offer testimony at the trial. With subpoena's in hand, Bill Flanagan was off to Texas to get them served and, hopefully, speak with Stewart and Thomason again.

After arriving in Texas, Stewart was nowhere to be found. He had since lost his job with the Texas Department of Corrections. From what little information was made available, there had been some apparent issues between Stewart and some female inmates. Flanagan also learned that Stewart, knowing he was being sought, didn't want to be found. He was believed to be hiding out somewhere in Florida until the trial was over. Thomason, on the other hand, was back in prison again, having been sent back on a parole violation. Bill spoke with Thomason at length before serving him with his subpoena. After being served, he told Bill that we may be able to force him up there but couldn't force him to testify. But then he continued to deny any involvement with Michele Harris, insisting that Stewart was the one sleeping with her.

Thomason's judicial trial subpoena, signed by Judge Mott, was legally compelling for him to appear and offer testimony at the trial. However, compelling the Texas Department of Corrections to produce him was another matter. I never learned the real reason, but the short answer was, Thomason would not be making an appearance at the trial.

I thought Bruce had been rightfully aggressive with many of the 'interested' witnesses in the third trial. But as Martin began presenting his case in the fourth trial, using the same parade of witnesses, Bruce's cross became even more aggressive. Especially with those whose memories and testimony seemed to have improved since the last trial.

Before Gregory Farr was called to testify, the defense argued that his testimony should not be allowed. After losing that argument, Farr was called to the stand. He admitted that he was a convicted murderer. He then testified that while in Auburn state prison with Cal Harris, he overheard him threaten another inmate by saying, "I'll make you disappear, just like I did my wife." But before Farr could be cross-examined, the court adjourned for the day. Meanwhile, defense investigator Jay Salpeter, contacted Farr's family to alert them of what Farr would be subjected to under cross-examination.

The following day Farr was again escorted into the courtroom by corrections officers and took the stand. This time, however, before answering any questions under cross-examination, he said, "Under the advisement of counsel, I'm not going to answer any more questions." That was it. Immediately after that, Judge Mott ordered Farr's entire testimony be stricken from the record.

So far, I was very impressed with Judge Mott on the bench. Unlike Judge Bartlett during the third trial, Mott clearly had things under control. I admired the way he took charge of the proceedings with his no-nonsense type approach that, by design, kept the trial moving forward. He reminded me a lot of Judge Smith, who always ran a tight ship. Mott, at times, with his often brusque and decisive remarks, made it perfectly clear who was in charge.

The other new prosecution witness was blood expert Patrick Laturnus. Briefly, for the most part, the testimony of Laturnus followed the scripted testimony of Dr. Lee, which I'm certain he had read ahead of time. His testimony was markedly similar, and he stayed within the professional boundaries set by Dr. Lee. With respect to the blood evidence, nothing had changed regarding volume or age. And once again, the only significant disagreement between opposing sides were their opinions regarding dilution and clean-up. Laturnus had done a respectable job testifying, but comparatively speaking, he was no match to Dr. Lee or defense expert Terry Laber.

With Gregory Farr out of the picture and other than their new blood expert, the prosecution's case remained unchanged. It simply followed the same script that led to the first two convictions and the latest mistrial. For the defense, however, especially with Mott's approval for a limited introduction of third-party culpability, there were some significant changes.

Defense Begins

In opening-up his defense theory in support of third-party culpability, Barket called a trio of key defense witnesses to the stand who knew Stewart or Thomason. Julie Brinkman, who testified briefly at the third trial, again testified about her brief relationship with Stewart. During that time, as mentioned previously, she testified about some of the incriminating comments Stewart had made to her. Most importantly, his admission to her that, "I was the last person seen with her (Michele) alive." And, "I know how to hide a body."

Barket's next witness was Terra Wade. She also testified consistently with what she told defense investigators previously, regarding her relationship with both Stewart and Thomason. Then specifically, about the conversation she had with Thomason in 2011 when he told her about going to Stewart's house with his girlfriend covered in blood. Claiming he told her he had "killed a deer" and got blood on his clothes and "you can't get blood out of clothes." She testified that Thomason also said, "he thought Stacy killed her because Stacy was sleeping with her." But since Cal Harris had been convicted, "neither he nor Stacy were worried about it anymore."

Chris Thomason's estranged wife Melissa Devries was called to the stand. Her testimony was also consistent with what she told defense investigators earlier. That during the spring of 2013, Thomason told her 'out of the blue' about a woman from New York who was murdered in September 2001, and her body had never been found. He then said, "Stacy probably buried her in concrete."

With the three defense witnesses that just testified, Barket had set the stage for the next phase of his defense theory. His next two witnesses were students from Mercyhurst University in Erie, PA, who were called to offer their testimony about the archeological dig and the items of circumstantial evidence they recovered from the burn-pit on Stewart's former property.

Jacob Griffin and Alyssa Harrison both testified about being students that worked alongside Dr. Dennis Dirkmaat, who oversaw an archeological dig of a burn-pit on the former property of Stacy Stewart. Both Griffin and Harrison described and identified the items that were found. Included, as previously mentioned, was a knife blade, house key, coin, fragments of blue and tan colored cloth, a button, and a navy-blue strap that looked like it was from a sports-bra.

Barket moved to have the items received into evidence, arguing that the items were both relevant and consistent with witness statements about bloody clothing being burned on that property. The prosecution objected, arguing that the items from the dig, "looked like garbage."

In his motion, Barket argued that the defense's circumstantial case against both Texas men was stronger than the prosecution's case against Cal. In further support of his argument, he added, "Imagine if witnesses came forward to disclose that Mr. Harris admitted burning bloody clothing in the days following Michele's disappearance. Now imagine the defense arguing that all of that evidence should be excluded because it was not relevant." My thoughts exactly. Without a doubt, had that same exact evidence been discovered in a burn-pit on Cal's property, the prosecution would not be saying that it "looked like garbage."

Unable to prove conclusively through DNA that the items were linked to Michele, Judge Mott initially, except for the bra-strap, denied each of the items from being received into evidence. But then later, denied the bra-strap as well.

Without proof-positive that the items from the burn-pit were Michele's, the defense was not offering them as direct proof. Instead, the defense offered them for the circumstantial value that linked them to what witnesses were saying about the burning of bloody clothes. How is that not relevant circumstantially?

Being denied the burn-pit items was a very real and disappointing blow for the defense. Barket and his team were struggling to understand how they could be denied since there was such a compelling argument in support of their circumstantial value. Later, when speaking with Bruce about the decision, it was his legal opinion that by law, the items should have been received into evidence.

For the fourth time, Kevin Tubbs offered his testimony about what he was doing and what he saw at the foot of the Harris driveway early that morning. This time, Tubbs was a more experienced witness who had matured considerably. Despite the prosecutor's aggressive attempt to discredit his testimony and credibility, he held up remarkably well. He maintained his composure and suppressed the anger and animosity he once held against Jerry Keene.

Under cross-examination by Martin's assistant, Paul Clyne, still pursuing the 'brown paper bag' full of money theory, asked Tubbs if he ever received any financial benefit in exchange for his testimony. Tubbs calmly denied that ever happening. Clyne then asked if he ever told anyone he would get paid by Cal Harris or anything in relation to the trial. In response, he said he didn't want anything from the defense or Calvin Harris. He then added that even though the defense had offered, he paid for his own hotel room and gas to get to Schoharie. During his re-direct, Bruce asked if he had ever received any benefit for his testimony. Tubbs replied, "No, but I have received a lot of shit."

Unlike many of the prosecution's 'interested' witnesses, whose memories and testimony seemed to improve over time, the testimony of Kevin Tubbs remained remarkably consistent time-after-time.

Some SP investigators, including lead investigator, Sr. Investigator Susan Mulvey, had never been called to testify about their involvement in the case. But as part of his defense strategy, Barket decided it was time they did. After that, Mulvey and two other investigators, all since retired, were called to the stand.

Retired Investigator Robert DelGiorno took the stand and was questioned about his interview with Michele's hairdresser, Jerry Wilczynski, shortly after she went missing. Wilczynski testified during all the trials, claiming to have overheard a call to Michele on her cell phone from Cal with this threat: "Drop the divorce proceedings. I will fucking kill you, Michele. Do you hear me? I will fucking kill you. I can make you disappear. Drop the divorce proceedings." When asked, DelGiorno said Wilczynski never mentioned the death threat when he was first interviewed. DelGiorno added, "Mr. Wilczynski told me Cal had refused to give Michele money for school clothes for the kids, and she should drop the divorce and come back to the Harris fortune."

Under cross-examination by Paul Clyne, DelGiorno said, "We didn't know it was a homicide at the time." Obviously, the prosecution was trying to argue that the threat was not disclosed because, at the time, Michele was only considered a missing person. That was nonsense. By the time Wilczynski was first interviewed, Michele had already been missing nearly two weeks. So, either way, whether missing or murder victim, a death threat would have been extremely relevant. We know from speaking with Mulvey, it wasn't until the day after Cal was indicted, four years later, that the money threat he initially told DelGiorno about suddenly turned into a death threat.

Retired Investigator Scott Pauly was called to the stand and asked questions about his lead to identify and interview some steelworkers at Lefty's. Pauly testified that Stewart's name came up during his assignment to interview steelworkers who possibly drank with Michele and others who frequented Lefty's, where she worked. When Barket asked if he had drawn any conclusions about Stewart's relationship with Michele, he said he had not.

Rather than conclusions, I may have asked whether he had any concerns about Stewart or his relationship with Michele. It was apparent from the lead that there had been concerns. Otherwise, Stewart would not have been asked to take a polygraph.

When retired Sr. Investigator Sue Mulvey was called to the stand, her discomfort was palpable. She did not want to be there. When asked by Barket, she testified about a helicopter search for Michele that was conducted in November 2002. More than a year after she went missing, above the Royal Ford dealership and the area over and around the Harris home. She testified that as they flew above the Harris property, Cal Harris could be seen outside, shaking his fist and pointing a video camera at them. She claimed that the FBI had advised the SP to continually search from the ground and air to help steer law enforcement towards new leads. Then she added, "Every little bit helps." Where have we heard that before? Under continued questioning,

Mulvey admitted that in all their search efforts to find Michele's body or a murder weapon, nothing was ever found.

In my review of every lead, there was no mention of the FBI ever giving that search advice to the SP. In fact, according to their own leads, the first consult with the FBI didn't take place until 2004.

After close to 30 days of testimony, the proof phase of the trial was completed. Both sides had rested their cases. But before deliberating, Judge Mott would listen to their closing arguments. Barket for the defense would go first, followed by Martin, who would offer the final word.

Closing Arguments

As in the previous trials, the respective closings were very lengthy, thorough, and strategically designed, with each side laying out their opposing views and interpretations of the evidence presented during the trial.

Once again, Barket masterfully attacked and repeatedly tore apart the prosecution's evidence and witnesses, one-by-one and piece-by-piece. Whether it was the blood evidence or the testimony from those 'interested' parties, nothing escaped his wrath. I had listened to his closing in the third trial, which was phenomenal, but this one was even more compelling. He pulled out all the stops. While his aggressive criticism that he directed towards the 'interested' witnesses and lousy evidence was noticeably apparent, so too was his emotional connection to the case. At times, some of his emotional outbursts appeared to be triggered by raw emotion. For me, it was an authentic demonstration of his sincere belief and the cause he was fighting for – that being, the life, and freedom of his innocent client, Cal Harris.

During his closing, Barb Thayer and her husband were sitting just a few feet away from me. As Bruce opened up his attack on the veracity of Thayer's testimony, I started hearing some low moaning coming from the Thayers. Bruce continued his attack by addressing the lies surrounding her claim that she was the one who made that 7:13 a.m. call to Michele. Then, he moved on to her other lies about the garage sale and her comment, "it's like Michele never existed." Bruce had clearly established how she lied about all those things. Now, he was hammering it home in his closing.

At one point, his rebuke of Thayer resulted in an audible outburst from her husband that was heard throughout the courtroom. Judge Mott quickly interrupted Bruce's closing, then turned and spoke directly to Mr. Thayer. Harshly admonishing him with a stern warning that if there were any more outbursts, court officers would escort him from the courtroom, and he would be banned from returning. When Mott asked if he understood, he just hung his head and nodded silently. Mott then turned and addressed the entire courtroom, firmly repeating the same warning.

Compared to the third trial, other than being a little more emotionally driven, Bruce's closing was markedly similar. This time, however, he added to his arsenal the new testimony from witnesses in support of third-party culpability. By including that element, he finished his closing with the defense theory that it was not Cal Harris, but Stacy Stewart and Chris Thomason, who were responsible for killing Michele.

In fairness to Kirk Martin, he too delivered an excellent closing, albeit a warped and flawed interpretation of the evidence and testimony presented at trial. Like Keene during the first trials, Martin was tossing make-believe evidence into the air, hoping the judge would latch onto it. From my perspective, it was really nothing more than a lot of smoke.

Deliberations & Verdict

After closing arguments from both sides, Judge Mott entered his chambers to begin his deliberations. I hung around in the courtroom, chatting with some of Cal's supporters, including his Aunt Merry, his children, his father Dwight, and others I don't even remember. I couldn't help but notice several of those who were seated behind the prosecution's table did not stick around but left the courtroom quickly. Shortly after, I joined Cal, along with Bruce, Donna, and Aida in the private defense room in the back of the courtroom. I had been in the courtroom all day, but this was the first time we had a chance to talk.

I learned that after both sides rested and before closing arguments started, Martin had approached Bruce and placed an offer on the table. He was offering to let Cal plea to First-Degree Manslaughter, in satisfaction of the Second-Degree Murder charge. Compared to murder, a sentence for Manslaughter would be substantially less. But it was now evident that his offer had been declined.

Judge Mott had a great deal to consider. There were thirty days of witness testimony, plus numerous exhibits of evidence that were received at trial. Considering his respected reputation for fairness, we were confident that by law, he would give both sides equal consideration.

Throughout all four trials, Cal's Aunt Merry, father Dwight, and his friend Rosemary were strong supporters and were seen in the courtroom every day. During the third and fourth trials, they were joined daily by Cal's four children. Two beautiful daughters and two handsome sons. All well-educated, responsible, and polite young adults. Together, they all stood in proud support of their father during his decade-plus-long quest for freedom.

Recall that shortly after Michele went missing, several of Cal's best friends and family had expressed concerns about the welfare of the children. They were also concerned about Cal's ability to care for them properly. Legitimate concerns at the time? Indeed. Admittedly, I shared similar concerns. But fortunately, our concerns were unfounded. Perhaps we all underestimated the love and commitment Cal had for his children, as well as his ability to meet their needs.

Fifteen years earlier, these same four kids, at a very young age, experienced the tragic loss of their mother – a mother who mysteriously went missing and had never been found. Since then, they also suffered the loss of their father as well, when he was yanked away three times. Yet they appeared in court, proudly supporting their father, still charged with the murder of their mother. Now, joined together as a family, they await the final decision. While waiting, their thoughts would bounce back-and-forth between fearful concern and hopeful optimism. They were anxiously wondering whether their family would finally be reunited or torn apart yet again.

As a defense team, we were confident yet cautiously optimistic that this fourth trial would put an end to Cal's fifteen-year legal nightmare with his acquittal. Of course, I had to remind myself of the confidence and optimism we had at the end of the first two trials. We were stunned when he was convicted. Not once – but twice.

We had obviously made some progress during the third trial when the jury could not reach a verdict. But with the fourth trial, there were many significant changes, especially for the defense – specifically, Cal's decision to waive the jury and go with a bench-trial. Equally important was Judge Mott's ruling, allowing the introduction of evidence in support of third-party culpability. Our level of optimism had also raised a notch or two after the proof phase of the trial when Martin made his plea offer of Manslaughter. That was a clear sign of their lack of confidence in meeting the burden of proof in the case. Our hope now was that Judge Mott would agree.

At the end of his first day, after deliberating for a few hours, Mott was seen leaving the courtroom, casually walking to his Jaguar in the parking lot and driving away. The next morning, he was briefly seen returning to the courtroom and entering his chambers to continue deliberating. Meanwhile, the clock kept ticking as the minutes turned into hours once again. A second day had come and gone and still no verdict as Mott was again seen leaving for the day. Was he at least getting close? No one had a clue. The waiting was brutal, as interested parties, including reporters, remained close to the courthouse. Some were seen reading a book, sitting on park benches, walking the streets nearby, huddled together in a quiet corner, or grabbing something to eat from 'Hot-dog Mike' from his cart in front of the courthouse.

Day three started the same as day two. Could this be the day, or would there be a day four? Like clockwork, Judge Mott arrived and, with nary a word, entered his chambers and went back to work. The morning passed, and it was now lunchtime. Still no verdict. The natives were getting restless. What was taking so long?

Finally, shortly after lunch, Judge Mott notified opposing counsel that he had reached a verdict. He would be announcing his decision shortly after 2:00 p.m., allowing time for everyone to regroup in the courtroom. As the courtroom filled to near capacity, Judge Mott entered from his chambers and took his seat on the bench. The already low-toned whispering in the courtroom turned to dead silence. At or about 2:13 p.m., in a brief, professional, and non-dramatic fashion, Judge Mott announced that on the single count of Murder in the Second Degree, "I find the defendant, Calvin Harris – Not Guilty."

Other than his finding, Mott offered no reason or explanation behind his verdict but simply returned to his chambers. He was thereby leaving the speculation door open as to what factored into his decision. But that was it. It's finally over. Just like that, Cal was once again a free man. His 15-year nightmare ordeal and legal battles were over. Never again could he be charged with the killing of his wife, Michele. But more importantly, the reunion with his children would now be permanent rather than uncertain.

Aftermath

As you might imagine, compared to the shocking results of the first two trials and the disappointment of the mistrial, this one was going to be dramatically and exclusively different.

Before the verdict was announced and from a historical case perspective, I had prepared myself for the worst. But when I heard the words "not guilty," I couldn't begin to find the words to describe the feeling. I wanted to rush forward to congratulate Cal and his legal team, but they were already engaging each other with joyful hand-shakes, high-fives, and lengthy bear-hugs. And tears were already flowing. I continued to watch as Cal's four children, who were seated directly behind their dad, jumped from their seats, rushed to greet him, and embraced him while wiping tears from their eyes. Overcome with emotion, Cal hugged his two daughters tightly. Then he hugged his two sons. All had tears flowing from their eyes. I was a bit choked up myself and found myself wiping away one of my own tears.

I decided to keep my distance and allow Cal this special moment with his family. As things started to settle down, I greeted some of Cal's other supporters. I saw Bruce walk over and shake hands with Kirk Martin and Paul Clyne. After speaking briefly, Martin and Clyne left the courtroom, and Bruce returned to the celebration.

While all this was going on, there was near silence on the other side of the courtroom. The prosecution spectators began to quietly leave the courtroom. With the expressions on their faces, it was evident they were not pleased with the verdict. A few SP officers were huddled in a back corner, quietly talking among themselves, likely speculating about how this could have happened.

Outside the courtroom, the media was quickly lining up their cameras and microphones along the sidewalk in anticipation of some post-trial interviews and photographs. I didn't think the little Village of Schoharie had seen this much excitement since the Courthouse murder of Schoharie County Sheriff, Henry Stedman, in July of 1930. Another interesting story. But getting back to the media and their post-trial activities, anxious reporters were waiting, with mics in hand, for Cal to make his exit from the courtroom. Cal was still inside the courtroom, trying to control his emotions and regain some level of composure before making his exit. An experience I was quite familiar with.

Cal led the way out of the courtroom, neatly dressed as usual in a long-sleeve white shirt, red necktie, and tan slacks. Following close behind were his four children, then Bruce and his team. Cal took a position on the sidewalk in front of a large array of microphones that had been set up on tripods. When asked for his thoughts upon hearing the not guilty verdict, he said, "When he (Mott) first came out, I thought I was done. I was numb. And then when he came back with the 'not guilty' I was shocked. I was truly shocked."

During his media comments and questioning, Cal was seen breaking down repeatedly, with tears flowing down his face. Mostly, whenever he talked about his children, which was quite often. While speaking with reporters, he said now that this was behind them, he intended to take his children on a much-needed vacation. After turning to thank his defense team, the tears began flowing again as he turned back and said, "Three times, I've been ripped away from my kids, and that's been hard." Stopping momentarily to compose himself again, he said he was "robbed of my right as a father," then added, "If I don't have my kids, I don't have anything." Breaking into tears again. After struggling to regain his composure, he continued by saying, "Obviously, my children and I are grateful to have this chapter behind us. We can now finally move forward and make some plans in our lives as normal people do. But I can tell you there will be no celebration at our house tonight. There are no winners."

When asked if there was any sense of closure, he said, "Not until we find Michele. Not until we find the mother of my children and we get those answers, there won't be closure. And we should have those answers. There is no reason that we shouldn't. This isn't a mystery. It just wasn't handled properly."

After referring to the years he spent in prison away from his kids, his tears began flowing again. He said, "I missed some of the best years of my life as a parent, and I'll never get those years back. It was like being kidnapped in broad daylight, and no one could help me. I was helpless." This reminded me of what Cal told me earlier about his time in prison. Having his children visit him regularly was the only thing that kept his spirit alive and prevented him from giving up. He couldn't wait to see them come walking through those prison doors every week-end. He loved having them there, but their time together always seemed to go too fast. But the biggest downside and hardest part was watching them leave. While his children were there, he'd always done his best to put on a strong face to appear upbeat. But as soon as they were out of sight, the depression rushed back in, and he turned to mush, often isolating himself in his cell for days, crying himself to sleep.

Cal was followed by Barket, who started by saying, "We couldn't be happier. Overjoyed. 15 years. It's hard to describe what that must have been like for Cal and his children." He then added, "The cause for celebration for Cal's freedom is there, but Michele needs to come home." He then offered a special thanks saying, "Thank God and thank Judge Mott for finally putting this to an end – the criminal prosecution." Then in a final comment said, "This is the fourth trial for Cal Harris. 15-years later, the prosecutors and the state police, with all the resources they have. They have put in tens of thousands of hours of work into trying to prove something that Cal didn't do."

The media reporters had also been waiting for a comment from Kirk Martin. After all the excitement surrounding Cal began to fade, Martin made his appearance to address the media. In his politically correct response, he started by saying, "We presented our evidence in this case. This is how our system works. The judge found the defendant not guilty, and we will, of course, abide by the verdict of the court." Later, he said he believed law enforcement officials did a thorough and complete case. I would have to respectfully disagree. Later, he continued his politically correct comments after reporters asked if the prosecution would look at defense arguments that another man killed Michele Harris. Martin said, "Michele Harris is still a missing person, so to the extent that if we had any credible evidence to the location of her remains or anything of that nature, we would certainly follow up on it." How much more credible evidence do they need?

News reporter Wendy Post had been covering the Cal Harris case since before the first trial. She was the crime news reporter for the *Owego Pennysaver*, a small weekly newspaper. I had spoken with her several times over the years. I remembered seeing and speaking with her after the first trial, shortly after Cal was convicted. She told me shortly after word of Cal's conviction was announced, crowds of people stood on the lawns and lined the streets outside the courthouse, cheering and yelling, "Guilty! Guilty!" In my understanding, Wendy herself was never convinced Cal had killed his wife.

I ran into Wendy again on the sidewalk outside the courthouse after Cal was found 'not guilty.' She had a pleasant smile on her face, so I assumed she was pleased with the verdict. We had not seen each other in quite some time. We really didn't have time to talk, but later, I called and spoke with her on the phone. We spoke briefly about our respective interests in telling the Cal Harris story. Without any prompting from me and somewhat out-of-the-blue, I was pleasantly surprised when she offered her independent opinion regarding the testimony of Kevin Tubbs. After explaining that she covered all four trials, she said, "Out of all the witnesses who testified over the years, I found the testimony of Kevin Tubbs to be the most consistent." In response, I said, "I'm glad to hear you say that because I would totally agree."

Cal's 15-year ordeal had been like a living hell for himself and his children, whom he had tried to shield through most of it. With the not guilty verdict, a weight had been lifted from his shoulders – a wonderful feeling. One I had experienced years earlier myself. But now, Cal was finally on his way home, reunited once again with his four children. This time, a free man.

PART VII

REIGN OF INJUSTICE

"There is no crueler tyranny than that which is perpetrated under the shield of the law and in the name of justice."

— Charles-Louis de Secondat, Baron de Montesquieu, 1742

50

JUSTICE DENIED

W ith Cal's acquittal, the case against him was officially closed, and the story should have ended there. But this story involved more than just the case against Cal. His acquittal had done nothing to solve the mystery of Michele's disappearance.

The conflict and controversy surrounding this case attracted and divided interested observers from every domain of society, not just friends and family but members of the entire community at large, including both local and national media. It even extended to judges at the highest level of New York State's Courts. When Cal and his family pulled away from the little village of Schoharie, many were left questioning whether justice had been served. Others likely asking, "Did a guilty man just walk free?" After all, Michele was still missing, and the man many still believed killed her had just driven away. And even though the defense did not prove Stacy Stewart and Chris Thomason were Michele's killers, suspicion had clearly been established that they were. Therefore, the pursuit of justice and answers to the 15-year mystery remained elusive.

For Michele's family and friends, Cal's acquittal left them convinced that justice had not been served. Cal himself, suspected and accused over 15-years, fought an uphill battle against a double-edged sword. He fought to prove his own innocence, while at the same time investigating to find out who actually killed his wife and mother of his children. So, when listening to his words after he was found 'not guilty,' it was no surprise to hear him say, "there are no winners," and there would be "no celebrating at our house tonight." And, on closure, "Not until we find Michele. Not until we find the mother of my children and we get those answers, there won't be closure."

Frustrated after the mistrial, Greg Taylor said during one of his interviews with CBS *48-Hours*, "She's not coming back, so it's not ever going to be over." He also said, "We want the person responsible for her (Michele) not being here to held responsible." I couldn't agree more, even though we have opposing views as to who that was.

The bottom line – justice had not yet been served.

So here we are, fifteen years later, right back to square one. And depending on who you ask, views and perspectives about justice or injustice will vary. For those who still believed in Cal's guilt, this was an injustice. But for those who believed Cal was innocent and the ones who killed Michele were never held accountable, this too was an injustice. So regardless of your viewpoint, justice had not been served.

What little justice there was, came in the form of Cal's acquittal. But like he said, "there are no winners," and there would be "no celebrating." All those interested parties seeking, demanding, and deserving of justice, remain unsatisfied. Because justice can only be served when those who have engaged in wrongdoing are held accountable, properly punished, and the voices of those victimized have been heard. Therefore, unless or until that happens, the public's faith and trust in the system continue to decline among false hopes, broken promises, and elusive outcomes. Thereby reinforcing the common legal maxim, "justice delayed is justice denied."

Despite the strong circumstantial evidence presented by the defense during the third and fourth trials implicating Stewart and Thomason as Michele's killers, Kirk Martin and the SP expressed no interest, nor took any action to pursue it – a direct contradiction to Martin's media response after Cal's acquittal, quoted earlier. Equally confusing was another of Martin's comments to the media saying, "My obligation as District Attorney is to seek justice, and I will continue to do that." So, he admits he has an 'obligation' to seek justice. Yet when presented with credible evidence, there's a conscious decision and refusal not to. And I am not the only one asking why.

51
BRIEF RECAP

What happened to Cal Harris should never have happened. Starting from day one and for the next 15-years, he was targeted, hunted, and pursued by any and all means available. Nearly to the exclusion of anyone else. Police claimed the investigation that took place, under the direction of Sr. Investigator Mulvey, was done evenhandedly in the interest and pursuit of justice. When considering everything that had taken place, including what I learned from my own investigation, the words 'evenhanded' and 'justice' in describing Mulvey's pursuit was anything but. Instead, it was a pursuit driven, not by professional interests but rather, a personal vendetta, with all the ingredients of malicious vindictiveness.

In the early rush-to-judgment, Mulvey clearly set things in motion for her vengeful pursuit of Cal Harris, even before the blood was found. Recalling the day, she walked into attorney Drazen's office, looked him right in the eye, and said, "I know Cal killed her, and I'm going to prove it."

As the prime suspect, Cal was immediately placed in Mulvey's crosshairs. During the early stage of the investigation and for a good reason, that was perfectly understandable. In the years that followed, extensive and exhaustive search efforts to find Michele were carried out repeatedly. Yet as we know, Michele, a murder weapon, or any evidence of her demise was ever found. Unfortunately, the searches were strictly limited to include only those areas known to be associated with Cal Harris and never expanded to look elsewhere.

Equally extensive was their pursuit of evidence that would help prove Cal was the killer. But other than those tiny specks of blood, just like their search for Michele, they found nothing. But after four years, it was decided that 'win-lose-or-draw,' they needed to move forward anyway. After that, they continued to embrace their deceptive, 'fake it till you make it' interpretation of what little blood was found. Even while knowing that an innocent explanation was likely, police convinced themselves that the Harris home was a crime scene. Compounding the matter further were the photographs that were later 'doctored' and used to misrepresent the evidence. Evidence that would allow them to continue calling the Harris home the 'scene-of-the-crime.' Even though the 'real' crime scene was at the end of the Harris driveway.

The rush-to-judgment against Cal was clearly established from the get-go. As the investigation unfolded in the weeks, months, and years that followed, it became clear that the direction and driving force behind Mulvey's pursuit of Cal Harris was personal. In-as-much, the essential components needed in an investigation, including objectivity, open-mindedness, honesty, fairness, and, most importantly, professional integrity were nowhere to be found.

The investigation dragged on for four years before Cal was finally indicted, arrested, then two years later, tried and convicted. But that was not the end. Rather it was a new beginning when Kevin Tubbs came forward with his revelations. A major turning point that ignited and prolonged the case against Cal for the next several years. In an aggressive effort to salvage the conviction, Mulvey chose the low road once again by taking her investigation into a disturbing and troubling new low.

Kevin Tubbs and John Steele, unknown to each other, had unknowingly corroborated each other's stories with their independent revelations of what they had seen at the foot of the Harris driveway. For coming forward, they were targeted and pursued much like Cal. They had committed no crime, yet they were treated like suspects rather than eyewitnesses who were trying to 'do-the-right-thing.' They had absolutely no motive to lie. They were placed under a wide-angled microscope, where the only effort was to destroy the messengers. Remember? If you don't like the news, 'kill the messenger.'

Ironically, the SP had spent countless hours, professionally and responsibly chasing down numerous leads involving rumors, sightings, visions, premonitions, gut-feelings, psychic readings, even jail-house snitches. All, to no avail. Most notably, spending three days chasing down a 'premonition' and searching for Michele in that swamp near Van Etten.

There was an ugly picture developing. Whether you liked or disliked Cal Harris wasn't important. What was happening here was wrong. Very wrong. I could understand why the police were doing what they were doing. But I couldn't understand why they were not doing the things they should have. Something was seriously wrong, and they were doing nothing to make it right. In fact, it was just the opposite. It became painfully obvious that salvaging Cal's conviction was their only goal. And justice be damned. From my perspective, they knew, but were in denial of 'an uncomfortable truth.' Yet there was way too much at stake here. As such, all they really wanted was another conviction. As troubling as it was, all I was hearing them say was, "To hell with Tubbs and Steele. To hell with Stacy Stewart. Do we really care if someone else did this? And to hell with Cal, we convicted him once, we'll convict him again. Let's put that scumbag back behind bars where he belongs." Likely, the name David Beers was included in there somewhere. Believing he had truly gone to the Dark Side.

During my investigation, once I made the connection to Stewart and Thomason, shortly after the revelations of Kevin Tubbs, they became 'persons-of-interest' rather quickly. Once I got started, I just followed the evidence trail and noticed red flags were popping up everywhere. From there, it just seemed to snowball, picking up one piece after another along the way. Everything was falling into place. And the more I learned, the more suspicious I became. Later, that suspicion included the missing or hidden documentation associated with Stewart and Thomason. Not just the missing results of Stewart's polygraph or the reason he was asked to do one, but also the missing or hidden documentation of the interviews of him and Thomason at the

Trackside Bar. Investigators told them that they'd been seen on video-tape with Michele at the Guthrie Inn. That further raised suspicion that there was a videotape, and that too was missing. From my perspective, they had moved from persons-of-interest to 'viable suspects.'

With much hesitation and reluctance, I presented my findings to the SP, encouraging and hoping they would take the lead. To pick up where I left off and continue the investigation of their suspected involvement. Instead, they chose to abbreviate or strictly limit their investigation by using a 'low-key and friendly' approach.

When comparing Stewart and Thomason's several interviews over time, their stories were always changing and becoming more bizarre. They couldn't keep anything straight and would make things up as they went along. With their back-and-forth finger-pointing, combined with their nonsensical and bizarre explanations, one doesn't need to be a psychologist to recognize psychobabble when you hear it. These two clowns even lied about things they didn't need to. When their stories were disputed by credible evidence, the lying and denying still continued. It was no real surprise to learn that Stewart, knowing he was going to be subpoenaed for trial, went into hiding. Talk about a 'consciousness of guilt.'

The cumulative evidence supporting Stewart and Thomason's involvement in Michele's disappearance had become far more compelling than that against Cal. Moreover, and perhaps most recognizable, were the contrasts between the two of them vs. Cal Harris, specifically the lies. With an overabundance of proof that both Stewart and Thomason had lied, repeatedly, each time they were interviewed.

In contrast, Cal had cooperated right from the get-go by agreeing to be interviewed and providing written consent for the search of his home, property, and vehicles. When requested, he voluntarily turned over all business, telephone, and financial records and then allowed his children to be interviewed. Later, he voluntarily submitted his DNA and surrendered his home computer. Whenever asked, Cal made himself available for lengthy police questioning over a three-day period. Moreover, he never refused to answer their questions, never asked for an attorney, and never once lied to them. In fact, when he was asked what he thought may have happened to his wife, he attempted to steer them in the right direction by answering, "I know she's hanging around with the wrong crowd in Waverly," and suggested they, "pump the shit out of them." He also told them, "Michele probably knew the person at the end of the driveway, or else she would not have gotten out of her van." Unfortunately, this, too, fell on deaf ears, never to be pursued. Why did they even bother asking?

52

ALTERNATIVE THEORY

So, what exactly did happen to Michele Harris? After all these years, she has never been found. Presumably, she is deceased, and someone killed her. The mystery surrounding her disappearance has just been rekindled by the recent acquittal of her husband, Cal. Therefore, the mystery surrounding her disappearance continues, and the demand for justice remains.

Throughout this saga, the police's theory that Cal was Michele's killer and his home was the scene-of-the-crime was made abundantly clear. Also made clear was the fact that their entire theory was built on nothing more than speculation, guesswork, and wishful thinking. Using evidence at times that was 'crunched' to make it fit. But when that wasn't enough, they threw Cal's character and personality flaws into the mix. With nothing further, they moved forward regardless to solidify their theory and lock it in stone.

In fairness, when considering my own investigation and knowledge of the case, I should be allowed to do the same. Unlike law enforcement, my speculation does not carry the same risks. So, by using my training, experience, and knowledge of this case, I will offer an alternative as to what might have happened to Michele, including who may be responsible, and why. A preponderance of evidence revealed in my investigation will support my alternative theory.

Author's Note: What I'm about to reveal is not necessarily a theory but rather a reasonable hypothesis that can be drawn from the evidence and a good-faith assessment of other known facts and information developed during my investigation. Therefore, it should not be construed as being factually accurate in its entirety, as any number of variations are possible.

Michele first started working at Lefty's around the same time Stacy Stewart and Chris Thomason arrived from Texas after being recruited by NUCOR. Initially, they were working 12-hour days and were being housed at the Guthrie Inn. In their search for a place to eat, drink and unwind after work, they quickly discovered, then became regular patrons at the nearby Lefty's Bar/Restaurant.

Stewart's attraction to Michele began immediately and later evolved into an obsession. Stewart and Thomason were often joined by their friend and co-worker, Wright Childers. They were all attracted to Michele. After working long 12-hour days, they were not only thirsty, hungry, and ready to unwind, they were also ready for some off-duty action. For young single guys, this meant some female attention. After eating, their only interest was drinking beer and getting laid. In-as-much, the heads on their shoulders were no longer the ones in control.

And there she was. Michele Harris. A patron favorite with beautiful golden blonde hair, a cute shapely figure, a friendly smile, and wearing fine, expensive jewelry. A real jackpot who was not only physically attractive but personable, fun-loving, flirtatious, and just fun to be around. They couldn't keep their eyes off her and insisted on being seated at one of her assigned tables.

Michele enjoyed and loved playing along, in what she perceived as innocent, fun-loving flirting that often included sex-related joke-telling. The benefits of which were usually some nice sized tips. Believing it was all just harmless fun, and being somewhat naïve, she was clueless of the trio's real objective, to get in her pants.

Stewart's obsessive infatuation towards Michele grew steadily. As a Lefty's regular, he would often leave $100 tips, then wait and buy her a drink after she finished work. Over time, he learned a great deal about Michele. Her marriage, children, pending divorce. Even her boyfriend and the co-workers she went out with. At times, he would learn where she was going and just show up. If she went to the boyfriend, he stalked her, lurking carefully from a distance, while circling through the neighborhood, watching. He even followed her home to learn where she lived.

Stewart tried hitting on Michele many times, but she'd never showed any interest. Even though he met and started dating Lisa Demtrak, he never gave up on Michele. He continued his pursuit at Lefty's and showing up at her favorite hangouts. Usually, the Night Train Lounge at the Guthrie Inn.

Despite the trio's best efforts, Michele had shown little or no interest in starting a relationship with any of them. Although they never stopped going to Lefty's, they did start pursuing women elsewhere.

Bare Facts, the local strip-club that featured total nude dancing, was where our trio from Lefty's became regulars. They all met and dated some of the dancers. Later, after Stewart bought his cabin in the woods, they brought their 'dates' there to party. The parties would regularly include serious beer drinking, large bonfires, pornographic movies, and sex. The stage was set for what was about to happen.

That Tuesday, shortly after NUCOR shut its doors at 6:00 p.m., our trio made their way to Lefty's and, as usual, asked for one of Michele's tables. With the terrorist attacks earlier, the normal flirtatious environment had mellowed somewhat into a more subdued atmosphere.

During a somewhat more serious conversation, Michele was invited to join the trio when she was done working. They were going to the Night Train Lounge at the Guthrie Inn, where they'd first met. Michele liked the idea but had a commitment after work. She could perhaps stop in later.

Lefty's closed at 9:00 p.m., and our trio made their way to the night club. After sharing a quick drink with Mike Kasper after work, Michele left to see Brian. Along the way, Nikki called, but Michele didn't answer. She left a message. Minutes later, Michele listened to her message but didn't return her call. Knowing that Nikki would never approve of her plan unless, of course, it included her.

After leaving Brian, Michele headed to the night club. By the time she arrived around midnight, the trio was already partying and very much under the influence. But the minute she walked through the door, their eyes lit up. She was like a magnet, as they immediately swarmed around her, each insisting on buying her a drink. Michele graciously accepted, and the partying continued. Between drinks, they danced and then drank some more. Michele was starting to unwind and enjoy herself, but she too was getting drunk.

Being a weekday, 'last-call' came early. They ordered and finished their final drinks before the doors closed. As they were leaving, Stewart invited Michele up to his cabin, where they could continue the party. By now, they were all highly intoxicated.

Michele was just starting to have a good time enjoying herself with some harmless fun. Not yet ready to go home, she accepted the invitation.

Outside the night-club environment, the situation was much different. Michele found herself in a small cabin, in the remote woods, at night, with three men she knew from Lefty's for several months and thought she could trust. Unfortunately, not long after the beer started flowing again, that trust became short-lived. The night club experience with music, dancing, and even some fun-loving drunken behavior, quickly changed. Michele suddenly found herself trying to fight off the drunken and persistent sexual advances of three strong, aggressive, and very horny young men.

Fearing physical injury to herself if she tried resisting, Michele acquiesced to their sexual demands, becoming the victim of an aggressive sexual gang-assault. When it was over, Childers and Thomason left for home, leaving Michele alone with Stewart. Sometime later, still sobbing, Michele promised not to say anything as she dressed and hustled out the door to her van. No sooner had she closed the door when Stewart had second thoughts and yelled for her to wait. She quickly jumped in her van and headed for home. But as she looked back, Stewart was following her. Her ordeal was far from over.

Stewart quickly caught up and was trying to get her to stop, but she just kept going. Upon reaching the end of her driveway, feeling a bit more comfortable being close to home, she decided she'd better stop to see what he wanted. Stewart pulled in behind her, leaving the rear of his truck angled out in the road.

Standing outside their vehicles, Michele continued to sob as she renewed her promise that she would not say anything. Just wanting to go home and pretend it never happened. Stewart began demanding she come with him. Continuing to cry, she started begging for him just to let her go home, promising over and over, not to say anything. Stewart only became angrier and more demanding.

Enter, Kevin Tubbs with his hay-wagon. After making eye contact with Stewart, he noticed Michele appeared to have been crying. Shortly after, John Steele drove by slowly and heard, "Just get in the car. Just get in the damn car." Once he was out of sight, Stewart's angry demands worsened. Michele tried standing her ground, but Stewart wasn't backing down. In his growing anger, he loses his patience and snaps as he reaches his breaking point. At this time, he pulls out his knife, threatening, then abducting her at knifepoint, forcing her into his truck and starts heading back to his cabin.

While staring at the knife, Michele continued her plea, insisting he didn't need to do this and renewing her promise not to say anything. But at the same time, she was carefully watching and waiting for any opportunity to escape. Knowing that her chance of survival would not be good once they reached his cabin. Deciding that it was now or never, she made her move. In her desperate life-or-death struggle, she fought viciously and heroically. But Stewart, being much stronger and armed with a knife, quickly overpowered her and, in his angry rage, repeatedly stabbed and killed her. During the struggle, one of her diamond earrings was ripped from her ear and fell to the floor.

Arriving at his cabin, a panicking Stewart called Thomason for help and then called in sick to work. Later, Thomason arrived and helped him remove the body from the truck. Then, they removed all the jewelry from her body and her purse. Later that night, under cover of darkness, they permanently disposed of her body, any proof, including their bloody clothing.

After advising Childers of what happened, he was reminded if anyone were to find out what happened, including his own involvement earlier, they would all go to prison. After that, the trio made a pact, swearing to keep their mouths shut and never to speak of it again.

53

REIGN OF INJUSTICE

I n the eyes of the greater community, Cal was presumed guilty shortly after Michele disappeared, which was solidified after his arrest. The cards were stacked against him right from the start. Later, he was tried and convicted by a jury tainted by their preconceptions of his guilt.

The wrong only worsened after Kevin Tubbs entered the picture. Realizing their case against Cal was in jeopardy, a renewed, aggressive investigative pursuit was launched by the SP. Not in pursuit of anything Tubbs had seen but rather, a pursuit of salvaging their case against Cal. Any professional integrity that existed was now non-existent. Personal and self-serving interests replaced it. Exclusively designed to save face and protect the dignity, character, and egos of those involved and the agency they worked for.

With Mulvey's known conflict of interest, her personal bias was obvious. As lead investigator, it was her decisions that established, controlled, and directed the investigation from start to finish. Accordingly, she was the front-line 'bag-holder' of responsibility. However, she did not act entirely alone. The investigation was a team effort that was often united in their decisions, including those known to be wrong. Therefore, there was a shared consensus of wrongdoing, designed to protect what I just described. As such, the level of responsibility goes beyond Mulvey to include all those who supported those wrongful decisions.

The levels of responsibility can and should be extended to a higher level, where the ultimate responsibility falls upon the higher-ranking echelon. Even though they had an ongoing responsibility to oversee and maintain accountability for the activities of its rank-and-file members, they failed to do so.

A clear example of that failure was specifically demonstrated in this case as follows:

In a State of New York, Court of Claims decision handed down on February 2, 2000, Mulvey had been judicially admonished for her illegal, unprofessional, and egregious acts of official misconduct. Specifically, while serving in a leadership capacity, which led to the false arrest, conviction, and imprisonment of an innocent young man." Despite the Court's decision, Mulvey was not only allowed to continue serving in a leadership capacity, but she was also promoted and granted even greater authority and responsibility.

The irony surrounding the issues of professionalism and integrity are identified and can be found on the New York State Police web site ***www.troopers.ny.gov***. Here, they identify their Vision, Mission Statement, Mission Priorities, and Values. Under the Values category, there are five sub-categories, one of which is Integrity which reads:

> **Integrity:** To Live and Work in Accordance with High Ethical Standards:
>
> - Have the physical and moral courage to do what is right
> - Be Honest and truthful
> - Do not tolerate unethical behavior

Although Integrity has been specifically identified as one of their core values, they chose instead to shamefully ignore, not just one, but all three of its underlying principles.

The New York State Police recently celebrated its 100th anniversary from its start in 1917. Under the command of George F. Chandler, the first Superintendent, the first vision and mission statement was established with the basic underlying principles still taught and used today. Interestingly, during his address to the first graduating class of troopers, one of the more notable things he said was: "One slip by any member of this command will do more harm than one hundred good deeds can efface. Human nature, unfortunately, is not constructive but likes to tear down. One mistake or unworthy act on the part of a trooper will subject the whole body to criticism."

Ideally, I would have preferred a better ending to this story. One where Michele had been found and brought home. One where the demands of justice had been met. One where all affected parties could experience some semblance of closure and begin the healing process. Unfortunately, nearly two decades now and Michele is still missing, and those responsible continue to dodge the sword of Lady Justice.

Given all the evidence unearthed, developed, and lined-up by the defense, in support of a strong circumstantial case against Stacy Stewart and Chris Thomason, I believe justice may still be attainable. I would go as far as to say it could be (indicating) 'this close.' But for every month and year that goes by, the chances of that happening becomes less. Unfortunately, the 'uncomfortable truth' has blocked the path of justice in this case unless those in authority are willing to swallow some pride, set-aside their egos, and restore some professional integrity. If that doesn't happen, Michele will never be found, and her real killers will continue to enjoy their freedom. The status quo will remain, and the reign of injustice will continue.

Although I bear little optimism that justice will ever be served, I do hold on to that tiny sliver of hope that perhaps one day, a final chapter can be written – one where all that went wrong will be made right.

AFTERWORD

Over a period of 15-years, three-and-a-half of which was spent in prison, Cal Harris went on trial four times before finally being acquitted on May 24, 2016. Thereafter, on August 22, 2017, a ten-count civil complaint was filed on his behalf with the Northern District of the US District Court in Syracuse, New York. Named defendants included the County of Tioga and Tioga County District Attorney Gerald Keene, along with several named and unnamed members of the New York State Police. The major allegations included Malicious Prosecution, Failure to Investigate, Fabrication of Evidence, Suppression of Favorable Evidence, Supervisory Liability, Civil Rights Violations, and Character Defamation. More recently, in August of 2019, the presiding Federal Judge found sufficient cause for the complaint to move forward by seeking a response to the complaint from Tioga County officials. The matter remains pending.

Unconfirmed but worth mentioning…Shortly after the first release of my book, I received a call from an interested reader who happened to be a close relative of Steven Greene, who has since passed. If you recall, it was Greene who identified Stacy Stewart and Chris Thomason from NUCOR, who were rumored to have been with

Michele Harris the night she went missing. According to the caller, he/she had learned from Greene, that in the days immediately following Michele's disappearance, Stewart was in possession of a Rolex watch and asking co-workers if they were interested in buying it. The caller said, "It wasn't until I read about the Rolex watch in the book that I remembered him telling me that."

ACKNOWLEDGMENTS

To Anna, my wife of 47 years and still in love, who lived and breathed this case as long as I did. A strong supporter throughout, as well as my go-to person when looking for a second opinion. She was there just to bounce something off, even in the middle of the night. At times, sensing my restlessness, she would wake and say, "You're at work, aren't you?" Busted. In particular, I always valued her perspective as a woman, which wasn't always what I was thinking. It was only through her encouragement that I chose to write the book. She wanted me to tell the same story to the rest of the world that I told her all along. Love you. Thanks for being there for me.

A special thanks to my investigative colleagues Frank Roney, Larry Brown, Jay Salpeter, Peter Smith, Mary English, Tom Brennan, Bill Flanagan, Natalie Beyer, and Pat Whelan. We were always on the same page, believing in Cal's innocence, which motivated our pursuit of the truth. I couldn't have done it without you. Well done, my friends. I truly enjoyed working with you.

Thanks also to Cal's dedicated legal teams over the years, starting with his first team of Joe Cawley, Sue Mertens, and Bill Easton, followed by his second team of Bill Easton again along with Terry Kindlon. Then, his last team of Bruce Barket, Donna Aldea, and Aida Leisenring. They, too, were driven by Cal's innocence and were utterly committed to defending him. Remarkably well, I might add. It was a pleasure working with all of you.

An added thanks to our forensic experts and consultants including, Dr. Peter DeForest, Dr. Lawrence Kobilinsky, Dr. Herb MacDonell, Paul Kish, Terry Laber, Karl Williams, and Owen McDonnell. Well done.

To all my early readers, for their interest, valued suggestions, and honest opinions. Starting with my wife Anna but later included Frank Miller, Al Motsko, and Jim Corbin. I hope I've answered some of the questions you've had over the years that I couldn't answer until now – much appreciated – thanks. Perhaps, a beer at Jonathan's might be in order. I'm buying this time.

To all the crime reporters and editorial staff of the *Binghamton Press and Sun-Bulletin*, but especially Nancy Dooling. And to Wendy Post from the *Owego Pennysaver*. Thanks for your accurate, honest, and unbiased reporting from start-to-finish. Commendable work. It did not go unnoticed.

A special thanks to Kat McCarthy, for her editing and designing skills of my book cover and website. For her patience and willingness to work with a first-time author. A great professional I look forward to working with again in the future.

I mustn't forget my weekly golf partners, Bob DuBrava, Teddy Okoniewski, and Father Ed Zandy, for their friendship, interest, support, and encouragement over the years. Also, for supplying the beer before starting the back nine. Even though double-bogey's, mulligans, and searching for lost balls is a routine part of my game, we still have fun, and I look forward to continuing. But it does help that we can now hit from the gold tees. Thanks, guys.

I've always had a strong faith and spiritual component in my life. Although some would disagree, I strongly believe our Almighty God is not only a mysterious and loving God, but also a God who loves justice. He didn't always answer my prayers on my timeline, nor in the way, I thought they should have been. Yet I was still amazed when I finally realized He did answer, just not how and when I expected. And for that, I give thanks.

DEAR READER

Thank you for reading *Reign of Injustice: The Cal Harris Story*. Your support means a lot to me!

If you've enjoyed this book, I would be very grateful if you'd take a few minutes to write a brief review on whatever platform you purchased it from.

Reviews are one of the most powerful tools when it comes to book ranking, exposure, and future sales. Honest reviews of my book help bring it to the attention of new readers.

Thank you so much,
Dave

ABOUT THE AUTHOR

David M. Beers holds a Bachelor of Professional Studies Degree from Empire State College. Previously, he served six years in the United States Marine Corps before being honorably discharged at the rank of Staff-Sergeant. After that, Beers became a sworn member of the New York State Police. As a trooper, he excelled in his regular duties and became a police instructor, helping to develop, implement, and teach a state-wide highway drug interdiction program. After being promoted to the rank of Investigator, Beers received additional training and experience and served in several specialized venues, including narcotics, major crimes, violent felony warrants, and forensics. There, he attained knowledge and proficiency in several forensic disciplines including, evidence collection and preservation, crime scene investigation, fingerprinting analysis, arson awareness, fire cause and origin, and bloodstain/pattern analysis. Over several years, he received numerous commendations while routinely maintaining excellent and outstanding performance evaluations.

Beers' career in law enforcement ended prematurely as the result of what later became known as the New York State Police Troop 'C' evidence tampering scandal. Beers, was initially cleared of any wrong-doing but was later falsely accused of a host of crimes related to his work as a police officer. After a two-year legal battle that included two trials, Beers was completely exonerated of all criminal charges. But having been tainted by the criminal accusations, Beers was fired from his position as a police officer. His law enforcement career may have been ripped away, but his training and experience had not.

Over the next two years, Beers transitioned his training and experience into the private sector, where he became a licensed private investigator. With his collective experience as a marine, police officer, defendant, and now a private investigator, Beers developed a unique perspective of the criminal justice system. From scratch, he organized and started his own investigative business he justly named, New Perspective Investigations, specializing in criminal defense investigation and consulting. Since then, he has worked on numerous high-profile murder cases, including the one detailed in this book, as one of the most unique and challenging cases of his career.

Contact David

Email at davidmbeers.author@gmail.com

Visit his website at davidmbeers.com

www.ingramcontent.com/pod-product-compliance
Lightning Source LLC
Chambersburg PA
CBHW072039020426
42334CB00017B/1329